THE
FORESTS
OF THE
SEA

Life and Death
on the Continental Shelf

THE FORESTS OF THE SEA

LIFE AND DEATH ON THE CONTINENTAL SHELF

by John L. Culliney

Sierra Club Books   San Francisco   1976

The Sierra Club, founded in 1892 by John Muir, has devoted itself to
the study and protection of the nation's scenic and ecological resources—
mountains, wetlands, woodlands, wild shores and rivers.
All club publications are part of the nonprofit effort the club carries on as
a public trust. There are some 50 chapters coast to coast, in Canada, Hawaii
and Alaska. Participation is invited in the club's program to
enjoy and preserve wilderness everywhere.
Address: 530 Bush Street, San Francisco, California 94108.

Culliney, John, 1942-
    The forests of the sea.

    Includes bibliographical references and index.
    1.   Marine biology—United States.
    2.   Continental shelf—United States. I. Title.
QH104.C82   574.92   76-21296
ISBN 0-87156-181-6

Book design by Adrian Taylor
Line illustrations by Bonnie Laurie Russell
Maps by John L. Culliney
Production by David Charlsen & Others
Printed in the United States of America

Contents

Toward an Oceanic Philosophy

Acknowledgments

This book owes its existence to countless scientists and authors whose work has gradually revealed the shape, substance, and life of the continental shelf. The references at the end of the book can only touch the surface of this immense and ongoing work.

My direct personal debt for understanding and the opportunity to explore the marine world extends to former teachers such as Willard Hartman, C.G. Bookhout, Orrin Pilkey, and Ruth Turner.

Ashore, at sea, and in the magic world below, many individuals have personally influenced this writing by contributing ideas and special knowledge of the continental shelf, and by sharing rare sights and encounters. Even a partial list of these friends and colleagues is long; they include: Bob Backus, Dan Berman, Robert Black, Don Bourne, Paul Boyle, Carl Burger, Ed Carpenter, Dick Cooper, Ned Crockett, John Farrington, Nick Fisher, Fred Grassle, Perry Kearney, Robert Livingstone, Ted Loder, Alan Michael, Bruce Miller, Berrien Moore, Susan Peterson, Orrin Pilkey, Eric Radack, Gil Rowe, Howard Sanders, Leah Smith, John Stegeman, Ruth Turner, Joe Uzmann, and George Woodwell.

Special thanks go to Carl Burger, George Hampson, Orrin and Charlene Pilkey, and Joe Uzmann who read and criticized sections of the manuscript.

The library staff of the Marine Biological Laboratory in Woods Hole, Massachusetts, was always accommodating and usually tolerant of my closing-time requests to use the copy machines.

The happy circumstances under which this writing was done were fostered in large part by my wife, Barbara, who helped during every phase of the evolution of the book.

In gratefully acknowledging all who helped, however, I assume the traditional responsibility for any errors, unattributed opinion, and expressions of zeal.

For my Mother and Father with love and thanks

The continental shelf is a special environment. In many ways it belongs both to the land and to the sea. Marine geologists regard the shelf as the rim of the land, barely declining offshore to a perceptible edge where the continental slope begins to descend more steeply toward the abyss. In most places the outer boundary of the shelf now lies under about 200 meters of water—1/19 of the average depth of the world's oceans. The shelf environment appears as a thin strip indeed at the very edge and surface of the sea. On numerous occasions in the past the continental shelf has been reclaimed by the land and the world of air, bright sunlight, grass and trees, rain and snow, rivers and glaciers. During the most recent glacial period the sea level dropped over 150 meters worldwide. Probably just as frequently in the past, the waters rose, flooding great valleys, and the continental shelf expanded slowly inland, doubling its present width over portions of the United States' coastal plain.

The geophysical dynamism of the continental shelf is more than matched by its biological vigor. The shelf environment comprises an extremely productive aquatic habitat, the sea's green-water rim, contrasting with the clear, relatively sterile blue of the deep outer ocean. Earth's life may have begun on some ancient continental shelf off some dark mineral shore of unutterable remoteness. Now with an extravagant bounty, the shelf supports every class of creature from bacteria to mammals.

To discuss thoroughly all of the interlocking geological and physical factors, living communities and ecosystems, and man's influence on the continental shelf would require many years, volumes, and authors. I have tried only to give a glimpse of this hidden world, a glimpse into the lives of a few of the varied creatures of the shelf, and an overview of several aspects of modern marine ecology in five large regions surrounding North America.

I have been concerned chiefly with exploring the perspectives and problems facing the creatures of the shelf. The sea otter's apparent ecological control of its environment; the reaction of a shrimp to the turn of the tide and what might be carried in the turbid current; the sensitivity of menhaden to an infinitesimal warming of the water: these are among the important phenomena of the continental shelf, and most of them are still poorly understood. Marine ecologists generally agree that their science is in its infancy. Reliable answers to many questions concerning the distribution and abundance of life and the more subtle factors governing the functioning and health of ecosystems await years and perhaps decades of patient work. Some questions, it appears, may never be answered in an absolute manner, but may be couched forever, like weather forecasts, in the language of probability.

I have tried to key major coastal and offshore environmental problems to regions where their impact is, or will likely be, severe. This helps to avoid repetitive accounts within each geographical area, but it is important to note that pesticides and heavy metals are building up in New England coastal waters as well as in the Gulf of Mexico and off southern California; spilled oil will have much the same effect on organisms off Cape Canaveral as off Cape Cod; PCBs have already been spilled in Puget Sound as well as on Florida's Gulf Coast.

The list of sources at the end of the book is selected from a huge, nearly unmanageable body of publications dealing with the shelf environment. All of the publications listed were used in writing this book, and I have tried to emphasize fairly recent references. These in turn usually cite earlier works, and anyone wishing to delve deeply into the history of a specific subject can backtrack from the mid-1970s through the vast understory of scientific literature.

Much factual information and numerous interpretations and projections were obtained in conversations with scientists and from seminars and conferences held from 1974 to 1976. For this reason and for the sake of readability, I have not included footnotes. Anyone interested in detailed scrutiny of the topics discussed in this book is not likely to be content with a single citation anyway. Such a person should visit a university or other science library and begin to browse with an appropriate index, or with titles from the list of sources in this book.

Quantitative descriptions are largely rendered in the metric system because it is the way of the future. In the "Impressions" chapters, however, I have retained many uses of the English system. Even in scientific activities, quantitative thinking often employs a kind of numerical pidgin. Oceanographers continue to ask for a five-foot piece of rope to fashion a bridle for their one-half-meter plankton net. Fishermen continue to recognize a three-pound lobster more quickly than one weighing 1.3 kilograms.

Readers will occasionally encounter discussions that are highly speculative, for example concerning intelligence in cetaceans and flying in squid. Although apt to cause raised eyebrows among scientific specialists, these sorts of things are fun to think about, and in informal, unguarded moments are thought about by at least some specialists.

The scenarios dramatizing animal behavior are based on actual experiments and observations, a few of which are my own, and the rest gleaned from others' verbal and written accounts. In attempting to convey the feel of another creature's world, a writer tends to teleologize, and his interpretations of life underwater are hopelessly limited by effects of scale and inadequate senses. Nevertheless, in gross ways, many creatures of the sea are like us in that they see and feel and taste, make long journeys, have strong preferences and dislikes, make choices and mistakes and learn. However, none but man seeks knowledge of the sea for long-range goals and projects his imagination past the present.

Knowledge of and imagination on an oceanic perspective have become vitally necessary. Now that the power of human technology rivals the forces of the planet itself, man has become largely responsible for the fate of the continental shelf and the whole living Earth.

John Culliney
Waimanalo, Hawaii
June, 1976

Swim to a Strange Land

Only a few miles from a major city in the northeastern United States lies the edge of one of the least explored and most important wilderness areas in the world. It is a unique place of immense space and shifting light and shadow. Rugged peaks and canyons and vast, dark and silent plains teem with a rich variety of wildlife.

These environs have existed almost unchanged since the early ages of the earth, yet their boundaries and subtleties of physical and biological form have shifted and altered continually through the long glacial winters and other, more profound behavior of the restless earth.

An explorer in these regions encounters unusual environmental conditions. One's sense of direction and even one's own bodily orientation are often in question. Boundaries, such as those between day and night, lose their sharpness and become subdued. Hidden colors are a surprise and delight to the eye. One must be receptive to newness. One must adapt. Even the seasons are muted.

The intriguing natural history of this place and its beauty and solitude rival those found anywhere. There are challenges here too, and dangers for the unprepared. More than in any other area on the earth, man is only a visitor here; he cannot remain.

This wilderness is also as fragile as any other. Its relatively pristine condition has so far been maintained only by virtue of its awesome inaccessibility, but man is finally encroaching. With new technologies he is already probing and thrusting, ferreting in every remote corner. So far, human activities have created only minor blemishes on this part of the planet, yet the potential for severe disruption is growing perhaps faster than the realization that maintaining this great natural ecosystem in its primal state of health is vitally necessary for the survival of the earth itself.

I first went out to the edge of this New England portion of the wilderness of the continental shelf with a companion one brilliant afternoon in midsummer. We were still in sight of the city when we coasted to a stop and turned off the boat's engine. I remember how the sudden silence made the scene unreal and remote, even though we were near civilization. Together we sorted and arranged our gear, finally hoisting it onto our backs. Then, balancing on opposite sides of the boat, we simultaneously rolled backward into the cold, green water.

I joined Ned, my diving companion, at the anchor line ahead of the boat to make last adjustments of equipment. Ned was well qualified as a guide to the country we were about to explore. As a professional underwater instructor and photographer, he had been in this area many times and had described its scenery, both physical and biological, to me in glowing phrases. Just the fact of Ned's presence in the water promised an interesting trip. Once submerged, he is transformed into a marine mammal. Moving along the sea-bed, blending with its contours, or stalking a lobster among the boulders he gives the impression of being preternaturally aquatic. Although I am not a novice, having had several years of diving experience, Ned's way in the water is that of a mountain man to my weekend backpacker. These thoughts ran rapidly across my mind as my field of vision, now entrained in two dimensions, inches above the sea surface, again took in the distant skyline of the city. From here, the sense of remoteness had perceptibly increased.

We began to purge the air from our buoyancy compensating vests and sank slowly in the water. Then we were below the surface, drifting, feet down in green glassy space. Looking up, we appeared to be receding from a huge, gently undulating mirror. We had gone through the looking glass and emerged into a slowed down world, a languid new dimension. Looking down, I saw Ned, a few feet below, exhale a slow cascade of bright silver bubbles which, long moments later, moved past me quivering toward the surface. Then, unexpectedly, we landed on our feet like parachutists, but very gently, waist deep in a field of slowly waving kelp.

Our landfall was about twenty feet below the surface, the top of a ridge with deeper water on either side. Kelp extended in every direction, but the impression of its great expanse was illusory because the field of visibility at this level had a radius of only about ten feet.

A field of kelp is one of the commonest of sights at relatively shallow depths off the rocky New England coast. This large, brown, strap-like alga is found in cold waters throughout the world. New England plants are small by kelp standards, usually less than twenty feet long, while a different species grows over 100 feet in length off California. Still larger kelp has been reported from Chile. Here we stood near the lower boundary of the plant's zone of luxuriant growth. In these waters it can still be found sporadically down to fifty or sixty feet, but usually as small isolated plants.

In the sea, as on a mountain, different plants and animals are found at different levels or zones, each of which corresponds to a broader range in latitude. Even in tropical lands, high mountains can serve as island-like refuges for boreal and arctic-adapted species because cold climates are duplicated at high elevations. In the ocean the zonation is inverted. With increasing depth the water grows colder and stays colder for more of the year. Hence marine life from high latitudes is found to occur deeper and deeper as the equator is approached.

However, in local waters, under relatively turbid conditions, the kelp zone is probably defined less by temperature than by the distribution of light. To the plants, only the very skin of the sea, the uppermost layer of a few hundred feet, is inhabitable. Within this layer the range of variation is great, from the broad green and brown waves of shore algae—less than a short city block away, as the stone falls—to the hardy vestiges which, at the edge of abyssal night, extract the last dim blue quanta available for photosynthesis.

To animals, light can also be a determining factor in zonation, and their behavior becomes a game of hide or seek. Many creatures of the open ocean seem to prefer a constant level of very dim light. At night they are abroad near the surface, attracted to starlight; they remain slightly deeper in moonlight and descend into the depths again just before full daybreak. Near the shore, nocturnal animals hide in rocky areas or reefs or burrow in the bottom until dark. Waters that by day appear nearly barren may swarm with life at night.

Many of the best known marine animals are diurnal. These include primarily surface-layer creatures which depend on eyesight for recognizing food. Some fishes and many sea birds actually seem to go into a state of dormancy resembling sleep at night. Ecologist-aquanauts have found that coral reef fishes divide the diurnal cycle into sharply defined shifts. At the dusk and dawn transition periods, the nocturnal and daytime groups of species replace each other quickly and with precise timing from day to day.

Finally, probably the largest group of marine animals may be active night or day. Relying on a variety of senses, these species perceive their surroundings by means of odors, sounds and echos, and textures, as well as details of light and shadow. They include a wide variety of organisms from protozoa to whales.

Thus, along with the vertical spatial zonation controlled by the marine climate, is a temporal division in the activities of different species that accords with their sensory adaptations. Size may be an important regulator here too. In the watching sunlit shallows, a small creature has a very short life expectancy.

Now Ned and I faced each other and again checked our gear, but before moving down off the ridge, I wanted a look beneath the dense canopy of kelp. I found a place at the edge of a steep drop where I could peer in under the waving brown layer of plants. Beneath the canopy of fronds was a more or less open space, about four feet high, containing stems of the kelp plants with their peculiar stubby rootlike holdfasts gripping the rock. The smooth whiplike stems, about 3/4 inches in diameter, were fairly widely spaced, and I could wriggle in between them along the bottom. Immediately I noticed the water seemed crystal clear and perfectly still. Currents and wave action were effectively screened out by the thick mat of vegetation above. Light was also subdued, and I was reminded of the dim world beneath the canopy of a climax forest on land. In a similar way, other plant life is largely excluded beneath the kelp. The main understory vegetation in this marine jungle is hardly recognizable as a plant, or even as alive. Called coralline algae, it grows in a thin brittle layer over stones, shells and other hard surfaces. Most often these objects appear as if someone had painted them a delicate shade of pink. Lichen-like, the coralline algae may cover large rock faces in patches and blotches and seem to thrive in shadowy places.

Animal life beneath the kelp seemed scarce, but this was another illusion. A closer inspection of the apparently bare rock revealed a highly variable surface texture, an interweaving of soft, bristly, crusty, and leathery patchiness. With my eyes at their minimal focusing distance, more details began to appear, flashes of movement, minute tentacles, regularly spaced pores leading down below the matted surface. Worlds within worlds, a whole diverse microfauna lived here, thousands or perhaps millions of individuals per square foot. Only a powerful microscope could fully reveal the biological depths of this place.

3

Slowly moving groups of snails were the only common animals. They inched across the bottom and up and down the kelp stems. Occasionally a hermit crab in its used snail shell scuttled by at a speed startling in this nearly motionless world.

I sprawled like a giant in a rain forest as I exhaled clouds of bubbles that fought to escape through the thatched ceiling until only a light dusting of silvery motes remained. Rather quickly the sensations became mildly disturbing: it would be possible to develop weed claustrophobia in such a place. I began to crawl out carefully the way I had come in.

It is embarrassingly easy to become entangled in kelp and can be dangerous if a diver is panicky. Even small kelp is nearly impossible to pull free from its grip on the rock. Nearly always it is part of the gear that hangs up. Stopping immediately and backing up will usually free a diver. Otherwise a few seconds of work with a knife will do the job, but be careful; the air hose back over your shoulder feels just like a kelp stem. Often the stems are brittle enough to snap in one place, if bent sharply, or after being bent back and forth become so frayed they can be pulled apart. The last resort is to unbuckle and slip out of your gear, turn around and see where the problem is. If your air runs out, you will have to abandon the equipment, but it is easy to slip through the vegetation to the surface without the projections and protuberances of the diving gear.

I emerged from the kelp and hung onto the edge of a nearly vertical rock face. Again there was the slight surging motion produced by surface waves, distinct but gentle at this depth. I could not see Ned, but I knew where he was, for out from the cliff, barely within range of my limited eyesight, were long columns of bubbles rising slowly from below.

Before going deeper I had to check my equipment. The tank gauge showed that my air supply was only 1/4 gone, but I realized that at greater depth I would use it faster as greater and greater pressure is required to fill the lungs. Also it was necessary to trim off. The buoyancy in a neoprene wet suit is reduced steadily with depth. When I left the surface I was nearly weightless; now I was definitely heavier, clinging to the steep pitch like a rock climber on some low-gravity planet.

Two breaths of air in my buoyancy compensating vest were enough. Transformed, I stepped away from the rock and turned to look at it as I hovered effortlessly. Spacewalking must be like this. I was drifting, comfortable in any orientation. Normal sensations of up or down had faded into a feeling of dimensionless freedom.

At the edge of the cliff I slanted downward, moved my fins briefly and glided. At once the water grew colder. It was a sharp change, and on my lips and the small amount of exposed skin around my face mask, it felt as if a bitter January wind was suddenly blowing. This was the thermocline, a boundary marking the depth to which the summer sun had so far succeeded in warming the surface waters. Swimming through this border zone, a few feet thick, I had literally returned to winter. Along this coast the thermocline begins with the first warm days of May or June as a thin, warm layer of surface water forms. This layer tends to float and remain coherent since it is lighter than the cold waters below. The stirring winds may destroy it at first, mixing it into the depths, but it always reforms. As the season progresses the warm layer gradually thickens, gaining stability, and its lower boundary, the thermocline, remains sharply defined. Below the thermocline the water reached its present temperature during the past winter, and it remains a season apart, while the hectic pace of the summer sea goes on a few feet above. Then with the cool weather of autumn, the stability of the surface layer breaks down. As water cools quickly at the surface, under frosty autumn nights, it sinks and destroys the thermocline. For the first time mixing takes place with the deeper waters, and the temperature below reaches the highest level of the year. Thus spring comes to the depths in the fall, and there will be no summer.

I felt the cold vaguely. The water temperature had dropped from about 65° Fahrenheit to near 40°, but the chill seemed to remain at a distance beyond my wet suit. The sensation was that of having a thick insulating layer of nerveless skin, and I was essentially comfortable.

With the sudden drop in temperature, the clarity of the water had increased enormously. I now could see perhaps forty feet, and as if a fog had lifted, spectacular surroundings revealed themselves. I was floating down into a most beautiful canyon, a marbled canyon whose sheer, surrounding, white, almost luminescent walls had a strange, quilted appearance. It was lovely and its loveliness eludes description. Like the kelp world, this place evoked fantasies, but they were of soaring and lightness, lyrical extensions of spirit. Fantasy merged with reality here too because I could see that the walls were alive. They were covered with living sheets in the form of a smooth, white, rubbery-skinned colonial creature known as a tunicate. By dividing and regenerating its body, multiplying by the thousands, this unique animal rapidly grows over large areas of rock. At depths between twenty-five and fifty feet it may completely cover flat, nearly vertical surfaces, and once established, virtually nothing else grows over it or feeds on it. There were a few small kelp plants growing up from crevices in the wall, but everywhere else the living marble glowed in splendid purity.

The bottom of the canyon was narrow, just a few feet wide, containing silty gravel, and I raised a small cloud of sediment as I landed. Trimming off again, hovering now about forty-five feet down, I swam slowly down the steep sloping floor. The walls, opening widely, fell away and merged with the larger mass of the ridge.

I moved along the base of the ridge, sixty feet below the surface. On the left the cliffs, deeply fissured by other canyons and clefts, rose in shining silence. To the right the bottom sloped rather gently downward as far as I could see. Everywhere were boulders that had apparently fallen from the rock massif above.

In this chaotic terrain were endless small caves and niches that seemed to promote a much greater variety of life than on the beautiful but monotonous walls. There were sponges of several different shapes; some were globes the size of my head; others grew upright, gracefully branched like multi-armed candelabra. Also anemones, of the kind you see in pools along the shore where they are the size of your thumb, here grew as large as saucers, crowning the rocks. Huge starfish prowled slowly over the bottom seeking mussels and other prey.

A natural community of organisms such as the one spread out before me can be described ecologically in several different ways. One simple way is to look at the feeding occupations of the inhabitants. The nearshore marine environment has several common occupations. First there are the producers or photosynthesizing plants. The most important of these are not the kelp or other conspicuous seaweeds but rather the single-celled algae, diatoms and others, the microscopic foliage of the sea. The producers form the base for virtually all marine food chains or food webs, the complex systems of linkages that relate prey organisms with their predators. Even life in the greatest depths, subsisting on the thin rain of leftovers that have often been digested several times during the long downward passage, ultimately depends on the photosynthesizers in the sunlit waters miles above.

Next come the filterers or suspension feeders, perhaps the most numerous marine animals. Many of these fix themselves to one place and have evolved ingenious ways of trapping small particles, especially the single-celled algae, from the water flowing past. These particles are sorted, and those that are digestible are used for food. The indigestible ones are packed together with mucus in strands or pellets and rejected, a sort of automatic-conveyer rubbish disposal system.

Another large class of animals is formed by the grazers, to whom the sea floor appears as an enormous carpet of food. But it is a complicated patchwork carpet, and the problem for many grazers is to locate their preferred patches of food efficiently. These specialists among the grazing animals live on certain kinds of bottom algae or prey on specific animal components scattered and clustered in the diverse bottom communities. Others may indiscriminately mop up organically rich films and sediments, digesting what they can.

The active predators form still another group. Their highly developed nervous systems enable them to detect prey from a distance and secure it, often with rapid and precisely coordinated bursts of energy. The distinctions between predators and grazers, and even filterers, are not always rigid. Starfish could be considered either predators or grazers. A medusa or jellyfish is a predator which feeds somewhat in the manner of a filtering organism. Many other creatures which fit rather loosely between grazers and predators might best be called scavengers. Animals as varied as crabs and sharks fit into this opportunistic group.

The last major group, called reducers, are hidden creatures. These are the agents of entropy, never obvious as a presence, though at certain times and places they vastly outnumber every other kind of organism. They perform the last important function of the biological community, breaking down complex matter, recycling, supplying the vital chemicals to the next generation of life. In the sea, as on land, bacteria and fungi are the most common reducers, but specialized worms, clams, crustaceans and others are also at work, turning stone, shell, and wood into dust. These creatures work unobtrusively, often from within, and their actions at times can be disagreeably surprising to man, as when shipworms fell a wooden bridge or dike or the boring sponge decimates an oyster bed. However, the total absence of these reducers from the natural scene might prove disastrous because the buildup of refractory materials such as reefs and waterlogged wood in coastal waters would occur with astonishing speed.

My inspection had carried me slowly along the base of the cliff, and I was approaching a jumble of several huge boulders lying against the vertical wall. Some of them were nearly the size of automobiles. About halfway to the top of this rockpile a pair of black legs, ending in swim fins, sprouted surrealistically from a crevice. The fins kicked and twisted briefly, then disappeared completely from sight. On the bottom, near the boulders, I noticed another movement; something was alive but behaving oddly. Moving closer, I saw it was Ned's collecting bag, a sack of nylon netting with a snap closure at the top. Now, secured with a cord around a head-sized stone, it quivered and gyrated and lunged spasmodically. Through a blur of legs and snapping tails and claws, I counted four fine lobsters, all vigorously trying to escape, but their combined activities in different directions roughly cancelled each other, and the bag danced and fought in a little circle on the bottom.

At the opening where Ned had disappeared, I looked into darkness that gave an impression of space beyond. Then there was a circle of light moving several feet inside, indicating a sizeable cave below. Suddenly the light disappeared and seconds later I was face to face with an enormous lobster thrusting out through the opening, firmly gripped behind the claws by Ned's gloved hand.

I took the lobster from him, and he wriggled free of the cave's mouth. We both examined the creature. It was well over two feet long, with claws bigger than a man's hand. Then Ned pointed to the broad fan of the tail, and I saw two notches cut in the leaf-like sections of shell that form the tip of the tail. I remembered that this was a mark the lobstermen use to designate a known egger, a female of high reproductive capacity. This one had been caught and released twice, after being notched, to alert other conservation-minded fishermen.

We released the big female at the cave entrance, and she backed slowly out of sight. I hoped the next human predators to come this way would also leave her in peace to produce her enormous broods of lobster babies.

Despite the best efforts of the lobsters, human activities in their domain are taking a heavy and often wasteful toll. On Georges Bank, one of the prime lobster breeding grounds, dragging by fishing vessels of more than a dozen nations is resulting in indiscriminate destruction of lobster populations. Most of the trawlers are actually after bottom fish, but they don't often throw lobsters back. Even if they did, the lobsters and their eggs, which are carried beneath the female's abdomen, have probably been so battered and crushed along with the tons of fish in the nets that most do not survive.

Very young larvae of lobsters are especially vulnerable to oil slicks because they live at the very surface of the sea, often clinging to tiny pieces of flotsam. Now with the prospects looming for oil drilling off the New England coast, especially on Georges Bank, the life expectancy of young lobsters will decrease considerably.

The recent discovery that adult lobsters are strangely attracted to certain refined petroleum products, notably kerosene, is another danger signal. The animals can detect kerosene at fantastically low concentrations in sea water. The stuff so powerfully stimulates searching and feeding behavior that lobstermen have begun using kerosene-soaked bricks to bait their traps. A large spill of kerosene could well affect lobsters over hundreds of square miles of ocean bottom. The animals would be induced to come together in unusual numbers and to fight unnecessarily among themselves. In addition, increased daytime activity would more often expose these normally nocturnal animals to predators such as sharks, rays and other large fish, seals, and man.

In this era of the multiple use and abuse of dwindling resources, the oceans are an increasingly important source of food, but have at the same time paradoxically become carelessly operated mines, grossly littered highways, heat sinks, and cesspools for industrialized society. The worldwide threat of pollution to marine fisheries is an ominous sign to a protein-hungry world. The continental shelf areas most heavily threatened are precisely the richest zones for potential food production, and the problem is growing as fast as technology.

The lobsters in Ned's bag had slowed their frantic activity as we stood again at the base of the cliff. Each of us had air for a few minutes more. Ned pointed to the gentle, boulder-strewn slope which extended down into a fluid gloom. I nodded. We both wanted to see where it met the level plain.

With the bag of lobsters in hand, Ned glanced at his wrist compass and pushed off. I followed watching the play of his light along the bottom. Its beam showed a seemingly endless rock garden of exotic shapes and colors. We might have been astronauts, slowly drifting, casting a searchlight across the nightside of some fantastic planet. Beyond the small moving circle of light existed a greenish pall that reclaimed all the bright colors instantly as the beam swept on.

Without the light, even the most detailed scrutiny of the landscape would yield only a few shades of color from gray green to black. Here the depth of water over us filtered out the brighter end of the spectrum, but, artifically illuminated, the true colors of the organisms inhabiting this rocky slope were revealed. They covered an amazing range and formed a concentration found in few natural areas on earth. The variety of color was not as great, nor as densely aggregated as on a tropical coral reef, but numerous variations of yellow, orange, red and purple could be seen within a radius of a few yards. Most of the flowerlike forms were in fact animals. Growing singly or in interconnecting colonies, upright on stalks, or covering the rocks like moss, these creatures come close to idealizing the concept of the biosphere as a thin skin of life, stretched tight around the surface of the globe.

I stopped briefly, lying on the bottom, my face mask inches from a rock, and watched a delicate spotted nudibranch or sea slug, an inch long, gracefully occupied in reproducing its kind. Undisturbed by Ned's light, the cream and lemon dappled creature flowed slowly back and forth, leaving a slender transparent rope that adhered in loops and whorls to the stone. Inside the rope, which was made of a clear gelatinous substance, were hundreds, perhaps thousands, of tiny pearly eggs. Over a number of days the eggs will develop into microscopic motile larvae, the young of the species. These swim for a time within their gelatinous stronghold, safe from most grazing animals and predators for reasons that are unclear. (Maybe the slimy protective coating tastes bad to small fish and other predators.) Then when they have reached the peak of their lilliputian vigor, the larvae escape from the confining jelly, again by uncertain means (some species seem to dissolve or digest their way out using enzymes) and join the swirling plankton.

Now the larvae are part of a vast drifting world. The nudibranchs and myriads of others, all different yet strangely, functionally alike, flicker through the water, drawing infinitesimally small particles of food—mostly single-celled algae—into vortices produced by circular bands of tiny, rapidly beating hairs called cilia. Aware of primitive cues, perhaps the intensity of light, temperature and pressure, the drifting babies of the sea respond only by vertical movement. They are powerless to direct their movements against the flows of water that are measured as currents. Drifting passively and waiting, the larvae thus fulfill the evolutionary urge for dispersal. As a larva grows older it will take on a new active role, testing the bottom, exploring for the subtle characteristics its ancestral memory knows are right for future exploitation. For some larvae, caught up in the offshore currents of equatorial Africa, the right conditions will not appear until they have reached the rich shallow waters of the continental shelf off northeastern South America, but unless eaten or attacked by disease, they will wait.

When the time comes and the food, temperature, and other necessities are of the preferred kind and intensity, a marine larva will metamorphose into its adult form, often with more bizarre effect than a caterpillar into a butterfly. Feeding methods, locomotion, the adaptations to the three-dimensional world must be exchanged for ones fitting the nearly two-dimensional existence of the bottom. Filter-feeders may turn into predators or scavengers; tiny swimmers become burrowers or crawlers, or simply fasten themselves in a selected place for life. Many species are gregarious, their larvae responding to concentrations of their own kind. Thus large adult populations build up, and reproductive success is assured for the future.

The settling of larvae, however, hardly depopulates the planktonic community. There are other kinds of drifting organisms that do not have such a dichotomous way of life and never settle to the bottom until they die. These permanent denizens of the open sea are known as holoplankton (from Greek *holos*, meaning whole or entire) as distinguished from the larval forms which are called meroplankton (meaning partly planktonic).

Whatever their classification, the plankton, taken collectively, has an essential continuity with all life in the sea. The life-supporting conditions which sustain the swarming, drifting communities must be protected, not only to maintain the nursery and dispersal system for organisms as varied as sponges and swordfish but also because of the vast and intricate linkages in the marine food web that depend on these unseen living galaxies. Marine ecologists are becoming concerned about dangers to the plankton communities from waste disposal, entrainment by power plants, oil spills, and other modern technological phenomena. It is possible this problem will prove to be more important than the highly publicized fish kills.

Ned and I continued our way down through the lower animal kingdom. We passed sponges, coelenterates, bryozoa (the moss animals), worms that looked like miniature feather dusters poking out from under rocks. We saw mollusks, brachiopods with shells like Aladdin's lamp, sea cucumbers with parasols of red tentacles, barnacles, tunicates. Many of these animals I immediately recognized from collecting trips along the coasts of northern Maine and Canada's maritime provinces. There they are seen intertidally or in the shallows near the shore, but here we were finding these cold-loving species in a distinct lower zone, excluded from the warmer layer above the thermocline.

To describe this flourishing community simply as a biogeographic zone, however, misses much of its significance. The place was also a living museum, exhibiting numerous relics preserved in life from the dark ages of the geological past. Many of these creatures have descended in basically the same form through unimaginable stretches of time, while continents and oceans lived and died in unknown places; while mountains rose sharply and subsided slowly; while the polarity of the planet reversed itself countless times. On occasion, glacial chill was remotely felt even in tropical seas, and everywhere waters rose and fell embraced by complementary waves of ice. The sea absorbed all changes, and its creatures could always find regions of stability and abundance. By contrast, land species lived and died at a frantic pace, a step ahead or behind the fire and ice and drought, erosion and upheaval. In the sea they drifted down the eons, with relatively little impetus to change in basic form and function, continuing to filter the dark waters and comb rich bottom oozes as they had done since the remotest invertebrate past. The ocean environment seems to have fostered a more gentle evolution than the land. Experiencing only faint echos of the sudden large-scale extinctions and replacements of terrestrial faunas, the oceans have gradually accommodated new types of life, and at the same time retained many of the ancient ones.

Of course the local marine environment had had a relatively complex recent geological history. I knew that this submarine landscape we were exploring had experienced great and disruptive changes, and I wondered how the surroundings had looked after being ground and scoured under millions of tons of slowly moving ice. During the last glaciation, the level of the sea had been lower by some 350 feet, all over the world, as liquid water became locked in ice. Much of the present continental shelf, far to the east, stood dry and exposed, untouched by the ice, while here under the great weight of the glacier, the terrain had warped downward. As that weight melted back to the north the land, elastically, began to return to its original position, while the sea crept in more slowly, keeping pace with the dying ice.

Ecological recovery was probably rapid in those centuries, about 10,000 years ago, when the North American icecap was in full retreat. This deep cold place must have been part of a broad shallow bay, no more than twenty feet deep, and studded with small islands which now are the numerous drowned ridges and knolls of this area. There would have been an abundance of marine life as the waters warmed seasonally, responding to the new mildness of the ice-wasting weather. There would have been an unparalleled diversity of water birds, probably more than at any subsequent time, as breeding sites were contested, not only by the present local species but also by those still unable to find suitable ice-free areas to the north. Seals, walrus, whales, and their kin probably sought these shallow, island-rich waters which promised seclusion and security for rearing young as well as an abundant food supply.

But the sea continued inexorably to rise and finally gained ascendency over the rebounding land, which came to rest first. By about 3,000 years ago the shoreline stood close to where it is now. Even then, after what was on a natural time scale a rapid and profound change, the coast of North America must have presented an incredible display of biological richness.

Within the last several decades, however, the shoreline has been transformed by miles of summer houses and resorts, interrupted here and there by fields of giant stacks and tanks, garbage dumps, and oily harbors. Future paleontologists will no doubt contrast the transient and reversible ecological effects of the great glaciers with the period of degeneration that followed soon afterward—an ecological decline of unprecedented swiftness marked by a huge and nearly instantaneous wave of extinction. This decline will be clearly attributable to a brand new kind of destructive geological force, the activity of a social, aggressive species which promotes catastrophism, squanders resources, and excretes massive quantities of incompletely processed wastes that overload the natural recycling processes. Man, the all-dominant land animal, has very recently become an important member of the marine ecosystem, and it is doubtful that there will be time to accommodate him.

According to the gauge on my wrist, we had reached a depth of ninety feet. The boulders and cobbles on the slope had become fewer and fewer, and at this point the bottom leveled off. Ahead was a sandy plain reaching farther than we could see. Resting, I tried to become aware of the surroundings. The sound of my breathing had become strangely hollow and seemed sharply defined, as if cut cleanly at the edges and without a trace of echo. Vision now had a late twilight quality, but the water was very clear, and we could see a small cluster of rocks looming ahead on the dark plain like a small kopje. All around was an incredible stillness, an imposing force and weight of silence far more intense than in any terrestrial vastness I have known. Standing in that spot, probably the first human to do so, between the jumbled slope with its tiers of alien life and the open watery plain, I felt an utter solitude.

My reverie ended as I noticed Ned nearby, occupied intently. He had found a flounder on the bottom, and he hovered motionless close above it. Ned appeared to be totally absorbed, studying the creature's remarkable camouflaged pattern which made it blend nearly perfectly with the textured shading of the bottom. My approach from the side was a little too fast. I saw the flounder cock one of its eyes in my direction. Ned flinched with surprise when the fish departed with electrifying suddenness. It whipped its body into rapid undulations and flew out over the plain like a startled bird. We followed slowly as it disappeared somewhere beyond the rockpile in the middle distance.

Scattered on the sand, fairly glowing against the dark, were mollusk shells of all sizes. Most were rather typical clams, but a number of large, empty scallop shells attracted my attention, and I looked around carefully for the living animals. Their dark mottled pattern made them much harder to see than the dead whitened shells, but I found one that must have measured eight inches across. This was the northern ocean scallop, a black-eyed relative of the blue-eyed scallop known to stalkers of wild edible delicacies. The black-eyed scallop is also delicious, and three or four large specimens will make a meal. When fresh, the adductor muscle is wonderfully tender, a sort of molluscan chateaubriand. This scallop is common along the coast of Maine, even in five to ten feet of water, but here it too seeks its comfort range by going deeper.

Scallops are lively creatures by shellfish standards. The one I held suddenly clapped its valves together, jetting a stream of water sideways out from between the shells. The powerful thrust spun the animal out of my grasp and, flapping its valves rapidly like living castanets, it fluttered and spun to a landing several feet away. This spastic form of swimming serves the scallop as an escape mechanism to avoid slow moving predators such as starfish, and at times humans. With a bag full of lobsters for dinner, I was no longer in a predatory mood.

The visible inhabitants on the open flat bottom are either cryptically patterned and hard to detect like the scallop, or can flee from danger with the flounder's speed. By far the majority of inhabitants here are safely hidden within the sediment. A whole community of burrowers—worms, mollusks, and others down to the microscopic level—lived in teeming galleries just a few inches out of sight. I am the most conspicuous object in the area, a lightning rod for any predator large enough to be interested. Of course, the chance of meeting a dangerous shark is small, especially in waters as cold as these. Still, the possibility lends underwater exploring a sense of excitement like that felt by a hiker in grizzly country. The dark silent places provide powerful occasions for self-discovery. Here on the deep watery plain, one readily perceives the frailty of humanity but also learns to purge the small unreasoning fears that come with too much glancing over the shoulder at indistinct shapes.

By the cluster of rocks, Ned was waving the light in circles, attracting my attention. There, under an overhang, barely fitting into a small dark recess, was a large cod. In the beam of bright light it appeared to be resting, breathing in measured gulps, eyeing us solemnly. Then I noticed a wound in its side, up high and two-thirds of the way to the tail; it was an obvious puncture that could have been caused by too small a fish spear. Moreover, the wound seemed to be partly healed. We crouched about six feet away watching, curious, but not wanting to disturb the creature in the quiet process of healing itself. But there was more to the tranquil picture.

On the bottom, almost directly in front of the fish and grotto, as if placed in offering, was a beer can. It was unblemished, brand new, and aluminum—a technologically perfect artifact that contrasted violently with every irregularly shaped stone and the flowing contours of the fish. This was the first piece of pollution we had seen, and its silent impact was so great I wished for a camera to record the scene, a casual insult, an intruding presence confronting the injured fish.

This was to be our last discovery of the day. We were both nearly out of air and could stay no longer. Ned glanced at his compass, adjusted it, and pointed back the way we had come. We swam together in the direction of the unseen cliffs. Navigating underwater was a precaution. We could have ascended directly from ninety feet and swum to our boat on the surface, but since the boating traffic was unpredictable in this area, it was safer to go up closer to our anchor. We reached the base of the cliff at the rock caves where earlier we had encountered the large female lobster. Here from sixty feet we began to ascend. The dark bottom vanished, patches at a time. Then we soared slowly beside the strange marbled cliffs, as our passage became an effortless upward drifting toward a growing green brightness. I let some air out of my buoyancy vest, slowing my ascent like a balloonist in windless, unbuffeted calm. We were beside the kelp fields, then above them, and the water grew suddenly warm. My ears were growling now as expanding air rushed through their inner passages. The view became featureless, but continuously brighter. Exhaled bubbles shone as they preceded me toward the light.

We emerged into bright, late afternoon sunshine, a few yards from our boat. The sky was cloudless except for the vapor trail of a distant jet, which neatly bisected the skyline of the city. I rested, hanging from the side of the boat, and watched the approaching plane trace its needle path in the blue. Our dive had lasted about fifty minutes and covered a distance that those other technologically equipped humans in the sky would travel in perhaps fifty milliseconds. What could they see from that exalted, accelerated perspective, gazing down on the suburban seaboard? Did they notice the shriveling of the wetlands, recognize the fossilized land beneath asphalt, marshes that once lay broad and fertile, stirred by living rivers in the migrating seasons? Did they appreciate the unheard of ecological phenomenon of a single animal species, in a trice of evolutionary time, dominating the physiography of the land as far as they could see? What of the forgotten lands from which we had just returned? Could they imagine the submerged valleys and ridges they were about to pass over, the longseamed, sloping flank of the continent descending to plains of boundless silence, and finally, far beyond the featureless horizon, the very spine of the planet, the mid-Atlantic Ridge, awesome in its immensity, rising to pierce the mid-Atlantic?

The plane was a tiny silver dart, thrusting swiftly eastward through its own rarefied ocean as I, still watching, lay buoyed by gentler forces. Perhaps among the passengers overhead one or two were aware of the natural order of the vista they surveyed. Nowadays there are people who know many facts about the ocean—the shape of the sea floor and its dynamics, the composition of sea water, its circulation, and about marine life in even the greatest depths. Humans are good fact gatherers. The scientists and engineers and their computers have become wonderfully adept at storing and juxtaposing a growing stream of facts. But only rarely, in a sapient flash amid the constant low-voltage noise of scientific research, are some of the facts synthesized into a meaningful view of nature.

Humanity's ecological dilemma has occurred largely because technology has outpaced the understanding of nature. Robert Browning's exhortation for the individualist, "Ah, but a man's reach should exceed his grasp. . .," becomes dangerous for a modern society. Man's reach has become so extensive and aggrandized through technological muscle that it is presently capable of altering the physical geography of large portions of the earth. Realigning ocean currents, blocking major straits, effecting large-scale climate modifications, all are in reach; but the normal functioning of phenomena such as currents and climate is still incompletely understood.

Humans must resist the temptations of doing some things just because they are possible. It is necessary to understand the consequences that societal activities will have on nature. Compared to man, the rest of nature has narrow limits: physical limits of time and space for the occurrence and maintenance of vital processes, interwoven with infinitely more numerous and subtle biological limits. With new technological knowledge must go a willingness to respect the limits of nature, or man's future is as imperiled as that of the environment. If we lose our small paradise, there is nowhere else to go.

Watching the decaying contrail overhead, now diffuse and puffy at the edges, I wondered how soon the megalopolis would reach out here—an offshore oil terminal, or a new floating airport—to annex and smother the natural communities that stretched away around and beneath us. The man-made clouds are thickening tendrils, encircling the world in the air and on the water. The storm is still coming, a peaking of wasteful economies and outlaw technologies in the years ahead. Can the growing destructive onslaught be seeded in time with understanding and careful planning to prevent collapse of many drastically simplified and unstable ecosystems? The oceans are the planet's last great living wilderness, man's only remaining frontier on earth, and perhaps his last chance to prove himself a rational species.

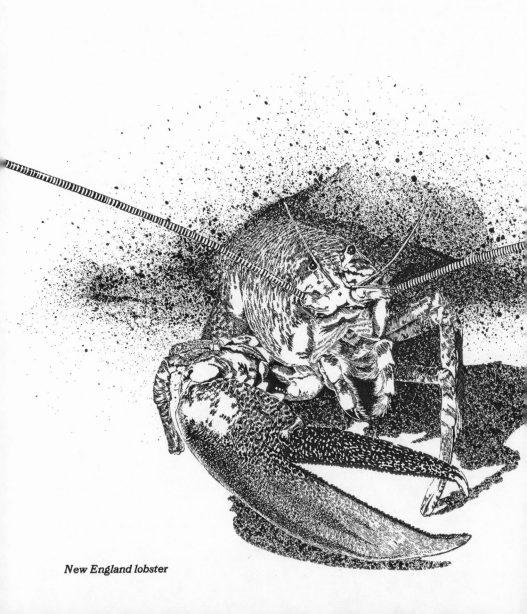

New England lobster

The Yankee Crustacean

I t is spring off New England. Over and through the chill waters shuttle numerous travelers, many of them in artificial conveyances moving on purposeful missions at various speeds and altitudes. Commercial ships of every variety stipple the sea off the shores of this heavily populated and industrialized region. Electronic eyes search the sky and sea for everything from military secrets to swordfish. Here and there may be spotted early harbingers of the summer pleasure throngs, such as the diehard weekend sailor wetsuited against the wind and spray. A careful observer might also see cormorants, eiders, harbor seals and many other birds and mammals returning from their winter habitats to breed among the northern rocks and coves. Even the most perceptive observer, however, would be unable to see one of the most remarkable phenomena in these waters: the spring migration of lobsters (*Homarus americanus*) over the continental shelf from their winter refuges on the rugged contours along the outer edge of Georges Bank to the shallow boulderlands close to shore.

For little-known reasons, the urge to travel is felt by creatures which at first glance seem too primitive and ill-equipped to exhibit such behavior. From depths of more than 200 meters (600 feet) on the submerged edge of the North American continent, the migrant lobsters walk to the coastal shallows of New England. They cover as much as 10 kilometers (6 miles) a day over vast stretches of sand interrupted by occasional boulders, fossil stream beds, remnants of ancient peat bogs, drowned glacial moraines, and elephant graveyards.

The long march of the lobsters was discovered by Dr. Richard Cooper and co-scientists of the United States National Marine Fisheries Service in 1970. Small-scale movements of coastal lobsters had been known previously. In late fall the animals move out of very shallow water, especially along far northern shores, to escape freezing, and they return again in the spring. The round trip is a matter of only a few kilometers. But Dr. Cooper's recent research shows that two distinct populations of lobsters exist: an inshore, essentially static population and an offshore one whose members move as much as 300 kilometers each spring and fall. The traveling lobsters, moreover, do not seem to make halfway efforts. In the central region of the broad continental shelf off New England no significant resident lobster populations have ever been found.

Tracking a lobster across the continental shelf is an impossible job, and Cooper's research team did not attempt to emulate the biologists who follow grizzlies to which radio transmitters have been attached. Instead they considered only two points—where the lobster originated and where it was later found—and used a simple but ambitious method to chart its migration.

Over 5,700 lobsters from eight locations along outer Georges Bank were captured and measured. Sex was also recorded. Then a small plastic tag was attached below the shell of each animal in such a way that even after molting (shedding the shell) the tag was retained. After the tags were in place the animals were released in their original locations. Although only a nominal reward was offered fishermen—market value of the specimen plus one dollar—a sizeable reservoir of curiosity and goodwill among lobstermen from New York to Nantucket resulted in 400 returns over a two-year period. Interestingly, none of the recaptured specimens came from north of Cape Cod.

Measurements of the recaptured migrant lobsters showed that they grew faster than those from inshore resident populations. The growth of a cold-blooded animal is known to be closely controlled by temperature. On the New England outer shelf the temperature near the bottom remains close to 10 degrees Celsius (50°F.) all year, partly because of the depth and partly because of the nearness of the tropical Gulf Stream. Thus migratory lobsters are not slowed in their growth, as are coastal animals, by months of near freezing winter temperatures.

Reproduction, however, is also controlled by temperature, and several degrees in excess of 10°C. are necessary for reproductive success. The optimum is around 18°C., a temperature the bottom dwellers find only in summer in relatively shallow waters along this northern coast. Cooper and his colleagues found that a majority of the migrants are female, and the scientists believe that the long trek to summer shoal waters is reproductively motivated.

How did the migrations begin? It could be that over 10,000 years ago the ancestors of the marching lobsters lived in boulder-filled shallows at the edge of a bleak Pleistocene coastal plain that would become Georges Bank. As the glaciers waned, waters grew gradually deeper and the bottom environment experienced less and less seasonal warming. To find summer shallows for spawning, the lobsters had to move north and west, just a short distance at first along the relatively steep bottom at the point where the gradient of the bottom changes suddenly between the continental shelf and slope. But after a few centuries they were traveling farther inward over the flooding flank of the continent as the sea advanced a few meters per year.

The migrations, if they evolved in this way, would not have extended north of Cape Cod because here the shoal-seeking animals would have been blocked by deeper water in the Gulf of Maine. Instead they lengthened their trek slightly decade by decade, over countless generations, in the direction of Long Island, Rhode Island, Martha's Vineyard, and Nantucket. Some eventually ran out of true shoreline. Today those lobsters farthest east of Cape Cod migrate only as far as the shallowest levels at the top of Georges Bank where depths of fifteen to twenty meters are found.

Theories about the behavior of organisms in the vanished past can never be more than speculation, and the evolution of the lobster migrations will remain an intriguing mystery. But the fact of the migrations instills a sense of wonder, and we may imagine that no more intimate racial knowledge of an immense terrain exists among earth's animals than that which has been

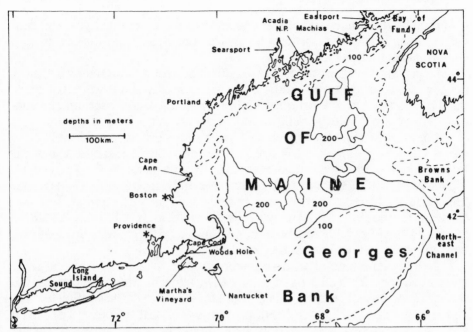

The New England Coast and Continental Shelf.

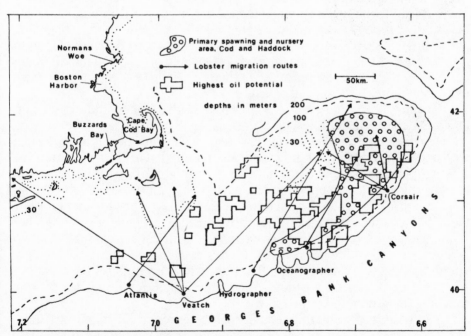

New England Continental Shelf: Georges Bank area, showing zones of potential oil development and ecological sensitivity.

absorbed by the sense-studded antennae, stalked compound eyes, and delicate walking legs of the northern lobster as it moves across the continental shelf to perpetuate its kind.

Information on the breeding of lobsters has been accumulating for many decades, and biologists now know many of the details. If one were to witness the inception of a new lobster generation in the creatures' natural environment, the action would probably conform closely to the following scenario.

For most of a day the big female struggled to cast off her old shell. Now she is crouching exhausted in the gray-green twilight just inside her lair formed by an overhanging ledge. Her old shell lies a meter away like a ghostly replica of herself, perfect in every external detail. In a while she will devour the old husk and recover its remnant organic and mineral content. But now she waits for the new shell-skin, which is still pliant and not fully expanded, to harden and give her body renewed support and room for growth. She may also be waiting for renewal of another kind.

From behind a boulder three meters away a male lobster appears. He moves back and forth on a zig-zag track as he plays his antennae through the water in broad gyral patterns. He is about half the size of the waiting female, and at first it appears he will continue on his way past the cave. Then, as if sensing some invisible emanation, he canters about and zeroes in on the entrance.

One meter from the still motionless female he stops, not hesitatingly or warily, but as if in recognition of the attainment of a goal. Then suddenly a new mode of activity possesses him. Antennae begin a lateral rhythmic switching resembling a repetitive semaphore signal. Giddiness seems to come over him, and he prances on the very tips of his walking legs, while rapid movements of his maxillipeds (small feeding appendages located around the mouth under his body), suggest an excited state, perhaps a primitive expression of relish over an imminent crustacean pleasure.

Eventually the male directly approaches the female and circles her, exploring every part of her with ceaselessly active antennae. After several minutes she seems to rouse, reciprocates sluggishly, and begins to stroke him with her antennae. But her ardor does not match that of the male. After the antennal play, he moves close to her side. Gently he starts to roll her over with his walking legs. Still appearing half asleep or hypnotized, she assists her smaller consort by extending her cumbersome claws forward and crossing them, like a dancer with crossed arms overhead. Her claws aligned with her body, she goes over easily. Abdomens meet, intricate reproductive structures mesh, and within her body the female collects and stores a quantity of sperm that she will carry for months. For up to a few minutes the creatures mate in a head to head position as the male balances with his large claws touching the ground on either side.

Knowledge of the mating behavior of lobsters comes chiefly from studies of captive specimens in marine aquaria. A powerful crustacean aphrodisiac called a sex pheromone is emitted by a molting female. Such chemicals, detected by smell and taste, are now known to function in a wide variety of aquatic and terrestial animals, including man. They promote mating at the optimal fertile period of the female. In lobsters the range and acuteness of chemical senses are still unknown, but they may act over a considerable expanse of sea floor.

Size restrictions on the mating of lobsters are one-sided. A large male cannot mate with a smaller female, but successful mating of large females with considerably smaller males does occur and may be commonplace. Impregnation of the female always occurs within a day or two, and usually within hours, after her molt. Once her new shell has hardened mating is physically impossible, and a female will usually fight with any male she encounters. Sperm is stored by the female in an internal pouch until eggs are produced, sometimes more than a year after mating. The eggs are fertilized as they are laid. They move in a fluid stream from the twin ovaries by way of small tubes and emerge through a pair of openings underneath the abdomen.

Prior to laying her eggs, a female spends several days in nearly continuous grooming activities. She retires to a quiet place and, propped up by her tail and large claws, she assumes a tripod-like stance. In this position with her underbelly well above the bottom, she painstakingly removes every particle of dirt and debris from beneath her shell and tail. The posterior walking legs used in this cleaning operation combine the features of pick, comb, and brush.

Only when her entire lower abdomen and the small feathery appendages called swimmerets are spotless does the egg laying begin. The female lies on her back, tail curled toward her head as thin strings of fertilized eggs emerge into the cradling cup formed by the tail and abdomen. Gently she rakes the eggs together and they coalesce, adhering to each other and to the maternal shell and swimmerets. Adhesion is assured by the presence in the emerging egg-stream of a mucus that sets rapidly on exposure to sea water to form a tenacious glue. Depending on her size, a female lobster will lay between 5,000 and 100,000 eggs at one time. When carrying eggs she is said to be "in berry" and from the underside of her abdomen protrude what look like dense clusters of small, dark green beads.

Each tiny egg, about the size of a tomato seed, is a complete life-support system containing a lobster embryo. Special properties of the egg surface permit the entry of oxygen. Carbon dioxide and waste products diffuse out. Food, in the form of yolk, is self-contained in each egg. Early in the developmental period only a minute fraction of the space in the egg is occupied by the embryo, an inconspicuous blister floating atop a reservoir of food.

The growing embryo, at first nearly colorless, draws steadily on its supply of greenish yolk and develops bright red pigment cells. Late in the embryonic stage, each tiny protolobster forms a pair of large eyes which, like those of insects, are made of many separate facets. To an observer peering closely with a magnifying lens and spotlight, the massed clusters of embryos in their tiny translucent bubbles appear a wonderful constellation of living color. Against a dark green background of remnant yolk, the scattered points and concentrations of red pigment cells and bursts of spectral hues from the compound eyes create a dazzling illusion of peering into the infinite. The mind's eye probes an inward universe beyond the wrong end of the telescope, flashes past emergent molecular worlds, and finds a cosmic complexity. Up from universal chemical soup in a few short months, the tiny embryos are close to hatching. They are equipped for the traditional challenges of independent life in the ocean world. However, many new and sinister ones have appeared in the recent past, and the contest is no longer even.

A hundred meters off the rocky coast at Norman's Woe, on the south side of Cape Ann near Gloucester, Massachusetts, is a line of huge submerged stones resting on a ledge parallel to the shore and about twenty meters deep. Their close alignment is puzzling, but it is clear they are glacial erratics, carried here millennia ago on waves of ice from as far away as Canada. Left in this reef-like configuration, the stones now provide abundant caves and crevices for marine life, including many lobsters.

On the bottom in a narrow alley between two of the monumental stones and protected at the back by the abruptly rising terrain, a large female lobster has spent an entire midsummer night liberating her brood. Her formerly plump egg mass now appears ragged and deflated. More than half of its living contents has departed although the entire hatching process will not be completed for another day or two. Periodically, with vigorous flaps of her tail, she speeds the liberated larvae on their way in small swirling clouds, like swallows tumbling in gusty autumnal winds. Barely the length of a human eyelash, the baby lobsters resemble largeheaded mosquito wigglers. Immediately after emerging from the curled, confining embryonic existence, the larvae swim upward, impelled by an inborn attraction to light, including that of moon and stars, and an instinctual aversion to the force of gravity. Meanwhile the first hordes of lobster babies released in the night have reached the surface and drift in a dawn growing explosively bright and revealing a new dynamic world utterly different from the former dim, bottom-hugging existence in the maternal abdominal sling.

At the sunlit surface of the sea a whole new set of life-governing factors appears, and the environment seems to present more hazards than exist in the insulating depths. Solar radiation, turbulence, temperature shock, sudden rainstorms, and the dabbling of petrels all impinge suddenly on the lobsterlings with varying intensity. Abrupt changes in temperature and a sudden reduction in surface salinity after a sharp cloudburst are among the worst calamities and may cause a kill over a wide area. Petrels—small, graceful seabirds which, robin-like, pluck tiny prey from the very surface of the sea—may also pose a great hazard to the larvae. But such incidents threaten any given individual larva far less than the myriad dangers within the marine jungle itself.

The ecology of animals has been compared to an existential game with clearly defined losers. Winners are rewarded merely with the opportunity to keep on playing. The strategy of the game for the tiny larval players is to grow as fast as possible, for in the world of the plankton chance encounters are decided by might and appetite, and lobster larvae themselves are known to be cannibals. Surrounded by food and, for a time, clear water, the lobster larvae drift on ancestral pathways along the shores of Massachusetts Bay.

From Cape Ann, summer surface waters flow slowly south and west among small rocky islands with scraggly vegetation, past Beverly Harbor and Marblehead. The new lobster generation travels with the current, for although the larvae are vigorous within their small waterspaces, they do not swim for long in any given horizontal direction. By the time the coastal flow skirts the Nahant peninsula and enters outer Boston Harbor some major changes have occurred in the animals and their environment.

During the passage, the lobster larvae that hatched off Norman's Woe have molted at least once and perhaps twice. As the creatures feed and grow, their tiny confining shells, like those of adults, become a progressively poorer fit. Unlike the adults, however, larvae grow very rapidly, and molting occurs at intervals of a few days. Before each molt a new looser-fitting shell has already formed beneath the old one, and the creature emerges from its cast ready for a new spurt of growth. With each molt the larvae enter a new stage which biologists keep track of by number. Larvae that began their planktonic voyage from Cape Ann thus reach Boston Harbor in the second or third stage. They have nearly doubled in length over the original eyelash approximation, but in appearance they have changed little. The outsized head gives them an ungainly predatory air, and the image of diminutive ferocity is appropriate for they consume several times their own weight each day.

The waters off Boston are a crazy quilt of cold clear ocean meeting unsavory patches of pollution. On a clear day, airline passengers approaching Boston's Logan Airport can see several sewage effluents on the deep blue waters, a spray of milky plumes aligned like accusing fingers pointing back toward the sprawling megalopolis. Off the town of Lynn just north of Boston Harbor, one of the most prominent outfalls spreads from a source six meters wide into an enormous fan nearly four kilometers in length and two in width where the milkiness finally merges with surrounding waters. Ninety-five million liters of primary sewage (untreated except for screening on a ⅜-inch mesh) flow into the sea every day from this source alone.

On the water itself, the view is equally disturbing. Tidal ebb and flow create sharp fronts or boundary zones marked by floating oil, bits of garbage, plastic, rubber and other unidentified materials. The tidal fronts extend vertically into the depths. Divers report the fronts form virtually opaque walls. Other descriptions of the fronts include the phrases "brown curtain" and "brown snow." The fronts pervade even the local atmosphere, and the smell of an urban sea may suddenly assail the nostrils of a sailor inbound from the outer ocean.

The lobster larvae enter the polluted waters apparently unprotected by either an evasive instinct or natural defense mechanism against the new threat. The stately pace of evolution cannot possibly match the rapid changes in the new industrial ocean. Indeed, the surface-seeking larvae are particularly unsuited to this environment because the uppermost layer of the sea accumulates the highest concentrations of many pollutants.

Some of the pollutants—for example, the metals—have always been there, but in small quantities. In little more than a century since the beginning of the short Age of Oil, petroleum, which consists of thousands of individual compounds toxic to marine life, has appeared in increasing concentrations in coastal waters. Worldwide human petroleum contamination now vastly exceeds that from scattered natural seeps. Still other materials such as the insecticide DDT, the industrial pollutants called PCBs, and their many chemical analogs have appeared during the past two or three decades. The rapid accumulation of these substances in unprecedented amounts has not allowed sufficient time for a scientific assessment of their potential ecological effects, either singly or in combinations. And the suddenness of contamination at the surface of the sea has allowed no time for adjustment by such creatures as lobsters.

By late summer, lobsters all along the New England coast have spawned and many larvae have begun to settle. The seasonal events circumscribing the lives of lobsters, however, do not occur simultaneously all along the coast. In the warmer waters south of Cape Cod the reproductive cycle and development of larvae is at least a month ahead of these processes in the chillier bays of Maine. Water temperature, the prime regulator of life functions of aquatic invertebrates, is optimal for the growth of lobsters (both larvae and adults) in the range of 15–20°C. (60–68°F.). The present poor status of the lobster fishery in southern New England waters, from Buzzards Bay to Long Island Sound, cannot be blamed on temperature conditions that are far more ideal than in Maine.

Early in June, swarms of lobsterlings begin to appear in the plankton along the Rhode Island coast. Like those off Norman's Woe they are caught up in a slow southwesterly flow. They move in a coastal band past industrial harbors and eroded rocky headlands, beneath solitary silent mansions and newly affluent suburban hillsides. Through their season they share the watery highway with mounting numbers of boats that leave a wake of oil and garbage through the summer months. In places it is so thin as to be invisible to human eyes, but it can be devastating to lives measured in millimeters.

By the time they reach the approaches to Long Island Sound, the larvae have been in the plankton for perhaps three weeks, and many are about to metamorphose into the fourth stage. For most the coming molt will be the last in the surface environment.

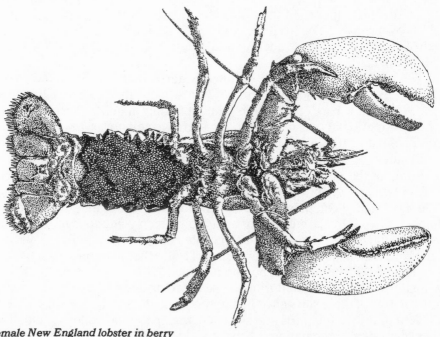

Female New England lobster in berry

Fourth stage lobsters make an abrupt transition in form. In one molt they emerge from the mosquito wiggler shape and become miniature lobsters. At this time the tiny animals, still only half as long as a safety match, begin to behave differently as well. The original light-seeking instinct disappears, and attraction to solid objects, crevices, shadows, and other hiding places becomes apparent. Fourth stage larvae and even older ones are sometimes found clinging beneath bits of straw, wood and other flotsam. But most of them, although powerful swimmers and perfectly capable of remaining afloat, sink slowly down toward the bottom.

The settling larvae have something in common with wartime parachutists dropping into a strange territory teeming with a variety of enemies. The fortunate larvae come out of the shrouded midwater regions over rocky bottom, and upon landing they immediately seek the nearest available cover. Others find an open sandy bottom which offers few hiding places. Many of these unlucky ones are quickly eliminated by small flounders and other roving predators. But even among the rocks the baby lobsters are far from home free. Most moving creatures of equal or larger size are potential enemies, and so are some that appear motionless. Crustacean relatives, chiefly crabs and larger lobsters, are especially dangerous. Aggressive fish an inch or more in length are everywhere, and tentacular traps lie hidden in every crevice. Years will pass before the newly settled lobsters achieve greater status as predators than prey in the bottom world.

Marine bottom communities on the New England shelf have been studied intensively, perhaps more than those lying off any other region of North America, yet our knowledge of the natural assemblages of organisms that live in these hidden sands and rocks is far from complete. Marine ecology, whose purview encompasses the living dynamics of underwater creatures, their populations of a single species, and communities of many interacting species, is far behind its terrestrial counterpart. Accessibility is a crucial problem. The close and direct observation of events beneath a canopy of kelp is far more difficult than a parallel exercise in a land forest. A long time will pass before humans acquire an adequate ecological understanding of the sea floor.

Recently, however, off the coast of New England and eastern Canada, marine ecologists have elucidated an interesting problem of ecological balance in a bottom community involving four levels of the food chain, beginning with kelp and other seaweeds.

Although not among the largest species, New England kelp is among the most productive in the world because of its extremely rapid growth. One species is capable of annual growth to twenty times its initial weight. However, this growth is not sustainable as a net increase in size because extensive breakage and erosion of the long thin blades or fronds of the kelp occurs in its typically turbulent habitat near the coast. Even more inhibitory to growth is grazing by snails and especially sea urchins.

Sea urchins are highly destructive to kelp and other seaweeds and strongly influence their distribution. On rocky bottom off northeastern North America, diving biologists are finding striking barren zones in the normally lush kelp forests. Within these cleared areas sea urchins are often eight times more numerous than they are on the general surrounding terrain. The prickly hemispherical animals, slightly larger than a halved tennis ball, have been seen moving slowly along in dense herds, grazing everything in their path down to the bare rock.

Some scientists believe that marine pollution in the form of sewage may be partly responsible for the expanding urchin populations: young sea urchins find nourishment in sludge deposits and other areas enriched by sewage fallout. However, another impact on the New England shelf is more clearly linked to the urchin explosion.

Lobsters are the major predators of New England sea urchins. The powerful armored crustaceans crunch up their spiny prey and dine at leisure on the pasty, tangy innards, of which the egg mass or roe is delectable even to human taste buds. Current estimates are that a single adult lobster consumes hundreds of sea urchins per year. Rock crabs also prey on urchins, but they eat fewer and smaller individuals than lobsters. Lobsters also eat crabs, so the ultimate controlling predator on the urchins appears to be the lobsters. Biologists now believe that overfishing of lobsters in coastal waters has favored the outbreaks of damage to the kelp forests by sea urchins. Thus predation at the fourth level in the chain: seaweed—urchin—lobster—man, seems to be strongly affecting the first.

Man's predation on lobsters and other species in New England shelf waters is growing rapidly, and the impact of ecological imbalance even to the level of algae is startling. However, the apparent impact of overfishing on the general coastal habitat represented by kelp forests is only the first to be discovered, perhaps because it is happening close to shore in a region where competent aquatic biologists are highly concentrated. The next problem concerns what is happening away from the coast where New England's enormously rich fisheries are being exploited as if there were no tomorrow.

What's Wrong
with the Fishing

N ear the edge of the continental shelf south of New England, the sands of Georges Bank seem all-encompassing, with only low rippling relief and an occasional glacial erratic boulder. There are places here, however, where the expanse of sea floor reveals scars and scrapes left by no natural process. A variety of artifacts lie haphazardly on the sand as if left by some modern glacial force. One of these artifacts, resting under 170 meters of water, is an old, battered but still intact lobster trap made of gray, plastic-coated wire.

Within the trap is a single living occupant. Antennae drooping and claws at rest, the lobster crouches in a corner. It has been imprisoned for over three months. A few shards of former companions, both lobsters and crabs, lie on the sand outside. Every edible morsel in reach, including pieces of shell, has long been consumed by the starving animal within.

Attached to the trap and extending over the sand and out of sight in opposite directions is a white rope, faintly luminous on the dark bottom. The rope, called a groundline, runs unseen for 500 meters west and curves more than 1,500 meters to the southeast where it ends close to the head of Atlantis Canyon near the shelf edge. Evenly spaced along the rope every twenty meters are over 100 lobster traps. The traps and the lobsters in them are lost; the captive animals will neither contribute to coastal seafood markets nor to reproducing their kind because all lines connecting the traps to the surface have been missing since Russian trawlers towed their heavy fishing gear through the area.

Originally the string of traps had been twice as long. Small anchors held the groundline in place at either end, and from these points buoy lines ran up to the surface. The first trawler intercepted the groundline about halfway along its length, and the rope snagged on a sharp metal-edged piece of gear and parted almost immediately. Then a second vessel about a kilometer east of the first began a run along the upper flank of Atlantis Canyon and caught the groundline near its anchored eastern end. With irresistible power the trawl attached to the ship tore the light anchor from the bottom, and the string of traps followed the fishing gear like the knotted tail of a kite. Then the groundline and a cluster of traps caught in a group of boulders. The line snapped, and a two-kilometer string of traps remained behind in the wake of the trawl. The twisted anchor and a few tangled traps continued on, perhaps eventually to be unraveled from the gear amid salty Slavic curses and distributed piecemeal over the bottom many kilometers distant.

Having been set only hours before the trawlers came on the scene, the lost traps contained fresh bait and they fished well. Within a few days many held two or more fine lobsters. The bait rotted, and slowly the captives began to starve. Occasionally a jonah crab that entered a trap or a small lobster was cornered and eaten by larger relatives. Death from disease also began to take a toll of hunger weakened animals. Those that died were consumed by the others, but they also served for a time as new bait and attracted new lobsters.

Eventually a large proportion of the resident lobsters over several square kilometers had been caught in the ghost traps. Many migrants had also been intercepted by the string lying across the seasonal route to and from Atlantis Canyon. After a year, poor returns from this area and the frequent presence of the foreign fleet encouraged lobstermen to try their luck elsewhere.

On a bright day at noon, the lone lobster in the ghost trap at 170 meters has a slatted view of featureless gray space above. The sandy bottom is illuminated to a surprising degree, enough to see outlines well, but details are lost in shadow. The lobster becomes aware of throbbing vibrations that swell until they seem intolerably compressed into the surrounding space. Mercifully the sound peaks and starts to diminish, but then, off to one side, an enormous school of fish materializes; they mill about in confusion and perhaps fright, and proceed past as if driven by something as yet unseen beyond the fifteen-meter radius of visibility. Suddenly, bounding and bucking along the sand on a course parallel to that of the fish, is a huge wooden slab. It is nearly the size of a barn door and dragged by cables that slant upward toward the receding thunder. As if precisely aimed, the otter board scores a direct hit on the ghost trap and disappears into the gloom. Miraculously the lobster remains, crouching unscathed in the wire mesh wreckage as the huge trawl passes.

Simple methods marked the beginning of the New England lobster fishery. The crustaceans were simply picked up by hand along the shore at low tide. They were so abundant in the rocky beach pools and under large stones that no one bothered to hunt for them in open water until about 1840. After this date depletion of the shoreline stocks led to the use of lobster fishing gear that had already appeared in Europe. Through the mid and late 1800s, New England lobstermen and seaside residents wishing a lobster dinner used a catching net that resembled an umbrella held upside-down. From a rowboat in two or three meters of water, the hoopnet was lowered on a rope. An old fish head tied in the center of the net served as bait. Looking down through the clear water, fishermen could see their quarry's every move; often within minutes several lobsters would materialize from under boulders and ledges and climb into the net. At the fashionable seaside resorts of the day, a chef could order lobster fresh from the ocean on an hour's notice, the same as vegetables from the gardens.

The familiar wooden lobster trap came into wide use on the New England coast around the turn of the century, although it appears to have originated in Holland as early as 1713. It is still common today, along with similar traps made of plastic-coated wire. Trap fishing for lobsters on the outer continental shelf began barely a dozen years ago and blossomed at the turn of the last decade when numerous salty entrepreneurs equipped their forty-footers with extra fuel tanks, high-powered winches, Loran navigation, and radar in order to locate tiny marker flags 200 kilometers out. Now the commercial trap men working the outermost grounds are hard-pressed to make a meager living, and they are cutting back. Even some of the pioneers on the outer shelf have quit, in a few cases with quiet monetary compensation from the United States government for damages laid to Soviet trawlers. Meanwhile the remaining trappers and the trawl users continue to interact in a destructive manner that impinges heavily on both fishing equipment and the lobster populations.

Within a couple of years, new regulations on the Georges Bank fisheries will probably prescribe separate alternate lanes for trap and trawl fishing. The lanes will be ten to fifteen kilometers wide and follow paths running shore-ward from the edge of the shelf. This arrangement will help avoid international disputes and damage suits, and the trapping lanes should serve as much needed refugia for severely overfished stocks of finfish. And the localization of trap strings in established zones that are off limits to trawlers should, with other measures, alleviate the problem of lost traps, which the fishermen call ghost traps.

On 25 January 1975, a consortium of Rhode Island lobstermen operating out of Newport announced the loss of $150,000 worth of traps and associated equipment on outer Georges Bank. Overnight several foreign vessels, believed to be Russian, had run through their gear set 240 kilometers off Cape Cod; all surface connections had been lost. This case of instantaneous creation of 3,000 ghost traps, affecting hundreds of square kilometers of rich lobster bottom, is the largest single such incident in history. But the aggregate of smaller losses of traps every year is far larger, and the problem is growing in both offshore and inshore waters.

Estimates of traps lost in Maine's nearshore fishery range up to 300,000 yearly. On the average each ghost trap collects and eliminates from ecological and economic service at least several lobsters. A very conservative implication is that well over a million Maine lobsters are destroyed by each year's crop of ghost traps within the year of their loss. And it is uncertain how long an average trap lasts. Unlike traps that are periodically hauled to the surface, bounced on a hard deck, and tossed overboard again, those resting undisturbed on the bottom last a long time, perhaps many years. Wooden ones finally rot or succumb to shipworms, but the plastic-coated wire traps are virtually indestructible.

Lobsters and crabs continue to be caught even in the absence of bait because these animals instinctively seek shelter. Festooned with encrusting and filamentous growth after a few weeks underwater, a trap becomes an attractive crustacean hiding place. In addition weak or injured captives and even those that happen to molt may serve as bait to entice others to enter.

Ghost fishing involves not only traps but also other devices such as gill nets which, remaining in the water, may continue to catch fish even after all control over them by fishermen has been lost. Outside New England, ghost fishing is of growing concern in the Caribbean where it affects the spiny lobster, and it is already serious in the Pacific Northwest. In the latter area, Alaskan king crab, dungeness crab, and sablefish (a gill-netted fish) are the major species affected.

Conservation measures to curtail the impact of ghost fishing are evolving gradually. Automatic release mechanisms for traps are simply contrived: a twenty by twenty centimeter square panel of cotton twine or netting on one side of a trap will rot after two or three months underwater. Such escape panels in crab traps are required by law in the state of Washington, and New England states may soon follow this example. A lingering problem, however, will be to convince fishermen that modifications and maintenance are necessary in the interests of conservation. Scofflaws are often eventually caught, but enforcement tends to spread itself very thin in the fishing areas.

It is probable that even in the absence of ghost fishing the United States lobster industry would find itself in decline. The number of fishermen increases every year in response to inflated prices, while landings go down. In Maine, for example, the catch declined from 10 million kilograms in 1962 to 7.4 million kilograms in 1972. But over the decade the value of the catch rose from $11 million to more than $18 million. The Canadian fishery has also been in eclipse during recent years. Unlike the United States, Canada imposes licensing restrictions that keep the number of fishermen roughly constant. Some biologists believe the Canadian lobster stocks are in a temporary slump due to colder than usual water temperatures rather than excessive predation by man.

Fishing pressure on the New England shelf is endangering more than lobsters. Entire offshore stocks of finfish are imperiled, and perhaps, over the long run, a whole ecosystem. From June to December, the season of most intense offshore fishing, ships of more than a dozen nations simultaneously cross and recross Georges Bank. Electronic fish finders run continuously. Night and day the great nets go down and come up creaking and groaning with fish of numerous species as well as crabs, lobsters, squid, scallops, starfish, and many others. When the trawl breaks surface and is slowly hauled up the steep stern ramp, all but a few individuals near the top of the load are squeezed by intolerable pressure. Eyes pop; eggs and viscera burst forth; even lobsters and crabs are crushed. Fishery statistics are misleading, for although the catch may be listed as a certain weight of cod or yellowtail, an enormously greater amount of protein, reproductive potential, and infrastructure of the sea floor ecosystem has been lost.

It has been estimated that 80 percent of the catch is commonly thrown away on American trawlers, an indication of the finicky attitude toward seafood in the United States. Far less conscious wastage is the rule among the European fleet, which caters to more catholic, old-world palates. The Japanese, weaned on seafood for centuries and perhaps today prompted by the pressures of life on a crowded island, seem to get more for their efforts than any other. Entrails and fish scraps are processed into animal feeds and fish meal concentrate, a source of protein that is becoming important in the hungrier parts of the world. Even Georges Bank squid are sought by the Japanese fleet for home consumption as well as for closer markets such as an expanding one in Italy. What little squid the American boats bother to save goes to the bait industry. Ironically, many kinds of fish Americans would never buy on sight return from foreign processors in the form of fish sticks and similar concoctions.

Despite advances in avoiding commercial wastage, the sheer intensity of the fishing effort, combined with modern technology, poses great danger to marine fisheries. The increase in fishing over the past decade was difficult for the marine biologists to grasp until they began bottom surveys on the Bank in small submersibles and saw the profusion of otter board scrapes, roller marks, and dredge-scour trails extending in every direction across the sand. The cumulative effects on the offshore food webs from years of saturation trawling are as yet unknown. No impact studies on effects of trawling have been done in these offshore waters. Many smaller fish, including the young of commercially important species, depend on worms, clams, small shrimp, and other inhabitants of the sandy bottom. The massive bottom disruption by fishing could conceivably promote a gradual decline in the ecosystem of the Bank region.

The trawls are designed to catch everything in their path on and near the bottom. Some of the giant nets would cover half a football field, with the tail end tapering into the stands. Opening vertically as much as fifteen meters (forty-six feet), the mouth could swallow a large two-story house. A trawl fishes by virtue of ingenious engineering. A bridle consisting of twin cables attaches the net to the main towing cable played out by the ship. The long bridle lines run to either side of the net's mouth, but about midway along each line is attached a large rectangular or oval slab, usually made of wood with metal edges and reinforcing. The two slabs, called otter boards, are heavier than water. When they go overboard they are aligned in the direction of the ship's movement and enter the water side by side, with the net streaming behind. At first they sink vertically, but not for long, for they are attached to their respective cables like kites to a string. As the ship moves forward the towed boards are forced apart. They resemble sideways flying kites, and they stretch the mouth of the great net open in a horizontal plane. Along its lower edge the net's mouth is weighted with closely spaced lead slugs the size of coffee cans. At intervals between these giant sinkers are hard rubber rollers like small wheels which aid towing over rough ground. A string of floats along the upper edge keeps the mouth open vertically.

When fishing for flounder or sole, the trawlermen hang "tickler chains" from the upper edge of the net, which can be made to overhang or lead the lower edge by a few meters. The chains drag through the sand and scare up flatfish, which often lie partly buried and remaining so might not be caught. But the chains usually miss some of the fish, and these survive to breed another generation. Modern electrical ticklers, now appearing on some vessels, are not as faulty, however. Similar to cattle prods, these brush the sand, and their continuous discharge brings up all the flounder in the vicinity. Yet this is only a fairly primitive example of the power of technological fishing.

Modern trawlers have underwater eyes and ears that in some cases can pinpoint the identity of fish in a school far below the surface. The latest developments include side-scanning sonar which can detect schools of fish day or night at horizontal distances up to 13 kilometers from a ship. On the open outer shelf, fish literally now have no place to hide.

The sonar watcher recognizes the fish from the shape and density of the school, its distance above the bottom, its orientation to currents and known bottom features, and its rate of movement. All of this information is translated into visual patterns of dots, blotches, and smudges on a steadily unrolling chart of paper aboard ship. Even so, mistakes are sometimes made, but now the latest research in fine-grained sonic probes has reached a breakthrough stage: an individual fish passing through an invisible search beam of sound waves can be identified. The data need not be displayed in chart form for close scrutiny. The new system features a special seagoing computer which receives the complex reflected acoustic pattern and instantly translates it into fish.

Such equipment will allow the ultimate in selective fishing, which may pose problems for some ecosystems. What happens after large-scale removal of a few important species, usually predators near the top of the food web? There comes to mind a possible marine version of what happened in the Grand Canyon when the removal of cougars by man permitted an extraordinary increase in the deer population. Severe impacts on certain vegetation resulted because of overgrazing by hordes of deer until they died in catastrophic numbers from lack of food. Signs of this sort of phenomenon may already be appearing on Georges Bank with a recent significant increase in abundance of sculpins, a northern relative of the scorpion fish. Haddock (*Melanogrammus aeglefinus*), which have been drastically overfished on the Bank, are believed to feed on sculpin eggs. No one knows much about what sculpin prefer as food, perhaps herring eggs—and so it goes.

Haddock illustrate a classic fisheries success story turned disaster. Living primarily on remote offshore banks, the species was never as traditionally important in New England waters as its close relative the cod. In the 1920s, however, the invention of powerful new marine engines permitted routine exploitation of the remote grounds, and haddock began to enter the market in force. A rapid onset of overfishing led to a sharp decline in the catch by the late 1920s. Then during the Great Depression, economics dictated a much reduced fishing effort and a low-level harvest. From the thirties to the early sixties fishery biologists believe the haddock off New England were being taken in numbers close to the maximum sustainable yield—a term that implies the rate of catching a species matches its natural reproductive and survival rates.

In fishery science reproductive and survival rates are combined into a statistic called "year class strength," a measure of the abundance of each year's crop of new fish of a given species. Using the statistic, obtained by counting selected samples of recognized ages (in temperate regions the age of a fish can be told by annual growth rings which are deposited in scales and inner ear bones), biologists can predict the near-term success of a fishery. Haddock, for example, begin to enter the fishery when they are close to three years old and about forty centimeters long. But many of this age still slip through the regulation twelve-centimeter (4-1/2-inch) mesh nets. Estimation of year class strength for haddock most accurately predicts the felicity of fishing for four-, five-, and six-year-old fish, as these are the year classes that make up the bulk of the catch. However in their computerized auguries, the scientists also detect declining regional populations, and in the case of the haddock quite possibly the end of the Georges Bank stocks.

Ironically, the stage was set for the present collapse by the fish themselves. The 1962 and 1963 year classes of haddock on the Bank were enormous, an astounding seven to eight times the average strength noted in previous years. These fish began to enter the fishery in 1965 and Russian trawlers, which had just begun to operate in the area, wallowed into the haddock with single-minded fervor. Abetted by the presence of huge factory ships, extremely heavy fishing continued through 1969, when collapse became starkly evident. Stocks fell far below previous levels. In 1967 alone, the 1962 and 1963 year classes contributed 90 percent of the entire catch. By the end of the decade there were barely any adult fish left to spawn. Since 1963 no new strong year classes have appeared, and researchers at the United States National Marine Fisheries Service believe the haddock's chance of recovery is very doubtful.

The recent history of haddock fishing also illustrates the glacier-like pace of reaching international regulatory agreements, a pace that is inappropriate for the rapidly developing technological fisheries. The International Commission for Northwest Atlantic Fisheries (ICNAF) was formed in 1950 and consists of representatives of seventeen countries that fish on the continental margins of the eastern United States and Canada. The group is loose-knit, having numerous ideologies and little subordination of national self-interest. Furthermore, there is no central authority to enforce its regulations.

In the mid 1960s, only mesh sizes of nets were specified by ICNAF for the taking of many species including haddock. What was clearly needed at that time, according to scientists, was a limit on the total catch of each species, a limit of fishing effort, or both. Finally in 1970, a quota system came into effect for the first time. The haddock quota was set at 12,000 metric tons per country per year.

In 1972, the plummeting projection for future haddock stocks on the Bank brought the quota down to 6,000 metric tons. Since the average weight of a netted haddock is about 1.5 kilograms, the tonnage allowed each country in 1972 translates into roughly four million fish.

ICNAF planners finally faced reality in 1974. Since that year, purposeful fishing for haddock has been banned, although a 10 percent incidental haddock catch is allowed in fishing directed toward other species. But many biologists believe it is too late. Even in the absence of fishing, several strong year classes would be necessary for the recovery of the Georges Bank population beyond 1976, and these have not appeared. It is likely that natural causes of mortality and incidental losses to the fleet will continue to keep haddock exceedingly scarce or else wipe them out completely.

Although the haddock is presently the most severely impacted of Georges Bank's commercial species, most others are being taken at the maximum sustainable yield. Nevertheless, cod, pollack, several species of flatfish, hake, herring, mackerel, squid, shrimp, and scallops still abound on the Bank and in the adjoining Gulf of Maine. In the face of such abundance, the human mind finds it difficult to comprehend depletion, but one remembers the history of bison on the western plains. Like the bison, the haddock is a gregarious species inhabiting a dangerously open terrain. The apparently boundless populations of both creatures were decimated only a few decades after being discovered by man with technology in his service. Now, poorly regulated trawling on the Bank could severely reduce the rest of the fisheries in a few years. Only a relatively few international agreements coupled with haphazard and undermanned efforts at enforcement of them stand in the way of a quiet catastrophe.

Presently ICNAF regulations are enforced by the boarding and inspection of vessels at sea. ICNAF patrols include ships of all member countries. United States National Marine Fisheries Service personnel carry out many of the inspections with the aid of the Coast Guard. Sometimes foreign violators are caught after a tip from an American boat in the area, or a Coast Guard spotter plane may report a trawler in a restricted zone such as a known haddock spawning ground. In recent years most of the known American fishery pirates have been caught by Canadian patrols. But in practice very few ships are checked, and much fishing is done at night. Finally, red-handed apprehension is no guarantee that justice will be done. Punishment is the prerogative of the offender's homeland, and wrist slapping is usually his worst fate.

Somewhat better enforcement has prevailed in the particular case of poaching on bottom creatures on the shelf, including lobsters, crabs, and clams, which have been protected by United States law since 1973. Although grandiosely titled the Continental Shelf Fishery Resources Act (CSFRA), this federal law was primarily aimed at conserving lobsters in the Georges Bank canyons. So far only a handful of violators have been prosecuted, but some have paid a high price for their illegal catches. In June 1975 a Bulgarian trawler with 500 pounds of lobsters aboard was seized by the Coast Guard. The case was tried in Federal District Court in Boston, and resulted in a settlement of $425,000 paid to the United States.

Nevertheless, the CSFRA was vague and incomplete. Its initial enforcement provisions listed marine creatures only by local common names (surf clam, tanner crab, queen conch, etc.) which often vary from place to place and sometimes refer to more than one species. Omitting scientific names, which are specific and recognized worldwide, invites international confusion in a matter that demands precise understanding. The list of protected bottom species also revealed some glaring omissions—for example, scallops—of which two species represent extremely important and endangered fisheries on the United States Atlantic shelf. Even at best the law was a halfway measure, ignoring entirely the pelagic (non bottom) creatures on the shelf, as well as the realities of big fishing which show that tossing back crushed lobsters and crabs is wasted motion.

On April 13, 1976, President Ford signed a new law entitled the Fishery Conservation and Management Act. It is tentatively scheduled to go into effect in March, 1977, and it will extend United States jurisdiction over all fisheries within 200 miles (310 kilometers) of shore. Arrangements with neighboring countries (Canada, Bahamas, Mexico) remain to be completed.

However, the new law has not entirely eliminated fuzziness from the regulation of offshore fishing. One of its key provisions is that foreign fishermen will be permitted to enter any region where there are more fish than American fishermen can harvest. Estimates of fish stocks are vulnerable to statistical sleights of hand and political interpretation. No changes in potentially destructive methods of fishing are likely to ensue.

Responsibility for enforcing the fisheries law belongs to the United States Coast Guard, which must come up with many more planes, ships, and recruits, and train the latter in new skills. Maintaining constant vigilance in peacetime over millions of square kilometers of the continental shelf will be an unprecedented activity for the Coast Guard.

Many new England fishermen look forward to the new regime. The 200-mile limit will extend United States control over most of the Georges Bank fisheries. Unfortunately, this development may have little effect toward conserving fish. The continental shelf will probably continue to see the same parade of foreign trawlers and factory ships whose owner-nations will be granted most-favored-fisherman status by the American State Department. Truly efficient regulation and enforcement on the proprietary continental shelf may come too late to save the ravaged offshore ecosystem.

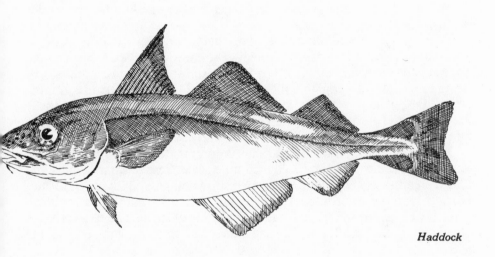

Haddock

Oceanic Oil: Sensitivities

T he quiet regions now crossed by New England's lobsters every spring and fall have had a surprisingly tumultuous history. Since the underlying geological features of the continental shelf were formed about 150 million years ago, the sea level has fluctuated frequently; warm waters have alternated with cold, and ecosystems have waxed and waned with the vagaries of the weather and ocean currents. In the wealth of time since the opening of the North Atlantic Ocean, which separated North America from Europe and North Africa, sediments contributed by the once lofty Appalachians and by the ocean itself in the form of minute shells, of plants and animals, have covered and depressed the original plutonic coastline. In some areas off the eastern United States this sedimentary layer is over 13.5 kilometers (45,000 feet) thick.

Those originally attempting to reconstruct the pattern of continental drift were confused by present-day shorelines. The contours of best fit were found to lie beyond the outer edges of the shelf on the steeper continental slope. Marine geologists now consider the shelf as wholly belonging to its continental mass. Basement rock layers underlying the shelf are continuous with those to landward, and the overlying sediments are predominantly derived from the land.

The terrain of the New England shelf is dominated by features that have formed very recently on the geological time scale. The submarine hills and valleys, steep ridges, boulder fields, and drowned gravelly beds of former lakes and rivers were all sculpted by mountains of ice that came from the north and northwest about 18,000 years ago. At the line of farthest advance, the ice formed a ragged edge often within a few dozen kilometers of the edge of the shelf.

The most prominent large-scale feature off New England is the Gulf of Maine, a huge depression nearly enclosed by the continental shelf. The central Gulf forms an irregular bowl with interconnecting basins that reach depths of over 300 meters. In several areas the Gulf is deeper than the rim of the shelf formed by Georges Bank, which lies far to the southeast. Rising abruptly along the outer edge of the Gulf of Maine, Georges Bank projects eastward like a giant thumb. It is a portion of the outer continental shelf that remained after active snouts of ice from the northwest scoured the deep basins of the Gulf of Maine, moved in an anticlockwise half-rotation, and reached the sea to the northeast. There at the eastern end of Georges Bank a classic, glacially carved U-shaped valley now lies partially filled with sediments 250 meters below the sea surface. Named Northeast Channel, this was once the most southerly departure point for thousands of icebergs that drifted, slowly melting, into the Atlantic.

Even as it began its retreat, which occurred through the process of melting and not physical movement, the glacier worked the land. Mighty unnamed rivers rushed forth from its core, carved the shelf into broad channels and deltas, and eroded the heads of the present submarine canyons at the shelf-slope break. Between the main rivers, great blocks of ice broke off the main body of the glacier. These blocks melted in place and formed kettle-hole ponds and lakes that slowly smothered in vegetation and became bogs.

The environment of this area was harsh. At first only tundra plants survived. Most animals, with the exception of true denizens of the arctic, must have stayed far to the south. Eventually enough forage grew to support herds of wooly mammoths and an occasional wandering mastodon. Perhaps these large animals migrated seasonally north and south along the exposed outer shelf, for their bones have appeared in fishermen's nets off New England to Georgia.

Thus for some time the New England continental shelf, especially Georges Bank, has been a place of more than merely local interest. Presently Georges Bank is of interest for its rich concentration of nutrients and for its moderate underwater weather serving the entire spectrum of marine life. Its reputation as a fishery extends far beyond New England and back in time through many past generations of gannets, auks, dolphins and whales, and a few of fishermen. Lately Georges Bank has become of interest because its sediments in some areas lie 7.6 kilometers (25,000 feet) thick, a first sign of the hidden presence of petroleum.

On 9 December 1974, Dr. V. E. McKelvey, director of the United States Geological Survey (USGS), addressed the winter meeting of the Interstate Oil Compact Commission at Phoenix, Arizona. Dr. McKelvey's speech carried his listeners a long way from the dry mild climate and clubby executive atmosphere of wintertime Phoenix, for his topic was oil on the outer continental shelf on the other side of the United States. According to McKelvey, the Geological Survey's best estimate was that between 10 and 20 billion barrels of oil and 55 trillion cubic feet of natural gas may be recoverable from the Atlantic shelf (extending from shore to the 200-meter contour, and from New England to Florida). He reminded the assembled petrocrats that the estimates were based entirely on echo-sounding records which indicated only the presence of probable oil-bearing zones, usually buried thousands of meters below the surface of the sand.

Later, in 1975, the USGS would revise its oil and gas projections downward, but on the subject of marine geology, McKelvey was most informative. He outlined for his listeners the structural framework of the United States' Atlantic shelf that snakes in a northeast-southwest direction, now constricting, now bulging in width between 80 and 350 kilometers. Imbedded along the edge of the continent like a 3,000-kilometer fossilized sea serpent, the Atlantic shelf visualized in depth takes on a segmented form. It is composed of a succession of deep sediment-filled basins or troughs separated by arches or platforms of rock with little sediment cover. The depth of sediment in the basins ranges from 3,000 to over 13,500 meters, or nearly nine miles, and the deeper the sediment the more likely that oil will be found.

Underlying Georges Bank is the northernmost deep sedimentary basin on the United States' east coast. The Georges Bank Basin is roughly oval, about 300 kilometers long and 130 kilometers wide (185 by 80 miles). Its center lies about 200 kilometers southeast of Cape Cod, but prospects for oil are greatest in the southern portion of the basin in a strip parallel to the edge of the continental shelf. Here the sediments are thickest, and drilling engineers are comfortable with the 60- to 100-meter depths of overlying water. Present geological information suggests that Georges Bank is one of the two or three most likely sites for oil on the Atlantic shelf.

Perhaps no more controversial, broad-scale environmental and economic issue exists in New England today than the development of offshore oil. Town meetings, public hearings, special governors' conferences devoted to the discussion of this issue have been commonplace for years, and the pace is accelerating. New England uses 430 million barrels of oil yearly to meet 84% of its energy demand. All of the oil is imported, much of it from foreign sources. Developing offshore oil would mean more jobs, and there is an understandable economic concern and even desperation in a region that consistently suffers unemployment far in excess of the national average. At the same time, New Englanders pay high fuel prices and must contend with a more rigorous climate than the majority of their countrymen. There is naturally an increasing sensitivity to criticism from the south and west that New England must contribute its share in offshore reserves and refinery production to assure that the country can continue to use petroleum at an increasing rate.

It is also clear that sensitivity on another level exists in coastal and marine environments threatened by development of the oil industry in the region. Unique and interlocking problems and dangers exist in the development of a major oil field on Georges Bank and the building of refineries and superports along the deepwater coasts of New England, particularly northern Maine.

In 1973, studies of the results of hundreds of massive oil spills in New England waters were published by the Massachusetts Institute of Technology after scientists at that institution had monitored the rates at which the oil spread and the effects of winds, currents, and cleanup efforts for periods that ran into many weeks. The oil spills were simulated and they caused no actual damage. The areas affected, the oil, tidal currents and tossing swells, the urgent activities of men and pollution fighting equipment were all contained and controlled within a giant computer.

The MIT researchers concentrated first on the offshore region where production of crude oil would be expected. Choosing four locations that roughly bracket the expected oil-rich zones of Georges Bank, they programmed the computer with data on seasonal wind and current patterns. Hypothetical oil spills representing blowouts from producing wells, tanker collisions, pipeline mishaps, and other accidents were then allowed to occur and studied in simulated waters during different simulated seasons of the year for periods of 150 simulated days.

Currents and winds over the shelf in the New England area are probably better known than in any other comparable place in the world, but any attempt to model a complex environment, even by the most sophisticated computer, suffers from a crucial lack of attention to detail. In all fairness to the MIT study, the results do show probable movements of oil in the offshore region, given the average wind and water conditions. And the study candidly suggests that reliance on average conditions does not make for accurate forecasting—an observation that can be corroborated by anyone familiar with New England weather. Also, as any astute gambler knows, results based on average conditions are only accurate when one deals with large numbers of trials or events, decidedly not a hoped-for condition when it comes to oil spills.

Relatively few of the simulated spills on Georges Bank ever reached the coast. Under winter conditions, oil never came ashore during numerous trials within the 150-day time period. (The choice of 150 days as a limit was based on a few studies of actual rates of degeneration of spilled oil in the sea. After this amount of time the only visible remains of a crude oil slick are floating tar balls.) The simulated winter results were gratifying because brutal maritime weather is common at this time of year and makes oil containment and cleanup difficult, dangerous, and often impossible.

In summertime trials, however, up to 5 percent of all Georges Bank spills reached the New England coast in as little as thirty days and mainly in the Cape Cod area. This result was not gratifying from the standpoint of potential economic impact on the coastal towns at the height of the tourist season. In addition, the computer analysts hedged noticeably on the chances of spills reaching Canadian shores, although the MIT report concluded that relatively small shifts in ocean current patterns might bring the chance of spring and summer spills reacing the Bay of Fundy up from zero, as predicted, to 10 percent.

Unfortunately, little analysis and discussion in the MIT report dealt with the potential effects of spilled oil on the rich pelagic and bottom environments of Georges Bank itself. After indicating that the hypothetical spills didn't seem likely to reach shore, the report assumed an out-of-sight-out-of-mind attitude which left hanging numerous unanswered questions pertaining to effects of oil on commercially important fish on the Bank and on the beleaguered New England fishing industry.

What the MIT report lacked in detail and authority in dealing with potential offshore petro-disasters, however, it made up considerably in discussing coastal oil pollution. After establishing a "worst case" condition for a refinery location in northern Maine—which would entail transporting crude from a Georges Bank field or elsewhere by tanker-barge rather than by pipeline, the former method having historically contributed far more spillage than the latter—the MIT analysts presented horrifying computerized scenarios of oil spills extending for scores of miles along the coast of Maine and into Canada.

Once again summer spills were found to have the greatest potential for drifting and reaching remote shores. Given a normally slight southwest current of one-tenth knot, a large but conceivable spill of 3.8 million liters (one million gallons) at a point one mile off Machias Bay could easily reach Acadia National Park, Penobscot Bay, and on occasion, Portland. Remnants of the spill, mainly tar balls, were projected to hit even the northern Massachusetts coast 10 percent of the time. If the southwesterly current were halted or reversed by winds, the computer predicted the 100 percent certainty that a million-gallon spill off Machias, pulled by powerful tides, would reach Canadian shores in the Bay of Fundy.

Computer simulations of oil spill trajectories near the coast, however, are usually oversimplified, especially when they deal with northern Maine. For mathematical and programming reasons, a computer deals best with straight shorelines without bays and peninsulas. A simulated shoreline lacks one other important feature that renders northern Maine forever irreconcilable with the oil industry: hundreds of large, and small islands and intertidal rocks lie scattered thickly along the coast from Penobscot Bay northward. One imagines a slick several kilometers across drifting in a strong tidal current. It approaches an island, separates as the island intercepts some of the oil, and becomes two slicks, which in turn are intercepted by other islands along the drift path. More and more patches of oil result as the slick reaches the shorelines, and containment and cleanup difficulties explode into impossible magnitude.

The MIT study rates the presence of islands in areas of strong tidal currents as one of the most serious physical environmental limitations on site selection for coastal refineries. Even so, the computer experts were unable to attempt any reliable simulations of spills in specific bays and harbors because of the lack of tidal current information for the Maine coast.

Although the physical aspects of oil spills have been quantified and computerized, dissected and projected in numerous academic papers, government-industrial reports, special commission proceedings and the like, relatively little in the way of incontrovertible fact and reasonable figures is known of the potential biological effects of oil in the sea. In many cases even "ballpark" figures (an expression, currently in wide use among technocrats, meaning a numerical estimate of rather poor accuracy but at least within reason) are missing.

There is a certain irony in the biological threat of spilled oil, for the material is derived from life itself. An incredibly complex mixture of chemicals, petroleum is the residue of even more complex configurations of matter and energy that flickered into life and died eons ago. During millions of years of slow decomposition, huge masses of plant and animal remains accumulated gradually in vast basins or pockets in the earth. Locked away from high temperatures and the spoiling influence of oxygen and bacteria, they became petroleum. A mistaken belief is that oil collects in large underground pools. Actually its presence in the earth is similar to that of groundwater, occupying the small interstitial spaces and crevices between grains of sand or minute channels in porous rock. Oil is most often mixed with salt water or brine. When a drill bit penetrates oil-bearing sediment far below the earth's surface, enormous overlying pressure forces the fluid from its crannied existence, and it seeps from miles around until it reaches the point of release, often with explosive force.

Petroleum is largely made of two elements, carbon and hydrogen, although small and variable amounts of others—especially oxygen, nitrogen, and sulfur—are also present. Atoms of the various elements enter into combinations. Each combined unit of atoms is a molecule, and molecules of the same kind, taken in aggregate, make up a substance known as a compound.

   Petroleum chemistry is based on the fact that carbon has a tendency to bond to itself forming chains of atoms. Hydrocarbons, the compounds which form the bulk of the petroleum mixture, are made up only of carbon and hydrogen, and the simplest hydrocarbon is:

Methane: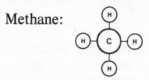

The series of petroleum compounds that begins with methane continues:

Ethane: Propane: Butane:

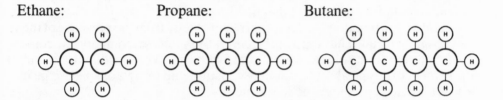

The compounds in such a series are referred to as lighter or heavier depending on the molecular size or weight. The lightest compounds including those depicted above tend to be natural gases, while compounds in a somewhat higher range of molecular weight are liquids at room temperature and atmospheric pressure. For any given series of petroleum compounds, the boiling temperature (at which a liquid becomes a gas) usually increases with molecular weight. Boiling temperature itself is often used to classify petroleum compounds and mixtures.

   The family of hydrocarbons that begins with methane is known to chemists as the paraffin series. This name comes from the largest molecules in the series which have 18 or more carbon atoms. These compounds are solid at room temperature and form the paraffin waxes. Members of the paraffin series constitute a major fraction of many crude oils. Fortunately these hydrocarbons do not dissolve readily in water, for while they are not acutely toxic they are known to have anaesthetic or narcotic effects on a variety of marine organisms.

   The chemical villains in petroleum come primarily from the family of so-called aromatic hydrocarbons. These result from the tendency of adjacent carbon atoms to form double bonds and to achieve chemical stability in rings of six carbon atoms. The simplest aromatic hydrocarbon is:

Benzene: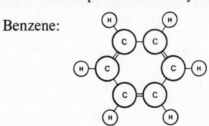

Like the paraffins, aromatic hydrocarbons proliferate in bewildering arrays by adding side chains and even multiple rings. Aromatics have a strong tendency to react with their chemical surroundings and to substitute atoms such as chlorine for hydrogen. Such substituted compounds dissolve more readily in water and thus make intimate contact with aquatic life to a far greater degree than do paraffin hydrocarbons. At the same time, the aromatics are far more poisonous.

It is difficult to imagine the fate of a lobster, fish, or other unwary creature caught in the clinging embrace of an oil spill. An analogous fate for humans might be the sudden introduction into the atmosphere of a new kind of killer smog, one that would gently adhere to and penetrate the skin, form a film over eyes, ears, and the organs of respiration, and cause loss of coordination, disorientation, and then rapid death.

Acute toxic reactions to an oil spill result chiefly from the presence of the light aromatics and their substituted derivatives. These compounds, commonly referred to as soluble aromatic derivatives (SAD), account for about five percent of a typical crude but may constitute up to 20% of some refined products such as gasoline and kerosene.

Lethal concentrations of SADs in sea water have been measured by scientists, who discovered that many marine creatures from seaweeds to fish succumb quickly to near-infinitesimal levels ranging from five to fifty measures of oil per million of water, or parts per million (ppm) as it is usually expressed. Pelagic shrimp are especially sensitive. Their threshold of toxicity may be as low as one ppm, about the equivalent of two drops in a full bathtub. Interestingly, common shore snails, the periwinkles, are among the most resistant creatures known. Their ability to produce copious quantities of mucus over exposed parts of their bodies apparently protects them, and periwinkles seem immune to encounters with SADs at concentrations more than a hundredfold above those lethal to shrimp.

Marine larvae—notably those of fish—appear ten to one-hundred times as sensitive as adults. This may be largely an effect of scale. The major nerve centers and respiratory and other organs of a tiny, paper-thin larva are so close to the surface of its body that poisonous substances reach these vital areas through the skin. By contrast, oil spilled on the skin of a human or other large animal immediately penetrates a few hair-breadths, but elicits no toxic reaction for the first line of defense is body bulk.

Larvae are also especially affected because of their feeble powers of locomotion. Powerless to swim against even the slightest current, larvae are forced to drift. They rely on the circulating ocean waters to bring them to the proper places until they are capable of directing their own movements. This arrangement has served them well for millions of years, but it fails in the presence of marine oil spills.

At the lowest levels of tolerance, subtle effects of SAD pollution are felt by the sensitive larvae. These are developmental defects called *teratogenic*—an ugly word that first achieved public recognition during the thalidomide tragedies and again in the Vietnam War when birth defects were linked to the military use of herbicides. At extremely low concentrations that were not immediately lethal, SADs produced abnormal development of cod eggs, which float at the sea surface. In experiments some embryos failed to develop heads, although torso appearance was normal. In many cases development proceeded regularly, but when the eggs hatched the larval codfish had a permanent curvature of the body. Others were spirally distorted like corkscrews. These larvae, though alive, were abnormally weak and unable to swim properly. All died soon after hatching.

Oil industry environmental spokesmen have long touted the supposition that the lower boiling aromatics evaporate quickly after an oil spill. They conclude that in ocean spills the dangerously toxic compounds are present for only a short period, usually no more than four days. At first glance the data look reassuring. The bulk of the volatile compounds does indeed disappear from a slick in roughly that time period. However, some of the most recent scientific observations indicate a more complicated fate for spilled aromatic hydrocarbons and a more sinister one for marine habitats in their path.

Two scientists at the Woods Hole Oceanographic Institution on Cape Cod, biologist Howard Sanders and chemist Max Blumer, have presented the most lucid picture to date of the behavior of oil in the marine environment. Both men, however, emphasize that far more remains to be learned. Unfortunately, their efforts so far, undertaken with minimal funds and no partisanship save a dedication to reproducible facts and objective analysis, have generated vituperative personal and professional harassment that seems to emanate from the dominion of big oil.

Gannet

Some rather pathetic attempts have been made to discredit the Woods Hole researchers in special reports couched in a scientific style. Such reports, pretending objectivity but straining credulity, are produced, printed, and distributed as tax deductible research projects by the industry. This private publication may in part be due to the likelihood that these reports would fail to pass the critical peer review required by standard scientific journals.

One of the scientific smear jobs, an attack on Dr. Sanders' work, contained literally dozens of glaring errors, and for weeks it was a laughingstock in Woods Hole. But the report was no light reading, filled as it was with authoritative-sounding data, jargon, and conclusions that glossed over and falsely represented new information on marine biological impacts of oil spills. Second only to Sanders' anger at the twisted representation of his research was his worry over the effect of the report on congressmen and federal resource rangers, who would not know that it was specious.

The research done by Blumer, Sanders, and their co-workers shows a surprising tendency of the SAD compounds to reach the bottom environment. This has been found to happen commonly in water ten meters deep, and in the presence of storm waves and turbulence these substances could reach far greater depths. After the February, 1970, wreck of the Tanker *Arrow* during stormy conditions in Chedabucto Bay, Nova Scotia, oil droplets were detected to a depth of eighty meters (260 feet). In the weeks following this spill, a dilute emulsion of oil from the *Arrow* reached seaward from the mouth of the bay as a plume ten kilometers wide and seventy kilometers long.

Not only do SADs dissolve in sea water to a greater degree than any other fraction of oil, but they also adhere to minute waterborne particles which exist naturally in countless numbers and form clouds, like dust in the air. The probable means of conveyance of toxic aromatics to the bottom is largely via such contaminated particles. Thus near an oil spill a rain of nearly invisible deadly detritus accumulates over the bottom and may rapidly spread from the epicenter of impact. Dr. Blumer traced the spread of oil over twenty square kilometers of the sea floor after a Buzzards Bay, Massachusetts, spill which was characterized as "small" in industry reports. The toxic wave creeping along the bottom left very little alive behind it; mortalities of worms, clams, burrowing shrimp, anemones, and others unable to move away quickly reached enormous proportions.

Hidden within sediments and marine food webs that reach all the way to man is another effect, a kind of lingering aftertaste of an oil spill that poses a public health problem fraught with emotion. The threat to health is cancer, and its agents are very high molecular weight compounds called polycyclic aromatic hydrocarbons (PAH). Heavy molecules composed of numerous connected aromatic rings, PAH compounds have extremely high boiling points and thus show negligible evaporation from a slick. They form a major fraction of the ubiquitous tar balls that remain floating or beached for months after a spill. PAHs also reach the bottom rapidly, where they persist in sediments for many years. Unlike the light aromatics, PAHs are not acutely toxic and are taken up by marine life in feeding and respiration and stored. Shellfish in particular accumulate high PAH levels in their bodies. In this way, even in an area originally denuded of life after an oil spill, these long-lived chemicals enter the food webs. As life begins to return, PAHs are first picked up by bottom feeders, then pass in turn into various predators, and finally to man through certain species esteemed as seafood.

Fortunately PAHs are not a major component in crude oils. However, it has been estimated in a study at Scripps Institution of Oceanography that a spill of 3 million gallons (11 million liters) could release 100 to 200 pounds (45-90 kilograms) of known carcinogenic material into the environment. This excluded many specific PAH compounds which have not been tested and whose associated carcinogenic risks are unknown. Even incomplete estimates, however, are unsettling in light of current medical theories suggesting that no safe threshold is known for potent carcinogens, and the etiological findings that long-term exposure to low levels of the substances often induces cancer.

Filter-feeding marine life such as oysters, clams, scallops, and some finfish concentrate sublethal petroleum residues quickly and form the most likely route for direct effects of oil spills on public health. The problem of petroleum affecting the taste of seafood is known as tainting. In the case of oysters and clams the situation is critical because each organism filters up to 300 liters (80 gallons) of sea water per day, and a seemingly insignificant concentration of oil in the surrounding sea could theoretically be magnified more than 20,000 times and retained by the animals.

The shellfish themselves are becoming ill. In 1971, a fuel oil spill occurred in Penobscot Bay, near Searsport, Maine. Large mortalities of clams ensued almost immediately. Then, in 1974, studies by biologists from Maine's Department of Sea and Shore Fisheries revealed a high incidence of gonadal tumors in clams which had survived the acute effects of the spill. The tumors were malignant neoplasms. The clams in a wide area around Searsport are still prohibited to shellfishermen.

On the New England continental shelf, the future of the lobster is a special area of concern. If fishing pressure, both corporeal and ghostly, has driven the lobster fishery in the direction of collapse, offshore oil development may finish the job.

Recent experiments have shown that lobsters are strangely attracted to certain petroleum fractions. Soluble branched-chain cyclic compounds (BCC) and aromatic hydrocarbons attracted lobsters when concentrations were known to be less than 60 parts per billion in sea water. Lobsters in laboratory tanks attacked and ate paper strips soaked with kerosene, which is a mixture of hydrocarbons rich in BCC. Further observations indicated that unidentified components of one type of crude oil interfered with the lobster's sense of smell. The effects of pollution on the behavior of aquatic animals is a new field of study, and scientists feel they have hardly scratched the surface. Lobster watchers will have to perform many more experiments with different crude oils and various fractions before the effects of spills, seeps, and chronic discharges on wild populations can be predicted accurately. Before these studies are done, however, it appears that the oil industry will barge ahead on schedule into an area of great sensitivity.

The suspected oil-bearing portion of Georges Bank lies in a strip that crosses most of the major lobster migration routes that run from the edge of the shelf toward Long Island, Connecticut, Rhode Island, and Massachusetts. A large oil field in this area might involve dozens of platforms, each with multiple wells. A major spill would affect the fisheries to an unknown degree, but even the routine operation of the oil field may threaten the marching lobsters. Estimates from Coast Guard data indicate that a large field at peak production loses up to 100,000 gallons (378,000 liters) per year in small incidental spills. Even more oil may enter the sea yearly as discharges from oil-water separators on the platforms. The oiliness of the discharge varies with the amount of brine mixed with the oil in the underground deposits. Still another—and potentially by far the largest—source of contamination around the production sites will result if tankers and barges are used to transport the crude instead of a pipeline. Oily ballast water discharge from the ships serving a large field could result in the equivalent of a daily oil spill of 2,100 gallons (8,000 liters).

One imagines the migrating lobsters approaching an invisible wall on the dark sea floor—a ragged and rarefied chemical curtain over 200 kilometers long and topped at intervals with production rigs resembling watchtowers on a hostile international boundary. The lobsters will be stopped, diverted, attracted to the sources of the daily chronic discharges. Few of the animals will be fatally poisoned, but hundred of thousands of invertebrate junkies may become hooked and remain in the oil field, their collective mission to the spawning grounds aborted for the first time in its long history. Even a short delay could disrupt the delicate timing of spawning with eventual fatal results for the larval broods.

No one knows where new recruits come from to stock the large lobster populations at the edge of the shelf. Joseph Uzmann of the National Marine Fisheries Service believes that larvae spawned in the shoal areas atop Georges Bank may be the prime contributors to stocks all along the outer shelf. The prevailing currents would tend to return the lobster babies in a long sweeping arc over the canyons. If oil fields are developed on the outer New England shelf, the larvae will have to come through thin chronic slicks and perhaps larger spills. These tiny surface-drifting creatures are probably more sensitive to oil than the bottom-hugging adults.

Oil development on Georges Bank threatens more than lobsters. The surface-dwelling larvae of finfish such as haddock and herring are extremely sensitive to films of oil barely detectable by human instruments. Although the main spawning grounds of these fish are near the eastern end of the bank, their larvae, like those of lobsters, are at the mercy of currents. The MIT computer that predicted the drift of hypothetical oil slicks could have been programmed with equal precision to trace the probable movements of clouds of haddock larvae relative to a fixed oil field. Although this was not done, it appears that the circulation pattern which curves south and west will frequently bring a large proportion of the helpless hatchlings drifting right through the area of maximum expected production.

In light of the negligible knowledge of the long-term effects of petroleum on offshore ecosystems, the casual attitude toward oil spills and chronic pollution which has been apparent in impact studies of the Bank area is inexplicable. Even the federal Council on Environmental Quality (CEQ), in its 1974 report "OCS Oil and Gas, An Environmental Assessment," ranked Georges Bank as a region of minimal impact and top priority for petroleum development. Encouragingly, an independent review by the National Academy of Sciences blasted the CEQ report for ignoring the offshore fisheries in its analysis and ranking procedures.

The voice of reason is firm, but quiet and difficult to hear amid cries for immediate economic gratification. Claims by the oil industry of the perfectability of its transport and transfer operations were punctured by a number of large spills in 1974 and 1975, including one that "could never happen" in the showcase terminal at Bantry Bay, Ireland. The economic rewards from a few years of oil production on Georges Bank must be weighed against the risk of destroying or severely depressing the fisheries for a far longer period, and perhaps indefinitely. There is a chance that after some years of truly thorough study of the effect of oil production on offshore ecosystems, together with real advances in pollution control, a limited and safe oil field on the bank can be a reality. At the present time we just don't know. Oil in the ground is secure and indestructible. Fisheries and the environment off New England are perishable and debilitated, but they might be restored if the powerful natural curative forces are allowed to work. So far they have been progressively overwhelmed. In all probability, the next decade will be decisive for the future quality of the environment on the hidden ground off New England, and as goes New England's shelf, so may the rest of the continent's underwater borderlands.

Winter flounder

Great Plains of the Sea

In her book *The Edge of the Sea*, Rachel Carson called the coastline of the southeastern United States a "rim of sand," and this term can be applied as well to the continental shelf from New York to Florida. On the northern portion of the shelf only occasional iceberg-rafted stones are found. Farther south occur widely scattered outcrops of coquina rock (a conglomerate of naturally cemented shells), and a fossil reef lies at the shelf edge. But these form only microscale relief lost in a 150,000-square-kilometer wilderness of sand.

To professional earthwatchers, this Atlantic continental margin is known to be geologically mature, or senescent: volcanic activity is presently unknown and earthquakes are rare. Unlike the Pacific rim of the continent, the east coast of North America is far from crustal spreading centers and the clash of earth's tectonic plates. South of New York the offshore history differs from that of the region to the north in ways that are only skin deep. Off both the New England and Middle Atlantic coasts, huge basins or troughs have been slowly filling with sediments for over 150 million years. The latter region, however, has never borne the great weight and scouring effects of the Pleistocene glaciers.

The continental margin includes zones of the continental shelf proper, the slope (which is defined by a steeper bottom gradient), and the continental rise—the deepest zone, which descends gradually from the base of the slope to the flat abyssal plain some five kilometers below the sea surface. A brief survey of the continental margin seems important in order that the shelf zone can be seen in geographical perspective. Events that occur on the shallow ocean borderlands may result in contamination of a much wider environment.

Looking at a map of the submerged eastern lap of the continent, one can appreciate its areal extent (all of the east coast and Appalachian Mountain states could be arrayed within it). The dimension of depth, however, is difficult to grasp. Accommodation to the printed page demands vertical distortion in maps of the continental margin in scientific as well as popular publications. This distortion is especially misleading in the case of the continental slope, which is not at all clifflike but in reality has a very gently grade. Humans, having evolved for a long time as surface creatures, but who have recently learned to fly and to dive in the ocean, are just beginning to comprehend the lay of this immense hidden land.

To achieve a crude but relatively accurate mental picture of the continental margin as a landform, one might imagine the view from an airplane gradually descending toward a landing from an altitude of roughly 4,500 meters (nearly 15,000 feet). At the start of its approach, the plane is in the same relative position to solid ground as an object at sea level over the lower continental rise. The illusion of the ground slowly rising to meet a descending plane becomes a reality, albeit in slower motion, from the vantage point of a ship located say 300 kilometers east of Cape Hatteras and heading for land. Here the ship floats in the deep blue water of the Sargasso Sea, a huge body of warm sea water, without strong prevailing currents, which forms the near-surface layer of the Central North Atlantic. But if a view of the sea floor on the lower continental rise were possible to the unaided eye, the scene would be essentially featureless. From a plane at 4,500 meters' altitude, objects the size of houses are barely visible.

From a ship, however, the small scattered, 10- to 50-meter-high knolls of this area would appear as minute stippling on the ground, and the largest living creatures in the great depths—for example, greenland sharks, which may reach 10 meters in length—would probably be invisible.

Imagine for the sake of illustration some sort of underwater telescope, perhaps an acoustic device that permits viewing through miles of water and darkness. As certain marine mammals "see" with sound, a person looking down from a ship would find a world of life suspended in space: fish, shrimp, squid, and other smaller creatures hover like clouds of every size and shape down through the middle depths. Near the bottom the overall abundance of life increases. A much-magnified view (comparable to that obtained by a deep-sea camera) reveals a variety of animals and signs of animals. Although mounds, tracks, and burrows occur rather sparsely, there are many different shapes and forms, and the makers of these natural artifacts represent all major groups from protozoa to fish. Indeed the deep-sea floor has one of the most diverse living assemblages on earth.

Droning on toward the distant coast, the ship passively loses "altitude" as the bottom rises very slowly at first; the average gradient in this area is only 1:100 or 10 meters per kilometer. A diver or an occupant of a submarine on the bottom at this point would be unable to detect the slope by visual means. Now, however, on its course heading due west, the ship is approaching a geological feature that dramatically breaks the monotony of the silent, sunless plain below.

The Hatteras Submarine Canyon is the most prominent feature on the continental rise and slope in this area. Its main branches run more than 250 kilometers from the northwest to the southeast. Its upper reaches consist of a fan-shaped network of widely-spaced tributaries on the upper continental slope that gradually flow together and merge in a large central channel. A ship positioned halfway across the continental rise floats some 3,800 meters above a main branch of the canyon. Echo-sounding gear that plots a chart of the bottom indicates that the channel itself is over 50 meters deep and a kilometer wide—a shallow U-shaped valley incised into the gently sloping terrain. In the upper canyon regions on the continental slope farther west, however, the channels are three or four times deeper and narrower, resembling true gorges with V-shaped profiles and steep sides.

A pilot's view of the ground below would still miss all forms of bottom

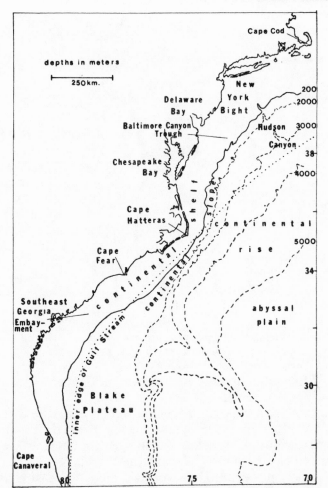

United States Atlantic Continental Margin: Overview from Cape Cod, Massachusetts to Cape Canaveral, Florida.

life, but ahead somewhere in the huge dendritic feeder system of Hatteras Canyon, given extremely good luck, one might detect a turbidity current advancing down one of the gorges. From a distance a turbidity current would probably resemble a great cloud of dust moving downslope. Similar to avalanches on land, these underwater mud flows arise from overburdens of sediment that accumulate near the heads of canyon tributaries. Turbidity currents combined with erosion by normal flows of water are believed to play a major role in the formation and maintenance of submarine canyon systems. Some marine geologists believe that new submarine canyons are formed by cascading masses of sediment brought to the edge of the continental shelf by rivers during periods of lowered sea level.

Nearing the continental slope, whose base lies approximately 2,000 meters deep in this area, we have entered the surface waters of the Gulf Stream. Only subtle changes in water chemistry and density distinguish this realm from the western Sargasso Sea which we have just left. But if we were to anchor at this position, the Gulf Stream would immediately declare itself as it

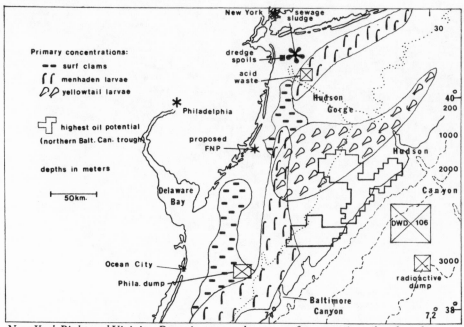

New York Bight and Vicinity: Dumping grounds, areas of prospective oil and nuclear power development, and representative zones of ecological sensitivity. Notes: FNP=Floating Nuclear Plant; DWD=Deep Water Dumpsite

raced beneath the stationary ship at seven or eight kilometers per hour and left a foaming wake to the northeast.

The main source of this major ocean current is not in the Gulf of Mexico, as nineteenth-century coast surveyors believed, but in the brimming waters of the western Caribbean Sea below Yucatan. By the time the flow converges to the north and east between Cuba and the Florida Keys, the current has become extremely powerful. However, it is along the east coast of North America that the Gulf Stream exhibits its most imposing velocity and volume. In the narrow Florida straits, the current reaches nearly eleven kilometers per hour (six knots), the fastest rate of flow in the open sea. It scours and erodes the bottom in this region, prevents sedimentation, and spills over the narrow Florida shelf. Air travelers approaching Miami or Fort Lauderdale from the sea often notice the deep cobalt blue of the Gulf Stream contrasting with cloudy greenish coastal water along a sharply defined border. From a jet this looks impossibly close to the beach, and indeed the distance may at times be as little as two or three kilometers.

Humans, with their terrestrial bias, forget that the "rivers" in the sea are no mere surficial features such as the Mississippi or Amazon, a few tens of meters deep. The Gulf Stream alone contains over a hundred times more flowing water than all the terrestrial rivers on earth. Off the southeastern United States, the current reaches more than a kilometer deep, filling a vast invisible water-valley whose fluid walls are up to eighty kilometers wide, and it touches regions that are still more remote to human experience than the moon.

Beneath the Gulf Stream, the continental slope off Cape Hatteras has a much rougher bottom than on the deeper lands farther to the east. Eroded channels, slump structures (remnants of massive undersea landslides), and ledges of rock are common. The ground, which rises noticeably now with a gradient between one in ten and one in twenty, slides past a few hundred meters below the ship. If we were in an airplane at this "altitude" we could begin to see large fish near the bottom, but as we approach the shelf-slope break the sprawling fan-shape of the upper Hatteras Canyon system would become obscure because of the low angle view. Only a few of the nearest channels would be apparent, lying one beyond the other in the distance off either side of the ship.

On most approaches to the continent, the boundary between shelf and slope is unmarked, merely a narrow zone where there occurs a sudden significant change in the grade of the bottom. Near the outer edge of the North Carolina shelf, however, is a peculiar limestone reef which meanders south, and finally disappears off southern Florida. No more prominent than a raised thread on a wide bolt of smooth cloth, and always close to the same depth, 110 meters (350 feet), the reef arose during a low stand of the sea in the last ice age. Its peculiarity is related to its formation, not by corals but rather by calcareous algae, an indication that relatively cool and shallow water prevailed in former times near the shelf-slope break. Now the tables are turned; the fossil reef, standing too deep for significant algal growth, lies at the inner edge of the Gulf Stream and colorful Caribbean corals (although not the reef-making type) festoon the former vegetable-rock. Exotic tropical fish, mollusks, starfish, and many others have settled here hundreds of kilometers north of their usual haunts. Most of them arrived from the Caribbean via the Gulf Stream and fortuitously found this last jumping off place on the shelf before the warm current veers easterly into the deep North Atlantic.

The rich reef is visited by larger and more independent creatures, too. Dolphins and whales must know well its sinuous course along the outer shelf, and sea turtles probably browse in its shadowy grottos and rise periodically to breathe and nibble at Portuguese men-of-war on the azure surface.

Far beyond the sea-level horizon where the land begins is another geological thread. Paralleling the outer reef and roughly matching it in relief is the chain of low barrier islands and dunes that forms the present inner boundary of the continental shelf between New York and Florida. The dune lines are more ephemeral features than the reef and more abundant. Vestigial parallel chains of former coastal dunes have been found submerged on the present shelf as well as far inland of today's shoreline. During the slow epochal excursions of sea level the continental shelf has remained a long time between the slightly raised edges of a vast, imperceptibly sloping plain of sand with complex geological and biological properties. Already a large part of the once and future Middle Atlantic shelf, the present coastal plain, has been pillaged by modern man who, since the time of Sir Walter Raleigh, has consistently designed against nature. Now the invasion of the outer shelf is beginning. It will be swift and massive and potentially disastrous, for far less understanding has accrued to the underwater environment than to that landward of the barrier dunes.

The bald physical appearance of the sandy shelf conveys a deceptive impression of utter uniformity. The composition of even the sand itself changes greatly from place to place. The amount of calcium carbonate, biogenic material in the sand, increases from north to south in the Middle Atlantic region. Shelly sediment on the shelf at first increases only gradually as one proceeds south from New York, but shows a sharp rise off Cape Hatteras, and increases again along the Florida coast. Finally off Miami, sands are primarily derived from the limy skeletons of sea creatures ranging from coralline algae to clams. Where strong currents sweep the bottom only a residual sea floor of coarse shelly gravel may remain, all the fine grains having been winnowed away. Beneath quieter waters fine white sand may accumulate. Unlike the tawny material of similar texture that covers northern shores, this semitropical sand is, when seen under the microscope, instantly recognizable as chips and flecks of once-organized beings. Magnified to the same degree, a pinch of New Jersey sand is a lifeless-looking collection of irregularly worn pebbles.

Off the mouths of major rivers, some of which no longer exist because they have merged with others or eroded new pathways to the sea, scattered patches of unusual sands have built up. High concentrations of heavy minerals have accumulated here, probably during times of lowered sea level, as veneerlike placer deposits on the continental shelf. These sands are usually mixtures of dark colors—green, purple, and black. The mineral content in some cases may be high enough to attract commercial mining interests in efforts to recover such metals as titanium and nickel. Duke University geologists have discovered a rich deposit of granular phosphorite a few kilometers off the mouth of the Cape Fear River on the North Carolina shelf. Phosphorite is a valuable raw material for the fertilizer industry, and mining companies have expressed interest in further exploration of this area.

The presence of these sands is in no way related to pollution. Their accumulation was a natural process engendered by the weathering of faraway deposits on land, followed by river transport of eroded sediment to the sea. Metals that are serious pollutants in the refined form used by man are harmless in the mineral state, locked as they are in inert chemical compounds that are virtually insoluble in water. If the mineral sands are mined and processed, however, the disturbance of the bottom, the resultant quantities of silt, and the disposal of tailings or by-products of the refining process pose serious threats to the shelf environment in the area. Together with offshore oil development, mining of the shelf sands may represent man's first massive encroachment in the underwater frontier of the Middle Atlantic region. Industrial utilization of the shelf is likely to go beyond the inital extraction of resources with a rapidity that will make the taming of bygone frontiers seem lethargic. Permanent installations such as offshore port terminals and nuclear power plants are on the drawing boards; floating airports and even cities are proposed. With the wave of exploitation, as always, natives of the reclaimed wastelands will first receive pious benedictions and then short shrift.

Between Sand and Sky

T he use of space and other environmental aspects of the continental shelf by its native creatures varies enormously. Movements of many can be measured in meters or even centimeters after larval settlement and metamorphosis. Some may not move at all as adults, remaining irrevocably fastened to solid rock. At the other end of the spectrum are creatures that exhibit a lifelong wanderlust, but even these have physical limits to survival and often preferred zones of habitation along the continental shelf.

The Atlantic coastal waters of North America are unique in possessing well-defined zones of marine climate that are related to prevailing currents on the continental shelf. The zones are termed biogeographic, implying a spatial organization of life. The location of these zones of life is predominantly determined by the shape of the shoreline, which is largely responsible for directing the paths of coastal currents.

Four major marine biogeographic zones or provinces lie off the eastern United States, fairly discretely separated by three sandspits: Capes Cod, Hatteras, and Canaveral (also known as Cape Kennedy). In the north, Cape Cod's sixty-kilometer barrier projects seaward and deflects and diminishes the southward penetration of the frigid waters of the Labrador Current. The degree of difference in marine flora and fauna north and south of the Cape is particularly noticeable on the inner shelf. Many boreal and arctic organisms reach their extreme southern limit on the north side of the Cape, while creatures from the warm-temperate Atlantic penetrate to the south side. Ecologists believe that summer water temperatures account for the high degree of segregation. North and south of the Cape in summer, ocean water differs at least by a sharp 5°C., and this appears to stimulate provincial preferences among species ranging from algae to fish.

At Cape Hatteras the phenomenon repeats itself. Known as "the Graveyard of the Atlantic" for its turbulent, ship-snatching shoals, the Cape is an area of sharp contrast where three different bodies of sea water vie for dominance on the shelf. It is strange to think of masses of water flowing together yet remaining separate, butting heads, so to speak, across broad fronts that shift back and forth along the shelf, yet this is essentially what happens. Only slow mixing occurs because of differences in temperature, salinity, and other related physical properties. Off Hatteras, the cool Virginian Coastal Current flowing from the north meets the warmer more saline Carolinian shelf water. The two bump against the tropical, highly saline Gulf Stream, whose inner edge sometimes meanders within a few tens of kilometers of the beach.

Normally both the Virginian Current and the Gulf Stream are deflected seaward by the wedge of shoaling sands that extends well offshore. Occasionally, however, strong northeast storms force Virginian water south of the Cape. At such times the so-called Hatteras barrier is said to have broken. This break occurs most often in late fall and winter, and may be belatedly detected by an interesting biological event. Northern planktonic larvae such as the blue mussel appear far south of their normal range. They settle and grow in North Carolina bays and harbors all the way down to Cape Fear, but as summer begins the water temperature becomes intolerable to the northern immigrants and their populations die to the last individual.

Once upon ten thousand summers some mussels may survive, having acquired a hidden beneficial mutation, perhaps a crucial enzyme that can endure high temperature. More likely, there may be a general southward extension of cold water creatures during an ice age. Then a slow reversion to the original climate over several centuries may allow a gradual adaptation to evolve. This kind of adaptation might proceed more quickly in microorganisms such as bacteria, some of which produce a new generation with potential favorable mutations and adaptive qualities every twenty minutes. Of course similar advances, retreats, and colonizations by pioneering organisms proceed in both directions. Tropical creatures arrive continuously at least as far north as Cape Hatteras, where they settle chiefly on the outer shelf.

Most tropical marine life is restricted to waters farther south. On the Atlantic coast of Florida a transition occurs from true tropical communities to those with temperate affinities. For poorly understood reasons, Cape Canaveral forms a significant boundary to the ranges of numerous species of nearshore algae, but animal distributions are not as sharply curtailed along the narrow sandy shelf in this area.

Although one is accustomed to think of sand as a relatively sterile biological medium, on the continental shelf this impression is incorrect on almost any scale. Smallest among marine bottom animals (although larger than bacteria upon which they often feed) are members of the interstitial fauna. These animalcula include numerous species of protozoans, as well as bristly gastrotrichs and the slow-moving tardigrades or water bears and non-parasitic nematodes or roundworms. Beyond basic details of anatomy, biologists know little of these creatures' lives. They are largely unrelated and dissimilar in all but their tiny size and unique habitat, which is the spaces between grains of sand. In some areas the interstitial animals are extremely high in number and of great diversity; vast cities of them sprawl in a few cubic centimeters of sand, and ecologists are intrigued by the dynamics of these lilliputian communities.

Although fleetingly short, the lives of interstitial organisms are nevertheless productive because they contribute to food reserves of certain larger sand dwellers that indiscriminately swallow everything in reach, remove the organic contents, and leave mineral grains cleanly washed by powerful digestive juices.

The inhabitants of the sandy shelf may be classified as *infauna*, those which remain nearly always hidden below the surface of the sediment, and *epifauna*, those which live on the surface. Both ways of life are represented by some kinds of animals, for example the tube-building worms. Some species live within the sand; others fasten tubes to a rock or shell above the bottom. Many of these worms fashion living quarters from the sand itself and seen through a magnifying lens the tubular dwellings are remarkable works of natural art. Individual grains of sand are chosen by the worm. No doubt some essential criteria of selection are lost on human observers, but uniform size and perhaps texture seem important. A mucoid glue secreted by skin glands cements the grains together, and the structure takes on the bodily contours of the animal. The highly magnified view is of often beautiful, sometimes breathtaking forms resembling segments of modern architecture, mosaic constructions having functional designs that may last a hundred million years.

Other worms roam through loosely constructed mines well below the surface. Heavy feeding at one spot causes cave-ins, producing craters in the sand surface above. Castings or fecal pellets pass to the rear and upward to the opening of the worm's burrow, which often has the appearance of a miniature volcano. The deep miners keep the sands in a state of biological turmoil. They loosen the topsoil of the continental shelf, return nutrient substances to the surface layer, and improve conditions for other creatures living nearer the surface.

Within the sand too, relying on environmental sanctuary in addition to organically-derived armor against prying jaws and claws, are the bivalve mollusks—clams, cockles, and their relatives. Most of the clams are filter feeders. Two fleshy tubes called siphons project from the rear of the shell-encased creature up to the sand's surface. Sea water is sucked into one of the siphons; inside the clam, the stream carrying plankton and other bits of edible flotsam passes across a sievelike gill. On the surface of the gill a remarkable sorting process selects and rejects particles according to size. The bits of food are driven into channels by rows of millions of rapidly beating tiny hairs called cilia. The animal prefers very small particles and these go toward the mouth. Coarser material is shunted toward the rear and eventually flushed out. Meanwhile the original flow of water has passed through the filtering gill and exited via the other siphon. Thus a continual stream of water from the unseen sea above passes into and through the buried animal. A similar system serves other permanently committed burrowers, including many worms and crustaceans. Besides bringing food, the circulating water carries vital oxygen and removes metabolic wastes.

Bivalves lead a double life. Like many other sedentary bottom creatures, most bivalves produce planktonic larvae. About the size of the smallest grains of beach sand visible to the unaided eye, the larvae resemble tiny clams, but with a striking difference. They swim by means of a unique embryonic organ called a velum, a flattened lobe of tissue shaped like an inverted parasol. In action it looks like a pinwheel or helicopter rotor, although the appearance of a whirling velum is illusory. Swimming power is provided by rapidly beating cilia all around the edge of the velum. Moreover, as the larva, called a veliger, moves through the water it uses the velum to feed. Tiny particles are caught and sorted by the velum in a manner similar to that of an adult clam's gill.

The enemies of veligers are legion. The tiny larval clamshells are easily crushed by larger antagonists or else give way to dissolving digestive fluids. The most dangerous time, however, comes when the veligers settle to the bottom to metamorphose and grow to adults. The velum degenerates and drops off, and the feebly motile clam fry must seek shelter from predators now concentrated in a nearly two-dimensional environment. Most often there is no place to hide except among grains of sand. Of the millions of offspring spawned by an average female clam, perhaps ten survive the first year of life. Survivors, however, grow very fast, and the odds of survival improve greatly for larger individuals. They simply outgrow many kinds of mouths that relish tender baby clam meat. Nevertheless, some predators retain a taste for clams all the way up to chowder size, and the ubiquitous bivalves, along with worms, often seem to be the "specialty of the house" in benthic food webs.

Highly motile and predatory sand dwellers of the open shelf include burrowers, skimmers, stalkers, and leapers. Large snails, notably whelks and moon snails, hunt buried prey, usually clams. In action, the moon snail or shark's eye, a few centimeters in diameter, with its smooth rounded shell and huge rippling amoeboid foot, resembles a creature or machine from science fiction. It cruises the bottom just out of sight, except for a pair of sensory tentacles that project like tiny periscopes above the sand; only a slow-cresting sand wave marks the animal's passage. When the snail detects prey, its foot turns downward and the creature flows into the sand to find a hapless clam, sometimes 50 centimeters or more below. Unlike the larger whelk, which grinds its bivalve victim's shell open with its own, the moon snail uses a little drill. The carnivore cuts a small round hole in the shell of its victim, which may even be a smaller moon snail, for these animals are avid cannibals. The carnivore inserts its probing mouth into the hole and feeds as if it were sucking an egg. The signature of the moon snail—a neatly tooled hole with a beveled rim—may be seen in empty shells cast up all along Middle Atlantic beaches.

Skimmers, stalkers, and leapers that roam the surface of the sand come in a variety of shapes and sizes. Skimmers include the sand starfish and the fast crabs that half-run, half-swim across the bottom. Swiftness is common. Even the starfish have a smooth tip-toed walk that makes them speedsters when compared to their sluggish, rock-hugging relatives in the north.

One of the stalkers on the temperate Atlantic shelf is the mantis shrimp, *Squilla*. These creatures have an enlarged pair of anterior legs, each tipped with an armored segment called a dactyl. These specialized legs fold next to the body and resemble those of a preying mantis, but the *Squilla*'s armament is more formidable. Despite their small size—known species of mantis shrimp range from 1.5 to 30 centimeters—they are spectacular predators.

Marine biologists recognize that the numerous species of mantis shrimp belong to one of two different hunting guilds, the spearers and the smashers. The spearers catch fairly soft-bodied prey with barbed dactyls each ending in a chitinous lance. Some species strike at speeds up to 1,000 meters per second, one of the fastest animal movements known. A large spearer can transfix a human finger with a flick of its wrist, and can catch and consume fish up to eleven centimeters long.

The smashers have a greatly enlarged and heavily shelled knuckle at the base of the dactyl. The larger species of smashers use this knuckle to deliver karate blows with a force approximating that of a small caliber bullet. They have been known to break an aquarium constructed with two layers of safety glass. They also shatter a moderate sized clam's shell with one blow. Other smashers have been observed attacking crabs. The mantis shrimp usually stalks its fellow crustacean from behind and delivers an initial stunning blow. Then it deliberately smashes both of the crab's claws before dragging the prey off to a burrow in the sand or among rocks.

For *Squilla* and other stalkers, such as flounders and the octopus, whose lair is usually found by some stark rock outcrop or shipwreck, speed is a factor that matters for survival. Most of these animals, whose roles shift minute by minute, from hunter to hunted, possess other useful adaptations as well— color camouflage, or the ability to burrow quickly—and despite the seeming precariousness of life in this environment a great living fabric woven with invisible threads graces the bare and level sand.

Above the sand in open water roam the largest, fastest inhabitants of the continental shelf. Most of these are fish, although squid, marine turtles, mammals, and birds may be present at various times and places. Within this spacious world, as full of motion as the sub-bottom environment is static, animals fit into the usual hierarchical system of prey and predators. The most vulnerable prey live near the sea surface and often band together, apparently for protection. On the temperate Atlantic shelf, one of the most characteristic of these is the menhaden, *Brevoortia tyrannus*, a fish which forms enormous schools and provides fare for millions, including man.

At birth a school of menhaden exists only in prototype, a filmy shadow left by the mass spawning of its parents. It is a dense patch of tiny floating eggs lost in the waters of the mid shelf. Within hours swells disperse the eggs over several square kilometers, and after two days when the eggs hatch, all semblance of a unified population has vanished. There are only scattered small larvae making their individual ways in toward the estuaries along the middle and southeastern United States coast.

Larvae from the first wave of spawning in October arrive along the coast in late fall. They are followed by wave after wave of others of their kind, particularly in the southern range below Cape Hatteras, where spawning may continue into the spring. If the coastal water is still mild, the larvae enter the estuaries—large ones like Chesapeake and Delaware Bays and smaller ones like those lying behind the Carolina outer banks and Georgia's sea islands. In severe weather the shallow upper estuaries rapidly become cold and may even freeze. Under such conditions menhaden larvae will spend the winter in comparative warmth near the ocean inlets. In cold water a temperature difference of two or three degrees is undetected on human skin, but to a cold-blooded creature the difference may mean life or death. A juvenile menhaden in estuarine waters at 5°C. appears to be full of vim and vigor; after a cold night and a drop in water temperature to 3°C. it may be dead.

When they reach the estuaries, the menhaden are approximately three centimeters long and are in the juvenile stage. Bodily proportions now prefigure those of the adult fish, and locomotion has already come under active control. Remaining in the rich estuarine feeding area for several months, the fish grow rapidly, and their schooling instinct develops apace. At first by chance encounters they begin to flock together, and eventually in the relatively finite confines of the estuary the schooling process proceeds rapidly. Now can be seen the function of the initial breakup of the original dense egg masses on the continental shelf spawning grounds, followed by individual migration shoreward, for in the new generation a vital shuffling has occurred. Recruits to the juvenile schools come from the regional spawnings of many different adult schools and inbreeding is thereby effectively prevented.

As they leave the estuaries menhaden range from five to sixteen centimeters in length and are vulnerable to predators from above and below. Great reductions in the size of schools must occur at this stage before the fish outgrow a host of small sharp-mouthed enemies such as needlefish and terns.

Once abroad over the open shelf, a school's size and density form its only defense against larger predators. Occasionally at night or in murky water the huge shadowy presence of massed fish may startle potential enemies into fleeing. Hungry porpoises and whales, sonar-scanning for food from a distance, possibly mistake a school so close to the surface for a mat of driftwood and other flotsam. To its major finny predators, however, the school apparently presents a difficult, confusing target because of its bulk. An isolated menhaden or a few in open water could be focused on, pursued, and snapped up, but a milling, churning, near-solid wall of fish is different. One potential victim blends into several around it; there are no openings against which a single fish can be viewed. Perhaps the predator becomes confused and frustrated; at least this is what appears to happen. There may be some primitive recognition of inadequacy, the mouth feeling too small to function against such a gargantuan spectacle. A few slashing attacks are made; a few victims fall out along the edge, but instantly the wall reappears.

Inside a school under attack, recognition of peril seems to spread quickly. Terror transmits on an invisible wavelength; patterns of vibrations set off by panic-stricken swimmers on the outside edges carry the message. If the attack is concentrated in a specific quarter, the whole school may react by moving in the opposite direction. Under natural conditions predators nibble along the edges of the school and seldom remain long in pursuit. Under other conditions, because of the extraordinary instinct of menhaden to remain together under all circumstances, man catches a school to the last fish. This accomplishment may creditably reflect human technology in the design of a purse seine, but increasingly, to man's shame, it reflects an apalling lack of design in other kinds of equipment now being deployed on the continental shelf.

Some fishes of the continental shelf never experience the bright and turbulent world known to menhaden because they inhabit surface waters only briefly as larvae before taking up a permanent way of life on or near the bottom. On the Atlantic shelf, the bottom-dwelling fish that most immediately comes to mind is the flounder, of which there are many species.

The eggs of most flounder float to the surface, and the larvae enter life as tiny transparent spindles wriggling atop a larger attached yolk sac. Foraging begins as the yolk becomes exhausted. Flounder fry become voracious predators of plankton, but soon the little fish begin to seek bottom, where their diet changes to tiny worms and crustaceans. At first flounderlings are thin-bodied but typically fishlike in other respects. Then suddenly striking anatomical changes take place, and the creature's behavior becomes fixed for an essentially two-dimensional way of life.

Within a few days, the eye on one side migrates around the head to stop beside its twin. Now both eyes come to lie side by side on the same side of the head as the fish begins to swim with its flat sides oriented vertically. Deceptively inactive, the flounder frequently rests on the bottom until a small shrimp or worm comes too close. There is a whiplash rush and the prey vanishes into sideways opening jaws. This sideways motion of the jaw makes the animal seem almost unfinished, but one looks in vain for signs of an evolutionary twisting of the mouth to match the adaptive orientation of the flounder's eyes and body. The sideways snatching at prey is every bit as efficient as the normally aligned jaw closure of other fish.

Besides being fast swimmers in short bursts, flounder have a magical mechanism of camouflage by which they evade larger sharp-eyed predators on the open bottom. Special cells called chromatophores contain dark pigment, and the cells can be expanded and contracted by the fish at will. The expansion of these cells on the flounder's upper surface resembles an effect sometimes seen at halftime in a college football game. In the stands, a group of people holding colored cards or cloth over their heads can form a pattern that emerges strikingly from the neutral surroundings. A better analogy for the action of chromatophores is the slow opening and closing of massed umbrellas. A flounder uses this principle, but unlike the halftime crowd its aim is to remain inconspicuous. By contracting its pigment cells, a dark flounder can become a light silvery gray in sixty to ninety seconds. The extremes of overall light and dark, however, are not as often seen as are variations in a near-infinite range of mottled patterns that match the creature's stopping place of the moment.

Perhaps the most conspicuous fishes that roam the continental shelf, the ones closest to human sensitivities and most commonly chronicled in literature from Hemingway to *Field and Stream*, are the gamefishes.

By the time they reach adulthood these predators near the top of the food web have outgrown nearly all of their enemies. Man is a unique enemy, however, and tends to impinge on these fish in every phase of their life history.

The unintentional forms of human predation hit gamefish hardest when they are young, sometimes even before they hatch from the egg. Although relatively little is known concerning the breeding and early life histories of gamefish that spawn on the continental shelf, recent information has appeared on bluefish, *Pomatomus saltatrix*. This species, nicknamed "chopper" for its voracious habits, is a favorite with sportsmen in the middle Atlantic area. The major bluefish spawning grounds lie on the outer shelf over the southern Baltimore Canyon Trough, an area considered likely for the development of offshore petroleum. Large oil fields here will produce the inevitable chronic contamination. Bluefish eggs and larvae, like those of cod off New England, will probably be maimed by invisible films of petroleum.

On the average, bluefish populations will probably diminish.

In the Middle Atlantic region young bluefish migrate toward shore and congregate along the coast and at the mouths of bays. Schools of small bluefish may be especially susceptible to consumption by large power plants in the coastal zone.

Even the nobility among game species, the dashing billfishes, may not escape. Although very little is known about the geographical distribution of eggs and larvae of these wide-ranging creatures, there have been several sightings of one species, the Atlantic sailfish, *Istiophorus platypterus*, apparently spawning close to the beach along the east coast of Florida. Development of this region's inner continental shelf is proceeding apace and includes a number of large power plants and a recently proposed oil refinery near Fort Pierce. Before it is too late, an intensive scrutiny of the coastal zone is needed to see if sailfish habitually spawn in certain places.

Ironically, the gamefish have found a protector in the collective personage of their dominant predator. Sport fishing is big business on the temperate Atlantic shelf. In Florida alone, recent estimates put the value of marine angling at 2 to 4 billion dollars annually. Elsewhere, from early spring to late fall, thousands of Americans address the surf with striper plugs and related paraphernalia. Others take to the water in countless small craft and troll along the drift lines just offshore, while watching for excited flocks of birds that hover above shoals of feeding fish. Or in small and large parties, they hire ocean-going boats out of salt-water towns such as Rehoboth, Morehead City, and Fernandina. A day's charter fishing on the outer continental shelf now costs as much as $400. While most skippers still hold to the traditional guarantee of a big catch, some fear that leaner days will coincide with the industrialization of the shelf. Suddenly aware of the potentially imminent decline of their pleasure, sport fishermen, who have long been conservationists, are becoming environmentalists. Their concern for a handful of species is broadening to embrace the whole essential ecosystem of the continental shelf.

Hot Oil, Hot Water, and the Hazardous Atom

O n the east coast of the United States a headlong rush into frontier territory is on. The pioneers this time are not land-hungry farmers, but profit-hungry industries. Leading the new wave of eastward expansion are two energy giants, the petroleum and electrical generating industries.

The oil people have discovered that as with New England's Georges Bank, deep sedimentary basins lie below the surficial sands of the temperate Atlantic shelf. Now industrial, political, and environmental interests focus their attention on three potential repositories of offshore oil: the Baltimore Canyon Trough, the Southeast Georgia Embayment, and the Blake Plateau Basin.

A downturn of continental bedrock off Long Island forms the northern edge of the Baltimore Canyon Trough. Named for a minor submarine canyon near its center, the trough extends 650 kilometers south to near Cape Hatteras. It is about 200 kilometers across at its widest point off southern New Jersey where it reaches to the upper continental rise. Sediments along portions of the Trough's north-south axis, which roughly parallels the coast 100 kilometers offshore, are more than 13,000 meters thick (approximately eight miles).

Powerful seismic probes which map the subsurface structure of the shelf down to the basement rock of the continent have revealed what appears to be a huge buried reef in the Baltimore Canyon Trough. Originally mistaken for an upthrusting ridge of bedrock, the reef probably formed 50 to 100 million years ago. At that time the environment off the New Jersey coast was one of tropical water and slow subsidence. The ancient reef must have countered the sinking of the bottom by growing upward. Its huge mass leads marine geologists to speculate that it may have rivaled Australia's Great Barrier Reef of today.

This buried New Jersey reef is not to be confused with the thin ribbon of algal reef off the Carolinas. Lying along a strange wild coast, bordering a young and spreading Atlantic, the New Jersey reef lived in truly ancient times. Many of its creatures, now transfigured in stone, may be unknown to paleontologists.

In the Baltimore Canyon Trough up to 16 million acres of the continental margin are considered likely for oil and natural gas development. A conflict between fisheries and petroleum development is looming in the area. A variety of important species, including menhaden, flounder, and bluefish, have major spawning grounds here on the middle and outer shelf. The complete list of species whose floating eggs are concentrated in this area runs into the dozens, and oil spills or even chronic discharges from platforms and tankers may wreak havoc with sensitive embryonic fish and the beleaguered Northwest Atlantic fisheries.

South of the trough the basement rock rises gradually to form the Cape Fear Arch, centered off the North Carolina-South Carolina border. Then the basement descends again, reaching depths somewhat over 3,000 meters below the present sea floor in the Southeast Georgia Embayment. This area is still under intensive study, and relatively little is presently known of its petroleum-bearing potential.

About 250 kilometers offshore, the 180,000-square-kilometer Blake Plateau lies opposite South Carolina, Georgia, and northern Florida. It is actually part of the continental slope, a structural appendage left dangling by the rifting of America and Northwest Africa. Another reef once flourished at the outer edge of Blake Plateau. It was last at the surface 125 million years ago. Now the reef lies under 3,000 meters of water.

The outline of Blake Plateau has been softened through the eons by a thick cover of oceanic sediment and its contours shaped by currents, particularly the Gulf Stream. Petroleum reserves, if they exist in the Blake Plateau sediments, will not be tapped in the immediate future because of the difficulty and expense imposed by the overlying depth of water, which ranges from 450 to 1800 meters.

In April, 1974, the U.S. Council on Environmental Quality (CEQ), a federal advisory organization in the executive branch, sent to President Nixon its report assessing future environmental impacts of oil production on the Atlantic and Pacific continental margins. The CEQ report was garnered from several intensive and short-term (approximately one year) research projects by universities and commercial consultants in each area concerned. The MIT report on Georges Bank off New England formed part of the CEQ study as did similar research by the Virginia Institute of Marine Science on the Middle Atlantic shelf. Despite its considerable heft (five volumes form a stack twenty centimeters thick), the CEQ report has some major flaws, the worst of which may be a premature attempt to rank the expected offshore drilling areas according to net environmental risk.

On the Atlantic coast, least risk was assigned to Georges Bank with the southern Baltimore Canyon area a close second. The northern Baltimore Canyon and the Southeast Georgia Embayment were deemed areas of moderate risk. Calculations of net risk took into account estimates of regional onshore economic benefits, including employment and the value of refinery production, and also projections of regional energy needs. But as in the MIT study of Georges Bank, the only criterion of true environmental risk discussed in detail was the probability of an oil spill reaching shore. Potential effects of spills on the shelf environment itself, whether from massive accidents or low-level chronic releases of oil were ignored. Many details of continental shelf biology remain to be discovered, but little recognition and no sense of urgency concerning this fact appeared in the report.

Disastrous disruptions of the migration routes of fishes and larval dispersal patterns could accompany the development of large offshore oil fields, but the CEQ report treated the continental shelf itself as it might the surface of the moon.

Even if new discoveries of offshore oil do not measure up to full expectations, the continental shelf looms large in the calculations of U.S. technocratic planners for the years ahead. Certainly, like the Alaskan North Slope reserves, offshore petroleum production will not last long in an economy that threatens to need the equivalent of 17 billion barrels of oil annually by 1980. The key word here is equivalent—for oil alone cannot possibly fuel the commercial-industrial-military behemoth, and plans are well advanced to use the continental shelf both as a reservoir and a receptacle serving other energy schemes. Fighting to the last gasp to avoid the anathema of conservation, which implies a slowed-growth or no-growth economy, gross national producers will increasingly move toward hastily contrived and poorly built energy machines, some of which pose the greatest environmental dangers in the history of men, fish, and the entire ocean planet.

In the early 1980s a brand new line of super power plants is scheduled to come into operation in a number of places along the inner edge of the U.S. continental shelf. The middle Atlantic region will have a sizeable share of these seaside generating stations which will average 2200 megawatts of electricity produced. They will be predominantly nuclear powered, but the hazards of the peaceful atom form only part of their environmental threat.

A continuous flow of sea water will be needed to cool the big reactors. As it does its cooling job, the sea water will be heated and pumped back into the ocean. The green waters of the open shelf, which will both contribute the cooling water and receive the return flow, look limitless. The power plants, whether floating or ashore, look tidy and pleasingly small in the architects' scale drawings. It would be startling, therefore, if a similar rendering would show the cooling system as if it were a river entering the ocean at the plant site. Cooling water flows approaching 8 million liters per minute (4500 cubic feet per second) are envisioned by the engineers. Along the Atlantic coast more water will pass on its circular route through a 2200 MW power plant than flows at low stage (minimal seasonal flow) in some well-known streams, among them the Potomac at Washington, D.C., the James River at Richmond, Virginia, and the Savannah at Augusta, Georgia.

Intake tunnels for the giant generating stations suggest a contemporary version of the river Styx, redesigned to conform to modern engineering specifications, but still leading to regions of darkness, death, and a rare, purified form of brimstone. The terrible reality of atomic radiation is that its effects reach beyond its power to kill. All creatures touched ever so lightly by the careless atom may be changed by an insidious alchemy, and the damage is forever passed in the genes down the generations.

But first affected in a very straightforward manner are myriad creatures of the sea for whom the intake ports present no warning in the tradition of the words over the entrance to Hell: "Abandon all hope, ye who enter here."

Below is a hypothetical series of events that could occur frequently around one of the giant cooling systems to be placed on the shelf in the 1980s.

The school moved slowly in warm surface waters near the coast. Most of the time it seemed to inhabit a void, a moving hole in fluid space, greenish except for a silvery ceiling close above. The ceiling gave this world its only physical sense of character. Sometimes it heaved and foamed in powerful surges; sometimes it barely stirred and merely mirrored the school in its empty surroundings. But emptiness is illusory on the continental shelf, and as the huge pancake-shaped mass of fish slowly tracked southward, it fed continuously on the teeming plankton. Such was the density of the feeders and intensity of their filtration that behind the school a crystal clear wake appeared in the hazy green waters. Fishermen have compared the sight to a mowed strip in a field of grass, and before spotter planes became widely used in the fishery, they relied on the tell-tale track to guide them to the menhaden.

Schooling menhaden

At the first dim light of dawn the school was in a desperate behavioral state—drawn to the warm water field but increasingly panicky—and at this moment an enormous number of bluefish appeared. Approaching from the southeast, the "choppers" sensed the menhaden at once and launched into them. Like a herd of bison beset by Indians, the menhaden began to move as a single great ponderous tongue of fish. Reacting to the directional attack of the bluefish, they surged away toward the north, beyond the emergence zone of warm water, past the huge horseshoe-shaped concrete barrier-island protecting the floating power plant. In the half-light and murky water the leading edge of the school closed in on a broad shadowy form which may have resembled a detached lobe of the school itself. A faint rush of moving water emanated from its edge. Without hesitation the leading menhaden attempted to merge with it, and they succeeded. Assisted by inrushing currents running at close to a meter per second, a slow cascade of five hundred thousand fish disappeared into the power plant's special intake structure that rose above the sea floor like a giant mushroom.

Present designs of offshore intake structures include a huge pipe up to 5½ meters (18 feet) in diameter rising from the sea floor and reaching about halfway to the surface. On the gently sloping Atlantic shelf most of the structures will be less than five kilometers from shore and quite close to the surface, often within five meters. Atop the vertical pipe or shaft will be fitted a velocity cap. Looking like a broad-brimmed concrete sombrero, this device spreads the inrushing current into a circular pattern around the pipe and pulls water from the horizontal rather than the vertical direction. The idea behind the velocity cap is that fish are better able to detect horizontal currents than vertical ones. Fish tend to swim against the former, the best example perhaps being trout in a fast-flowing stream. A few studies sponsored by electrical utilities suggest velocity caps in use on the relatively small cooling water conduits of 1960–70 vintage power plants do reduce average numbers of fish killed. Velocity caps thus constitute a step in the right direction, albeit a small one, but they have never been tested on the gargantuan scale of intended use in the 1980s. Merely scaling up an existing device, no matter how successful, provides no guarantee of calculable function at a larger size. Also, the behavior of fish of the continental shelf is collectively far less well known than that of trout, and the currents experienced by the former are usually far less swift than will occur near the intakes.

Off the coast of southern New Jersey, a rapid succession of sharp cold fronts cooled the autumn surface waters by several degrees within a few days. Winds accompanying the shifting weather reached gale force, and unusually turbid conditions extended several kilometers offshore. The directional sense of the migrating school was unaffected, however, and the menhaden moved steadily southward until one mid-October night when they were in sight of the lights of Beach Haven on the outer coast. The response to warmth was impulsive, a thing of the moment. In the newly chilled surroundings it overruled the underlying directional urge of the school, but not all the fish felt it at once. The presence of warmth existed in long thin streamers, and the sensation of temperature change was a feather touch. A human swimmer passing through the interlaced thermal zones would have noticed nothing. Only the most sensitive of thermometers might have detected the changes, and even then could not have pointed to the source of the warmth. But the fish felt and knew, and the subtle emanations were seductive. Within a few minutes the entire school reversed direction in the dark water and headed north.

Somewhat before dawn, just five kilometers off the beach, the school arrived in the vicinity of the warmth. Across a swath of sea, hundreds of meters wide, plumes of warm water rose from the bottom 15 meters below and drifted south in a slowly spreading pattern at the surface. The warmth, now up to several degrees above the temperature of the surrounding ocean, was attractive to the menhaden. Several other manifestations in the area, however, odors and vibrations that filled the water, fostered a continual low-level nervousness in the school. In the field of warm fluid zephyrs was a subtle odor of death, for the plumes contained countless bodies of plankton, all freshly killed. But the school's anxiety rose mainly in response to the growing perception of predators. Never had the school felt and smelled and tasted such a surrounding concentration of predators. There were a variety of sharks, jacks, big kingfish, cobia, and others having southerly affinities which, apparently like the menhaden, had interrupted their fall migration by this thermal oasis in the sea.

Close to the entry vents velocities may reach a meter per second, a speed comparable to a fast flowing river and the swiftest of tidal currents. Except for the fastest swimming species, unsuspecting fish coming too close may be swept in before they react. The huge shaft and velocity cap, itself some 20 meters (65 feet) across the hatlike rim, may form an attractive nuisance on the open sandy shelf. Many kinds of fish are known to gather around large solid objects in the water. After its emplacement, an intake structure will rapidly sprout a garden of delicacies for underwater browsers, as well as a more refractory canopy creating an attractive reef-like aspect. There is the possibility that the intake pipe will become an enormous ghost trap which continually attracts new fish to its vicinity, then swallows them in an unguarded moment. Furthermore, continuous large-scale destruction of many species could occur as predators chase them into the intake. Examples of this phenomenon may already exist, but they have received scant attention in impact studies to date. And the sheer size of the new power plants suggests that this problem may become more serious by orders of magnitude than anything yet seen.

The swallowing of fish and other organisms by power plants is known as entrainment. At an intake the only physical barrier to entrainment is a grating made of heavy steel-alloy bars which is designed primarily to prevent the entry of large half-submerged logs, curious or suicidal divers, and other similar sized objects. Thus except for the largest marine organisms, every kind of inhabitant of the continental shelf may be sucked into the pipe.

Once inside there is no escape. Nothing save perhaps a salmon in its prime can escape the powerful flow which accelerates past the velocity cap to two or three meters per second. A continuous thirty-square-meter cross section of the living sea races in the dark past smooth and silent walls toward destruction. For many minutes nothing happens; there is no change in temperature or direction, no obstruction. Then suddenly the stream reaches the pumping station located on shore, and for most of the adult fish the journey is over.

They run onto the traveling screens with damaging impact. Pinned in place and powerless to move, they are plucked from the intake channel by the screen which dips only its lower portion into the rushing water and operates like an escalator carrying the fish upward. Fastened to the heavy-duty screen, like steps a meter or so apart, are shallow baskets. The baskets extend the whole width of the screen, and as the screen carries the fish above the cooling water stream they are released from the pinning force of the current and fall into the baskets. Slowly they ride the escalator to the top. Just before the screen turns over a giant roller to start down the other side, the fish are blasted from the shallow baskets by continuous jets of water emerging from a horizontal row of high pressure nozzles. The fish along with other flotsam filtered out of the cooling flow fall into an adjacent collecting pool. Usually located at ground level, the collecting pool connects by pipes or a natural channel to the sea, most often via a nearby harbor or bay. Theoretically, the fish are free to return to their environment without further incident.

But most return in exceedingly poor shape if at all. Many fish die of their injuries or shock before they leave the vicinity of the pumping station. Battered and bruised and often displaying "grill marks" where they were splayed against the screens, the rest are easy prey for enemies large and small, including disease-causing microbes which gain entrance on scraped and bruised patches of skin. Studies to determine the survival of fish repatriated to the natural environment via traveling screens are nonexistent.

Of course not all fish catch on the screens. Larvae and fry of most species are small enough to pass through the coarse, two-centimeter mesh and they, together with plankton representing every major division in the animal kingdom, plunge on toward the plutonic regions. Depending on the plant's location, the cooling water may travel unaltered as far as two or three kilometers beyond the pumping station, or it may continue only a hundred meters or so before life-destroying changes ensue rapidly. At the approach to the reactor, the giant conduit with its river of sea water splits into branches. As in a segment of an organic circulatory system, the branches grow finer and finer. Within a few seconds the enormous unified flow has entered a network of titanium-steel capillaries lying around a cavernous pressure vessel containing steam superheated by nuclear fires to several hundred degrees. The cool sea water does its job—almost instantly the steam inside the thick-walled chamber condenses and is ready for another work cycle; almost instantly the heat lost by the steam enters the cooling stream and its myriad forms of life.

Delta T (Δ T) is the thermal engineer's term for the gain in temperature of a cooling fluid in the operation of a power plant. For example, if the sea water enters the cooling conduit at 10°C. and is heated to 25°C., the Δ T of the operation is 15°C. Δ Ts as high as 25°C. (45°F.) in water released to the ocean have been proposed for the power plants of the 1980s. Environmentalists' objections and pressure on utilities and regulatory agencies have so far brought about only token reductions in ΔT, for example from 25° to 22°C.

Although thermal effects in the marine environment depend on many factors including age and species of organisms affected, season of the year, and rapidity of the temperature change, biologists agree that ΔT is more critical in warmer regions than in cooler northern waters. Marine life in the tepid summer sea off Florida may be living close to an absolute upper temperature limit. Thus a 5° to 6°C. rise in temperature around a thermal outfall might prove lethal to many creatures there, while a comparable kill would perhaps require a 10° to 12° increase in New England waters.

ΔT is inversely related to the volume of cooling water used. In relatively warm regions such as the Gulf of Mexico, power plants with once-through cooling must pump greater amounts of sea water to minimize the temperature increase and prevent the formation of large, lethally warm pools around the discharge zone. But an accelerated pumping rate is itself deleterious because of increased entrainment. Even if the temperature change were controlled at a non-damaging level, extreme turbulence in the vicinity of the pumps and condenser tubes would still severely damage most of the trapped organisms.

The implications of ΔT are misleading if one thinks only of the levels of temperature involved. The absolute number of degrees of change is usually not as important as the rate of change, which, in the cooling capillaries of a generating station, is practically instantaneous. In the jargon of the physiologist, an organism exposed to a sudden shift in temperature is said to undergo thermal shock. Even though the actual change is one that a creature experiences in its normal annual cycle, the sudden burst of warming or cooling is frequently injurious and may kill. Delicate systems of metabolism, activity of nerves and brain, the normal development of eggs and embryos—all are pushed to the thin edge of dysfunction by thermal shock. A living body, especially a cold-blooded one whose internal temperature matches its immediate environment, and quintessentially one inhabiting the continental shelf where the underwater weather shifts at a snail's pace through the year, cannot stand the pace of the new industrialized ocean.

As the network of cooling capillaries reconverges into a single trunk line on the outflow side of the plant, the now warm effluent carries the same stream of plankton, but every individual has suffered a sort of severe stroke, and many are dead and dying. In some of the early studies of entrainment effects, biologist consultants for power companies reported that a majority of plankters survived transits of cooling systems with ΔTs up to 15°C. But more recently observers have found these pronouncements to be premature.

Dr. Edward Carpenter of the State University of New York at Stony Brook on Long Island collected entrained copepods as they emerged from the outfall of a relatively small generating station at Millstone Point on Long Island Sound, near New London, Connecticut. Nearly all the tiny crustaceans, which had experienced a ΔT of 13°C., were alive at this point. Using the same plankton collecting net, Carpenter also obtained copepods of the same species from a nearby area well removed from the discharge.

These control animals, he was reasonably sure, had not passed through the plant. He then placed both groups in small cages of plankton netting immersed in sea water and began to keep careful notes on the copepods' behavior.

From the start, the entrained group showed signs of distress. Their swimming behavior was abnormal and feeble, causing them to sink 2½ times faster than the controls. After three and a half days about half the copepods which had passed through the plant were dead. After five days the mortality of this group had reached 70%, while 10% of the control population had died, perhaps of old age or of injuries sustained during their capture. The Millstone plant discharges into a deep coastal pond, and when Dr. Carpenter took samples from the deeper waters of the pond he found enormous concentrations of dead copepods still sinking slowly toward the bottom.

Dr. Carpenter believes that hydraulic or mechanical stress caused by turbulence is primarily responsible for the death of copepods and probably other plankton entrained by the Millstone plant. At one point the reactor was shut down, but the cooling system remained in operation. Copepods collected during this time showed the same behavior as the group exposed to the plant's heat, and after five days about the same number had died. The effect of thermal shock at the Millstone plant and others having higher Δ Ts remains in question, however, since, as Carpenter cautions, the copepods do not experience thermal stress without mechanical effects. In addition, the relative harm of turbulence as compared with temperature to other kinds of plankton is uncertain.

Using his data and the flow rate of the cooling system, Carpenter calculated that 610 billion copepods pass through the plant yearly. Such an astronomical number is difficult to comprehend. Further calculations indicate that it represents at least three-tenths of one percent of the copepod production (a measure of the formation of copepod flesh via growth and reproduction) over 333 square kilometers at the eastern end of Long Island Sound. Again, what the loss of this amount of copepod production means to the food web of fish and other interdependent creatures is difficult to interpret. One power plant may not consume enough copepods to cause a shortage, but what about two? Three in the same area? How many of these huge new predators can coexist with established food webs on the continental shelf?

Carpenter believes his data underestimate actual losses because zooplankton other than copepods are also probably damaged by passage through the plant. Scientific testimony presented before the U.S. Environmental Protection Agency in 1975 indicated that entrainment by a large power plant could wipe out most of an entire year's crop of veliger larvae produced by clams along a fifty-kilometer stretch of coast.

Even at the small Millstone plant, biological impacts were not confined to copepods and larvae. One week in August, 1972, an estimated 150 million very young menhaden passed through Millstone's cooling system and settled in a slow, silvery rain to waste at the bottom of the effluent pond. The fish were about three centimeters long, and at first they passed easily through the traveling screens. Incredibly, the mounting kill was either not noticed or ignored until the third or fourth day, when the traveling screens began to buckle from the weight of the fingerlings that had finally clogged the mesh. No outside scientist was present while the kill was in progress. The incident received almost no publicity in the local community. Dr. Carpenter arrived after the plant had been forced to shut down in order to clear tons of fish from its intakes. He observed men hired by the utility using pressure hoses to wash walls of fish from the sides of the tidal effluent pond. He estimated 150 million dead fish, which may make the Millstone kill a world record.

Extending several hundred meters across the bottom on the open shelf, perhaps ten to twenty meters deep, a cooling water outfall from a giant power plant takes the form of a perforated pipe. Called a multiport diffuser by engineers, the rig resembles the kind of lawn sprinkler with holes all along its length. In principle the device takes the concentrated deadly sting out of the massive hot water discharge by spreading it over a wide area, yet at the same time it creates a wide and no less potentially fatal field of attraction for marine fish.

Like the intake structure, a diffuser outfall is an attractive nuisance, but it operates in a far more subtle manner. Diffusers on the open shelf will at times be surrounded by a field of relatively warm surface water up to several square kilometers in area (one or two degrees above the normal local water temperature). The closer one is to the diffuser, the warmer the water becomes, reaching perhaps five or six degrees above normal. Fish are known to sense temperature changes of the order of several hundredths of a degree occurring over horizontal distances of a hundred meters, and the far-reaching influence of the thermal fountains in the sea are not even guessed at.

Fingers and tendrils of warm water may extend many kilometers in slow, prevailing surface currents. Some species, especially those that migrate seasonally, may be attracted to the warmth and even trapped there with the coming of winter. This phenomenon was responsible for some spectacular non-entrainment fish kills near existing thermal effluents. One example in January, 1972, involved menhaden near a nuclear generating station at Oyster Creek on the New Jersey coast. The fish do not normally occur in the area in winter, and they were probably attracted to the estuarine discharge site during the previous autumn. As in other similar cases the damage was done when the plant shut down briefly for refueling. Overnight the water temperature in the discharge zone plummeted from about 15°C. to near freezing, causing what is known as reverse thermal shock, which is just as devastating as the kind that results from elevated temperatures. To fish, crowded perhaps for months in a small area under conditions of probable semistarvation, it was lethal. Thousands of menhaden died and covered the shores of the tiny estuary knee deep in iridescent, putrifying bodies.

Local, out-of-season warming of the sea promotes some life-destroying changes that seem truly insidious. One of these is gas bubble disease. Water, when warmed, may become supersaturated or overloaded with dissolved air. Fish utilize some of this as oxygen, but the pressure of nitrogen entering the fish's bloodstream is higher than that in its body and the gas begins to fizz out of solution. Fatal embolisms often follow. Air saturation is naturally highest in cold Atlantic shelf waters during early spring. According to fisheries biologist J. B. Pearce, slight warming of the water around thermal outfalls poses the greatest danger for menhaden beginning their northward spring migrations.

On the continental shelf the thermal fields created by the new super power plants may attract astronomical numbers of fish of both resident and migratory species. While the fish may end up starving because of local exhaustion of food resources, their parasites and disease-producing microorganisms should thrive, which suggests a new, subtle, and potentially ecocatastrophic problem associated with the warm water discharges.

In temperate waters the thermal fields are like tropical oases in the sea. They form small but significant settings for the mingling of one biogeographic zone with another. Such pockets of warm water can serve as refugia and incubatoria for exotic organisms which survive close to the discharge in winter, then spread into the surrounding area in the summer. The situation is parallel to the periodic colonization of North Carolina waters by the northern blue mussel, but unlike that animal, which travels the natural seaways, comparable Caribbean creatures probably most often reach the Middle Atlantic shelf with the unwitting aid of man. Boats coming north carry veritable jungles of marine life attached to their hulls. No customs inspector probes, pinches, peers, and sniffs among the multi-colored growth that disguises a boat bottom like a beard. No regulation requires below-the-water-line cleaning of a fouled boat that crosses a biogeographic boundary, but this may soon become necessary if large thermal discharges proliferate in the ocean. Highly undesirable aliens have already begun turning up in force in the Middle Atlantic area, and scientists believe this may be only the beginning of a vast encroachment.

Oyster Creek, part of the Barnegat Bay estuarine system on the New Jersey coast, was the scene of the first known tropical marine invasion around a North American power plant. Jersey Central Power and Light (JCPL) began operating the Oyster Creek plant in 1969 and faced ecological problems from the start. One of these was the previously mentioned menhaden kill by cold shock, but many other difficulties centered on shipworms, two species of which occur naturally in Barnegat Bay. Several marinas on Oyster Creek itself, which received the thermal discharge, were severely impacted by the wood-destroying mollusks whose breeding periods were extended and activity heightened by the year-round presence of warm water.

As their docks collapsed, the marina owners sued JCPL for losses of business and capital investments. The legal action dragged on while the utility disclaimed responsibility and maintained that shipworms represented a natural phenomenon in the area. But in July, 1974, two new species of shipworms were discovered in Oyster Creek, and their nearest natural populations were known to occur south of Cape Canaveral, Florida. They apparently arrived with a wooden yacht sailing north with the spring, and they found ideal tropical conditions in Oyster Creek.

This dramatic development speedily settled the court case in favor of the marinas, but it posed unsettling problems for Barnegat Bay. After a year one of the tropical species had multiplied greatly and spread beyond the mouth of Oyster Creek into the Bay for more than 15 kilometers along the path of the thermal plume. Laboratory experiments by researchers at Harvard, who were involved in the case on behalf of the marina owners, revealed that at least some of the adults of this species could survive normal winter temperatures in the area, and they could probably breed away from the plume for most of the summer.

Presently a search is on for other exotic marine life in the area. The project is led by Dr. Ruth Turner of Harvard, who has studied the shipworm problem in Oyster Creek for several years and who now suspects that other invaders will turn up. She believes the same sort of process may occur wherever large thermal effluents are situated in the temperate marine environment. Even more damaging than shipworms in the long run may be diseases and parasites of commercially important fish and shellfish. The thermal fields could become loci of infections which might fester undetected for years, then under favorable conditions break out in a regional epidemic. In other cases migratory fish may become vectors of a disease, carrying it from one host to another. Within the perpetually warm blizzard of dead and dying plankton surrounding an ocean thermal outfall, many microbes may find ideal living conditions—a sort of crude bacterial incubator on an unprecedented scale. Some types of pathological organisms are very hardy, may well adapt to local waters, and even evolve into new strains. Unlike fish and other higher organisms, microbes possess simple physiologies that are little perturbed by thermal shock. Thus periodic shut-down of a power plant and a temporary return to ordinary conditions will not necessarily alleviate the possibility of disease, and the reverse thermal shock may only hasten the end of the fish.

One other thermal-related problem affecting fish and man has been envisioned by biologists from the University of Miami. In the Caribbean there is a spotty but widely distributed toxic condition affecting humans who eat certain reef fishes. This condition is termed *ciguatera* poisoning, and it originates in certain blue-green algae. Fish which browse on the algae become highly toxic to man, although the fish themselves seem little affected, if at all. The browsing species also pass the toxin on to their finny predators. Thus a jack or barracuda can be as poisonous, or more so, than its small herbiverous prey. If *ciguatera* should turn up in fish living around the industrial-tropical pools on the northern shelf, local catches of fish might have to be inspected carefully before they are sold for human consumption.

Giant intake structures and diffusers lying like small reefs off the heavily used beaches of the east coast could bring a threat more sinister and disturbing to local emotions and economics than periodic fish kills. The thriller *Jaws* raises a nagging question: why would a great white shark hang around a given stretch of coast in the first place? One reason might be the presence of intake and outfall structures with their rich attendant marine life. It is not unlikely that sharks and other predators will be attracted to the sea floor emplacements because of the foraging possibilities. From there, given present construction plans, it is only a short swim to the beach and to the peculiar fluttery vibrations humans make in the water, sounds which some scientists believe sharks mistake for their normal prey—wounded or disabled fish, seals and porpoises. At present, impact studies for electrical generating facilities on the continental shelf have not considered the *Jaws* connection. Perhaps they should, for it would be unfortunate to have to institute shark watches at once-safe seashore areas and force vacationing Americans to swim like trapped fish within giant antishark screens.

Recently a new use of the continental shelf has been suggested by the electrical power industry: the emplacement and operation of floating nuclear plants (FNPs). Although now only at the conceptual stage, the FNP concept has gained powerful backing from some federal energy officials and the nuclear industry.

Built in a "wet slip" at a coastal manufacturing site, each FNP as now conceived would consist of a barge or float surmounted by the power plant itself. The whole floating structure would be roughly square (about 120 meters on a side), draw 10 meters of water with a displacement of 145,000 metric tons, and rise nearly 55 meters above the sea surface. Quarters for a crew of 112 operating personnel are included in the design. The working part of the plant consists of a pressurized water reactor similar to ones now in use, having a generating capacity of 1150 megawatts of electricity.

Two or more FNPs might be moored together in water 10 to 20 meters deep. A massive concrete breakwater covering up to one-hundred acres would encircle the FNPs; two small openings in the breakwater would allow free circulation of sea water and permit access by boats for service and exchange of personnel. Designers of the FNPs claim that the breakwater would be built to withstand the worst acts of God and man, which are conceived, respectively, as the ultimate in hurricane waves and a collision and explosion such as might accompany the wreck of an oil tanker or liquefied natural gas carrier.

The first proposal for actual siting of FNPs came in 1972, from the Public Service Electric and Gas Company of New Jersey. Two FNPs would operate on the continental shelf just 4½ kilometers off the beach at a position 19 kilometers northeast of Atlantic City. A transmission cable buried in the sea floor would deliver power to the mainland.

Optimism over FNPs, however, has washed up cold and wrinkled on some notable shores. Henry W. Kendall, an MIT physicist and a leader of the Union of Concerned Scientists, has stated that a major accident involving an FNP might be worse than a corresponding mishap on land. Testifying before a congressional committee in 1973, Kendall said,

> . . . when the remains of the reactor core and waste products melt their way through the reactor containment structures . . . contact between this material and the ocean water will cause the certain release of a very large quantity of solid radioactive wastes into the world's oceans. Such an event is a catastrophe of a kind the country has never experienced. There is in a large nuclear plant, for example, enough strontium-90 to contaminate thousands of cubic miles of water above permitted AEC tolerance levels . . .

On a global scale, the great ocean currents communicate between countries and continents. They have been conveyors of climate and life throughout earth's history; now the arteries of the sea could be injected with dangerous doses of the most poisonous substances known. Slow-traveling underwater clouds spreading invisible death could have devastating effects on the rich Northwest Atlantic fisheries. Although oceanic water masses are slow to mix, the longevity of many radioactive pollutants would assure the eventual contamination of major current systems. The Gulf Stream branches after it leaves the United States' east coast, and its waters brush Iceland and northwestern European shores. Thus a release of radioactive material including strontium-90 and the extremely dangerous plutonium from a stricken FNP off New Jersey could at the very least damage international friendship.

The AEC (now NRC) considered Kendall's fears exaggerated and termed the possibility of a reactor meltdown "highly unlikely." However, the agency did concede that an accident such as the one envisaged by Kendall could poison the ocean over a wide area and observed that more study must be done on the behavior of hazardous nuclear material in the sea, especially plutonium. Despite the hint of official hedging that has surrounded this issue, it has nevertheless become unthinkable to treat high-level nuclear wastes according to the oft-repeated catch phrase: the solution to pollution is dilution.

In recent years there has been considerable controversy over potential terrorist activities directed at nuclear generating stations, fuel reprocessing plants, and transport facilities for uranium and plutonium. The unthinkable is no longer impossible now that the word is out that a college physics major with modest mechanical abilities can fashion a crude but functional atomic bomb with a chunk of stolen plutonium the size of a grapefruit. Since 1974, security surrounding nuclear activities in the public sector has increased greatly, and the Energy Research and Development Administration (ERDA) and the Nuclear Regulatory Commission (NRC) plan even tighter security in the future.

If the years ahead are as fraught with tension as ERDA and NRC seem to expect, then some sort of security coverage will have to be devised for the continental shelf. The naked ocean intakes of nuclear plants, which are likely to proliferate all around the United States' coastline, will be inviting targets for terrorists equipped with little more than fast outboards and scuba gear. Their threats might be backed up by a homemade depth charge or simply a large weighted slipcover made of industrial plastic. Once a plant's cooling water stops flowing because of a collapsed pipe or blockage of the intake, an emergency cooling systems (ECS) within the plant is supposed to operate for several minutes while a crew frantically shuts the reactor down. If the emergency system does not work properly, core meltdown ensues and deadly radioactive clouds can escape and spread as far as 100 kilometers downwind. ECS is the most controversial part of all commercial reactors now built or on the drawing boards because the system has never been tested under actual operating conditions.

Widespread nuclear power development points to a world totally dependent on man-devised controls of dangers which cannot be coped with by the natural resiliency and recuperative powers of earth's ecosystems. We are just beginning to question the use of nuclear energy in terms of environmental susceptibility, absorptive limits, dispersal characteristics, and biospheric health. To this should be added grave misgivings concerning social costs. The answers will not be immediately forthcoming, and some of them when fully known may forbid rational beings to proceed along certain paths. Beginning in the 1980s, it may become necessary for vulnerable continental shelf installations to be protected by patrol boats. Perhaps nearby beaches will be watched and "suspicious" fishermen searched.

Octopus

Spoiling the Sea

On the open shallow shelf of the New York Bight, within the delta-shaped pocket of an equilateral, 350-kilometer stretch of Long Island and New Jersey coast, an undulating horde begins to gather in the wintery waters of early February. The fish, averaging about a third of a meter long, alternatively move forward a short distance, then rest briefly on the gradually shoaling sands. When swimming, they resemble miniature flying carpets that stay just above the bottom. When resting, their flattened bodies seem to dissolve into their surroundings. They are not a schooling species and they pace themselves individually, while nevertheless heading shoreward as a broad diffuse wave toward the spawning bays and estuaries—Barnegat, Navesink, Raritan, Jamaica and many others.

They are winter flounder, also called blackback (*Pseudopleuronectes americanus*). The species characteristically inhabits the shallow inner continental shelf, and its annual migration into coastal estuaries occurs all along the Atlantic shore from Canada's maritime provinces to Cape Hatteras. The New York Bight lies near the center of the species' geographic range and historically has harbored large blackback populations.

Although the spawning adults enter estuaries of which none are pristine and many are grossly polluted, they encounter relatively little stress. First, the cold water of early spring automatically contains more dissolved oxygen than at other times of year. Second, the fish feed little or not at all during the spawning season and thus do not ingest toxic materials. Finally, much water-borne pollution, including oil, pesticides, detergents, and related chemicals, is concentrated in the surface layer. In an estuary, relatively fresh water often floats over a saltier layer below and a physical barrier of sharp density change, called a halocline (similar to a thermocline), impedes the intrusion of surface pollutants into the depths. A bottom fish can follow the so-called salt wedge (a clean lower layer that is continuous with the open sea) for considerable distances into estuaries whose upper two meters of water combine the qualities of discharges from a tanker's bilge and the sewer effluent of a chemical manufacturing plant.

Female blackback lay their eggs at night in dense clusters. Unlike those of many marine fishes, including other flounders, blackback eggs are heavier than water. The egg clusters also contain a sticky substance which causes small dense mats of eggs to cling to the bottom. Two or three weeks of incubation and microscopic activity pass before the larvae hatch into the still frigid tidal currents. They are two millimeters long, fragile bodied, huge eyed, and resemble soft glass figurines, as do all of their kind. For up to several weeks more they drift but remain with the estuarine system and always close to the bottom. During this time they draw sustenance from a bulbous, underslung yolk sac that slowly shrinks into more fishlike contours.

Before long the restless eye migrates around the head, and the little fish commit themselves to a bottom orientation. In motion their bodies begin to trace the contours of the sea floor; at rest they learn to mimic its color tones and patterns.

By midsummer most young-of-the-year flounder have left the channels and emerged in great numbers from the lightly polluted, and in lesser numbers from the grossly polluted, estuaries onto the inner shelf. All around the arc of coast at whose apex stands New York City the paths of young blackback are focused in the direction of the largest single concentration of marine pollution on earth.

For more than forty years, New York City and its urban satellites have officially used the adjoining continental shelf as a disposal area, although casual ocean dumping has certainly occurred there for a much longer period. Today, beginning only ten kilometers east of Sandy Hook, New Jersey, sewage sludge, polluted harbor muck, acids and other chemicals, demolition debris or "cellar dirt," and several other categories of civilized refuse are dumped in mountainous quantities. Farther offshore, obsolete munitions and other military wastes as well as exceedingly toxic chemicals and low-level radioactive materials have disappeared for decades beneath the waves. Separate areas have been set aside for each category of waste. This practice may permit the detection of specific impacts and help avoid combinations of ill effects on the environment, but serious attempts at regulation, monitoring, policing, and eventual phasing out of the varied dumping activities have only recently developed on paper. As watchdogs of the undersea dumps the Environmental Protection Agency (EPA) and the U.S. Coast Guard have been little tested. The EPA is responsible for determining biological effects in and around the massive dump sites in the area of New York Bight.

One of the dumps closest to shore, and perhaps uppermost in public sensitivities, is the sludge dump. Sewage sludge which is dropped from barges forms a thick, heavier-than-water slurry that spreads over the bottom. In 1974 alone nearly four million cubic meters of sludge was dumped in inner New York Bight.

Also in 1974 a serious flap was raised by environmental and recreational interests in the New York and northern New Jersey areas. Less than a kilometer from several swimming beaches, marine scientists from local universities had discovered what they called "black mayonnaise" (BM), an evocative euphemism for sewage sludge. The term accurately suggests the color, texture, and organic richness of the sludge. The EPA was apparently taken by complete surprise, and in a preliminary report declared that while patches of BM had indeed been found they were not from the main sludge dump ten kilometers farther off the beaches. Thus, declared EPA, the sludge was not being moved by bottom currents toward shore, as had been alleged by environmentalists. This reassuring statement, however, did not explain the presence of the nearshore sludge patches; a considerable amount of unscrupulous convenience dumping near the beaches must have gone on quite recently under the public's nose and that of EPA. The very fact of illegal dumping forbodes a large measure of futility in trying to carry out complex regulations concerning ocean waste disposal. The errant sludge patches, along with an occasional violator intercepted here and there by the Coast Guard, must represent the tip of the iceberg in illegal dumping, especially farther offshore where the designated dumping grounds are well over the horizon.

Two hundred forty kilometers south-southwest of New York's main dumping grounds other unsavory blemishes mar the clean floor of the Middle Atlantic shelf. Before 1973, Philadelphia's sludge dump lay just sixteen kilometers off Cape May, New Jersey, practically in the entrance to Delaware Bay. Now the dumping ground has been relocated sixty kilometers east of Ocean City, Maryland, and business is booming (700,000 wet tons slid into the sea in 1974). Furthermore, as in New York Bight, there is evidence of "short dumping." Alarming increases in heavy metal contamination of surf clams and scallops have been found by EPA and other scientists. The metals are clearly traceable to Philadelphia's sludge, and concern over a potential human health hazard has focused on some prime shellfishing areas.

Sewage sludge is a complex material, the combined effluvia of millions of bathrooms, kitchens, and domestic, commercial, and industrial sumps of every description. Most of the water from raw sewage is filtered away, leaving a viscous deposit of sludge that may be further dried or disposed of as is. Raw sludge is an incredibly rich mixture of largely organic chemicals, and when it is dropped in the ocean it forms a superb source of nutrition for simple forms of life and an ideal growth medium for bacteria. This role is a proper and normal one for concentrated organic material, and the same marine bacteria that accomplish the final recycling of dead fish and other similar matter invade the sludge.

Materials that are acutely toxic to marine life are fortunately uncommon in sludge, but the sheer *volume* of organic matter literally overwhelms the recycling capacity of the benthic environment. The immense populations of bacteria use up oxygen until it is depleted below the level necessary to sustain higher forms of life, and huge areas of "dead sea" appear over the bottom where sludge deposits have accumulated. Sometimes not only clams, worms, burrowing shrimp, and other within-bottom dwellers are killed, but even fish cannot penetrate the layer of water along the bottom where the dissolved oxygen content is close to zero. Occasionally such a layer of lifeless water, which has formed over the sludge dump, may begin to drift along the bottom. As if covered by an invisible subsea smog, marine life inhabiting areas downstream from the sludge will smother and die. This phenomenon has probably been going on for years, and it well illustrates the adage, "out of sight, out of mind." A comparable situation on land—say, a die-off of hundreds of acres of forest surrounding a disposal site—would have been intolerable long before EPA came into being.

While most marine bacteria are believed harmless to the environment and man, sludge in the sea conserves and harbors a host of man's own microbes for long periods. Reassuring microbiological studies have shown that typical human intestinal bacteria, the so-called coliforms, are rapidly killed when exposed to sea water, but these experiments did not duplicate the conditions of a massive sludge dump. More recent studies showed that within the protective incubating bulk of a marine sludge deposit after nineteen months on the sea floor were large numbers of man's most common intestinal affiliate, *E. coli* (*Escherichia coli*). Coliform bacteria were found within shelf sediments for eleven kilometers around the New York disposal site, and fecal contamination reached seaward over thirty kilometers along a shelf channel that connects to the Hudson Submarine Canyon. *E. coli* itself is not of concern here, for it is a harmless species. However, because it is abundant and easily recognized it serves as an indicator of significant human fecal contamination which could also harbor truly harmful microbes.

The viruses are among the worst microbes from the standpoint of longevity and resistance to sewage treatment methods. As proto-life below bacteria on the evolutionary scale, viruses are dangerously infectious in low numbers. The dumping of sewage sludge in shallow water near swimming beaches, or by accident or otherwise in areas where fishermen make catches for human consumption, poses a public health problem of still unknown magnitude. Shellfish, chiefly clams and oysters, are notorious for concentrating viruses, among them, polio virus, and outbreaks of disease such as hepatitis have been traced to contaminated seafood. The virus problem remains a major stumbling block to the recycling of sewage sludge for use in aquaculture. Even under laboratory conditions viruses cannot be purged adequately from sludge, and sludge is a primary nutrient source for algae, which in turn feed oysters. These concentrate even trace occurrences of pathogenic microbes to dangerous levels and deliver them directly to where they are most harmful. Using dried, treated sludge as a fertilizer for landbased crops is far less dangerous. And, in light of skyrocketing costs in refined chemical agriculture, the massive dumping of organic nitrates, phosphates, and other fertilizing compounds on the continental shelf is exceedingly wasteful.

The dumping of dredge spoils is similar in some ways to the ocean disposal of sewage sludge. Harbor muck is moved on barges and supposedly dumped in its own area surprisingly close to the north Jersey shore. On the bottom eight kilometers off Highlands, New Jersey, the polluted mud covers the clean sand in a sticky deposit that is physically similar to sludge. Dredge spoils too are often organically rich and promote natural bacterial growth resulting in oxygen depletion, but even in well-aerated water-dredge spoils have been linked to massive kills of bottom life. Unlike most sludge, the harbor muds contain abundant man-made toxic substances; oil, metals, acids, and other chemicals. Some areas covered by especially poisonous dredgings have been found to be azoic—without detectable life. The usual condition, however, is a severely reduced biotic diversity in the spoil areas; bottom communities become dominated by small, bristly, extremely fecund worms and a few other hardy creatures which are rarely found among the normal denizens of the sandy shelf.

For many years, fishermen working the waters of New York Bight have been aware of the dead zones in the vicinity of the sludge and dredge spoil dumps. Nevertheless, fishing on the shelf remained generally productive despite an increasing incidence of obvious skin disease in bottom fish all over the area. The disease, whose symptoms include hemorrhage as well as festering skin sores, now seems linked to the presence of sludge, spoils, or both. Some fishermen refer to the condition as leprosy of the sea, but the simplest descriptive term is fin rot. Recent scientific studies of the growing number of cases and the pathological portents for the bottom fishery over a wide area of shelf figured importantly in EPA's decision to end dumping on the shelf by 1981.

A similar form of wasting disease has been seen in lobsters, crabs, and shrimp taken in the vicinity of the dumping zones. Symptoms include black spots on the gills and deterioration of the shell, which assumes a scarred, burnt appearance. In the worst cases, legs and tail sections become thoroughly rotted and fall off. Normally, crustaceans possess a remarkable capacity for regeneration; legs and claws lost to predators or in mating battles readily grow back. But in the case of animals with eroded appendages taken from New York Bight and kept under observation in clean aquaria, regeneration did not occur.

The problem is not limited to conspicuous symptoms. Microscopic lesions and disruption of tissue in fish that appeared normal were frequently found by researchers. The etiology of degenerative disease in shrimp seems to involve certain bacteria which gain entrance via a minor injury such as a scratch or a scrape. These bacteria are termed chitiniverous: they dissolve and consume chitin, the tough, horny substance that composes a shrimp's shell. The cause of corrosive symptoms in fish, however, is not clear. If the fish are victims of a chronic chemical pathology, the short-term effects now observed may be followed by latent ones. Biologists should begin to look for tumors and other signs of chemically induced cancer even in fish showing no external signs of bodily damage.

Flounder, which are frequently in direct contact with the bottom, are the fish hardest hit by fin rot. Blackback, probably because they inhabit the most grossly polluted nearshore zone, show symptoms of disease more often than others of their tribe. But fin rot and microscopic pathology now appear in other flatfish, including yellowtail, summer flounder, fourspot, and windowpane.

In early spring, across an immense spawning ground on the Middle Atlantic continental shelf, newly fertilized eggs of the yellowtail float free above the submarine prairie. The eggs, unlike those of the blackback, are lighter than sea water, and they rise slowly toward the surface. These larvae become creatures of the surface plankton. They drift in sunlight in the clear, tumbling ocean, often beyond sight of land. As they drift the larvae go through the same changes as their cousins of the muddy estuaries. There occur the same shift of eye and perfection of control over pigment cells. And there occur the same small and large behavioral changes, adjustments of orientation and balance that prepare the way for descent and a permanent residence on the sandy shelf several dozen meters below.

The yellowtail flounder (*Limanda ferruginea*) is a fish of the broad midreaches of the continental shelf. Once this colorful species, up to forty-five centimeters in length with large irregular russet spots on its brownish or olive upper side, and a bright yellow tail, was so numerous on Georges Bank to the east that American trawlermen imagined that large areas of bottom were practically shingled with the flatfish. Now the yellowtail, especially in its former northwest Atlantic haunts, has declined drastically—sucked into the insatiable vacuum cleaners of the technological fleet.

In the middle Atlantic region a sizeable breeding population persists. A large spawning ground on the central shelf extends roughly from New York to Delaware. Like the inshore blackback, the yellowtail is a spring spawner. But beyond this superficial similarity the life histories of the two species are quite different.

Baby yellowtails remain in the surface plankton for several weeks as they feed on matter in the water around them. At the same time the tiny developing fish are preyed upon by somewhat larger neighbors of varying shape and form. Jellyfish, swimming crabs and shrimp, young squid and numerous kinds of juvenile fish exact the usual devastating toll that culminates ultimately in the purposeful predation of man. In the offshore waters of New York Bight, however, new and featureless dangers threaten yellowtail larvae and many others. Within the most dense pocket of yellowtail spawning is a large lobe of what may become the northern Baltimore Canyon oil field. Fishery biologists originally located the flounder spawning area in the late 1940s, long before impact statements were dreamed of. In the middle 1970s, however, the effect of oil on yellowtail reproduction remains unstudied, although biologists speculate that the teratogenic effects produced in cod eggs by even minute traces of oil may appear in many species of the continental shelf.

In studying the oil contamination of the bottom in New York Bight, marine petroleum expert John Farrington, of the Woods Hole Oceanographic Institution, has found anthropogenic petroleum hydrocarbons in the sediments all the way down to the lower continental rise. Farrington has said that shelf sediments off New York have become equivalent to natural petroleum-bearing sands, which they are not. Before any petroleum has been raised from the deep strata of the Baltimore Canyon Trough, a thin oily excrescence has expanded along the shipping routes and down-currents from dredge spoil sites.

Thirty-five kilometers east of Long Branch, New Jersey, acid chemical wastes are dumped in a designated area larger than the main sludge and spoil zones closer to shore. The acid wastes, which contain heavy metals and other impurities, come from a variety of industries located throughout the middle Atlantic region. The dumping occurs within a major band of menhaden spawning, but no studies of acute or sublethal effects on larvae and other creatures have been done.

Beyond the edge of the continental shelf is another chemical dump which dwarfs all the rest. It is known as Deep Water Dumpsite 106 because it begins 106 miles from the nearest shore point in southern New Jersey. DWD 106 is a disposal area for some of the most toxic wastes produced by American industry. In 1974, three dozen companies, including such giants as Dupont and American Cyanamid, discharged nearly 400,000 cubic meters of dangerous chemicals over the sector of the continental slope designated as

DWD 106. Toxic metals such as mercury, cadmium, and arsenic, carcinogens, experimental biocides, and neurotoxins are among the materials dumped at the deepwater site.

Dumping the deadly materials here may be better than flushing them into a stream behind the factory, but how much better? How seriously do the chemicals affect marine life over the lower continental slope? How quickly and in what quantities do they reach bottom? Is there any interaction between the dumpsite and nearby Hudson Canyon? None of these questions has ever been investigated. Scientists from Woods Hole Oceanographic Institution and the Environmental Protection Agency plan a detailed first look at the ecology of DWD 106 during the summer of 1976.

Just south of DWD 106 is another ocean dump which has been operated quietly since the World War II Manhattan Project, which led to the development of the atomic bomb. This disposal area has received low-level radioactive wastes from numerous civilian and military sources. As in the case of DWD 106, the ecology of the radioactive dump has long been neglected.

Larvae of fish in surface plankton off New York Bight and on the entire Atlantic shelf are beginning to encounter another hazard in the form of tiny plastic particles. These range down to microscopic sizes, and they come from sources that are just beginning to be identified. One major source is believed to be rubbish disposal from ships. Thousands of tons of plastic from this source alone enter coastal waters of the United States each year, and the material does not decompose. The chemical environment of sea water, warm temperatures, bacteria—nothing will make it truly disappear except perhaps decades of exposure to direct sunlight, even though styrofoam particles, a plastic bag, a six-pack collar, or a scrap of packaging may seem to disappear after a while. It gradually breaks up into smaller and smaller pieces. This physical disintegration is faster in relatively shallow areas, for example during storms, when waves stir bottom and fill the churning waters with abrasive sand. In the surf zone, breaking waves rapidly render unsightly plastic pollutants to invisible shards that are distributed by surface currents back over the continental shelf.

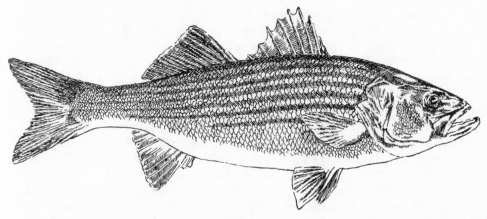

Striped bass

Ironically, this esthetic restoration has the most potentially severe environmental impact. Fish larvae and other plankton have recently been found with microscopic plastic particles clogging their intestines. Such industrial constipation cannot be classified as a minor malady; blockage of the gut by completely indigestible material is deadly to the larvae. The several cases of this problem found so far foretell the onset of an environmental disease of uncertain magnitude. Unlike a viral epidemic, the microparticles causing the disease are noninfectious, but they are extremely long-lived and widespread, and they seem to exert a fatal attraction on their victims.

Proposals for massive dumping of solid city refuse in baled form are being considered in several coastal centers. New York City is one of these with an enormous solid waste problem, and the ruling city custodians must often cast a wistful mental gaze beyond the smog and concrete toward the empty southeastern horizon. Thirty-seven thousand tons of solid waste (1974 figure) are generated *daily* by the city. Available land-fill sites for dozens of kilometers around have been used almost to capacity, and long-term disposal options are being sought with mounting desperation. One of these involves removal of the trash by rail to a remote upstate location, but the present rate of trash efflux projected thirty years into the future requires a land-fill disposal site whose area approaches that of the state of Rhode Island.

The sea floor thus represents to city managers an attractive solution to the trash problem from the standpoints of both economy and esthetics. However, no one can precisely predict the ecological effects of massive dumping of baled waste on the continental shelf, let alone in deeper waters. A major esthetic problem may still arise. So-called floatables, such as many plastics, foam products, some rubber, old light bulbs, and similar buoyant detritus tend to escape when bales absorb water and burst, or when metal banding surrounding a bale rusts and disintegrates. Only expensive stainless steel banding lasts indefinitely, although even bales bound by stainless steel eventually shrink and loosen up because of the disintegration of some components. Floatables finally leak out and reach the surface. From there it is usually only a matter of time until they end up on somebody's beach.

Shredding the refuse before bailing it largely eliminates the floatable problem, but escaping plastic particles may endanger surrounding marine life. This situation would be compounded by those storms whose waves reach bottom on much of the continental shelf. Abrasion and erosion of baled waste at relatively shallow depths may foster a chronic emergence of the minute plastic particles that could menace the plankton over hundreds of square kilometers.

Suggestions have been made that bale dumps might enhance fishing by serving as artificial reefs. Of course these would be impossible sites for commercial trawling, and contrary to expectations might be just as frustrating to hook-and-line fishermen, forever tangling their gear in trash. Such lumpish underwater mountain ranges would further disgust scuba divers. Who would enjoy exploring the murky cubist canyons and garbage-floored grottos of such a place? Many fish might indeed frequent the vicinity of such a dump. Some plausible arguments have been made for the compatibility of bale-dump sites with a gill net or a trap fishery such as exists for lobsters, but this suggestion deserves careful scrutiny. Problems of fin rot and similar indicators of environmental pathology in fish and shellfish, as well as on consumer appetites and perhaps public health, would be of concern.

The whole question of dumping on the shelf is likely to be moot by 1981 if the EPA follows through with its present intentions, but, as its interactions with the auto industry reveal, the agency can lose its grip on what it believes is best for the environment. Moreover, it seems at times to be unaware that with the onrush of time and economic growth, its options grow narrower for conserving significant, unspoiled portions of the natural world. In the face of a mounting garbage crisis in perennially unmanageable and fiscally tottering cities such as New York, interim permits for ocean disposal of solid wastes are conceivable in the near future. But where do we go from there?

Over the deep plains and mighty hidden canyons of the outer shelf and slope, another gathering of flounder begins in early summer. The orgiastic ritual of mass spawning and the setting of the gathering near the boundary of perpetual night and cold—portals of earth's vast biological underworld—seem appropriate to a creature known as the witch flounder (*Glyptocephalus cynoglossus*).

The buoyant eggs of the witch rise slowly through hundreds of meters of water and incubate at the sunlit surface of the sea. Larvae drift for an unknown period in surface currents and travel uncertain paths over the continental margin. Eventually they make their way back down to the nether regions of the sea. For a long time they drop through the greying waters like air passengers descending in fog. At last they coast silently onto a dim bottom. To the dark adapted eyes of the small fish the new two-dimensional world extends only a few meters in any direction, and at its brightest appears moonlit at noon. Lost to all eyes here, however, is a panorama of the most spectacular undersea landscape on the North American continental margin.

Aligned like an arrow in the bow of New York Bight, the Hudson Submarine Canyon begins as a gorge which runs as a deepening furrow across the outer shelf. The head of the gorge now lies on the inner shelf, but in former times it was continuous with the Hudson River Valley. Originally carved by centuries-long outpourings of glacial meltwater, the landward connecting portion of the gorge on the inner shelf has been filled with recent sediments.

From its solitary beginning the gorge widens and deepens and becomes the central channel of the huge Hudson Canyon system. On the mid and lower slope and upper continental rise, Hudson Canyon receives hundreds of tributaries large and small. The system's fan-shaped network embraces an area 300 kilometers wide on the upper slope. The overall form of the canyon complex is similar to that of Hatteras Canyon, but the Hudson easily dwarfs its southern counterpart by an order of magnitude. Beyond the canyon rim, which lies under 200 meters of water on the shelf-slope break, the main axis of Hudson Canyon plunges magestically downward as an impressive valley reaching depths of 1,000 meters below the surrounding sea floor and extending for more than 400 kilometers into the deep sea.

Biologists have trawled and dredged in the Canyon with special equipment, and they have viewed its muddy depths in photographs taken by remote cameras and the glare of running lights from small submarines. All reports so far indicate that canyon environs, including the myriads of tributaries, harbor a much greater abundance of life than is found on adjacent terrain of the continental margin. Large crabs, lobsters, and a wide variety of bottom fish are especially in evidence. Less obvious is the abundance of lesser creatures that supports the large conspicuous predators and scavengers.

Commercial fishermen are beginning to show an interest in the canyons. As shelf stocks are depleted, deeper-living species such as the witch flounder are being sought, especially by the foreign fleets, whose large vessels are somewhat better equipped for deep trawling than those of American registry. A modest trap fishery for lobsters and crabs already exists in upper canyon reaches. As yet, however, limitations imposed on standard kinds of fishing gear and boats by great depths of water have prevented over-exploitation of most canyon areas.

Biological richness in canyons, relative to the surrounding bottom on the continental slope and rise, probably derives from concentrated flows of nutrients moving down the channels from the bounteously productive continental shelf. The currents hug the canyon floor and may be related to the tides. Monitoring a time-lapse film taken for a seventy-two-hour period in Hudson Canyon, scientists detected a sudden shift from clear water to total opacity as a slowly traveling cloud of mud and probable organic matter passed the camera and appeared to move downslope. After a few minutes the water cleared again and in front of the camera a crab, like a suburbanite after a snowstorm, was seen clearing its burrow of fine silt.

Unfortunately the same mechanism by which a canyon funnels nutrients into relatively impoverished deeper waters may also serve to inject disease and pollution directly into the deep sea. This is especially true of Hudson Canyon, with its unique gorge on the shelf close to several dump sites. Some oceanographers are now searching for down-canyon transport of pollutants which may move directly via currents or more subtly via biological vectors and food webs. What is perhaps man's largest and most concentrated refuse heap is already tipping toward a slow avalanche into the heretofore most remote and pristine environment on our planet. At present so little is known about the dynamic functioning, ecological requirements and limits of deep marine ecosystems that continued massive waste disposal in the vicinity of a major conduit to the abyss is folly.

Even bottom sediments on the outer shelf must not be allowed to become further contaminated with pollutants—oil, toxic chemicals, leachates or particulate matter from solid waste dumps—that may threaten the canyons and their life. The canyons are unique in their own right and deserve to remain inviolate as land forms, but these rich areas may also serve as refugia for numerous overexploited species such as lobsters. Careful husbandry of the canyons in a more sophisticated ecological/technological age than ours may permit sustained harvests of food from their depths. Above all, before the remote and pristine regions of the sea floor as well as the overlying water mass are dismissed as worthless desert, let us recall that this term once was applied to most of continental North America west of Pennsylvania. Many impending decisions on offshore oil, nuclear power plants, ocean dumping, and other potentially massive impingements on the marine environment may forever be decried as tragic myopia by our descendants whose world view will, one hopes, reach far wider and deeper than our own.

Portraits in Veiled Waters

E xplorations of the hidden wilderness of the continental shelf are still in the primitive stage. Scuba divers can range over only a hundred or so square meters of the shelf at a time. Even the latest research submersibles are limited to a few hours underwater and cover less than a square kilometer on an average dive. Thus by far the dominant, large-scale, if hazy, perceptions of the continental margin come from the work of scientists groping through the concealing waters from specially equipped surface ships. Research at sea is difficult, exhausting, and sometimes dangerous, but it brings intense rewards—an excitement and exhilaration that only explorers know. More alien than any terrestrial domain, yet closer and more provocative to the human spirit than outer space, the ocean, which has pervaded and tempered man's cultural evolution from the beginning, will likely beckon scientists, explorers, adventurers and poets for a long time to come.

My first direct contact with the unified sweep and scale of the continental shelf came when, as a graduate student in marine biology, I participated in a five-day cruise off the southeastern United States. This is an account of that cruise which combined traditional sea-going experiences with a portfolio of impressions engendered by a slow, speculative passage through the teeming shoal waters of the Atlantic.

First Day:

Late on an autumn afternoon there was suddenly a heightened sense of anticipation on the ship. Wrist-thick hawsers were being loosened and cast off, and the vibrations of the idling engines became more powerful. Without warning there was a long blast of a deep-toned whistle, and the ship began to slide away from its berth.

I watched a crack between ship and pier widen into a gulf of smooth dark water. Along with my shipmates I waved and shouted goodbyes to friends remaining ashore. Two months after its acquisition by the university, the research ship was still enough of a curiosity that a small throng attended its comings and goings. Turning from the small harbor toward the sea, the ship loomed larger than it had next to the pier; here was home and office, work and play for the next few days. Already the clustered laboratory buildings nearby and the white-washed small southern town on the opposite shore seemed diminished in perspective, like places briefly noted on the way to some important destination.

In the inlet between two of the barrier islands that lie along this coast my last image of the land was of long marching dunes topped by plumed sea oats. As we left the estuary, the breeze was noticeably cooler; the air had lost its parched land-smell and seemed to flow in the nostrils with less friction. Long swells came out of the unbroken southeastern horizon as the ship began to respond to an ancient rhythm.

There are many, and I am one, who take some time to adjust to mother ocean's exuberant greeting. The spirit is willing and usually fiercely determined not to be seasick this time, but inevitably there is that feeling of surprise when the first queasy sensations reach the conscious level. Glancing around on deck, I guessed I was not the only one experiencing early warning symptoms. The onset of seasickness instills sobriety in the most boisterous personality, and several of my shipmates had rather abruptly ceased to socialize. In the manner of both ancient and very recent mariners they kept their own counsel, staring seaward or back toward the vanishing outer banks.

Now just before the dinner hour some had left the rear deck—either in anticipation of the fried pork chops that were to be served for dinner or to flee the odor of them which poured through the half-open entryway to the galley. For myself I resolved to skip dinner.

At the same time I moved forward to remain in the cool rush of air from the sea. Fresh air is essential to the cure. If one is at all unstable in the stomach the stuffiness of a ship's interior is bound to hasten the heaves. The problem seems especially acute when one attempts to concentrate on any set task.

Although I missed dinner, I remained well enough to feast visually and spiritually on a spectacular sunset. Soon a shipmate appeared, a fellow sufferer who said that he too did not relish the thought of eating that evening. We talked until the western sky was dark. Mainly the conversation concerned the ship, the cruise, and the unknown world that lay ahead of us over the next few days' horizons.

Our ship was small, only 120 feet long and 28 feet on the beam (widest point). She nevertheless carried a great variety of collecting and analytical gear, along with several kilometers of light and heavy steel cable. We could therefore obtain samples and photographs all the way down to the abyssal sea floor. Since the ship and research equipment were brand new, however, our operations could still be classified as a wetting of technological toes—mainly testing the temper of machines and men on the continental shelf.

Nominally all scientific aspects of the cruise were under the direction of one man, designated chief scientist. He had planned the cruise, his projects took precedence over others', and around him all the other scientists and students on board revolved like satellites in higher or lower orbits. Chief scientist on this cruise was a quirky oceanographer with an international reputation who was known to his students (behind his back) as RJ. This was in part an attempt to humanize a relationship with a reputation as well as a man. In most situations (and frontal orientations) he was addressed as "Doctor."

Although he cast a giant shadow, RJ was a smallish man, squint-eyed and intense, with a rare, unusual smile that could be mistaken for a grimace. He was also an egalitarian of sorts. Ashore and at sea he nearly always wore the same gray plumber's coveralls. RJ also insisted on personally attending to the minutest repairs and adjustments of his research equipment. And finally, though none knew for sure, RJ was rumored to be prone to violent bouts of seasickness.

The day before we left, RJ had briefed everyone on the cruise plan. We would first head south to a point on the edge of the continental shelf due east of Charleston, South Carolina, and opposite the northern arm of Blake Plateau. Then we would follow a zigzag track generally northeastward along the central and outer shelf to just north of Cape Hatteras. Most of our stations (preplanned stopping places for the taking of samples and bottom photographs) would occur along this zigzag run. There were geologists as well as biologists aboard. The geologists were seeking a variety of bottom sediments ranging from fine sand to shell gravel and also remnants of drowned reefs. Finally, depending on time, we would make one or two deep tests of equipment on the slope or continental rise off Hatteras and then return to port.

By now a velvety darkness had closed over the surface of the sea. Only the faintest glow remained in the western sky. The ship slid smoothly through barely discernable swells, if anything calmer than when we first emerged from the estuary. The land was far astern, long beyond vision. It was a balmy night; all around was a kind of huge soft fabric of air and sea disturbed only at our bow. I watched the faintly luminous white breakers spill away from the advancing ship, but our shearing passage seemed to leave little lasting trace. Night and ocean rapidly knit together again in our wake.

Suddenly the engines slowed. Simultaneously the forward deck lights came on, and my nocturnal musings ended. Instantaneously I was a captive of the lights, eyes fighting to adjust. Now on the inside looking out, I was unable to maintain contact with the night which had retreated beyond the glare that nearly surrounded the ship. It was time for science; we were on the first station.

RJ appeared carrying his new camera with the help of a technician. They brought the heavy contraption onto the deck, propped it on the rail, and began attaching it to the wire rope. Moments later I helped steady the camera frame against the slight rolling of the ship as RJ fished a screwdriver from his coveralls, made a final adjustment, then waved to the winch operator. Slowly the rig descended, held away from the rail by a covey of eager hands. Black water closed over the bright yellow frame resembling an upright ladder to which were attached, one below the other, the camera itself, a powerful electronic flash unit, and a device called a pinger, which sends back an acoustic signal useful in locating the vertical position of gear dangling far below a ship. All three pieces of working equipment were encased in pressure-proof cylindrical housings. The entire rig measured about six feet high by two wide. Watchers at the rail could make out the shimmering artifact reflecting the ship's lights from a long way down. "Must be seeing forty feet at least," someone said.

The camera shutter and flash were controlled by a torpedo-shaped weight hanging on a cord six feet below the frame. When the weight touched bottom the release of tension on the cord triggered the photographic units. The camera was preset to focus at eight feet and the angle of view was slightly off-vertical, thus avoiding shadow effects from the frame and trigger weight.

Each picture would encompass about forty square feet of the sea floor.

Together with several others I moved along the rail to a point roughly amidships where the bright lights from the forward deck and stern were cut off by the overhanging upper deck. Here also was cast a wedge of shadow on the water. The winch man now slowed the camera's rate of descent as it neared the bottom. On the deck just above us, RJ monitored the length of wire rope paying out, and he intoned numbers that estimated the distance of the camera off bottom. It sounded like a countdown for a spaceshot; I imagined him trying to watch the gauge and the dark patch of water below at the same time. Right on cue, in nearly perfect synchronization with the end of the count, a sudden brief pulse of light flared in the dark water. There seemed an element of magic in seeing the flash transmitted from near the bottom on the mid-continental shelf up through this thickness of dark water. RJ was leaning over the rail above and beaming in his peculiar way. The winch operator reeled in four or five meters of wire rope and slowly lowered again for the next picture.

I tried to imagine the scene fifty meters below, where nocturnally active fish, crabs, squid, and others prowled the sands with senses tuned to the finest pitch, alert to the possibility of food or danger. How did they react to the presence of the ungainly object that dangled and drifted through the watery night? Close up the flash must implode on the dark-adapted nervous system with shattering effect. Even animals dozens of meters away across the bottom must be startled by the sudden silent flarings in the dark. I wondered what would be the reaction of terrestrial creatures—birds, mammals, insects—if a similar object, perhaps scaled up in size, descended one day or night through the clouds and drifted and bounced slowly across the countryside as it flashed like an intermittent sun. Fright? Some might be curious, even attracted, and I wondered if any fish or squid followed our camera. Perhaps opportunistically they picked up easy prey in its wake— light-stunned worms and shrimp whose normal defensive reactions were temporarily lost or slowed by the fierce bursts of light.

The camera was going to be down for nearly two hours since the film magazine held seventy frames. For a while I watched small crustaceans and an occasional fish dart about in the lighted area near the ship. But suddenly I felt tired, and in the absence of further excitement decided to turn in for a decent stretch of sleep before my early watch.

Second Day: 0345

Someone was shaking my shoulder, and a bright light pierced the open doorway of my cabin. My mind, struggling up toward consciousness, registered unusual cramped configurations, and then I remembered where I was. I muttered something and heard a whispered "your watch." Then whoever it was left and mercifully closed the door. My shipmate in the upper bunk never moved. He went on watch at eight.

The deck undulated gently, and in the dark this was disconcerting. I switched on the bunk's small reading light and located my clothes in the locker beside the tiny sink. Bracing against the wall three feet opposite the bunk, I pulled on my pants. There was barely room to turn around: getting dressed could be a real adventure if we ran into rough weather.

My watch was from four to eight in the morning, not the choicest time slot, but I had been one of the last to reach the sign-up sheet. I consoled myself with the thought of seeing several ocean sunrises. My duty was to monitor the depth recorder in a little room that opened off the rear of the bridge. My shipmate of the previous watch was glad to see his relief, briefly showed me what to do, and sleepily departed.

I pulled a length of chart from the recorder's take-up spool and saw that for the last hour or so we had been crossing uniform bottom nearly eighty meters deep. The machine which whirred and clicked softly in one corner of the tiny room measured the time it took for evenly spaced sound impulses from the ship to return from the bottom. Reflected impulses were translated into blips on a slowly moving chart of paper, and the continuous train of blips were so close together they formed a smudgy line on the paper which was marked with a vertical scale representing the depth of water. My job was to mark the chart every fifteen minutes with the time and the ship's heading and speed. From this information there would eventually be constructed an accurate bottom profile along the ship's path.

This minor and monotonous bit of the ship's operation left me fourteen out of every fifteen minutes free, and I sought diversion by exploring the shadowy bridge and talking with the steersman.

Our conversation took place in a zone of near darkness where numerous dial faces glowed a soft yellow green. We looked out on a wide, dim expanse of ocean and a sky which featured a late thin moon, now high in the east off our port bow. I learned that he and most of the crew had been fishermen—shrimp in the summer, scallops and menhaden in the winter, weather permitting. Among them they had well over 200 man-years of experience seeking a livelihood in these waters. Several had also served locally in the Coast Guard, and in matters of seamanship they bruited a casual air of competence in an outer-bank accent which some linguists believe preserves elements of the speech of their Elizabethan ancestors. "Eh, myte, wot toime is it?" Or " . . . she'll be a very hoy toide t'night."

The crew were also practical marine biologists, and some knew the habitat and behavior of the fauna of the shelf better than the biologists. They had colorful local names for the fish, such as pogy (menhaden) and hogchoker (a small species of flounder), but they consistently distinguished even closely related species. Local trawler captains filled mental maps as well as conventional coastal charts encompassing hundreds of square miles of the shelf with data on types of bottom, locations of reefs and wrecks, unusual current patterns, and populations of animals. In previous years some of these men had been indispensable guides for scientists pioneering in studies of the underwater wilderness.

If the crew was composed of generalists with a surprisingly broad knowledge of the marine environment and how to deal with it on a practical level, the scientific party presented a fair contrast. The biologists and geologists on this cruise were specialists, each having a rather narrow area of interest. Although the scientists' powers of scrutiny, achieved through powerful instruments, were greater than those of the crew who knew the sea best through eyes, ears, noses, the soles of their feet, and the seat of their pants, I felt both kinds of knowledge were important. In fact both are probably necessary to reach an understanding of the real nature of the marine world.

Many scientists nowadays spend too much time behind laboratory walls while they explore the ecology of computers whose incomplete input derives from their own. Even worse, they become entrapped by bureaucracy. New Big Science demands the diversion of extraordinary amounts of career time to political strategies and grantsmanship designed to pry money from funding agencies. One wonders if potential Newtons, Darwins, and Einsteins are being quietly smothered by the bureaucratic octopus. We are losing the ability to stand and stare, and perhaps stifling the talent to reflect and review, integrate and synthesize. Even matters of great practical and personal importance to scientists in the real world are now often learned by accident.

0900:

Shortly after breakfast, of which I partook lightly, we made a station using the small biological trawl, a miniature version of the commercial otter trawl. We were near the edge of the shelf at our farthest point south, and the catch was exceedingly varied with a large admixture of colorful Caribbean life—starfish, crabs, large and small mollusks, and many fish, all inhabiting a shell-gravel bottom over 100 meters below.

The contents of the net were dropped into a large plywood trough, and together with several others I was pawing through the creeping, flopping mass when I came upon an interesting fish. It was small and strikingly ugly about the head with a leaflike flap of skin between bulbous jutting eyes. Most of its body was covered with small overlapping tabs or enlarged scales, giving the fish a shaggy appearance. But contrasting with these grotesqueries were the colors—mottled red and blue overall, and under each pectoral fin a large patch of pure yellow.

I reached down and picked it up and at the same time heard a hoarse yell, "Watch out, ee'll burn ye." Startled, I dropped the fish even before I knew the yell was directed at me.

A member of the crew who had been watching the sorting of the catch came over and pointed to the fish I had dropped. "He's a stinger, that one," he said. And then from some remote bit of book learning I recalled the characteristics of that fish. It was one of the Caribbean scorpion fishes having venomous spines along the back and in the pelvic and anal fins. This fish was not deadly, as some in the tropical Pacific are reputed to be, but I realized that I could have been painfully poisoned a long way from proper medical attention.

Somewhat sheepishly I thanked the man for his warning. The examination of the catch continued; however, everyone now proceeded at a noticeably slower pace.

1530:

The weather was certainly handling us gently. Scarcely a ruffle on the sea all day. My stomach had settled firmly into its familiar place; I threw caution to the winds, wherever they were, and enthusiastically indulged in a whopping lunch, then spent the high afternoon napping in warm October sunshine and began to acquire a rosy tan.

The camera appeared to be giving RJ a lot of trouble. He seemed in an unusually bad mood, and no one risked solicitous conversation with him for the time being. But it was known that during last night's initial testing there apparently had been a bit of moisture inside—not a leak, but water vapor trapped within the housing or camera itself before the equipment had gone over the side. This had condensed as a thin fog over the lens after submergence. All of the pictures were blanked out. RJ and his technician had dissected the camera into numerous parts which now resided in a low-temperature drying oven. They would reassemble it for testing as soon as possible.

The ship was now steaming in a northerly direction along the outer shelf. Standing at the starboard rail of the upper deck, I could see perhaps eighteen miles to the horizon, blue on blue this clear, warm fall day. My vantage point was located approximately on the west bank of the Gulf Stream, and I scanned this gently flowing world with a good pair of 7 x 35 binoculars.

On an oceanic map, the Gulf Stream is depicted as a straightforward river of tropical sea water, gently curving into the North Atlantic. But beginning here off the southeastern United States, the Gulf Stream frequently meanders in its course. At times a meander grows into an increasingly involuted loop. The flow follows an ever-more-circular path, eventually doubling back toward its starting point. Finally the main current is reconstituted at the junctures of entry and exit from the loop—which is itself pinched off and becomes a pond in the sea, up to 200 kilometers across with its own particular fauna and flora ringed by a circular flow of Gulf Stream water.

The loops are called Gulf Stream rings, and superficially they resemble the ox-bow lakes that lie scattered beside dusky coastal-plain rivers in the southern United States. However, unlike these earthbound features—products of centuries of erosion followed by slow senescence under soft sediments and rank vegetation—Gulf Stream rings form in mere days or weeks. In little more than a year they disappear gradually into their surroundings. Only their fish and other creatures are left as immigrants in a new pelagic environment.

Because the Gulf Stream separates water of the Sargasso Sea from that of the continental slope, rings that form on either side of the current have different properties. A shoreward ring encloses a volume of Sargasso Sea water. Surrounded by relatively cold slope water, this is called a warm-core ring. On the opposite side of the Gulf Stream, slope water intrudes into the pocket of a meander, and ring formation results in a cold-core ring injected into the Sargasso Sea.

Biologists now see the rings as areas of ecological confrontation between different pelagic communities. The sudden intrusion of a body of alien water as big as one of the Great Lakes, with its particular complement of life, to one side of the Gulf Stream or the other sets the stage for evolutionary change through competition, predation, hybridization, or other interactions. A crude parallel might be imagined if a patch of African savanna, a hundred kilometers or so wide, were transported to Nebraska. Many kinds of the introduced creatures would perish within a short time, but probably some surprising adaptations would occur. Usually the less-conspicuous members of the fauna, the generalists without showy ornamentation, specialized diets, restricted physiologies, or rigid behavior patterns, are the most successful colonizers. Certain microorganisms perform well in shifting situations, and their successes, at first invisible, may eventually alter the ecology of the new environment in subtle ways through nutrient utilization and excretions of biologically active substances.

Perhaps fifteen kilometers to our starboard, well within the Gulf Stream, the long blocky shape of an oil tanker lay on the bright water like a bacillus, magnified by the binoculars as in the field of a microscope. The tanker was also moving north, taking advantage of the four-knot boost afforded by the current.

Seeing the tanker made me think of potential regional petroleum development. I imagined the bottom below us at the edge of the shelf, the yawning lip of the ocean that dropped away steadily to seaward. Beneath the tanker it was twice as deep as here. Then just a few kilometers farther out the continental slope ended its plunge prematurely. The bottom flattened and broadened toward the south into the huge, unique Blake Plateau. Disembodied from the continent and lying under three to four times as deep water as the continental shelf, sediments of this 80,000-square-kilometer twilight wilderness are believed by the U.S. Geological Survey to be rich in petroleum. Development of the Blake Plateau is unlikely to occur until after oil reserves on the shelf proper have been exploited. I tried to imagine the surrealistic sight of a forest of production rigs on the remote horizon. If indeed it holds large volumes of oil and gas locked in deep interstitial embrace, Blake Plateau will probably be one of the last reserves developed in the U.S., and I wondered if in the end we would finally husband the precious resource as prudence suggested. Perhaps my mental image of forests of platforms here in twenty or thirty years, together with fleets of supertankers serving a still-frantic national economy, would not materialize. Perhaps the last of our oil would be treated more thoughtfully than ever in the face of a future without it.

2000:

Dinner this evening was a delight—broiled king mackerel—a big forty-pounder, freshly caught by one of the crew. Afterward I helped with some chemical analyses in the wet lab and kibitzed awhile amid card players and readers in the scientists' lounge. This pretentious designation referred to a room about seven by ten feet, with a table and padded bench along one long wall and a sparse bookshelf featuring paperback detective novels on the other.

It was a quiet evening. The next station was to be after midnight, but I rapidly tired of poker watching, and I didn't feel sleepy. After a while I went out on deck.

Nights at sea on a small ship can conjure primeval feelings, stir the consciousness deeply to levels below normal remembering. Given the proper mood there begins an upwelling of associations from some early organic existence; the mind projects itself backward toward an infinity of uncluttered space and unsullied flows of air, water, and life. Perhaps these feelings are enhanced by sensory deprivation—a reaction to the uniformity of existence in cramped spaces, seeing the same faces day and night, the seldom-relieved drone of engines. Perhaps they are partly caused by the random, round-the-clock pace of shipboard work.

Whatever the reason, there is a blurring of traditional referents, and going out on deck at night brings a rush of openness, a sudden release. The camaraderie and concentrated gaity of shipboard life evaporate instantly as one steps from the brightly lit interior and confronts the hypnotic face of the universe. Time and change, so fast-paced and elusive in the hectic routine of a land mammal, seem to wait for those who pursue them at sea. It is easiest to catch up at night. There is a feeling of expanded existence, as if one might live many lifetimes here. Under the spell of a vast oceanic night, one can lie on deck for hours, awash in soft air, and wander among the wheeling stars.

Third Day: 1430:

The weather was beginning to change. During the morning a breeze developed into a moderate southwest wind, and with it the sea began to come alive. Within two hours we were rolling in long swells measuring seven or eight feet high from trough to crest. Happily my sea legs seemed strong and sturdy, a definite feeling of relief.

Just after dawn we stopped on station when a small flock of birds appeared from out of nowhere. They were slightly smaller than quail and two-toned in color, black on the head, back and wings, pure white on the breast. Someone recognized them as dovekies (*Plautus alle*), an arctic-breeding species which winters on the open sea. This was farther south than most sightings, but the chubby little birds seemed at home. In the clear blue water they resembled miniature penguins as they dove and swam with rapid wingbeats. Flying underwater, they seemed to chase planktonic prey in the confused swash around and beneath the ship. Nobody saw the dovekies leave; after a few minutes they had simply vanished without a trace into the blue vastness.

Later in the morning I saw a pair of the most beautiful dolphins. They stayed well away from the ship as they arched powerfully side by side through the swells and maintained a steady course. Whenever they cleared the water their flanks flashed white in the sunlight, a beautiful sight against the deep blue backdrop. After thumbing through a book, I decided they were Atlantic white-sided dolphins, *Lagenorhynchus acutus,* a species of more northerly waters, relatively rare at this latitude.

Sometime after this sighting, we had just come on station when a small group of familiar bottle-nosed dolphins found us and made their normal close approach. As everyone scrambled for cameras, the dolphins swam slowly around us, and at times they seemed to be watching us as if we afforded them entertainment.

The most striking scenes of porpoise-watching-man-watching-porpoise occurred by the port rail where the long swells approached the ship broadside. As we would slip down into a trough, a glittering wall of water rose just off the rail, and from it the dolphins grinned fixedly at us eyeball to eyeball across a few meters of space and eons of geological time. The next instant as the ship rose high on the oncoming swell, the dolphins would seem to vanish only to reappear again magically in the same position as before. Occasionally a dolphin would race a swell beneath the ship and appear like a torpedo on the starboard side. But for many minutes the strange stereopticon series of eye-level contacts held everyone's attention while hard science was temporarily forgotten.

It was easy to imagine we were the ones on display here—specimens confined to a technological terrarium drifting in open ocean. The dolphins were the dominant creatures in residence. They could swim rings around the ship, even when it was moving at full throttle. They were obviously and consciously in full command of their freedom here, whereas we were not, and I began to envy them.

Envy seems to be justified in the presence of dolphins. Their world of the sea covers about three-fourths of our shared planet. Relying on natural attributes sharpened by evolution, they have not become trapped in a total reliance on technology for survival. Moreover, dolphins have never needed technology to achieve the good life. Imagine an environment in which one can live naked in almost total comfort, a fluid Eden where no one needs clothing or shelter, and everywhere is delicious food that can be snapped up at will. Travel opportunities are virtually unlimited. Communications are rapid and sophisticated, a function of both the dolphin's (and other cetaceans') capacity to generate and receive an incredibly complex repertoire of acoustic information, and unique physical conditions in the underwater world that often permit transmission of sounds over hundreds, and sometimes thousands, of miles. Here lies a pretty problem for the armchair anthropologist. How would a society of beings gifted organically with these attributes tend to develop?

Dolphins and their relatives have little in common with humans, and we may be incapable of imagining even the rudiments of their oceanic mentality. The two animal types have been diverging along different evolutionary lines, responding to different adaptive stimuli for tens of millions of years. An impartial observer might imagine that the huge-brained cetaceans long ago surpassed man in the ability to form abstractions. The brain of the bottle-nosed dolphin, *Tursiops truncatus,* is slightly larger than man's and has more fissures, folds, and convolutions, indicating at least the same order of complexity as the human brain. The great whales carry a crown of intellectual tissue up to six times the size of ours. By way of interesting contrast, some of the largest dinosaurs got by with brains little bigger than walnuts.

It may be permissible to speculate that dolphins and whales use relatively little mental effort on controlling activities of their streamlined bodies and other basics of living in their benign, physically supporting environment. Specifically they must be far less distracted than we by the vicissitudes of climate, bread-winning, house-holding, job-hunting and the like. Assume also they are without the mentally paralyzing aggressiveness, insecurity, and paranoia developed by humans over millennia of dirty, crowded, and competitive terrestrial life-styles. In the dolphin's world, scheming and plotting for power and aggrandizement by individuals and groups is essentially meaningless. A war among these social animals is unheard of; even serious fighting among individuals within a species is unusual. Only the rapacious killer whales, or orcas, attack other cetaceans for food, and possibly sport. Perhaps the highly organized orcas consider other species as animals or sub-cetacean or we may be witnessing a period in which the orcas are asserting their dominance as did the most aggressive species of early man among several congeners and contemporary protohumans.

Of course many more kinds of cetaceans coexist in the world ocean than ever did hominid creatures on the African savanna. The sea simply may be so vast, and offer such a diversity of resources, that aggressive competition among dolphins and whales failed to develop to the extent that it did in man. It is also interesting that dolphins and whales rarely fight back when attacked by humans. They may fail to comprehend the predatory drive launched against them from above the sea surface.

If dolphins and their relatives are really free of the turmoil occupying so much of human thought, what does go on in their big brains? What do they think about? Mysterious, joyful wraiths, they materialize out of the great flowing ocean spaces and tease our imaginations. *What do they think of us?*

A number of scientists believe that dolphins possess a form of language and that eventually our two species may communicate. One of the reasons for attempting to communicate with dolphins, offered perhaps with tongue in cheek, is to prepare our human society for contact with beings from outer space. However, it seems reasonable to suppose that intelligent aliens will first contact the dolphins. After a brief survey of our planet, the extra-terrestrials might quickly rule out any other native life as being truly intelligent.

Fourth Day:

There were continuing problems with the deep-sea camera system. We had made eight camera stations to this point, and none of the results was satisfactory. RJ's mood had settled into a stoic calm. I think everybody admired the endless persistence of the man.

After the initial problem caused by condensation in the camera had been corrected, the strobe unit suddenly failed. Many of us probably would have given up and sent the damned thing back to the factory for repairs, but RJ and his research assistant, thumbing a technical manual like a Berlitz phrasebook, soon had the strobe's wiry guts exposed. To be on the safe side they first dried the whole thing as they had the camera, then, with an electronics testing kit and tackle box of spare parts, performed mysterious rituals in the dry lab below the main deck. In the end it worked.

Late yesterday the first well-exposed photos were obtained, but they were all out of focus. At first we thought it was merely a matter of shortening the cable attached to the trigger weight, thus bringing the camera closer to the bottom when the shutter tripped. The cable was shortened, then shortened again, but the degree of improvement was minimal, and it was clear that the camera lens itself had been preset far short of the proper focusing distance.

Once again the heavy housing and seals would have to come off.

With all the concern among the biologists over the camera, many of us hardly noticed that one group on board was garnering success and samples at every station. The geologists, using simple sand and rock dredges, were filling up a corner of the large wet lab just off the forward deck with gritty fragments of Pleistocene history which had once lined the shore of a shrunken sea. The most interesting samples, sporting yellow tags giving latitude, longitude, and the depth of water, were chunks of porous limestone rock. Encrusted with coral, sponges, and representatives of most of the rest of the animal kingdom, these were pieces of a formerly flourishing algal reef that bordered the shallows at the edge of a regional coastal plain once twice as broad as it is now.

I found myself wondering what rivers had run their extended courses to the ice-age ocean which must have foamed and crashed ahead of a thousand unnamed hurricanes on the now-silent reef ninety-five meters down. Far south of the ice this low flat shoreline, then almost in touch with the Gulf Stream, must have possessed a moderate climate and immense marshlands, a wilderness of birds and grass blowing to the horizon. What forests and savannas back of the coast had known the wandering Pleistocene herds—mammoths, llamas and camels, bison, and their spectular predators, the saber-toothed cats, which made their last stand in this region just a few thousand years ago? Finally when the sea rose to reclaim its continental shelf, did it play a crucial role in sending to extinction the last North American populations of these animals? As the sea rose, they would have been concentrated ever more vulnerably into the slaughtering range of ascendant man.

2100:

We were sailing due east. Since midafternoon we had been just north of Cape Hatteras. At our shallowest station I could see the big, black and white, candy-striped lighthouse which watches over the dangerous shoals and narrow continental shelf here—only 30 kilometers wide. This was an ideal area to attempt some deep-water work, but time was running out. Now that RJ thought he had fixed everything, he desperately wanted some deep-water pictures. Our next station was to be the ultimate camera test.

There was some concern over the weather, however. All day the wind blew strongly—twenty-five knots from the southwest, with gusts to thirty-five. The sea ran in impressive swells, and the ship danced over and through them with some very complicated moves. Fortunately no one seemed to relapse into seasickness, although appetites waned noticeably and everyone tried to avoid tasks that demanded a high degree of concentration. There was also a conscious avoidance of cramped, windowless spaces below decks where walls crawled sickeningly and the floor dropped away with an unexpected twist one moment only to return forcibly the next.

At 1800 hours we had all heard the Coast Guard's thorough weather report which issued small craft warnings because of an approaching cold front. In addition the report mentioned that some severe squalls might be expected along the fast-moving front, which would pass off Cape Hatteras in the early hours of the morning.

Some of us speculated as to what severe meant, but we reassuredly agreed that the ship didn't quite qualify as a small craft.

We were due on station in an hour, and I was curious to see how the camera operation would go in rough weather. RJ was nowhere to be seen in the more frequented parts of the ship, and I imagined he was making final adjustments to the much-refurbished camera. The ship was really rolling now, and I had to brace myself when walking. Any kind of coordinated work would be getting difficult. With these thoughts I found myself passing the top of the narrow stairs leading down to the dry lab.

There was a strange strangling noise below, out of sight. Vaguely concerned, I started down the stairs just as a stench of vomit suddenly materialized. On the floor below in a corner was RJ. He had braced himself against the wall. A large screwdriver clutched in his right hand, he faced the camera frame, itself wedged between two heavy crates in front of him.

RJ and the camera frame and the small stuffy room swayed and rolled in concert with the ship, and between wrenching bouts of essentially dry heaves he set bolts and turned the screwdriver with saltatory efforts of his whole body.

I offered my help, held and turned the heavy frame to give him the best access. In silence and mercifully quickly the work was finished. With a muttered thanks and ". . .I just need a half hour. . .," RJ disappeared in the direction of the chief scientist's stateroom. I struggled back to my own bunk, lay down, and turned the blower on full as the nausea and wooziness gradually subsided. Without intending to, I fell asleep.

Fifth Day: 0345:

Once I was on my feet, I came awake quickly, motivated by self-preservation. The deck was heaving like a convulsed living thing. But I noticed the powerful tone of the engines was absent. Why weren't we underway? I knew no station was scheduled at this time.

Congratulating myself for having slept in my clothes, I searched cautiously in the dark for my shoes. During a brief lull in the violent motion, I found them, got them on, and stumbled into the blazing light of the lounge. A lone geologist was there before me.

"What's going on?" I asked, bracing against a wall. "Are we on station?"

"This is the second camera try," he answered. "I got the word a few minutes ago when I got up. We haven't moved since 10 o'clock last night. The first time it came back with the film magazine jammed."

I shook my head in disbelief. "What's the depth?"

"1800 meters; it takes three quarters of an hour for the goddamned thing just to make the round trip."

"Where is it now?"

"Coming up; we probably better go out." He gestured toward a rack of slickers and rain pants. "You're definitely going to want that foul-weather gear."

We stepped from interior quiet and light into roaring murky night. Apparently we were in the middle of one of the line squalls accompanying the shifting weather. Rain mixed with salt spray tasted brackish and drove in horizontal sheets through the beams of the deck lights whose brightness seemed much diminished over former occasions. Off the rail, the near view displayed a riot of hissing swells, white tops rising well above our heads, foam whipping off in the wind. The exact position of the sea surface in such conditions seemed a matter of conjecture.

The camera was being run off the stern winch this time, and I carefully made my way across the deck to a corner by the rail and stared at the slim steel cable emerging from the black depths and reeling into the ship at slightly over two kilometers per hour. Then, as I started to turn around, I was startled to see a bright, fat, arrow-shape appear out of the black source of the wind. Briefly, reflexively, it resolved into a squid about the size of a cucumber. It flew straight as if from a bow, without a trace of arc across the lighted deck, passed within six feet of me, and vanished into the receiving night. As I retreated to the semi-shelter of an overhanging portion of the upper deck, this apparition put the raging weather into a brief positive perspective. I had a vivid mental picture of squid over many square kilometers of ocean around us launching into the storm as the normal boundary of their world expanded into a new and exhilarating realm.

The gliding of squid has been known for some time. I had read about it, but this didn't prepare me for the powerful image of the animal hurtling through the storm. I wondered if I had witnessed a moment in the evolution of natural flight, which has occurred only a handful of times in the history of life on earth.

Surrounding a squid's body is a tubular envelope, the mantle, which contains a powerful set of muscles and controlling nerves and allows the forcible expulsion of water through the tube's only opening, a narrow flexible nozzle, the siphon. The squid embodies the organic origin of jet propulsion. Add flexible fins to this system, and air gliding results when the animal reaches escape velocity at the sea surface.

If the squid is ever to achieve true flight, some major adaptations must occur involving masculature and supporting skeletal structures to make wings of fins. Problems of dessication and even sunburn might also be formidable. However, the creature's gliding abilities already suggest well-developed bodily coordination in the air. Furthermore, one imagines that with relatively minor adjustments of its sophisticated optical system a squid could see as well in air as in water. Invertebrate anatomists will rightfully consider all these thoughts highly speculative, but the shaping forces of spectacular evolutionary change have focused in less likely spots than a squid's eye and remarkably versatile body.

Evolutionary theorists considering these matters might speak of pre-adaptations and selective pressures. As a macropredator, the squid has a potential advantage in seeking food from the air that would be wasted on fellow gliders, notably flying fish which myopically consume various bits of organic minutiae. Both squid and flying fish apparently glide to escape predators, but if indeed they could spot prey from the air, squid would be able to take advantage of flight in another vital activity. Competition among several species of squid on limited feeding grounds might provide the selective pressure, perhaps leading a small species through many small internal and external changes and numberless generations to eventual sustained flight in the manner of soaring seabirds.

"In sight"—a bellow from my companion who was staring intently down along the emerging cable. On cue the winch operator throttled down. The camera came up slowly, shimmering yellow against black water. The rolling of the ship caused the dangling frame to swing wildly. I reached for it and missed twice. On the third try, I caught it and received a shock. My hand, acclimated to the tepid rain and Gulf Stream spray, contacted icy cold metal, a reminder that a few hundred meters down the inner edge of the Gulf Stream abutted frigid slope water. As we hauled the camera in, struggling to control it against the tossing ship, I had a long faithless moment of speculation on the device's likelihood of having functioned in the cold crushing environment nearly two kilometers below us.

To my surprise, RJ himself emerged from the shadowed winch operator's cubicle and helped us carry the rig over the rolling deck into the wet lab. He seemed a lot better than last evening, and he smiled his grim smile, but his eyes looked exhausted. Inside we set the frame on the floor. Quickly he wiped the camera's housing dry with a rag, snapped open a catch, and muttered, "Well, the winding worked this time."

I couldn't tell if his voice was hopeful or not. Half expecting him to take the film out and head for the darkroom immediately, I was surprised when he seemed to read my thoughts.

Wearily he said, "I don't think I could pour hypo into a bathtub right now; I'll leave the film until morning." We tied the camera frame to some wall brackets in the lab. It was 0430.

0830:

It was a beautiful morning. Seas were still running high, but they were once again ranged in long regular swells, and the ship's movement was less violent than on the previous evening. Overhead an intensely blue sky showed between small, scudding clouds. The air was much cooler and dryer, with a crisp, freshly washed feel. Whenever the sun broke through, the sea shone blue as the sky.

We were heading home. A few shelf stations were still to be made by the beaver-like geologists, but there was relatively little to do now. After the heavy weather and intensive effort of yesterday it was a good feeling.

I was in the lounge with a number of others when RJ entered holding the spool of film, still glistening wet from the last processing bath. Conversation and random activity ceased in the room. RJ pulled a length of film out from the reel and held it up to the light. There were regular rectangular frames, definitely even exposures. Several of us crowded close to see better. There were images! Sediment ripples, linear tracks, mounds, burrows, a fish!

All showed clean clear definition.

"Hallelujah," he said.

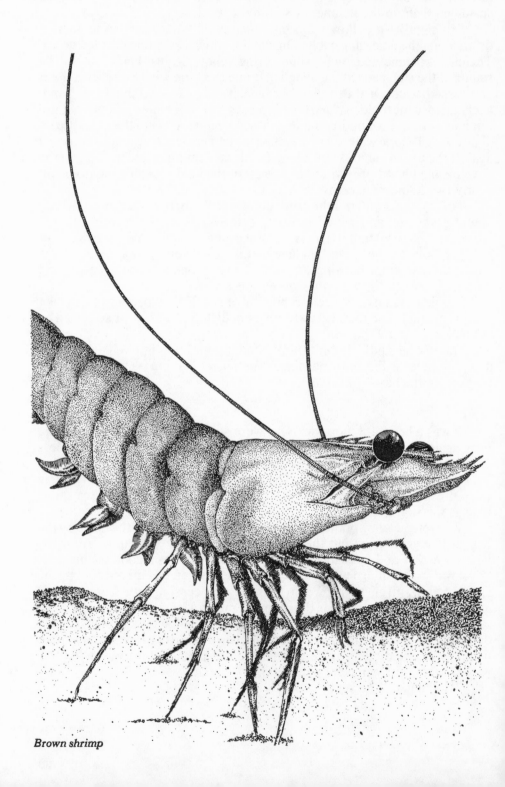

Brown shrimp

Sea of Diversity

The continental shelf of the Gulf of Mexico probably exhibits greater diversity than any other area of similar size within North American epicontinental waters. The composition of shelf water and its circulation are complex because of the admixture with rivers draining half of the contiguous United States. The bottom terrain is exceedingly variable. The fauna and flora combine temperate Atlantic and Caribbean elements in proportions which shift locally and seasonally. A departure point for an exploration of the shallow Gulf is difficult to choose. Perhaps it is best to start at a place that maintains a unique connection to the Gulf's remote geological past, yet presently reflects the region's concentrated biological wealth. This place might be called the hill country of the continental shelf.

Strewn like miniature monadnocks across the broad submerged apron of the northwestern Gulf of Mexico are an uncounted number of underwater hills. Many of the hills stand far out on the imperceptibly deepening shelf. Others occur still deeper on the continental slope and beyond. The submarine climate here so far from land is essentially oceanic, typified by clear water, a stable salinity, and minimal temperature flux. The dominating biological influences are Caribbean.

Covered with a continuous living fabric, a carpet of many colors, the hills have been called "flower garden banks" by some scientist-explorers. They are inhabited by numerous tropical creatures, some of which here make their northernmost permanent settlements in North American waters. The hills are not true coral reefs, although reef corals live on them. So do waving groves of gorgonians, or whip corals, sea fans, anemones, plumed worms, and vaselike sponges. These are seascapes straight out of the tropics. In the shaded galleries, beneath dense canopies so rare on the open shelf, and in the relative security of the water surrounding each hill's reassuring bulk, a million swimmers seek safety and sustenance.

The origins of these peculiar hills are rooted in thousands of meters of sedimentary rocks and in tens of millions of years of geological time. According to reconstructions by earth scientists, events leading to the presence of the hills probably unfolded as follows.

For untold eons during the time called Jurassic, climate belts around the protean Gulf of Mexico created arid conditions. Extremely low regional rainfall and the millenial desert sun caused rivers to dwindle and die long before they reached the huge inland sea that extended considerably farther north and west than at present. Evaporation exceeded the renewal of water.

Only a shallow opening, partly filled by a massive barrier reef complex, connected the deeper basins of the Gulf with the sea to the south. Only an influx of sea water from a narrow Atlantic, which had just formed in the rift between Africa and America, prevented the area from drying up completely. Then as now the opening to the Gulf lay between the Yucatan and Florida peninsulas, which some geologists believe originated as mega-atolls— countless cubic kilometers of coral rock which coalesced upon remarkable, region-wide stipplings of volcanoes.

Tens of thousands of centuries passed while the reef-hindered inflow to the Gulf evaporated like the northern rivers. Particularly in the northwest, vast stretches of the ancient sea, including present dry land areas in Texas and Louisiana, reached a critical level of salinity. Salt began to crystallize from the briny water and form deposits on the bottom. Sustained by time and enough seawater to continue the process without dissolving what had already accumulated, broad belts of salt built up to thicknesses of hundreds of meters.

Much, much later the era of excessively high salinity ended. The sea deepened, and circulation of its surface waters improved. The climate became more humid. Biological productivity along the northern margin of the Gulf increased tremendously as rivers returned chemical nutrients and blanketing sediments to the area.

Under a slow blizzard of sediment the salt deposits, called evaporites by geologists, were buried. For a long time, moreover, circulation in bottom waters of the Gulf must have remained poor. Only near the surface was there an abundance of oxygen capable of sustaining life, and eon by eon particles of that life, everything from diatoms to leviathan reptiles, died and sank into the abiotic depths. Slowly great concentrations of organic matter accumulated below the reach of ravenous scavengers, which could not penetrate these oxygenless bottom waters. Mingling in mounting layers with sand and mud and salt, these mass graves of former beings became petroleum.

The formation of the hills began still later, a slow process that probably continues today. After their burial the salt beds initially formed stony deposits, seemingly as solid as the shales and sandstones that came to cover them. But as the inverted mountains of sediment grew, the temperature of the salt beds began to rise because of compression. By the time 2500 to 3000 meters of sediment had accumulated over the salt, its temperature reached 100°C. and the pressure 600 kilograms per square centimeter (or 8500 lbs. per square inch). Under these conditions salt becomes plastic—as soft as butter on a warm day. Squeezed like a layer of toothpaste beneath mounting layers of sandbags, the salt began to flow slowly in the direction of lower pressure, seeking fissures and weaknesses in the hot imprisoning layers of stone. Most of the time its direction of escape was upward.

Scientists believe that salt under these conditions travels only a few millimeters per year, but it keeps inexorably flowing. Its force is formidable, derived from the weight of thousands of meters of overburden. Finally, irresistibly, a column of salt approaches the surface and easily shoulders aside rock and sediment. The overburden thrusts above the surrounding terrain, and a salt dome is born. On the surface it lives as a hill of fractured stone, sediment and life; the salt usually remains slightly below. Upthrusting forces keep pace with erosion and dissolution until the salt ceases to flow.

Centered on the shelf of the northern Gulf is the dominant geophysical

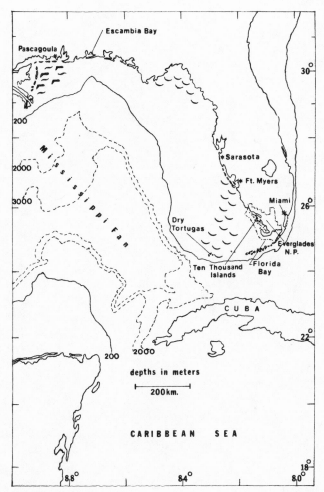

Eastern Gulf of Mexico.

and geochemical influence in the region. For eons the Mississippi River has flowed to this sea of diversity. Throughout its history Old Man River has been the greatest contributor of vital raw materials to the coastal and marine food webs of the Gulf. Each spring astounding ejaculations of the fertilizing elements—nitrates, phosphates, silicates, iron, potassium, and others down to trace materials too numerous to mention—have poured in opaque floods to the semitropical sea. Heavier sediment settles quickly in deltaic deposits before reaching the open Gulf, but dissolved material and weightless organic debris continue out over the continental shelf in mighty plumes.

The virility of this father of waters must have been especially impressive during the epochs of wasting continental glaciers which stood mile-high across the upper Midwest. The annual floods of those centuries were probably protracted affairs lasting at peak flow through the summer and the inundations were probably greater by an order of magnitude than any witnessed by modern man. Recently marine geologists discovered evidence of an episode of massive glacial melting and discharge from the Mississippi

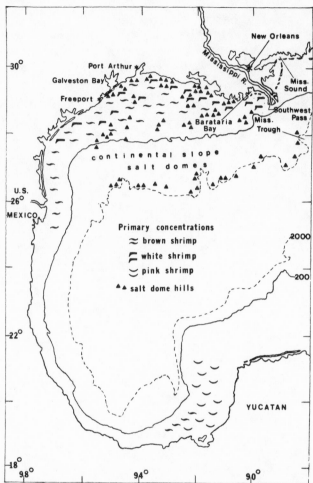

Western Gulf of Mexico.

dated around 11,600 years ago. The scientists suggested that this discharge may in part have caused the legendary coastal flooding at the dawn of human civilization in several regions of the world. Handed down orally from primitive societies, the legends were ultimately recorded by Old Testament writers, Plato, and others.

At times the River must have filled the entire alluvial plain that reaches from Missouri southward, and the present-day continental shelf may have been one vast everglades from Florida to Texas. The highest ground in the region probably comprised the peculiar salt-dome monadnocks of the Texas-Louisiana shelf, from which the sea had retreated over seventy-five meters below its present level. Huge deltaic areas, former levees, dikes, hillocks, and channels can be traced in an area some 300 kilometers wide on the outer shelf. Most of these features have been obscured, their profiles blurred by the combined effects of erosion and sedimentation, which accompanied the rising sea level and later submarine currents. A broad valley incised thirty kilometers into the outer shelf extends outward into the deep sea as the Mississippi Trough, believed to be the nearly filled remnant of a mighty submarine canyon. Extending far beyond the shelf is the greatest reminder of the River's past power and glory. Dwarfing the Trough, the so-called Mississippi Fan, or Cone, is an enormous tongue of sediment about 216,000 square kilometers in area which reaches in a long, shallow slide out into the deep Gulf. In the northeastern Gulf, the Fan has buried a large portion of the continental slope, and has lapped across the sea floor to the latitude of South Florida. Many geologists now believe that much of the Fan formed relatively recently and quickly during the glacial floods.

In modern times the River has taken a more sedate pace. Its average flow, however, is still over 14.5 million liters (500,000 cubic feet) per second, sufficient to fill the New Orleans Superdome in 2½ minutes. In spring the Mississippi's peak flow may be as high as 45 million liters per second. To set these figures in a broader perspective, more than 70 percent of the United States' freshwater runoff reaches the sea at the Mississippi Delta.

One hundred fifty kilometers south of Galveston, Texas, a cuspate hill with a long root of salt rises from the smooth submarine plain to within thirty meters of the surface. This hill stands near the edge of the shelf; its flanks fall away steeply to depths of over 100 meters. Although nearly a kilometer across on the longer axis of its roughly oval summit, the hill is unmarked on navigation charts. Its lovely tropical gardens and teeming populations of fish live in anonymity a few meters below the passing hulls of the world's largest ships. The hill itself is not unique—it is one among many in the northwestern Gulf—but because of its location, its beauty, the diversity of life on and around it, and its as yet pristine surroundings, it can serve both as a symbol and an introduction to the natural history of the regional continental shelf.

Flowing past the hill is a slow current conveying all manner of pelagic life from Yucatan and beyond. The strength of the current and the abundance and diversity of its denizens vary from year to year and season to season. As the current passes, the hill extracts its due in the manner of a toll station housing millions of collectors which sweep the plankton-laden waters. Relieved of a token quantity of its living burden, the flow is at the same time enriched by specific contributions from the hill's own web of life. Eggs, spores, and larvae begin life here and embark on their journey through the northern Gulf. For most of the planktonic travelers the journey is fleetingly short. Threats to life are numberless; the chance for survival of any given individual is miniscule but traditionally has proven adequate for the continuance of most species. However, in the modern era only the flow is guaranteed. Its path leads into a unique corner of the ocean, biologically and geologically, physically and chemically, a sea of diversity.

Trails in the Sea

Offshore in the western Gulf, currents generally trend toward the north. Shoreward branches may develop, carrying their drifting communities along the Texas coast. At times fish follow the plankton, and tropical species such as the white mullet, Mexican sea robin, and Mexican flounder turn up off Texas and occasionally Louisiana in summer.

Floating gulfweed (*Sargassum*) also washes up on these shores. A given bundle of yellow serrated fronds and small leathery bladder-floats may have originated in the far Atlantic east of Bermuda and traveled by a circuitous route to the Caribbean, there finally to be spun off into the western Gulf of Mexico. Cast up on Texas shores, the weed contains basically the same camouflaged community of hitchhiking animals that one finds in *Sargassum* blown in from the Gulf Stream along Atlantic beaches from Florida to Cape Cod.

From time to time the currents moving north from Mexico carry enormous broods of larvae produced by the mass spawning of some creature of the continental shelf. One of the most prominent denizens of the region is a shrimp of the family Penaeidae, known to biologists as *Penaeus aztecus*, or brown shrimp. "Brownies," as the fishermen call them, constitute one of three avidly sought species of shrimp in the Gulf. The others are commercial or white shrimp (*Penaeus setiferus*) and pink shrimp (*Penaeus duorarum*). All three occur in moderate numbers on the temperate Atlantic shelf, but they reach their greatest abundance in the Gulf of Mexico. Of the three, *P. aztecus* leads in the catch statistics for most of the Gulf Coast, and it also forms the basis for an important Mexican fishery.

On the middle shelf, perhaps near one of the salt dome hills, a spawning of shrimp begins after the dim submarine landscape is shrouded in darkness. With senses other than sight newly alerted, a horde of brown shrimp has emerged from the sand where they have been spending the day. Earlier, a visitor here must have seen a barren-looking sandy plain sixty meters deep. Only if he peered extremely closely, like an old Indian tracker searching for the minutest signs, could he have detected the shrimp. An indistinct breathing pore appears here with a sand grain or two moving from the slight exhalations of a hidden respirer; there, a pair of slim antennules, less than two millimeters exposed, twitches periodically for a fresh apprehension of the overlying water world; there again, an eyestalk boldly protrudes like a bulbous periscope, but as inconspicuous as a BB shot on the huge sweep of the shelf. A few hours later in the unbroken blackness of the submarine night, this bottom seethes with softly scuttling life engaged in its most important biological ritual.

Tiny eggs begin to issue into the watery darkness. Clouds of them, tens to hundreds of thousands from each female shrimp, drift slowly down the current. Gradually the dense drifting patches of eggs disperse as they cross the deceptively uniform terrain. On the scale of the egg clouds, a sand ripple induces turbulent atmospheric effects equivalent to those caused by a mountain range, and a passing fish occasions a slowly swirling tornado.

Within a dozen hours great changes are wrought within each egg. Thin outer membranes begin to fall apart in response to the struggles of a tiny emerging protoshrimp called a nauplius (plural, nauplii). The creature recalls a chubby insect with a tiny brownish cyclopean eye and a pear-shaped body from which sprout three pairs of swimming arms. Each arm ends in a tuft of long hairs which serve the nauplius's crude swimming efforts. Watching a nauplius in a drop of water under the microscope, an observer imagines trying to swim with the aid of threadbare whiskbrooms. At top speed the creature scratches its way jerkily through the water. Its progress, however, is hopelessly slow for the effort expended, and it frequently stops to rest.

Like many other drifters in the water all around them, the nauplii are virtually colorless and translucent. Their pallor is a defense measure against visually orienting predators which lunge at hints of pigment or sharp shadows. It is highly likely that numerous other senses serve defensive as well as aggressive strategies in the plankton world. The success of strike and counterstrike, pursuit and evasion, may depend entirely on the detection of lilliputian bow waves or turbulent trails, infinitesimal temperature shifts, haloes of electrical energy, or molecular-level body odors in a scant millimeter between chitinous fang and vulnerable membrane.

Most of the larval shrimp lead very short lives. As they drift northward over the Texas continental shelf, those in mid and surface waters are attacked by other travelers in the plankton, while those near the bottom face additional dangers. Yawning siphonal traps suck them below the surface of the sand where they are eaten by worms or bivalves and even other sand-dwelling crustaceans.

Elsewhere in this region, broad fields of sea whips and sea pansies, two kinds of soft coral, sprout from the bottom. Both sea whips and sea pansies are coelenterates, animated traps with stinging tentacles which paralyze prey at a touch. Both are colonial animals and like stony coral are composed of thousands of small compartmentalized individuals called polyps. On first sight the sea pansy (*Renilla*) looks strikingly like its terrestrial namesake. A supporting stalk is capped by a disk-shaped lobe of soft tissue in which the polyps crouch. The upper surface is usually a beautiful purple or amethyst color during the day when the polyps are contracted, but at night this same surface takes on a look of ruffled lace with a hint of superimposed geometry. Expanding and spreading over the purple disk, the polyps, each with precisely eight tentacles, form an intermeshing sheet. The colony now appears ghostlike white. Alive with multiple arms and mouths it is a diaphanous, deadly web that waits for the tiny drifters. Each vaselike polyp serves the double function of catching food and digesting it, and has a formidable capacity. Its soft walls are highly elastic, and in times of good feeding dozens of newly hatched shrimp nauplii can be stuffed into each of *Renilla*'s tentaculated digestive sacs.

Within a week an estimated 80% of the shrimplings are gone. But the remaining larvae have gone through several molts involving pulses of growth and changes of form. In the manner of their relatives, the lobsters, the young of shrimp go through strikingly different stages of development, but while the lobster makes only one quantum transformation with its fourth molt after hatching from the egg, shrimp lead more complicated lives.

In less than two days, the nauplii molt four times as they grow from roughly 3/10 of a millimeter to 6/10 of a millimeter in length. With the fifth molt the spidery creatures suddenly sport a noticeably lengthened tail and enlarged head with new spines and bristles. The whole animal at this stage begins to look a little like a bottle brush, if one ignores the stubby pair of dark compound eyes that have appeared for the first time. Interestingly, the shrimp larvae, now called protozoeae (singular protozoea) resemble the larval form of crabs (termed a zoea), and they also appear somewhat similar to the youngest larvae of lobsters.

Compared to the bristling, aggressively scuttling protozoea, the primitive nauplius seems hardly more than a feebly animated egg. Indeed its development is sustained by a form of yolk, just as are the lobster embryos, which pass through the equivalent of the nauplius stage while still in the egg. The only adaptive advantage for shrimp in releasing naupliar offspring seems to be that nauplii are cheap to produce, physiologically speaking. If, like lobsters, shrimp were to manufacture more sophisticated larval models at the protozoeal stage of design, the shrimp might quickly become extinct. It is probable that the small-bodied shrimp could not produce and carry enough of the larger, later-hatching eggs to assure the survival of significant numbers to adulthood. The game of numbers is the first consideration in any animal's reproductive strategy. On the average over the generations, a species must produce at least enough young to attain zero population growth (ZPG, the replacement of each pair of breeding adults per generation), or its doom is sealed. Species that manage to exceed ZPG for a time also get into trouble, but their error is inevitably self-adjusting when they begin to outstrip vital resources.

The most significant behavioral change accompanying the graduation of the larvae from the nauplius to protozoea is that the latter begins to feed. At first, however, as with the young of many animals, feeding is a myopic exercise. The larva must literally bump into its fare and seems to subsist largely on passive phytoplankton and possibly organic detritus. A well-coordinated behavior involving the approach and seizure of edible items in the water has not yet appeared.

Protozoae pass through three stages, becoming progressively larger at each stage, but, excluding spines and appendages, still measure only three millimeters at the longest. The third protozoea enters its molt predetermined to emerge in a striking new guise.

The new shrimpling is termed a mysis because of its external resemblance to a primitive order of crustaceans, the mysidaceans, or mysids in taxonomic shorthand. The mysidaceans may have arisen long ago by the retention of embryonic characteristics in the adult organism. This process, called neoteny, seems to occur through a retardation of the rate of development, while growth proceeds. Sometimes a few, sometimes many organs and aspects of morphology are involved. The lost evolutionary history of mysids and men (who as adults retain numerous physical characteristics of the fetal ape) appears to embody elements of neoteny.

Until the appearance of the mysis stage, marine biologists have great difficulty in distinguishing the larva of brown shrimp from a bewildering variety of its cousins which also inhabit the waters of the Gulf. During the season of greatest spawning, from spring to late fall, nauplii and protozoeae of more than a dozen species of shrimp drift in anonymity along the continental shelf, but with the molt to mysis each species begins to reveal unique characteristics, many of them about the head in the manner of antlered mammals.

In some species the mysis has become an almost caricatured study in ferocity. What a pity the Aztecs or the Romans did not possess plankton nets and microscopes. Given the inspiration of the mysis, an Aztec or Roman artisan's rendering of war gods' or soldiers' helmets might have routed a barbarian army at a glance.

The leading feature of the mysis head is a thick spine. In some species it is straight and unadorned like a lance; in others it is jagged and looks like an idealized model of a lightning bolt. Projecting straight forward between and beyond the eyes, the mysis's rostral spine would be extremely impressive in bronze, magnified perhaps 2,000 times. An improvement on the protozoea's stubby optical equipment, the mysis's eyes are large and prominent. Bulbous, faceted ends on stout stalks project nearly forty-five degrees to each side of the centerline.

The mysis's body is more elongated than that of the protozoa. Functional legs sprout from the thorax behind the head; at the tips of the legs tiny claws can be seen. The abdomen, now definitely discernable and shrimplike, forms the longest portion of the body. At the posterior end, stout overlapping plates spread into a fanlike tail. The appearance of the tail confers a significant new behavioral advantage on the animal. The capacity for powerful short bursts of back-swimming, an escape reflex, has developed.

Some evidence from Gulf of Mexico plankton studies suggests that mysis-stage shrimp become more strongly influenced by the diurnal cycle than their larval predecessors. They swim close to the surface in daytime and descend toward the bottom at night. There they may begin to use their diminutive claws, dabbling delicately for tiny edibles in the sand, but alert and hesitant like nervous mosquitos, whose size they now approximate. At the merest whiff or wisp of danger, the marvelous safety reflex of the arthropods, mediated through giant nerve fibers and a snapping tail fan, activates. In a split instant the mysis is away from the bottom, once again falling free through black watery space.

During the first drifting phase of a shrimp's life, different populations of larvae spawned on the shelf all across the northern Gulf fill the ephemeral highways and byways. They go where the currents take them in this sea of diversity; they pass over drowned capes and barrier islands similar to those on the Atlantic shelf; they glide over hundreds of reef-capped salt domes and buried submarine canyons. Enormous numbers of larvae move through and within the tremendous zone of influence of the Mississippi River.

A week after spawning, the new shrimp generation has dispersed widely across the continental shelf. With the further passage of time, however, the process of dispersion begins to reverse itself. At some point, probably in the mysis stage, the larvae first become sensitive to certain compelling nuances in the water around them. Just what guides the behavior of the tiny creatures is uncertain. Chemical cues are possible, as are physical ones such as temperature plumes. The result of a potentially complex behavior, however, is straightforward. The larvae of brown shrimp, white shrimp, and others all begin to move toward the mouths of estuaries all around the northern Gulf.

It is intriguing to speculate on the motivations and mechanisms underlying the migration of the tiny shrimp. It is probable that many estuarine emanations penetrate far out onto the shelf. Certain of these may be detected at low concentrations by the shrimp. But there is a formidable problem: while the senses are adequate (and the spirit willing), the locomotion is feeble. A larva's swimming abilities still do not permit sustained travel against the currents.

Picture the environment twenty kilometers off the Louisiana coast. Currents are capricious. They generally flow parallel to shore here, but this basic pattern is enormously complicated by winds, fluctuating river discharge, bottom topography, and perhaps lesser factors that operate at levels unnoticed by man, but which are nevertheless of significance to plankton. The one directional aid to movement that remains essentially stable and dependable is the tidal cycle. Offshore the tides are weak, but they are capable of moving hordes of larvae; the water drifts a kilometer or two toward the coast, then ebbs back again.

Picture a mysis larva suddenly entering a wafting of faint land scents on the open shelf. All its young life it has known only the relatively odorless, highly saline flow of oceanic water across its gills, or at least it has not yet recognized the exotic new stimuli that now bathe its senses. Perhaps the mysis is induced to seek bottom to feed, or merely to cling to some stationary bit of algae or shell. If so, it will remain in essentially the same place while the ebb flow continues to carry the rank, pungent tastes of a coastal estuary. But when the tide turns, these stimuli will dissipate and there is again a shift to the bland olfactory environment of the open sea. Again the mysis may begin to swim in a sheet of water which now moves gently shoreward. A repetition of these events over several tidal cycles would bring the shrimplings by a lazy but continually one-way series of fits and starts into ever-stronger tidal flows, and finally to the muddy mouths of the estuaries.

The behavior described is speculative, and no one knows if larval shrimp actually move inshore from the open shelf in this manner. Other kinds of larvae, those of annelid worms and mollusks, are known to react strongly to emanations from preferred kinds of sediments and food sources. They settle from the water onto the bottom as if a narcotic had been added to the water. After a while, if the stimulus was a weak one, they begin to swim again. In the case of mysis larvae, a cunning pattern of adaptive behavior related to the tides, which carry a great variety of potential directional cues, is not unlikely when one considers the antiquity of coexistence of tides and shrimp.

Whatever the mechanism of their shoreward movement, the shrimplings begin to appear in coastal waters such as Escambia Bay, Mississippi Sound, Barataria Bay, and Galveston Bay as soon as two weeks after spawning. At this time, too, most have molted from the third mysis into the first postlarval stage. This molt again qualitatively changes the appearance of the animal, but less radically than in earlier transformations. Postlarvae retain the mysis's striking frontal armament, but its effect seems diminished because the rest of the head now bulks noticeably larger. The animal's body is longer than before and proportionately still more slender than an adult's, but this creature is more clearly a shrimp than in any of its previous guises. The fragile sylphlike swimmers straggling in from the continental shelf are approximately one centimeter long.

An early morning flight in a light aircraft over a remote part of the northern Gulf Coast recalls viewing an immensely rich and panoramic tapestry. The dominant feature in this osprey's-eye view is the pattern of water interlocking with the land. The dominant colors below are dark and underworldly: dark maritime forests of live oak and pine; dark water swamps of black gum and cypress; dark winding bayous. Browns and gray greens of tidal shallows grade into uniformly dark depths in the larger bays and channels. Occasional surprises stand out sharply against the somber hues. An oyster reef brushes a bay's surface, runs a sinuous 200-meter course across the tide, and descends into opacity. It appears flat-topped, dull white, a caricature of an Atlantean causeway beginning and ending in water the color of mud. It is also an invertebrate metropolis designed with nature by humble architects, but its foundations are in the Pleistocene. More surprises: a thin white ribbon of beach ahead, a spray of snowy egrets in flight above a blackwater slough.

The second impression of this water-knit wilderness is its flatness. It is certainly easy to imagine that with a steady rise in sea level—perhaps three or four centimeters per year, a rate known to have occurred in the past—much of what passes for dry land in this region could again come under the purview of the continental shelf in two or three human generations.

After a while it is possible to shut out the drone of the plane's engine and to feel the silence flowing from the waterscapes below. This dimension, however, is better appreciated when one is actually down there, adrift in a boat on a calm estuary morning among quiet flows of plankton and small fish, floating seeds and rafts of decomposing marsh grass, birds and a breakfasting family of dolphins. On the water it is difficult to tell where the continental shelf ends and the terrestrial influence begins. Man tries to classify and compartmentalize, but the environmental extremes are stitched together with a million different threads along a wonderfully flexible seam.

The concentration of food for the postlarval shrimp in the organic sink between land and sea is several times higher than any previously encountered. At the same time the danger shows a corresponding increase. For the first time the baby shrimp are subject to significant predation from above the water's surface. If they stray into the shallows, young herons and egrets may pick them off with a flick of a rapier bill. Too near the surface elsewhere, young shrimp may be snipped from the fluid fabric by the bill of a feeding tern, kingfisher, or black skimmer.

It is likely that the adult behavior of burrowing into the bottom during the day and foraging at night begins soon after the shrimp enter coastal waters. Any deviates which ignore this diurnal pattern must be quickly eliminated, not only by birds, but also by a great variety of aquatic predators: fish, squid, and fellow crustaceans such as the fast-swimming blue crabs.

While the day and night changes in behavior are mediated by responses to light, the shrimp appear to possess senses that seem truly bizarre. Recent studies on another crustacean species, the red ghost shrimp (*Callianassa*) revealed that the animals detect X-rays. The ghost shrimp flee a field of invisible radiation and seek shielded areas of the environment, simulated for the study within a laboratory aquarium. This intriguing realm of almost-ESP is totally alien to humans who feel absolutely nothing when the dental or TB clinic's technician presses the button. Many questions arise. What do the ghost shrimp experience—a searing brightness, uncomfortable warmth, pain? Over how broad a spectrum does the detection of ionizing radiation extend? Do other crustaceans have this capacity? The likelihood is good, for the researchers have tested carpenter ants, and these terrestrial anthropods are even more sensitive to X-rays than the ghost shrimp.

The avoidance behavior toward ionizing radiation may be a holdover trait of great antiquity. Perhaps at some time in the incredibly remote past this singular trait was adaptive in an ancestral arthropod threatened by high solar flux or radiative bombardment from another source. If that is true, then X-ray avoidance could be among the most conservative specific behavioral reactions known, for the ancestors of ghost shrimp and ants entered divergent evolutionary paths hundreds of millions of years ago.

One also speculates that in the unhappy event of global nuclear ecocide, all will not be lost. Those creatures that can detect the dangerous radiation in water and air, and which can find small refugia for a few decades, will be in the best position to inherit the earth.

Brown and white shrimp which survive in the estuarine jungle grow extremely rapidly. During the summer in blood-warm brackish water the shrimp, which assume the adult body form after three postlarval stages, increase their length by twenty-five to forty-five millimeters per month. Estuaries are among the most productive natural systems on earth. Tidewaters from Texas to Florida consistently have provided the proper conditions—temperature, chemical factors, and abundant food—to bring the shrimp to marketable size in less than six months.

At some point during their period of estuarine residence, the shrimp begin to develop a gregarious urge, and like so many kinds of marine creatures, both motile and sedentary, they seek each others' company. The common rule holds that species of a kind flock together, and assemblages of brown shrimp segregate from those of white shrimp with great fidelity.

Before they are sexually mature, the hordes of shrimp leave the estuaries and return to the open shelf. Usually the estuarine exodus takes place within six or seven months of the initial larval incursion from the sea. Often the shrimp are hurried by winter. Strong horizontal temperature gradients are typical in the northern Gulf. During January much of inner Mississippi Sound may be a chilly 12°C., while a few kilometers offshore the water is a relatively mild 18°C. (For comparative purposes, the latter temperature represents the summer maximum for New England shelf waters north of Cape Cod). In the winter, temporary reverse thermoclines form along the Gulf coast where warmer, more saline offshore water undercuts colder but fresher surface layers. Later in the spring, the true thermocline rapidly forms under the powerful equinoctial sun. The shrimp always prefer warm water to cold. Thus adults may move far out on the continental shelf during a particularly severe winter.

Here the shrimp come full circle, arriving at the point of reproducing their kind. The crustacean equivalent of puberty is reached in the open sea; communal mating and spawning follow. Given the chance, female white shrimp, and probably other species as well, spawn as many as four times in a year. Until recently this prodigious rate of reproduction has maintained shrimp populations at high levels in the wake of sporadic natural disasters such as floods as well as increasing predation by man. After the 1971–1972 fishing season, however, something began happening to shrimp across the whole northern Gulf. Despite increases in fishing effort, the catch declined precipitously. This decline was especially noticeable in the so-called fertile fisheries crescent (Pascagoula, Mississippi, to Port Arthur, Texas), where roughly 20 percent of United States' seafood, much of that shrimp, is produced. In Louisiana, for example, the shrimp catch dropped from a 1971 high of 92 million pounds to 60 million pounds in 1974. Louisiana traditionally has led the nation in shrimp fishing; this record reflects the incredible natural abundance of shrimp in the state's thousands of square kilometers of coastal nursery grounds.

Some scientists have ascribed the decline to regional bad weather, particularly the heavy rains in 1973, but this is probably only part of the story. Never before has there appeared such a massive drop in the entire region's shrimp catch, and earlier flood years have been worse than 1973.

Another possibility is that the intensity and ever-greater efficiency of fishing may finally have overwhelmed the shrimp's ability to maintain its natural level of abundance. If the present fishing effort were to remain constant, this would mean that ZPG for shrimp would readjust at a new lower figure, for the fewer shrimp on the continental shelf, the harder they would be to catch. But the power of technological fishing no longer guarantees this self-regulating principle that fosters conservation in normal predator-prey interactions. Man is on the verge of developing extensions of eye and ear, fang and claw that can detect and trap the last furtive shrimp school in the nighttime depths of the Gulf. Fisheries' quotas for shrimp in different parts of the Gulf may soon become as necessary as they are for finfish in the Northwest Atlantic. So far there are only short token winter and summer abstentions in the offshore Gulf shrimping industry.

Potentially far more dangerous to shrimp than climatic fluctuations and even modern fishing are the largely invisible, colorless, and odorless pollutants pouring into the estuaries and shallow shelf waters. These insidious incursions, focused on the Gulf like beams of destroying radiation, come from cotton fields, oil wells, cities, and numerous other sources. Silently, subliminally, some of the substances destroy larvae and other plankton on contact, and sicken nearly every other form of life. Many of the pollutants are brand new to the planet. There is no recognition of danger comparable to the ghost shrimp's response to X-rays, but as in radiation disease, no hint of pain and no obvious sign of damage may be noted in the Gulf until it is too late and the victim is terminally ill.

Many of the pollutants do not kill quickly. They are slow-acting poisons accumulating throughout the marine food web up to and including man. Many are specifically designed to kill insects, the shrimp's close relatives, and physiological effects on both are similar. Careful observations on shrimp survival should look beyond the mere provision of fishery statistics. Reproductive success, physiology and behavior should be monitored frequently. Such shrimp-watching may provide a distant early warning of impending pollution dangers within the shelf ecosystem in general. The fate of the sensitive crustaceans is woven into that of the whole living Gulf as incalculably as the paths of larval wanderings.

Snowy egret

Marine Woodlands

Infrequently among catches of brown and white shrimp there appears a third species, also designated by a color. The pink shrimp (*Penaeus duorarum*) completes the roster of shrimp species in the Gulf which are important from the standpoint of human consumption. The occurrence of pinks in the northwestern Gulf is a freak, for their normal haunts lie hundreds of kilometers away, predominantly along the southwest coast of Florida.

Like their northern cousins, pink shrimp spawn on the shelf. By far the greatest spawning concentrations occur near the Dry Tortugas, an area of reefs and coral-formed islets near the shelf's edge off Key West. Commercial shrimpers have worked these grounds for decades, but the importance of the Tortugas as a spawning site was not realized until the late 1950s.

At that time scientists from the U.S. Bureau of Commercial Fisheries and the University of Miami began to find evidence that adults which spawn at Tortugas come from the mangrove estuaries of the Everglades, and the larvae of *P. duorarum*, like their congeners off Texas, Louisiana and Mississippi, somehow make the return migration across 150 kilometers of open shelf. After ten days they turn up as diffuse clouds of post larvae at the entrance to Florida Bay. Then the many-jointed, translucent slivers of shrimp move into the backwaters to feed and grow until they too develop a social imperative, spawning urge, and seaward geographical fixation.

Despite its smallness, the southwest Florida region deserves to be included in any discussion of the natural history of the Gulf of Mexico. There is a qualitative difference in the marine environment here. The tropical manifestations are more permanent and pervasive than anywhere else in the Gulf, except perhaps the hill country.

Off southwest Florida, fish, invertebrates, plants, even the tempered seasons (wet and dry largely displacing warm and cold), all spill over with regularity from the adjacent Caribbean. Less tangible tropical essences also spread from the thickly overgrown coastal zone out across the shelf and permeate its waters by means of the tides. To pink shrimp and its fellow marine life large and small, one of the most important of these must be the flavor of mangrove.

Along the inner edge of the southeastern Gulf of Mexico stands the only significant mangrove forest in the continental United States. Three species of trees, known commonly by colors (red, black, and white) grow in close proximity. The coast of Ten Thousand Islands that borders Everglades National Park is the heart of the mangrove region, a continuous forest that extends inland for thirty kilometers along numerous waterways. Until violent hurricanes in 1935 and 1960, some red and black mangrove trees nearly thirty meters high, close to the world record, could be found here. Northward toward Fort Myers, the forests diminish in extent and the trees in stature. Above Sarasota there is further degeneration into shrubby copses. Under the control of severe frosts, their distribution expands and contracts north and south with climatic cycles.

Black mangrove (*Avicennia nitida*) is more resistant to winter cold than the other two. Having the ability to sprout from the stump, it appears sporadically as small thickets in Louisiana and Texas. Black mangrove is unique in possessing a peculiar "air injection" system which brings oxygen to roots growing in anaerobic muck. All around the tree, radiating in rows from the trunk, pneumatophores sprout from the mud like bony fingers. Sievelike in structure, they connect to the hidden roots and perform the aerating function.

White mangrove (*Laguncularia racemosa*) possesses an adaptation similar to *Avicennia*. Instead of pneumatophores, however, simple openings in the lower trunk allow air to reach the roots via ducts in the wood itself. Both of these trees tolerate exposure to a full range of salinity from normal sea water to fresh water, but rarely do they front directly on the sea.

The most conspicuous mangrove species is the red (*Rhizophora mangle*). This tree is the land builder which faces the sea in its fiercest moods and usually survives. It is a founder of islands that first lie scattered in the shallows, then gradually coalesce in an orgy of spindly but powerfully anchored trees. In the Ten Thousand Islands this process is continuous and dynamic. Every stage in the geobotanical evolution of a low tropical coast can be found. Most strikingly at uncertain times and localities there can be seen the effects of severe storms, which in mere hours erase or fragment a century's slow terrestrial budding. The result is that hundreds of kilometers of involuted, island-studded shoreline, amid a maze of tidal creeks and sloughs, are here raveled into a cartographer's ten-kilometer scale.

Storms are not the only destructive forces impinging on the lives of mangroves. Certain organisms which might be called marine termites are found in the marine woodlands. The shipworm, *Teredo* (actually a bivalve mollusk), and the wood-boring crustaceans, typically the isopod, *Sphaeroma*, belong to the ecological guild of reducers. Overall their role is a beneficial one. They initiate the recycling of wood in the sea, a process that is completed eventually by lesser creatures, the marine fungi and bacteria. Without the wood-destroying activity of shipworms and their ilk, coastal waters and beaches along wooded coasts would quickly become choked by enormous amounts of dead wood.

From time to time and place to place, the flattened, bug-like *Sphaeroma* and, rarely, the shipworm have been found attacking living mangrove trees. But even this may be beneficial; thinning the stands and keeping open the waterways assures a steady supply of trace nutrients and prevents extreme accumulations of waste materials.

The mangrove's great productivity in the intense photosynthetic environment of South Florida constitutes its main contribution to marine life. The rich detritus formed by decomposing leaves and wood constitutes the base of a whole new food web, one which parallels and intermeshes with the standard trophic system derived from phytoplankton. The creation of physical habitat, however, is also important—especially the huge networks of protected waterways. The mangroves are probably essential to pink shrimp and many other members of food webs on the wide, shallow continental shelf.

The best way to acquire a mangrove consciousness, or merely to open a scientific inquiry into this unique ecosystem, is to visit the shadowed winding waterways in a silent conveyance such as a canoe. Along the open coast, the forest seems impenetrable. Entry appears unexpectedly in the form of a small tidal channel. Cross the shallow sand bar at its entrance and the channel drops away to clean sand bottom a paddle's length below. The water is very clear; fish dart ahead of the canoe. Banks form. A curtain of shade drops. Squinting facial muscles relax, and a sudden coolness crosses the shoulders. The relentless south Florida sun remains behind.

If it is a windy day, a uniform rustling sound comes from the canopy above. Even in a gale there is little intemperate roaring and swaying of whole trees. The red mangroves along the little stream are so well buttressed they will stand stiffly until hurricane-force winds rip them from the muck at one stroke. At the level of the forest floor only light, intermittent air currents hint of high canopy winds ten or fifteen meters overhead. In insect season, one is well advised to enter the mangrove forest on a windy day. It is not that midges and mosquitoes are prevented from flying in the light breezes along the channels, but rather their heat-seeking guidance systems may be confused by the eddying airflows. Nevertheless, some of these anti-personnel missiles find their target under any conditions, and even in hot weather long sleeves and pants will be blessed.

The interior forest presents a different picture from the dense, sun-saturated barrier along the outside bay. So little light enters the interior that negligible understory vegetation exists. A great openness is the result, parklike in a sense that includes low tangles of *Rhizophora* buttress roots, widely scattered whips of young trees doomed to wither in the shade of their parents, and a druid's geometry of *Avicennia* pneumatophores surrounding muddy trunks.

At first the surroundings seem monospectrally gloomy, a Tolkienesque setting devoid of animal life, but as the eyes adjust and perceive the means and extremes of texture and color, signs of life appear everywhere. The second impression is that one has discovered the kingdom of the crabs. On the trees, black scuttling crabs the size of tarantulas run in small groups. They look like spiders, but they act like squirrels. Wonderfully agile, they race up trunks and out slender branches high above the canoe. To see the mangrove tree crab (*Aratus pisonii*) up close, one can pick almost any tree; reach high with one hand and slowly move it around the trunk. Invariably one or several of the small, flat-bodied creatures will sidle warily on pin-tipped feet around to the near side, affording the observer a clear view if he remains perfectly still. Up close the spidery look vanishes. The animal is hard-shelled, smooth, hairless, and appears encased in fine marble. The flecks of color on ebony or dark olive ground are yellow and red pigment cells, chromatophores, the same kind of adaptive cosmetology used by lobsters, flounder, squid, and others.

A tree crab's first choice of an escape route is upward; only if this route is blocked will one drop to the ground. In this event a crab will dash into the nearest hole or crevice among the roots. Only as a last choice is sanctuary sought in the water. Lurking by sunken logs and under the banks beside the clear, deep channel are powerful enforcers of such a behavioral hierarchy. In the trees the acrobatic crabs probably hold their own against birds and raccoons, but in the water against a light sand bottom or silvery undersurface, the wriggling black forms are an easy mark for a young snook or sheepshead.

Of course many kinds of crabs do live permanently in the water, but these possess adaptations such as heavy armor, cryptic coloration, secretive behavior, or high swimming speed. The last attribute is possessed by the familiar blue crab (*Callinectes sapidus*), a prized commercial species throughout the Gulf region and along the temperate Atlantic coast north to Cape Cod. As fast and elusive as many fish, these crabs are more common in the open bay, but may sometimes be seen stalking over the bottom of the clear mangrove channel.

On a sandy open bank in a small clearing are the burrows of fiddler crabs; hundreds of holes the diameter of a penny form a colonial outpost, the only such settlement along this stream. The tide is falling, and the fiddlers will soon move out to forage. From nearly every burrow, half-exposed crabs watch their world with small, stalked eyes.

Rarely seen, a large muscular-looking crab, red and black in color, moves among the prop roots along the stream. In this unusual forest, crabs appear to assume something of the roles of squirrel, prairie dog, perhaps even puma.

Less active than crabs, other residents along the channel's edge are nevertheless conspicuous for their numbers. Snails cling quietly to the trees above the tidal zone, as do oysters, with a firmer grip within the range of total immersion. Out in the open spaces among the prop roots and up into the canopy, a variety of spiders weave their snares, some of which reach nearly two meters in diameter.

Ahead, an area of intense light appears, and the canoe noses into a secluded, brackish lake surrounded by mangrove except for another wider passage to the outer bay a hundred meters along the shore to the right. The water is still, less than a meter deep, clarity diminished; mud bottom replaces sand. Around the lake the mangrove wall is a visually impenetrable wreath, unrelievedly green except for a distant cluster of trees where large birds rest in late afternoon torpor. One tree especially is overloaded, drooping with birds like outlandish fruit. Most of them are brown pelicans.

In a wide cove nearby the water is disturbed. A flurry of little fish spatter briefly out of their element, then disappear again like raindrops. There follow sharp, liquid tearing sounds and splashes. Around the canoe several small tarpon have materialized chasing the minnows. Suddenly two fish simultaneously leap clear of the water; then another and another. They are about half a meter long, and they reach a height of at least twice their body length.

Lifetimes could be spent in a place like this. An endless volume of practical and academic knowledge lies compressed in a few vertical meters from the forest canopy to the peaty muck of a mangrove lake. But if one is in a hurry, it is advisable to watch the tide. Even a canoe gets stuck on exposed mud.

Once begun, a trek across a mud flat is not so bad. The mud is like a plush carpet, and seldom does one go in over the knees. Imagination tends to people the mud with noxious or even deadly creatures, but the light and lyrical environment of a coral reef is far more dangerous, with its morays, scorpion-fish, fire coral, and sharks. The only real hazards in the mud are hidden oyster shells and, in the wake of civilization, broken glass. Both have the same effect, and edge for edge the shells may be sharper.

Nevertheless, one gains the sand shallows of the bay entrance with relief. Towing the canoe with a line, a wader revels in the firm footing beneath clear, warm water. The hard grainy hide of the wild continental shelf spreads beyond the curving mouth of the bay to the unseen submarine horizon. Out there, no encroaching hot dog stands, beach umbrellas, portable radios, smell of unguents, lifeguards. In the near view one reflects on artifacts of greater pedigree: the mounded squeezings of a hidden worm, the meandering track of a whelk, the sharp swift V of a ladyfish out toward turtlegrass. Late in the day a prehistoric flight crosses an upwelling sunset. Ibis glide like pterodactyls in over the mangrove and suggest the rich continuous history of this environment.

Still later in darkness, each homeward paddle stroke stirs liquid fire, a concentrated counterpart to the swirls of stars overhead. Galaxies of single-celled plants flare like microscopic pulsars; millions react within the space of one stroke's turbulence. Around them in the dark drift countless billions of others in a continuous web of plankton that stretches from the tangled mangrove roots out over the shelf and beyond. More significant in basic biochemical achievement than the ibis, the fish, the whelks and the worms, these tiny lives, bound up with sunshine and the essence of mangrove, are the foundation for higher expressions of consciousness, all the way to man. Nowhere on the thin membrane of the biosphere stretched tight around the globe can ecological isolationism be sustained. Nowhere is this principle better illustrated than in the Gulf of Mexico, where tropical and temperate zones converge in looping ocean currents, clouds of regionally flavored nutrients, and mingling life-streams that ebb and flow in three-dimensional hydrospace with the great cycles of the earth.

The Tainted Shelf

In spite of the fact that offshore oil was first developed in the Gulf of Mexico, there is an appalling lack of reliable information on marine ecology in and around the oil fields. To be sure, studies have been done, but they have dealt with effects of oil reaching the shore; or they have featured very hardy organisms; or they have left out consideration of delicate larval forms; or they have ignored community effects or sublethal effects. In nearly every case some filmy hedge oozes into the design or interpretation of these experiments. In nearly every case, too, the funding of such research comes directly or indirectly from the oil industry.

Numerous oil spills have occurred in the Gulf since the late 1940s. Many of these have been larger than the spill off West Falmouth, Cape Cod. Some have approached the size of the Santa Barbara, California, blowout. But nothing approaching the investigative efforts which ensued after these two spills has ever come out of the Gulf region.

Petroleum platforms and pipelines began to appear on the shelf off Louisiana in 1948. The development of offshore oil gradually accelerated in the northwestern Gulf until now there are many hundreds of wells producing oil and natural gas. In terms of potential superspills and widespread, even overlapping, chronic contamination, it is the massive scale of modern production that presents the greatest danger to marine ecosystems. In addition, some of the old pipelines are now known to be leaking. Many of these are abandoned. No one even knows where they all are.

The next probable stage in the regional industrialization of the shelf will be the appearance of superports. These are offshore tanker terminals consisting of giant mooring buoys, pumping stations, pipelines, and perhaps submerged storage tanks. Two superports have been planned for the northwestern Gulf. Three others are under consideration for the temperate Atlantic shelf.

In water some forty meters deep off the western Mississippi Delta, the proposed Louisiana Offshore Oil Port (LOOP) will accommodate tankers of 300,000 deadweight tons and larger ones, which will predominate in the 1980s and 90s. Most of these will bring crude from the Persian Gulf to United States' refineries.

LOOP is a cooperative project of nine oil companies. It is expected to consist of five disc-shaped mooring buoys, two pumping platforms, a crew-quarters platform, and five pipelines, each 1.2 meters (four feet) in diameter. Four million barrels of crude per day will pass through the terminal.

Fifty kilometers south-southeast of Freeport, Texas, a consortium of twelve oil companies is building another superport, Seadock, in thirty-four meters of water. Seadock will be nearly identical to LOOP.

Plans call for burying the huge pipelines traversing the shelf from the offshore terminals to tank farms on shore. But there is no guarantee the pipes will stay put. The restless offshore currents, aided by periodic hurricanes, shift the sediments in huge, slow waves which may be two meters high. A pipeline buried to this depth could be uncovered and covered alternately every three or four years. The inner shelf off Louisiana is especially unstable, with hummocky mud domes, usually having a core of upthrusting salt. The overlying mud here comes from the enormous efflux of sediments from the Mississippi Delta to massive bottom slippage, or slumping. This happened Geologists attribute the capsizing of two Shell Oil Company rigs off the Mississippi Delta to massive bottom slippage or slumping. This happened during Hurricane Camille in 1974. The movement of bottom sediment on such a scale could bend a 4-foot-diameter pipeline like a soda straw.

The new superpipes will be the largest ever used on the sea floor. Given present trends, initial quality-control inspections should be very thorough. In May, 1976, the U.S. Department of Interior announced that completion of the Alaska oil pipeline may be held up for months while thousands of potentially faulty welds are checked. Once the LOOP and Seadock pipelines are down and buried, it will be too late for second looks.

The giant tankers, which typically require five kilometers and fifteen to twenty minutes to come to a stop, pose incalculable dangers. Two safety features would greatly improve the chances for avoiding new world-record oil spills in the Gulf of Mexico: providing double (false) bottoms for tankers, and providing them with double screws or other means for better maneuverability. Even at the slowest speed, a supership, loaded with oil "to the skin," has so much momentum that disaster will ensue if it meets a fixed object. For the United States to demand expensive design features in all large tankers, foreign and domestic, which enter our coastal waters poses some difficulties, but the demand may avoid costlier reckonings later.

In the past, no attempts have been made to clean up oil spills on the shelf of the northwestern Gulf. Environmental concern surfaced only if slicks seemed likely to wash ashore. Beneath turbid waters, oil has been building up in sediments and organisms. What is hidden from the eyes and ignored by industrial-contract researchers becomes obvious to the tastebuds. Oil-tainting of various species of fish and shellfish, especially oysters, is well known in coastal Louisiana. Now the areal extent of the tainting problem may be expanding.

Many Americans are familiar with slick television commercials and other advertisements to the effect that oil rigs enhance the abundance of marine life, especially fish. But scientists, as well as fishermen, point out that on the relatively open bottom of the continental shelf, a rig acts like a salt-dome hill. Many marine creatures merely move in from the surrounding area because they like to orient to a solid, three-dimensional structure. A concentrating effect is more likely than a significant increase in the overall abundance of fish. Now the oil rigs attract record numbers of fishermen as well.

Over the years this may not turn out to be the benign example of resource sharing it is painted to be. The long-term hazards and final fate of small concentrations of petroleum compounds in the diet of fish eaters is only subject to intelligent guesswork. A unique fishery for red and silver snapper has grown up around the oil production platforms. Indeed by the late 1960s, the bulk of commercial snapper fishing on the Gulf's northwestern shelf had shifted from the natural snapper banks and salt-dome hills to the new artificial "reefs." Fish nurtured and possibly tainted in the shadow of big oil are marketed as far east as Panama City, Florida, and are distributed to retailers and restaurants all around the Gulf.

The coming of superports, more pipelines, and still more oil wells in the northwestern Gulf of Mexico demands immediate improvements in environmental safeguards, quality-control inspections of equipment, and independent ecological assessments. The Gulf's oil reserves will probably last only a few more decades. The living marine environment and the seafood resources of this region may not survive the age of oil without intensive care.

Crab and oysters in mangrove roots

The Poison Sink

Imagine the Gulf of Mexico, especially its broad continental shelf spreading east and west of the Mississippi Delta, as the canopy of a super-organism. Superficially the organism resembles an exceedingly luxuriant and productive tree. The leaves of the canopy are represented by phytoplankton, the microscopic foliage of the sea. The fauna living in the immense, diffuse canopy depends entirely on it for sustenance. The canopy, in turn, with all its associated life, depends on a major trunk with fluid roots which gather nutrients from the Appalachians to the Rockies.

The Mississippi's importance to the life of the Gulf of Mexico has always been directly related to its incomparable drainage area—a vast storehouse which continuously releases the essential nutrient elements. The delivery system traditionally has served a small ocean with just the right quantities for delicately adjusted metabolic systems and naturally structured marine communities. But the subcontinent that feeds the river has changed drastically. Numerous cities with unprecedented concentrations of industry now excrete their peculiar wastes directly into the flow. Many more additives reach the Mississippi system in slow-seeping ground water and surface runoff from millions of square kilometers of exotically salted farmland.

The river's new burden is silent and sickening. A glut of nutrients which produces corn and wheat in record abundance can choke the organically nurtured pastures of the sea. Much swifter sickness and death enter marine food webs in the form of man-made chemicals, toxins unknown in the history of life on earth until the latest microsecond of geological time. Like the stem of an enormous funnel, the Mississippi collects everything carried by flowing water from the northern Rockies to the Alleghenies. The effects of megatons of residue from the American way of life late in the twentieth century are perhaps immeasurable. In terms of the diversity of civilized effluvia, the Mississippi and its receiving waters must be the most comprehensively polluted in the world.

Currents in the northern Gulf of Mexico tend to be weakly developed. During calm weather in spring, Mississippi River water sometimes forms large coherent pools on the continental shelf. Such pools mix with sea water only slowly as they begin to drift along the coast. Usually they move to the west because the largest proportion of the river's flow reaches the sea through the delta's Southwest Pass. However, at times of high discharge similar pools may form off the delta's easterly passes. The floating pools are reminiscent of Gulf Stream rings. They sometimes remain detectable for several weeks and may travel a hundred kilometers. Marine life encountering a pool immediately detect the sharp change in salinity; those which cannot avoid or tolerate the fresher surroundings will not survive prolonged immersion. This is in the natural scheme of things; it may even provide a certain renewal in the manner of a limited forest fire. Lately, however, the huge floating blobs of river water have become much more dangerous to every creature in their path. Thousands of new residues are entering the sea and the food webs of the continental shelf. After the river water has mixed into the sea, the residues remain, largely at the surface where they first impinge on a special and little known environment, the oceanic microlayer.

Some marine chemists believe that the uppermost layer of the sea, an incredibly thin world between water and air, should be considered an entity apart from the entire remaining oceanic bulk. These considerations are based on the fact that chemical properties and concentrations of many materials at the very surface differ enormously from those in deeper waters over one millimeter down.

A variety of chemicals make up a natural floating film which is usually invisible to the casual human observer. Called surfactants, these chemicals are chiefly organic, and normally they derive from dead marine life. The surfactants are only partly soluble in water and form a film because of peculiarities in their molecular structure. Often one end of a particular molecule will be fully soluble or wettable, while the other end is insoluble. Such compounds tend to spread on water into films which may be only one molecule thick; they exhibit a chemical hydrophobia with, so to speak, the soluble molecular head ends in water and the tails sticking out into the air.

The films are suspected of having many properties governing interactions between earth's oceans and atmosphere. Meteorologists and oceanographers are only beginning to comprehend the rudiments of such interactions that affect, for example, the planetary equilibrium of carbon dioxide (CO_2). Presently, as in the past, the oceans absorb much of the CO_2 emitted into the atmosphere. A relatively constant and balanced amount thus remains in the air despite fluctuations in the rate of production of this gas. At least this has been true until recently.

It is clear to chemists that sea-surface films exert important effects on the absorbance of CO_2 in the oceanic sink. The chemical nature of substances in the film, the thicknesses of films, microtemperatures, turbulence effects, and the presence of organisms all affect the movement of gases across an air-water interface. So far this realm of research is so complex that no realistic understanding or model of transfers between atmosphere and ocean is possible. Furthermore, natural skin conditions on the oceans are rapidly being altered by unnatural additives. An unseen geochemical dermatitis may be only the beginning of severe planetary health problems, such as a steady rise in temperature at the earth's surface (greenhouse effect) from excess atmospheric CO_2. While experts in atmospheric physics such as Wallace Broecker of Columbia University believe that the appearance of a significant greenhouse effect may be a century or more away, other dangers focused on the biological environment at the sea surface are already acute.

Biologists also recognize the uniqueness of the microlayer and refer to its assemblage of minute organisms collectively as the neuston (from Greek, meaning surface-swimming). A startling perception of the special teeming nature of the neuston environment accompanied the discovery that more bacteria live in the top millimeter of the sea than in the 100-meter-thick layer immediately below. Such concentrations of bacteria are normal at the very surface. They are free-living marine bacteria. They accumulate here to feed on, or more correctly, absorb through their single-cell membranes, the wealth of natural oils, carbohydrates, proteins, minerals, vitamins and other nutritious chemicals that enrich the surface film. These benign bacteria are vitally important. Not only do they serve as food for larger creatures, but they also recycle basic nutrients to the single-celled algae. Bacterial breakdown of animal and plant remains and wastes replaces the nitrates and phosphates needed by the "foilage of the sea."

The oceanic microlayer supplies food to small consumers in another more unusual way. Frequently bubbles of air are forced below the sea surface by turbulence. Such a bubble's skin, having passed downward through the neuston zone, instantly becomes a microcosm of the sea-air interface, with a concentrated organic film and attendant bacteria. When the bubble bursts upon regaining the surface, its skin collapses into a shapeless bit of organic matter, a bacteria-coated tidbit that is probably highly nutritious to zooplankton such as copepods. Marine biologists estimate that bubbles of pinhead size on the average account for a continuous coverage over three or four percent of the world's ocean surface. This translates to about 10^{18}, or one-trillion-trillion bursting bubbles per second and potentially millions of tons per year of highly enriched plankton food.

At present the actual contribution of the bubble detritus to marine food webs is still speculative, although it must be less than the all-important photosynthesis of the phytoplankton. But both mechanisms which form the very basis for life in the sea are now being altered. Toxic organic chemicals and heavy metals are rapidly accumulating in phytoplankton, and bubble skins now carry thin coatings of many poisons.

The litany of man-made things found in surface films includes some familiar names: DDT, PCBs, cadmium, mercury; some are less well known: endosulfan, endrin, dieldrin, toxaphene; and many are brand new, more and more of them each year, named in the test tube by their organic chemist creators.

Since the appearance of Rachel Carson's book, *Silent Spring*, more attention has focused on chemical threats to terrestrial and fresh-water environments than to the sea. In the mid-1970s, however, marine food webs show compelling evidence of dangerous contamination at all levels. Measurable decreases in growth rate of marine microalgae, the smallest and most numerous varieties of phytoplankton, have been noted in the presence of organochlorine compounds such as DDT and PCBs. The waterborne levels of pollutants at which the effects begin to show up are miniscule—in the fractional parts per billion (ppb) range. But organochlorines are poorly soluble in water. These hydrophobic compounds are "swept up" very rapidly by particulate matter. They are especially strongly attracted to the fatty substances called lipids in the membranes of living cells. In laboratory experiments, 98% of the DDT or PCB stirred into a jar of seawater was absorbed by plankton in six seconds.

Concentrations capable of sickening the most sensitive kinds of phytoplankton have already appeared in some bays and harbors of the United

States. If these substances continue to build up and reach critical levels on the continental shelf, the collapse of marine food webs could begin on a gigantic scale.

The phenomenon of magnification shown by many long-lived pollutants in the natural environment begins with a very small concentration carried to the sea by a river, or from the atmosphere by precipitation. The compound, typically an organochlorine, is absorbed from water by micro-organisms, usually algae or bacteria. These in turn are consumed by some filter feeder such as a swimming copepod or perhaps a clam on the bottom. The filter feeders are eaten by larger predatory creatures, and there may occur one or two further consumptive steps by still larger predators. At each stage more and more of the pollutant is sequestered in living bodies.

One can think of this as a kind of vacuum cleaning process in which each succeeding feeder pulls in the pollutant from a wider area. An algal cell absorbs the poison from a few drops, perhaps up to a thimbleful of water; a small clam eats millions to billions of algal cells; a duck consumes thousands of small clams. By the time a duck hawk, or perhaps a man, has eaten several dozen ducks, the poison from up to a square kilometer or so of coastal water may have been funneled into one top predator. Of course most of this does not remain in a hawk's tissue, but the multiplication from the original trace of toxin in the water still reaches many thousands to millions of times.

This classic idea of the multiplication of pollutants in food chains was first conceptualized in the early 1960s when there were relatively few hard environmental data. Now many more details concerning toxic chemicals in aquatic ecosystems have come to light.

At the lowest levels in the food web, magnification factors have been found which seem astounding. In a 1975 study of aquatic bioconcentration of common insecticides by bacteria, one species magnified beta-chlordane from water by a factor of 55,900 times.

Such bacteria in the oceanic microlayer could transfer exotic poisons into food webs of the continental shelf much more rapidly than previously expected. The larvae of marine creatures, many of which include bacteria in their diet, are usually far more sensitive to toxicants than the same species as adults. The difference between larval and adult susceptibility reaches three orders of magnitude (or ten raised to the third power, which equals 1,000 times).

Food-chain magnification is not the only way in which marine animals accumulate toxic materials. Direct absorption of chemicals from sea water through skin and especially the gills is common in crustaceans and fish. Intake of poison in this manner sometimes even exceeds that from food.

Crustaceans, notably shrimp and crabs, which are related to insects, are among the hardest hit by insecticides and related compounds in the sea. Recently extremely disturbing information has appeared on crustacean poisoning, particularly in coastal waters of the Gulf of Mexico.

In 1969, high levels of Arochlor 1254, one of the common PCB compounds, were detected in Escambia Bay near Pensacola in the west Florida panhandle. Although similar to DDT in chemical nature, PCBs are not used as insecticides but as industrial refrigerants and in many manufacturing processes. The main source of contamination was a Monsanto synthetic fibers plant on the Escambia River where the concentration of PCBs reached highs in the hundreds of parts per billion. Although oysters and small fish were found to harbor the highest PCB concentrations in Escambia Bay, white and brown shrimp were also strongly contaminated.

In 1969, whether by coincidence or not, Escambia Bay s shrimp fishery crashed. In 1968 the catch had totaled more than one million pounds. A year later it was down to 234,000 pounds; then it declined again in 1970 to 52,000 pounds. Monsanto has since reduced the leakage of PCBs to the Escambia River, and the fishery has improved again. But residues of Arochlor.continue to occur in shrimp caught in the area.

Scientists of the Environmental Protection Agency's pesticides laboratory at Gulf Breeze, Florida, who discovered the PCB problem in Escambia Bay have extended their studies into the subtle effects (sublethal effects) of very low concentration of PCBs. One of these experiments involved the ability of contaminated shrimp to tolerate changes in the salinity of their water. When shrimp that had been kept in water of nearly full ocean salinity were placed in brackish water with one-fifth the salt content of the sea, those with traces of PCB in their bodies began to die. The researchers found the poisoned shrimp could not control the salt concentration of their blood. In contrast to uncontaminated shrimp, which remained normally healthy at the low salinity, the PCB victims' blood became watery and lost its essential balance of sodium, calcium, magnesium, and potassium. This experiment simulated a specific natural stress in a shrimp's life, namely the rapid dilution of estuarine water after heavy rains. The results indicated that even traces of PCBs diminished the shrimp's fitness for survival.

Another Gulf Breeze study of PCBs showed a selective toxicity of the pollutant to marine life. Concentrations of Arochlor 1254 from one to ten ppb in experimental aquaria containing a variety of organisms from Gulf coastal waters markedly decreased diversity over a four-month period. Numbers of species and individuals of crustaceans, mollusks, and bryozoans (colonial moss animals) were drastically reduced. However, no apparent effect was seen on the abundance of annelid worms and nemerteans (ribbon worms), coelenterates (sea anemones), echinoderms (sea urchins), tunicates (sea squirts), and brachiopods (lamp shells). In terms of abundance, the control aquaria (those not receiving PCBs) were dominated by crustaceans; a decrease in crustacean numbers appeared in tanks containing 1 ppb Arochlor, while in the communities receiving 10 ppb, sea squirts became the dominant organisms.

One and ten parts per billion PCB would be fairly high concentrations to find free in the marine environment, but localized coastal waters such as Escambia Bay, which lie downstream from potentially harmful industries, should be watched closely. In addition, PCBs are volatile and are rapidly distributed to remote areas via atmospheric circulation. Concentrations are slowly building up throughout the world's oceans. It is clear that this cannot be allowed to go on much longer.

The experiments on the alteration of natural communities, together with the study revealing PCBs' role in the disturbance of the shrimp's ability to regulate its blood chemistry in brackish water, point to a future of diminished prospects for many marine species, especially the crustaceans and mollusks that are so valuable as seafood. In the end, coastal communities dominated by worms, coelenterates, and leathery sea squirts seem an unappetizing, and probably naturally untenable, prospect.

Perhaps because they are hardier, less peripatetic animals than shrimp, and thus easier to keep under confinement in the laboratory, crabs have been more widely studied for their reactions to organochlorines, especially pesticides. However, the general effects are probably similar in most crustaceans, including shrimp.

In 1975, researchers described the effects of low internal levels of two insecticides on blue crabs (*Callinectes sapidus*), the most important commercial species of crab in the Gulf, as well as in temperate Atlantic coastal waters. The toxicants in question were DDT and Mirex, the latter a substance in wide use for the control of fire ants throughout the south. Again the scientists were interested in doses which do not kill outright but rather produce lingering, disabling side effects.

Trace amounts of both DDT and Mirex caused pronounced elevation of the crab's metabolic rate, a sort of invertebrate hypertension whose consequences are unclear. Further investigation revealed that Mirex was also extremely potent in disrupting the autotomy reflex, a crustacean defensive maneuver in which a leg or claw seized by a predator is simply dropped off by its owner, the intended prey, which then often escapes. The preprogrammed point of separation in autotomy is nearly bloodless, and the wounded animal has the fortuitous faculty for rapid regeneration of its lost limb. But this life-saving ability was inhibited in young crabs after they had accumulated only 20 ppb Mirex. Another finding was that Mirex caused a thinning of the carapace, the uppermost, exposed portion of the crab's shell. In the opinion of the scientists, both impairment of the autotomy reflex and thinning of the protective carapace could greatly increase the crab's susceptibility to predation.

Another 1975 paper by a different biologist described the behavior of blue crabs exposed to acute levels of waterborne pesticides. His vividly rendered observations of the doomed animals, "Acute exposure elicits wild swimming, hyper-irritability . . ., followed by loss of equilibrium, convulsions and death in 24 to 96 hours . . ." conjure macabre scenes which are becoming more predictable and imminent every year. The crustacean dances of death may be beginning in localized areas. Eventually they may involve millions of larvae and perhaps adults within whole drainage regions.

The possibility of unknown mass kills has recently been suggested by environmental scientists. The current theory holds that a crustacean ecocatastrophe might remain undetected if it involved primarily larvae and juveniles. They are small and inconspicuous, and their bodies would be rapidly consumed by scavengers. In the case of larger, more motile juveniles and adults, a localized pollution event might produce a kill out of proportion to the area of high toxicant concentration. Many crustaceans, especially crabs, are wide-ranging scavengers themselves. They would move in from surrounding areas to feed on their stricken relatives and a kind of slow deadly biological implosion, a regional population collapse focused on a small central zone of lethality, could occur.

Sharp declines in blue crab abundance have already occurred from New York waters to the Gulf of Mexico. Beginning in the late 1960s, the crab fishery through much of the southeastern United States suffered a sharp drop in production. Louisiana alone saw its crab landings halved between 1971 and 1972 (from 10.9 million pounds to 5.0 million). Scientists suspect pesticides, probably arriving in surges of agricultural drainage water, as a leading cause of the declining crab fishery.

Another class of invertebrates, the bivalve mollusks, have received considerable recent attention from researchers attempting to understand the effects of exotic chemical pollution in the sea. Studies of oysters, clams, and mussels are often focused somewhat differently from the research on crustaceans, for the bivalves are generally much more resistant to substances such as organochlorines and heavy metals. Also the bivalve's way of feeding, which is to filter minute particles of plankton and organic matter from the water, is at issue. The studies on bivalves have emphasized the concentrating power of these animals. Some examples:

Oysters concentrated DDT from 1 ppb in sea water to 7 ppm in their edible tissues, a multiplication factor of 7,000.

Oysters accumulated the toxic metals, cadmium and mercury, from experimentally polluted sea water respectively up to 750 and 916 times over the environmental level in a six- to ten-week period.

In a study of food-chain magnification of dieldrin, small brackish water clams, *Rangia cuneata*, were fed contaminated phytoplankton. The resulting concentration of dieldrin, a powerful carcinogen, in the clams exceeded 65,000 times that in the water.

A footnote to this last example is that *Rangia* clams are a major food of blue crabs in Louisiana estuaries.

In many studies of this sort, damage to the bivalves has not been obvious. However, sublethal reactions are beginning to be identified in certain bivalve species. Normally the common mussel attaches to rocks and other objects by means of a beard-like cluster of tough threads called a byssus. Now less than ½ ppm endosulfan, a pesticide, has been found to inhibit the formation of the mussel's byssus. Scallops, whose young also rely on a tiny byssus to fasten themselves to submarine vegetation, are even more sensitive to endosulfan than mussels. Further specific threats to bivalves will probably turn up. However, the overall significance of the bivalves immersed in a wide spectrum of marine pollution must concern their role in transferring toxic substances to the next level of consumer, which begins to include man.

In addition to pesticides, heavy metals are concentrated by mollusks as well as crustaceans. Environmental and public health problems associated with mercury are now well known. Less is known about other serious metallic pollutants, for example cadmium, which emanates from scrap metal dumps, lead mines, and industrial sources such as electroplating factories.

Very little is known about cadmium in food webs of the northern Gulf. A tendency of mangrove trees to magnify concentrations of cadmium and other metals has been discovered in south Florida. Mangrove leaves become enriched in cadmium which further increases in concentration, up to 200-fold, in estuarine detritus after the leaves decompose. Since organic sediment provides basic nutrition for the mangrove ecosystem, the bioconcentration of heavy metals gets a head start here. Extreme precautions regarding dumping, certain industrial developments, and other sources of metal contamination are warranted within mangrove watersheds.

The next trophic level above macro-invertebrates, typified by shrimp, crabs and clams, is inhabited largely by fish. Fish are probably the marine creatures of most widespread and direct concern to man. It is not surprising, therefore, that a huge and growing scientific effort is underway to assess the impact of human activities on marine fish. Recent findings from research in United States coastal waters are very disturbing. The results of fish kills around power plants and the depredations of technological fishing are fairly clear-cut, and ameliorating actions, or more often trade-offs, can be imagined if not always implemented. A cure for chemical intoxication of our most valuable marine resource is infinitely more difficult. The preponderant symptoms are subtle, sublethal, and already, like a malignancy in insensible tissue, devastatingly widespread.

Studies published in 1975 showed that concentrations of ten ppb of four insecticides—DDT, parathion, malathion, and Sevin—all retarded the healing process in injured fish. The underlying connections between wound healing and the chemicals were not explored, but the bald cause and effect reveals a sublethal pollution phenomenon never before suspected.

Sevin, also known as carbaryl, has been touted as a safe insecticide and came into wide use after the initial DDT ban in the United States. Unlike the organochlorines, which persist in the environment for many years, Sevin begins to break down after a few days in sea water. Unfortunately derivatives from the breakdown process are more toxic than Sevin itself, and they last much longer.

The same biologists who carried out the wound-healing study discovered that Sevin and its derived compounds disrupted schooling behavior in the silverside, an estuarine fish. When one-tenth ppm of these nerve poisons was present in the water, the fish did not maintain their normal close-ranked formation, but spread out, occupying twice the area of a normal school of the same size.

Sevin and its derivatives appeared to have a residual effect as well. After the experimental fish were placed in clean water, schooling did not return to normal for three days. Like Sevin, many other pesticides are nerve poisons, and they all should be tested for effects on adaptive behavior of marine life. Schooling fish in particular depend for survival on flawless perception and precise neuromuscular control which mediates their response as a single entity to a predatory threat. Deviants from the automatic group behavior are, to use the CIA codephrase, terminated with prejudice. Under normal conditions this behavior helps preserve the species' unified social adaptation for survival, but if a school itself falters in its ceaseless, time-honored pattern of defensive drills, it may be eliminated to the last fish.

Results of other studies reveal differential sensitivities in fish and bizarre symptoms:

As long ago as 1968, spotted sea trout, *Cynoscion nebulosus*, in Texas waters were found to contain enough DDT residue to cause concern over a potential impairment of reproduction.

Young striped bass appear especially sensitive to certain pesticides. DDT, endrin, endosulfan, and Dursban all were acutely toxic to these fish at levels below one ppb.

An eight-ppb concentration of toxaphene, an insecticide used by cotton growers across the south, was found to be lethal to mosquitofish, *Gambusia affinis*. Although ranking low in public recognition, toxaphene has been used in the United States in larger quantities than any other insecticide over the last eleven years. Present consumption is estimated at nearly 60 million pounds per year. Like PCBs, toxaphene is volatile, only more so. The latest studies of airborne toxaphene over the western North Atlantic show it to be twice as concentrated as PCBs and more than ten times as abundant as other pesticides so far detected in the atmosphere over the ocean. Toxaphene is extremely persistent, and, despite its intensity of use, its chemical composition remains largely undetermined because it is not one substance but a complex mixture of many polychlorinated organic compounds, making prediction of its environmental effects practically impossible.

Recently, however, sublethal levels of toxaphene in water have been linked to bone degeneration in fish, especially a severe weakening of the spinal column. The end result appears to be that fish break their own backs merely through their normal exertions. Although this strange malady has not yet been seen in marine fish, it should be looked for in the Mississippi Delta region. An epidemic of toxaphene-induced bone disease has appeared in fresh-water catfish in the Mississippi Valley.

With enhanced predator status comes ever-increasing exposure to many chemical toxicants. It seems probable that localized areas within northern coastal waters of the Gulf of Mexico now contain threshold levels of pollutants damaging to many fish and crustacean populations. Indirect evidence supporting this prediction comes from the recent fate of conspicuous members of the next higher trophic level.

Once boastful of an unparalleled wildlife spectacle, the official seal of the State of Louisiana is now commemorative. The seal features a brown pelican (*Pelecanus occidentalis*) which, according to a study published in 1922 by the U.S. National Museum (Smithsonian Institution), flourished in "immense" breeding colonies in the Mississippi Delta region. In 1922, Louisiana pelican rookeries were already established in federal sanctuaries, safe from human egg gatherers and duck hunters. This protection continued and even intensified through the decades, but it was of no avail when DDT, followed by a steadily growing array of analogs, began to flow into the pelican's feeding grounds. Gradually accelerating mortalities culminated in a massive die-off in the late 1950s. Suddenly the Louisiana state bird was gone.

Beginning in 1968 an ambitious ornithological experiment was undertaken by the Louisiana Wildlife and Fisheries Commission. Several hundred brown pelicans were imported from Florida, and for a while it appeared that a thriving colony had developed in Barataria Bay, just west of the Mississippi Delta. Successful nestings occurred several years in a row. But in June of 1975 disaster again struck the Louisiana pelicans. Reports of dead birds came from all over Barataria Bay. State wildlife officials were taken by complete surprise. Of the estimated population of 465 introduced pelicans, more than 300 had died.

At Louisiana State University six of the dead birds were analyzed for pesticides. The chemists found endrin, dieldrin, toxaphene, DDE (a toxic derivative of DDT), BHC (benzene hexachloride), and heptachlor, as well as PCBs. The concentrations of endrin alone were believed to be lethal to the birds. All but one had more than 300 ppb (considered a lethal dose by U.S. Department of the Interior standards). Even if the birds could have survived a relatively high dose of a single toxicant, the additive effects of the others would have sealed their fate.

Endrin had been applied heavily on Louisiana, Mississippi, and Arkansas cotton crops since 1973. The organochlorines in the Barataria Bay pelicans are believed to come primarily from Mississippi River water, silently, invisibly drifting to the west in huge deadly pools. According to an article in *Audubon* magazine, Louisiana wildlife officials have started restocking the Barataria Bay rookery. Suggestions by environmentalists that the birds should be moved east of the delta where they might have a better chance for survival have gone unheeded. Louisiana seems destined to go on borrowing pelicans and making them into modern counterparts to the caged canaries which were once taken into mines to warn of poison gases. *Audubon* quotes a Louisiana Wildlife and Fisheries Commission spokesman who seems to agree with environmentalists that it is only a matter of time until the next organochlorine overdose is mainlined into the state's coastal waters.

In this region the pelican's fate has been shared by ospreys as well as the once-prospering coastal populations of bald eagles. Both are primarily fish eaters, and the food selection process is subtly stacked against the birds of prey. Fish most often caught are probably slightly slower than normal, their reflexes and escape reactions dulled by body burdens of pollutants that are greater than average.

Many scattered reports of other seabirds suffering from organochlorine poisoning have been received from elsewhere in North America as well as in Europe. Outbreaks of strange birth defects have appeared in terns. Other birds have been found acting strangely—dizzy or dopey or unusually tame. These usually died soon after they were discovered and upon examination proved to have very high levels of PCBs or pesticides. Dead birds found washed ashore typically have high organochlorine levels and were also often in very lean condition, having little bodily fat reserve.

DDT, dieldrin, endrin, PCBs and other organochlorine compounds are known to accumulate in fat. Fatty tissue exerts a kind of chemical attraction for these substances which are held in solutions of natural oils. Thus large bodily accumulations of the pollutants can be stored in relatively harmless fashion. This storage becomes a biochemical time bomb if the animal experiences a sustained deprivation of food or a greater-than-usual need for energy. When an animal is under stress, stored fat will be used rapidly, and the poisons released from their chemical stasis. They then reach high levels in the blood stream, circulate through the body and interfere with crucial enzymes. Some of them accumulate around nerve centers and kill suddenly.

Like the pelican and osprey, man is a major consumer of seafood and is likely to become more dependent on this resource. Unlike these birds, humans generally have not yet built up acute levels of pollutants derived from the food chain, although some horrible effects have become evident in Japan. However, the present symptoms shown by wildlife in the Gulf of Mexico and elsewhere represent only the tip of the chemical iceberg. The ongoing contamination of shelf waters and biota with pollutants old and new is decades ahead of a proper scientific assessment of the hazards it poses to health. Not only are effects on man of most chemical pollutants unknown, but it is believed by many scientists that substances which singly are of little concern can act in combinations to produce additive and multiplied (synergistic) intoxication with lethal results. Simple mathematics will further show that from the thousands (perhaps hundreds of thousands if petroleum compounds are included) of physiologically active chemicals building up in heretofore unimagined concentrations in the Gulf, potential synergistic effects approach infinity. The astronomical possibilities perhaps should lead theoreticians to perform calculations similar to those assessing the chance for life among the star systems in our galaxy, except that in this case the numbers will indicate the probability for life continuing as we know it on this planet.

Too much supporting evidence has appeared for these speculations to be dismissed as science fiction. Of course the first synergistic pollution event with serious implications for man is unlikely to be acute. Cousteau-style catastrophism or the mutant marine "Andromeda Strain" once envisioned by Paul Ehrlich should probably be assigned a low probability. Sublethal and delayed-action effects are more likely, perhaps a teratogenic or mutagenic epidemic, Thalidomide-like in its element of surprise. Even greater is the likelihood of a gradual increase in the frequency of environmentally induced cancer. In the United States, regional victimization by forms of neoplastic disease related to marine pollution, particularly mediated through the eating of contaminated seafood, may occur first among populations around the northern Gulf of Mexico.

The combination of factors which supports this speculation includes:

This region traditionally produces and consumes a great amount of seafood, most of which comes from the inner shelf, precisely the area of greatest

Daytime behavior, brown shrimp in sand

marine pollution. For example estuarine dependent species account for more than ninety-five percent of Louisiana's catch, and one of the prime nurseries for shrimp, crabs, and oysters on the whole Gulf Coast is Barataria Bay.

Petroleum production, attended by chronic spillage of known potent and persistent carcinogens, has gone on longer and more extensively in the northern Gulf than anywhere else on the North American shelf.

The abundance and variety of industrial and agricultural chemicals entering coastal waters in this region is far greater than elsewhere.

Precedents of a sort are already extant. In 1973, two outbreaks of hepatitis on the Gulf Coast were traced to oysters from supposedly safe areas near the Mississippi Delta. The contaminated oysters were distributed to restaurants all the way to Texas. Dozens of people became seriously ill.

Chemical pollutants are probably distributed in much the same manner as the hepatitis virus. Seafood items such as oysters, crabs, shrimp, and inshore finfish are exposed to and accumulate the highest relative amounts of chemical residues. Distributions of toxicants in Gulf waters are not uniform, however, and perhaps edible species contaminated only at the present upper extremes of concentration are dangerous with respect to human consumption. But the extremes, as in the case of endrin, are reaching major fishing areas, and it is fortunate that people have never developed a taste for fish-eating birds.

Finally, when considering the dilute chemical soup pouring out of the Mississippi and lesser rivers, it is important to remember that the fish, oysters, clams, and crustaceans concentrate the dangerous residues to levels far above those which triggered the scare over drinking water in New Orleans and other cities. It may well be that a statistical increase in human cancer deaths related to heavy consumption of contaminated seafood is already in the incubation stage, which often lasts twenty years. As in Japan, environmentally induced disease should first hit poorer people who live near the most seriously polluted bays and depend on local fish as their primary source of protein. Like pelicans, they may consistently eat fish containing poisons magnified from the water by hundreds of thousands to millions of times.

A few programs of areal pollution monitoring have begun in the Gulf of Mexico, but the region is vast and the coverage spotty. Studies on synergistic effects have started recently, but the number of chemical combinations is hopelessly large. Perhaps more could be done in the public health arena: spot inspections on the docks or in the fish markets; close attention to species taken in suspect areas, such as around oil rigs; labeling of all fish and shellfish catches as to point of origin. In light of the overwhelming complexity of the problem, however, the best way to reduce the risks to human and environmental health is to cut off the pollution at its sources.

It is disconcerting to hear scientists like George Woodwell, one of the researchers who developed the biological magnification concept, state that DDT is still accumulating in the ocean because worldwide use is now as high or higher than during the peak U.S. production in the early 1960s. With fanfare the Environmental Protection Agency on paper banned the use of dieldrin and aldrin in 1972, and in 1975 began protracted plans to ban chlordane and heptachlor and perhaps Mirex and endrin. However, much of our pesticide problem began years ago. The U.S. National Academy of Sciences recently estimated that only a quarter of the organochlorines already present on land, in ground water, and in the air has so far reached the sea, and their half-lives are measured in decades. Thus even if the use of these compounds, at least some of which are carcinogenic, were to cease today, we would still have to sweat out perhaps a half century of geographically scattered risk. Perhaps through intelligent action we will avoid problems like those that have appeared in Japan, but should we continue our environmental habituation to dangerous chemicals, it may soon lead to condemnation of catches and eventually to long-term fisheries' quarantines over large areas, particularly in the northern Gulf.

From the standpoint of marine environmental health, a major limiting factor on industrial growth should be the careful testing of all chemical wastes. The substances which may do us in could be brand new ones, untested and unsuspected, already out there spreading malignantly through the creatures of the continental shelf. While careless tolerance of chemical runoff to the sea continues, time is surely not on our side.

In the Gulf of Mexico, time has always moved slowly, paced by long lovely sunsets and low rhythmic swells on a wide glassy sea. For eons time has been measured here by the slow bedding of sediments concealing gritty pools of oil, by the fertilizing floods, the return of tiny crustaceans to brackish bays and bayous, and by huge flights of birds. Now localized pools of pollution ring the northern Gulf like nascent rotten spots on the skin of a luscious fruit. The Gulf's natural flow of time seems to have suddenly reversed in an outflow of oil and a reduction of biological diversity toward a bleak and hostile era.

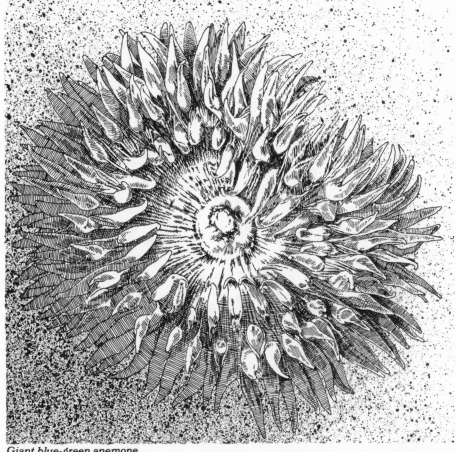

Giant blue-green anemone

Cycles of Stone

Along the Pacific coast of North America there is an illusion of permanence. To one familiar with the generally flat, sandy Atlantic and Gulf coasts, an alien hugeness pervades the scenery of Torrey Pines, Big Sur, Point Reyes, and points north. Rolling, rounded hills sweep inland in great waves from broad beaches. Massive cliffs squat beside the great-grandmother of oceans. Only the boulder taluses that have rolled down from the heights and occasional rock spires rearing above nearshore swells interrupt the expansive peace and timelessness one feels while exploring these green and golden shores.

Such scenes typify much of the California coastline. Northward toward Oregon, the maritime terrain becomes steadily steeper and more venerable. The coastal country begins to feature truly impressive mountain ranges, snow-capped much of the year, as on Washington's Olympic Peninsula. Beginning at Puget Sound and proceeding north, one encounters great flooded mountain valleys forming deep marine bays and inland passages with the characteristics of fjords. Elsewhere wooded slopes and mountain streams plunge to the open seashore, and there are places where one can pitch a tent fifty yards above the tide mark and hear a chorus of spring frogs against a background of booming surf.

Below the surface of the rolling Pacific, the topography is nearly as varied and dramatic as that on land. Occupying the position of an inner continental shelf, hills and valleys, cliffs, ledges, and interspersed areas of rock and sand form a markedly different kind of shallow sea floor from the huge, nearly flat mantle of sand which stretches nearly unbroken from New England to Texas. Along the Pacific border, numerous submarine canyons are incised into the nearshore continental margin. The canyons off southern California are better known than elsewhere. Their names reflect shore points near their heads: Hueneme Canyon, Mugu, Redondo, Newport. Sometimes, as in the case of La Jolla Canyon, they begin a few hundred meters off the beach and plunge rapidly down to slope depths.

Detailed studies of several canyons off southern California have shown that they are conduits to deep, bowl-like basins lying farther offshore. Turbidity flows carrying sand and gravel, nearshore organisms such as snails, organic remnants of kelp, as well as beer cans and many other materials cascade down the canyons and onto the basin floors.

The deep basins are also named for nearby locales (Santa Barbara, Santa Monica, Santa Catalina, San Pedro), and they have been slowly filling with sediment for eons. Typically their bottoms lie between 500 and 1,500 meters deep. Because the basins are recessed and cratered, ocean currents largely pass over them, and their bottom waters become stagnant. The oxygen concentration may remain near zero for years (even decades in the deepest parts of the Santa Barbara Basin). This effectively eliminates life along the bottom. It is known that occasional unwary schools of fish enter the oxygenless waters and perish *en masse*, as do unlucky creatures swept into basins with turbidity flows from above. At the same time, the natural anoxia fosters the accumulation of a scientifically valuable record.

Most of the sediment in the basins does not come from turbidity flows but rather falls as a constant light rain from overlying waters. Even in southern California there is enough seasonality—winter storms contrasted with summer calms—to change the character of the yearly fallout over the Santa Barbara and other basins.

Winter sediment is characterized by coarser material; by summer most of this has settled out, leaving very fine particles, high in organic matter, still settling slowly. Thus in the depths of an anaerobic basin, where no burrowers such as worms or clams disturb the bottom, the yearly sedimentary cycle becomes evident in the alternation from coarse to fine texture, which shows up as a thin band. Repetitive series of bands, each representing a year, have been studied by scientists, and the muddy archives now go back over a century. Within the sediments, to the very year in some cases, can be found the advent of DDT and PCBs in the marine environment and the beginning of significant human contamination of the sea with trace metals.

Also prominent along with canyons and basins on the steeply sloping western continental margin are submerged seamounts. These are usually solitary and volcano-shaped, but they are different from the way most people picture them. Where they exceed 500 meters in height, seamounts almost never have slopes exceeding 20° to 30°. Matterhorn-like peaks in the sea, where the erosive power of glaciers has never reached, cannot exist except in imaginative artwork.

The exceedingly variable and rugose nature of the terrain off the Pacific Border, together with the proximity of deep ocean to the land, have led some scientists to omit the term "continental shelf" and refer to the regional submarine environment as a continental borderland. The huge underwater features here—canyons, basins, seamounts—seem to match the traditional western psyche. The precisely defined, long-established zonation of the Atlantic continental margin—shelf, slope, rise—do seem somehow out of place, for in its most fundamental aspects the Pacific Border is still a brawling, unsettled frontier.

Furthermore, any imputation of hoary age and rock-clad rigidity to this region would be dead wrong. The somnolence of the big golden coast is subject to great fitfulness. Periodically on the human scale and frenetically on the geological, earthquakes provide reminders that for a long time this edge of the continent has been in complex and continuous upheaval. Along the Pacific Border upwellings of rock have produced the newest geological crust in North America. Beneath concealing and confusing veneers of sedimentary strata and sea water, two of earth's greatest crustal plates are in relative motion, one in contact with the other. The movements of these plates are responsible for the waves of hills, cliffs, taluses, mountains, fjords, basins, volcanoes, and earthquakes.

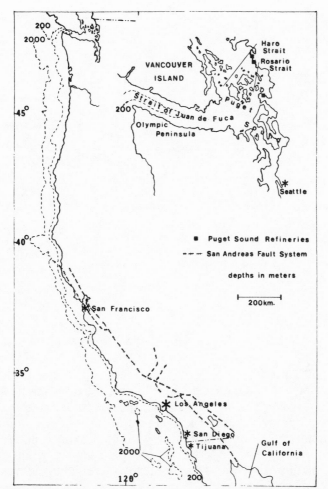

United States Western Continental Borderland: Puget Sound to Baja California.

What follows is not intended as a definitive discussion of plate tectonic theory. Elementary geology texts and popular sources such as Nigel Calder's *The Restless Earth* treat the subject in depth. What is of concern here is a survey of the influence of plate tectonics on the dynamic, magnificently jumbled Pacific Border—past, present, and future.

Like irregular reptilian scutes, the crustal plates form the solid hide of planet Earth. Large plates extend beneath ocean basins and underlie entire continents. Very small ones, mere fragments, also have been identified. What is wonderful and essential about the plates is that they are in motion.

Picture one as operating like an escalator, a very irregularly shaped and slow-moving one, which runs neither up nor down but rather horizontally from one place to another. The force driving the escalator-plate appears to be heat from the deep interior of the earth. Heat seeking a way out to cooler realms is manifest as molten rock, roiling up under the thin planetary shell.

Even solid stone, when heated and pushed against, will flow after a fashion. This plastic movement is called "creep" by the engineers. Not surprisingly, it is terribly slow, but with the constant application of heat and

143

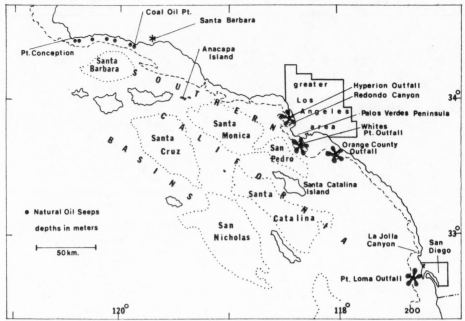

The Ocean off Southern California: positions of major basins, wastewater outfalls and natural oil seeps.

pressure it is inexorable.

The place where plates begin to creep is a rift or crack in the earth's surface. The greatest rifts meander across the sea floor and form an earth-girdling network forty thousand kilometers long. As lava wells up from below, new material adds on to the plates, lying back to back along a rift zone. Nearly continuously, this forces the adjacent plates apart, while at the same time, parallel chains of mountains arise in slow, wrenching heaves on either side of the rift.

Scientists have now listened to the moving plates. An instrument called a seismometer, which picks up very low-frequency vibrations, was lowered to the ocean floor near the Mid-Atlantic Ridge. Several recordings were made of crunching and crushing sounds. Very long and drawn out, these were below the level of hearing and beyond human experience, but when the sounds were speeded up thirty times, listeners reported that they were reminiscent of "the reverberations in a busy bowling alley." The speeded-up sounds lasted ten to fifteen minutes, followed by hour-long intervals of deep silence.

When a plate runs under an ocean, it will carry sediment, seamounts, islands, everything along with it. This process has been termed sea-floor spreading. A rift under land may remain hidden for millions of years beneath sediments, rivers, or large lake beds that form in the gradually widening valley. In time, however, the crack will allow entry to the sea, and a new phase of continental drift will have begun.

Since the plates are in close contact all over the earth, something, somewhere, has to give, and the places that give often lie close to the edges of continents. Where an oceanic plate moves directly toward a plate bearing a large land mass, the former is forced deep into the earth. At such places crustal material is consumed—heated, crushed, and metamorphosed by an unimaginable friction. This process, called subduction, is one of the major earth shapers. It has been especially important in contributing the present craggy features of the Pacific Border.

During a long period of time beginning in the Jurassic period, the major modern features of North America's west coast have settled hesitantly and, it seems, tentatively into place. Some aspects of this geological evolution at the ocean-continent interface make it appear as if a grandiose game is being played with the crustal plates through the eons by whimsical gods, one holding the continental plate, and one the oceanic. Even basic rules of play governing movement of the crustal counters have changed sharply. Or perhaps each player in turn makes his move at a very leisurely pace.

Between 85 and 150 million years ago, uplift of the Sierra Nevada occurred beside a Pacific whose sea floor spread from an ancient active ocean rift straight toward proto-California. Subduction of the ocean floor beneath the continent's western edge played a large role in this mountain building. The Sierra were once far higher than now. Numerous active volcanoes belched and blackened the sky along the chain.

One theory of Pacific Border evolution holds that the sea floor and oceanic crust which plunged slowly, irresistibly, and abrasively beneath the continental plate reached incandescent temperatures just a few kilometers down. Masses of melted stone, or magmas, squeezed upward through fissures or weak zones in the overlying continental rock. These magmas were the Sierra volcano makers, and showers of ash and rivers of lava must have frequently reached the coast of a narrower California whose ocean beaches lay at the foot of the Sierra.

Some other geologists are beginning to believe that the Pacific continental rim grew toward the west by accretion, or the progressive incorporation of chains of islands, called island arcs, whose origins may have been hundreds or perhaps thousands of kilometers distant. Island arcs are created by volcanic activity where two oceanic plates converge. The process is the same as that which stimulates volcanism along the edge of a continent. Because the plates move, island arcs may be swept into and incorporated in continental masses. It is possible that the foundation of the Sierra themselves was originally brought to North America in island-arc form.

Such ancient island-arc additions have been heavily eroded and otherwise hidden from casual recognition by sedimentary cover and later crustal upheavals, but subtle clues remain. One of these is the presence of sulfide ores of precious metals: copper, gold, silver, zinc, and lead. Large pure deposits of high-grade ore are characteristic of modern island arcs. Recognition of linear continental belts of such deposits, particularly in the western United States, has led plate tectonic theorists into a partnership with economic geologists.

At some point, which appears to have been several tens of millions of years ago, the direction of sea floor spreading began to shift in the northeastern Pacific. How long it took for the great eastwarding treadmill to come to a halt is not known. When the Pacific Plate ceased to underthrust proto-California, deep gashes, or grabens, were left where the ocean trench had stood beneath what are now San Diego, Los Angeles, and Santa Barbara.

These gradually filled with sediment and organic matter and became petroleum-forming basins.

The Pacific Plate then began to move toward the north. This directional change may have coincided with a corresponding shift in the spreading center, or perhaps merely greatly increased activity along the rift known as the East Pacific Rise brought on the new movement. Subduction was now centered along a great gash in the North Pacific sea floor which would be named the Aleutian Trench.

Instead of meeting head-on, the Pacific and North American Plates now sideswiped and scraped each other, edge to edge for thousands of kilometers. Instead of creeping evenly and relatively smoothly over the earth's gently curving surface, the two giant plates began to exhibit behavior aptly termed "strike-slip faulting." Frequently, they would lock edges here and there. Then decades, or at most a century or two, would go by, but with no halting of the unalterable forces which have rolled the crustal plates over their deep stony horizons for hundreds of millions of years. Eventually the strain would become too great. The locked zone, perhaps extending several kilometers down into rock, would give way in a massive earthquake, and the plates would slide two or three meters past one another, making up in one rumbling jump for all the years of standing still. Weeks or months of aftershocks might follow as enormous blocks and dikes adjusted to new positions deep in the earth.

Caught in the crush along the Pacific Border, like tiny bergs between two huge ice floes, are small crustal plates. Named for their localities (e.g., Farallon Plate, Juan de Fuca Plate), these miniplates may be broken fragments of their larger counterparts, and may be shortlived. The Juan de Fuca Plate now appears to be underthrusting Vancouver Island and will probably be consumed within a few million years. Its passing will be literally earthshaking, and may be marked by a new volcano or two.

To make things more complicated in this geological jigsaw puzzle, the active rifting zone of the East Pacific Rise has invaded western North America. Some four million years ago, this rift, which curves in from the equatorial ocean floor, snaked northward beneath the present site of the Gulf of California. The gulf is now spreading very rapidly, an estimated six centimeters per year. At the same time, because of the northward movement of the Pacific Plate, Baja California, which lies on that plate, appears to be getting shorter from south to north. Eventually Baja will be carried north of the U.S. border. Tijuana will have reached the latitude of San Francisco, while some portions of that fair city will have ridden far to the north in a long series of short jumps with each major earthquake.

Recently, geologists have come to suspect that an active rift zone is elongating beneath the state of California. Rifting continuous with that in the Gulf of California appears to have extended into the Imperial Valley. Heat flow in rock strata below the floor of the Valley has been measured by drilling through the sediments. High measurements of heat flow, together with other tests made on the young volcanic rhyolite domes near the Salton Sea, fit the theories of a rift zone propagating toward the north. In a few million years the Gulf of California may lap what is now Indio or perhaps Palm Springs.

The present prevailing pattern of continental drift, however, is most clearly seen in the shearing of maritime California along the great San Andreas Fault. Generally everything west of this fault lies on the Pacific Plate; land to the east rests on the North American Plate. But according to some geologists the exceedingly complex crustal movements in southern California are resulting in further slices of North America being crowded onto the Pacific Plate. These, along with the rest of "The Coast," the Channel Islands, and the submerged continental borderlands, appear destined to bump and grind their way north for a long time to come.

As humans have just begun to realize, the motion of land and sea floor along faults will readily crumple cities, nuclear reactors, refineries, and pipelines. All will be carried very slowly away. Taking the long view, one prominent earth scientist predicts that 50 million years hence the last refractory remnants of the oil rigs, power plants, Los Angeles, Santa Barbara, and perhaps San Francisco will cascade slowly into the awesome depths of the Aleutian Trench.

If the shade of John Muir continues to watch over the magnificent manifestations of nature on North America's Pacific Rim, appropriate sentiment for the final fate of California's coastal zone is assured. During the great Inyo earthquake of 1872, Muir tried to josh his worried neighbors out of their fears that the floor was about to drop out of Yosemite Valley. "Come cheer up; smile a little and clap your hands, now that Mother Earth is trotting us on her knee to amuse us and make us good," he said.

Muir himself did not believe in the extant geological theory of cataclysmic deepening of the Valley. But his neighbors were not in a mood for levity. So Muir took a more serious tack, concluding that, "In any case . . . so grand a burial was not to be slighted."

Somewhat over fifty million years from now, Mother Earth seems likely to be grandly burying the strangely concentrated stuff of the United States' west coast. But as in many a fabulous tale of transcendent events, endings are never as final as they seem. There will be renewal and recycling into ore bodies and volcanic ash flung around the earth on thin stratosphere winds. Predictably crustal plates will still creep and clash, though small ones may be gone or be replaced by others. The globe will still spin, though ever so slightly more slowly because of the moon's gravitational drag. The water planet will still stand out intensely, improbably blue and white in the void. The only question that appears totally unanswerable is: who or what will be here to know these things?

Cycles of Water

Off the rugged western edge of the continent is a broad band of flowing water. Unlike the Atlantic's Gulf Stream, it moves from north to south, and it is cold. Its origins could be said to lie in the far North Pacific below the Aleutians, but it is also true that it has no precise beginning or end. The huge flow nearly 600 kilometers wide is known as the California Current and is part of the oceanwide gyral system of currents which, in the northern hemisphere, describe great clockwise circles in the sea.

To an observer in space, dazzled by the rapidly revolving earth with its intricate shifting cloud patterns and seasonal color belts, this global pattern of oceanic circulation would appear strikingly stable. Over periods of at least a few thousand years, the large current systems of the oceans would stand out as an example of earthly permanence and precision. Such an observer, equipped to perceive the infrared end of the spectrum, would note temperature differences on the earth's surface as a splashy mosaic of unusual colors. But his attention would be drawn to the almost organic pattern laid over the ocean reaches—a panoramic display of the circulatory system of a living planet, boldly prominent as on an anatomical chart.

Along the continental coasts forming the western borders of ocean basins are the greatest flows of water on earth. Known as western boundary currents, these include the Gulf Stream of the Atlantic and the Kuroshio, or Japan Current, of the northwest Pacific. North of Japan, the Kuroshio curves in a spreading pattern toward North America. A branch of this flow eventually reaches the Pacific shores of Alaska, where its influence keeps many harbors such as Valdez ice-free all year. However, much of the wide subarctic drift derived from the Kuroshio bends southward and becomes the California Current, which dominates the northeastern temperate edge of this greatest of oceans.

Largely separated by the doldrums around the equator itself, the major wind and water circulation in the northern and southern hemispheres tends to remain apart. South of the Baja peninsula, the California Current begins to bend westward, and its waters soon become entrained by the trade winds, blowing from the northeast in a band hundreds of kilometers wide. This wind and current system has its counterpart below the equator, and the western boundary currents spring forth anew from recycled waters which are piled up by the trade winds of both hemispheres.

The oceans' great western rivers, however, are deflected from their poleward flow by the hidden contours of their continental banks and, more importantly, by the subtle effects of the earth's rotation. In the northern hemisphere, moving water is forced gradually to the right or clockwise; in the southern hemisphere, the flows trend anticlockwise. The resulting pattern of gyres and eddies forms roughly a mirror image in oceans north and south of the equator.

The spinning earth works its mysterious way on oceanic circulation through a tendency to turn out from under moving objects. This phenomenon is called the Coriolis Effect after a French mathematician who first described its unfelt but powerful influence on earthbound movement. As if by an invisible hand or magnet, a force appears to turn objects from straight-line travel into curving paths. Friction opposes the twisting force, and the Coriolis Effect is more noticeable in air and water than on land. The force is strongest near the poles and gradually diminishes in lower latitudes; it is absent at the equator. There are intriguing stories of lost polar explorers wandering in arcs, but these accounts were strictly anecdotal and unverified. However, artillerymen, pilots and astronauts, birds and fishes must compensate for the Coriolis Effect in their activities or miss their targets and destinations— sometimes by hundreds of kilometers following long traverses.

The imperceptible force of the planetary Coriolis Effect can be simulated and magnified greatly on small rotating systems, closer to the human scale of perception. Trying to draw a line with a straight-edge on a revolving phonograph turntable illustrates the Effect. A clearer example is to imagine, or better play, a game of catch on a merry-go-round. Two players on such a revolving surface will see the flight of a ball between them as a smooth curve. A merry-go-round rotating in an anticlockwise direction represents the northern hemisphere as seen from above the north pole. In this situation, the ball will be seen by the thrower to veer away in a clockwise arc to the right of its intended recipient. A ball game on a clockwise spinning merry-go-round (representing the southern hemisphere as viewed from the south pole) will be just as difficult, but the apparent deflection of the ball will be to the left. Strangely, an observer standing beside the merry-go-round sees no real deflection. In relation to the playground or amusement park, the path of the ball appears straight and true. In the same rather mysterious way, earth's Coriolis Effect evaporates if earthbound motion is examined from the stationary vantage of space. But reality is ever elusive, for astronomers would be quick to point out that the great wheeling galaxy, bearing our solar system on one of its rarefied outer arms, confers a Coriolis Effect of higher order on motion beyond our experience.

In the sea, the largest currents or gyres, directed by the Coriolis Effect, circle entire ocean basins and communicate between distant continents. Throughout earth's history the currents have been broad highways of biotic dispersal, migration routes, and avenues of discovery, traveled by fishes, seeds, floating trees, rafts, and similar conveyances bearing desperate animals and determined men.

This pattern of ocean circulation was probably a significant factor in the successes and failures of early navigators. Columbus's southern route to the New World followed paths of least resistance in the North Atlantic gyre. He sailed south with the Canaries Current, which bends slowly clockwise and joins the westward-flowing North Equatorial Drift in the trade wind belt. Recently, Thor Heyerdahl followed much the same route on his *Ra* expeditions. Heyerdahl has probably achieved more in the way of practical and primitive experience with ocean circulation than any other explorer for centuries. In the earlier *Kon-Tiki* expedition, he and his adventurous fellow raftsmen drifted over 7,000 kilometers, beginning in the Humboldt Current off Peru and curving westward into the vastness of the central tropical Pacific.

A few anthropologists have suggested that Pacific Northwest Indians reached the Hawaiian Islands in their seagoing canoes. Their most likely route would have taken advantage of subgyral eddies spun off the California Current in Mexican latitudes. But these currents are often weak and unreliable, and most such expeditions (if indeed they occurred) probably came to grief in the empty eastern Pacific.

Astonishingly, artifacts appearing to have Chinese cultural affinity have turned up in scattered sites along the Pacific Coast of the Americas from British Columbia to Ecuador. Most of these occurrences date roughly from the early centuries A.D. Archaeologists guess that these are traces of several waves of fugitives, perhaps religious outcasts, who set out in substantial craft to find a new home. First they found the Kuroshio and must have drifted for hundreds of days in a great circle around the North Pacific before they reached America via the California Current.

Without question the greatest ocean explorers were the Polynesians who came from the west out of Asia. These "vikings of the sunrise" spread across Oceania against the main flows of wind and water during the so-called Dark Ages in Europe. Within a few hundred years, the Polynesians touched most of the islands in the central and western Pacific, many of them infinitesimal specks lost in a universe of sea and sky.

By the time Europeans reached these waters, the winds and currents to be reckoned with probably became well-known to the seasoned explorers. Sir Francis Drake and Captain James Cook must have had extensive knowledge of the California Current, but early maps of such voyages, full of enthusiastic depictions of islands and continents, often omitted details pertaining to the circular connecting sea roads. Possibly the great captains were protecting their professional interests and reputations, or else, simply as stereotypic seafarers, they kept their own counsel on such matters that did not concern landlubbers.

The great flows of sea water provide a major mechanism by which the earth regulates its temperature. Feverish levels of solar heat received in equatorial regions are carried away by ocean currents, as well as mass movements of air toward the poles. The currents are climate makers, creating high latitude rain forests as well as the driest coastal deserts. Along the Pacific Coast, the California Current recycles water which has given up much of its heat in the far north. This flow of cold water provides a unifying influence for most of the west coast of North America and simultaneously creates a strikingly different marine ecology from that found on the Atlantic shelf. There is a conspicuous blurring of the biogeographic provincialism that is so sharply defined on the eastern seaboard. Other differences between the two coasts result from the combined effects of currents and topography. Relatively high fertility prevails all along the Pacific Border and out from the coast for hundreds of kilometers because the California Current conveys a huge and steady supply of nutrients from the rich North Pacific. On the Atlantic margin, rivers contribute most of the nutrients for coastal productivity, and the Gulf Stream is sterile by comparison with the California Current. Regional upwelling, which brings nutrients from deep water in close to the coast, is also prevalent on the Pacific Border, while it is virtually absent off the east coast.

As it carries cold water southward, the California Current becomes a dehumidifier. It steals moisture from the sea winds that blow toward southern California and Baja. At the northern edge of this desert coast, the dry, mild weather is largely responsible for a second-order effect of great portent: the attraction of an immense human population between Santa Barbara and San Diego.

It is thus clear that in a number of ways, interactions of this relatively steep and truncated margin with the California Current confer a regional uniqueness which only begins with the surficial geology and the physics of water movement. Off Pacific shores occur biological phenomena which are not matched elsewhere on the North American rim.

The Fluid Forests

At the base of the ocean's primary food webs are the phytoplankton, microscopic organisms which are at once single cells and whole plants. The phytoplankton have been called the grass of the sea, but it is also possible to think of this plant community as a forest, microcosmic in one perspective and vast in another. In most places this forest is thinly "treed," but it is distributed in a panoramic green wave across the surface layers of the sea. Whether under brilliant blue skies or scudding stratus clouds, gentle mists in sea fog, or wild storm turbulence, the invisible drifting forest mirrors in many ways the once unbroken carpet of evergreen trees that covered the northwestern coastal hills and ran far inland and upward to the limits of vegetative growth.

A figurative comparison of phytoplankton to forests seems a good way to approach the vastly different scales of events that govern basic aspects of life in and along the California Current. During spring and summer, strong northwest winds blow along the coast. Derived from atmospheric high pressure over the North Pacific, the wind flow parallels the California Current. Surface water near the coast, entrained by the wind and prevailing current and continuously forced into a clockwise turn by the Coriolis Effect, moves gently but massively toward the west. As this surface water is steadily eased away from the shore, it is replaced from below by an upwelling of deeper, colder water. Upon reaching the surface, this water in turn trends slowly offshore, and as long as the wind continues to blow the process continues. Following irresistible physical laws, it extends into a regional pattern.

Northern Pacific Coast upwelling occurs most intensely and with greatest continuity from late spring through the summer (May to September). The largest North American upwelling area extends from Point Reyes north of San Francisco Bay to the central Oregon coast. This phenomenon, however, is not confined to waters off the United States but occurs in numerous areas primarily along western coasts of continents. One of the world's greatest upwellings, which dwarfs that of northern California, lies off Peru. Large upwellings also appear along the Pacific shores of British Columbia, Baja California, and Panama.

Upwelling episodes, like major ocean surface currents, can be detected by thermally sensitive equipment aboard space satellites. However, the picture they provide is only skin deep. Perhaps some future imaging device based on a side-scanning principle will graphically portray the anatomy of an upwelling as it has been painstakingly pieced together by theoretical oceanographers and shipboard experimenters monitoring apparatus in the depths.

Water which moves away from the coast at the surface eventually sinks again. This downwelling, however, may occur many dozens of kilometers offshore from the zone of upward flow. After a short time, scientists believe, a continuous cyclic movement of water called a convection cell develops. In diagrammatic view it resembles a wide watery belt, slowly revolving in place along the coast. Developing with an advance of windy weather down the coast, the leading edge of an upwelling belt appears to trace a helical path. Once it is established, a coastal convection cell slowly circulates water until its driving force, the north wind, ceases for several days. Within a typical cell, water, nutrients, and plankton will return in one form or another to a given point, in a period of time ranging from two to four weeks.

Deep water that reaches the sunlit surface layer during an upwelling episode carries an abundance of plant nutrients. Compared to the normal surface environment, deep water is laden with nutrients which arise from the bacterial decomposition of organic bodies large and small that sink slowly into the sunless deep. Thus, upwelling brings to the light a kind of compost, thinly constituted to be sure, but rich and ripe for the stimulation of algal growth.

It is comparatively easy in this age of satellites to hold in the mind's eye an image of the upwelling belt centered off southern Oregon. We can even imagine the thickening concentration of nutrients pervading this wide strip of sea as the upwelling pattern boils silently southward with a corkscrew motion. The nitrates, phosphates, silicates, and so on, are stirred in from below.

It is fairly easy to picture all this on the broad scale, the huge table set for the first course in the bounteous banquet of the sea. But to comprehend what follows, it is necessary to jump back nearly to the other end of the scale.

Since the invention of the microscope in the 17th century, people have been insinuating intellect, imagination, and intuition down there among the phytoplankton cells. The many discovered facts have spawned many theories, but numerous facets and nuances of life in the microscopic milieu remain puzzling, and perhaps many more are still beyond the reach of ponderous sampling gear or else too subtle for even the most sophisticated and sensitive analytical tool which is confined to an abiotic, air-conditioned, oceanless laboratory.

For a glimpse of the biological frontier of inverted inner space, one must imagine his frame of reference shrinking. Familiar forms loom to outlandish proportions, then pass beyond ordinary experience. Physical laws feel vastly different to creatures so small that some can thread the arch of a needle's eye as humans might swim beneath the Golden Gate Bridge.

Within the phytoplankton milieu are some unexpected manifestations of biophysics and biochemistry. These tend to elude the ponderous perception of humans, but they are basic life governing forces to beings that measure on the order of 1,000 to 10,000 to the centimeter.

Shape is tremendously important and varied. Each species has opted genetically for certain characteristic expressions of external features. But a phytoplankter's "choice," or rather the bodily expression of its genes, is not whimsical. It is dictated by vital necessities such as buoyancy and the efficient uptake of nutrients.

Thus an elaboration of surface area by means of flattening, the growth of protuberances, or indentations—in short, any feature which causes the body's shape to deviate from a simple sphere—may have multiple effects. Phytoplankters such as diatoms, without means of propulsion, depend in part on cell shape to retard their sinking rate. Functionally they resemble self-contained sea anchors. Increasing their "drag" in the water aids such species in remaining in sunlit surface waters.

Seemingly outlandish shapes also may help in the rapid exchange of vital substances through the cell wall. By a crude analogy, a spherical sponge will not absorb water as fast as one of the same volume which is slab-shaped. Add projections or leafy appendages and the potential absorptive rate becomes even greater.

Internal adaptive mechanisms of phytoplankton are also simple, but packaged beyond the dreams of human engineers even in this age of miniaturization. Diatoms have no obvious means of motility like the whiplike propulsive devices possessed by another major phytoplanktonic group, the flagellates. Yet some diatoms appear to be able to change the density of their internal fluids. The production of gas vacuoles, small internal pouches, serves the same function in some blue-green algae—very primitive micro-plants which embody many characteristics of bacteria. Other suspected ways in which phytoplankters change their density are through accumulations of fat and mucus droplets, both of which are lighter than water. By means of one or another, or possibly combinations of these cunning mechanisms for buoyancy control, inactive-appearing phytoplankton may not only hold their vertical position in the water, but conceivably migrate up and down.

An organism on the phytoplanktonic scale, however, experiences limi-tations and obstructions to movement that humans never dream of. These often have to do with changes in the density and viscosity of water. Density refers to the weight and hence the physics of displacement of water. Cold water is denser than warm; salt water is denser than fresh. Plankton can be trapped below a density discontinuity such as the thermocline. Like a balloon at ceiling altitude, such a microorganism may be physically unable to reach upper rarefied waters. Viscosity, which is a measure of cohesion of a fluid, may also vary considerably in the world of the phytoplankton. Organisms the size of humans feel the power of these environmental factors only in extreme or abnormal circumstances, swimming in the Great Salt Lake (density), for example, or in a swimming pool filled with molasses (viscosity).

On nearly any scale of measurement, the dilute chemical soup that is sea water is never very thoroughly stirred. This is especially true with respect to the algal nutrients, which tend to concentrate and dissipate locally in re-sponse to many forces. Upwelling, which operates on a gross level, is only one of these forces. Using one or another means of vertical locomotion, phytoplankters may encounter patches of high nutrient concentration, al-though it is not known if they actively seek such areas. Once surrounded by an ample supply, however, algal cells are known to absorb nutrients such as phosphate faster than they can be used. This "luxury consumption" results in a stored surplus. Later in leaner surroundings the surplus can be used by the cells to maintain a high rate of growth.

Some phytoplankters in the thin oceanic soup take advantage of meatier chunks than simple nitrates and phosphates. Although these creatures, called autotrophs, normally practice photosynthesis, they may also live as chemotrophs. That is, they absorb and digest dissolved substances such as sugars and amino acids, which exist in low concentration in sea water. Chemotrophic nutrition may occur largely at night, and it seems to permit some phytoplankton to inhabit areas which are shut off to strict autotrophs. For example, certain flagellates are often as common at great depths in the sea, far below the last vestiges of sunlight, as they are near the surface. It appears these do not live permanently in deep water, but make periodic excursions of one or two kilometers between the surface and the depths. But while they are away from the light, they must subsist entirely by chemotrophic means.

To most kinds of phytoplankton, light is absolutely necessary for existence. But the daily renewal in the dawn across the long-shadowed swells touches only the blue skin of the sea. Despite clever mechanisms providing buoyancy, the tiny creatures of the light are in a precarious situation. They cannot usually remain long in conditions of ideal illumination.

Light in the sea attenuates steadily with depth. The average depth of the photic zone in which algal cells receive enough light to maintain growth is 200 meters. A given phytoplankter will live most efficiently at a specific depth, usually near the surface. Some species have achieved a remarkable ability to get along well under suboptimal lighting. Cells growing in dim light rapidly increase their chlorophyll content. Thus in deeper parts of the photic zone, stocking up on this alchemical substance keeps the solar-powered factory, which converts carbon dioxide and water to simple sugar, running at a high rate. The more chlorophyll that is available, the more available light energy that can be trapped and used to effect the chemical conversion. When these cells return to a more brightly lit level, the excess chlorophyll disappears, probably digested by the tiny plant.

Sea lion cow

Conversion from low-light cells to high-light cells can take place within a few hours, or one cycle of division. Thus during an upwelling, versatile phytoplankters, riding the convective circuit, regulate their solar-powered manufacturing process at maximum efficiency. Going up or down, they employ a kind of automatic choke, and the tiny organic engine turns over smoothly without strain or wasted effort. The response of the microalgae to variable light intensity again recalls the image of a forest in the sea, for this adaptation corresponds to the production of "sun" and "shade" leaves by higher plants.

A mystery surrounds the use of light by planktonic algae at different times of day. Throughout most of the sea, the productive part of the phytoplankters' workday is the early morning, particularly near the equator. Tropical marine phytoplankton taken from the sea and placed in incubators with uniform lighting show bursts of photosynthesis up to six times greater at 8:00 A.M. than they did at 7:00 P.M. This fluctuation decreases steadily going north from the equator, and finally ceases entirely at latitudes between 60° and 70° N. Scientists have no firm explanations. They speculate about cell fatigue or accumulations of waste products, but the actual reason why algae are more active in the morning remains to be determined.

The growth of phytoplankton populations is largely controlled by available resources. Even with a cell's capacity for adjusting its chlorophyll content, the reproductive rate eventually slows in dim light. In very dense populations, also called blooms, shading of lower cells by those above may occur. This also tends to stabilize the population size. Zero population growth, or ZPG, becomes self-imposed.

Within well-lit near-surface waters, however, the availability of fertilizing chemicals often provides the limits of growth. In shelf waters the element that is usually in shortest supply is nitrogen, which occurs in sea water primarily as dissolved ammonia and nitrate compounds. Nitrogen is the key element in amino acids, the building blocks of protein. Protein is normally the main product of photosynthesis, but cells which experience a nitrogen deficiency switch over to producing predominantly carbohydrate. If prolonged, nitrogen deficiency results in an algal apathy, which recalls that experienced by humans existing on a diet of junk foods. Cell division stops. The rate of photosynthesis drops, eventually reaching five percent of the normal level.

Nutrient balances are of major importance in the success certain phytoplankton species have in competition with others. At the beginning of the spring growth period or an upwelling episode, the water is rich in nutrients. A few rapidly growing species become dominant. As a result of this growth, the common mineral fertilizers become partially depleted, and organic wastes, chemicals figuratively "perspired" by the first wave of algal cells, begin to appear. At this point other species, partial chemotrophs which are able to use organic matter in an otherwise less fertile milieu, first become conspicuous. With time, phytoplankton communities become obvious melting pots, as greater numbers of species share an increasingly complex resource base.

This process offers another analogy with the development of a terrestrial forest. Pioneering plants on open ground usually consist of a few rapidly growing species. These are followed by other species, for example, ones that can grow in partial shade, and saprophytes, which live on the organic production of their autotrophic neighbors. Eventually there is formed a diverse and integrated community of organisms. But unlike the dark green swells that sweep over pristine coastal ridges and up the flanks of the Cascades, the forests flowing in a temperate sea evanesce and reform every year.

The seasonal succession of different kinds of phytoplanktons is still something of a mystery. At any particular place and time, one or a few species usually will far outnumber all the rest, but this dominance is temporary. Within a matter of days or weeks those formerly most abundant will fade from the scene (although never disappearing entirely), their place taken by another species or two or three. Shifting nutrient concentrations must play a large role in choreographing the diverse parade of organisms involved in succession, but it is probably not the whole story. Most knowledge of phytoplankton ecology is derived from lab studies of one or two species growing in culture flasks and does not offer a true picture of life in the ocean.

Competition among certain species of phytoplankton finds expression in the release of complex organic substances into the water. Some of these are pheromone-like (acting as external hormones), and speed up the growth of the cells releasing them in the area. Others, however, are chemical warfare agents that interfere with the growth of competitors.

The grazing of zooplankton forms another major controlling influence on the growth of phytoplankton. It takes a while for the zooplankton to get going in the spring, but as phytoplankton blooms reach full flower, the animalcules begin to react. Dominated by copepods, the zooplankton populations finally increase rapidly to find an immense feast awaiting them.

Copepods are small crustaceans resembling delicate wingless insects. They dart with impossibly rapid antennal strokes hither and yon through their fluid medium. A strobe light flashing faster than 1/1500 of a second is needed to freeze on film the swimming motions of some copepod species.

Although these little creatures are typically classified together as vegetarians or primary consumers in the marine food web, the lives of two given species may be as variable as those of an elk and a rabbit. The overall picture of copepods as gentle grazers is also misleading. Several species are known to be voracious predators, attacking and consuming other copepods and especially small fish larvae. One of these diminutive carnivores is *Labidocera*, which becomes abundant at times in the California Current. Bristly and powerful, *Labidocera* grows to be several millimeters long and preys heavily on larvae of the California anchovy. Striking randomly at anything that moves in its path, *Labidocera* kills far more than it consumes. Disabled and dying anchovy larvae, with chunks bitten out of them, littered the bottom of an aquarium in which biologists studied the behavior of this rogue copepod. Such studies have led to reasoned speculation that *Labidocera* takes a huge toll of each year's crop of anchovy babies.

By the pyramidal ecological law of food supply and demand, however, there are far more herbivores in the plankton than carnivores. It has become clear that most of the grazers have highly particular tastes in their feeding habits. Many kinds of copepods select algal cells within a narrow size range, automatically rejecting particles that are too large or too small. Newly hatched larvae of the California anchovy appear to depend overwhelmingly on a single species of flagellate. The evidence is that spawning of the fish is delicately timed to coincide with blooms of this phytoplankter. The veliger larvae of mollusks such as abalone consume the smallest algal cells, but these creatures too are selective.

For years plankton ecologists have routinely measured the presence of phytoplankton in terms of overall primary production or chlorophyll concentration. This was done largely for convenience. It provided a quantitative measure; it avoided time-consuming sorting and scrutinizing through microscopes; it fit the growing trend to employ modern automatic chemical analyzers incorporating radioactive tracers such as Carbon 14. What was lost was the predictive power to relate phytoplankton abundance to successful grazing for key organisms higher in the food web. Now it is believed that fish larvae such as the California anchovy will starve in the midst of abundant "chlorophyll" if a particular phytoplankton species is not present. The late J. D. H. Strickland of Scripps Institution of Oceanography, an astute scientific explorer of the plankton world, summed up the problem succinctly: "Animals do not eat primary productivity or C14 or chlorophyll or anything else. They eat plants. And they are very concerned about what sorts of plants they eat." It appears that the microscope will remain an essential tool in phytoplankton ecology. This will be particularly true for studies having implications for fisheries and those assessing impacts of pollution on key organisms in food webs.

As the submarine growing season becomes well advanced, selective grazing, together with shifting nutrient balances and releases of organic substances, bring about a growing dynamism. Copepods dart and twist through the vast canopy like swallows in a prairie sky. Veligers drift in clouds near the water's surface and recall swarms of gauzy-winged insects on a summer evening.

The upshot of the seasonal maturation of the fluid forest community with many species of interacting phytoplankton and zooplankton is a bewildering heterogeneity, or patchiness. Relentless grazing effects a conspicuous pruning and thinning. Wide clearings appear. Although dense aggregations of diatoms or flagellates may still form where an ideal concentration of nutrients exists, sooner or later the grazers descend and such patches are stripped by hordes of hungry animalcules.

Divers have reported seeing horizontal bands of concentrated plankton only a centimeter or so thick. Laser holography, a technique newly applied to marine biology, has allowed scientists to take a picture of a cubic meter of sea water. Probing slowly downward through the compressed image with magnified technological vision, they come upon dense clusters of creatures surrounded by relatively vast, empty water spaces.

On broader scales in the open sea, close-spaced water samplers and plankton-collecting devices show the ubiquity of patchiness. Off California, long ribbonlike plankton patches form parallel to the shoreline. In these waters, many meters below the surface, oceanographers also find well-separated layers green with phytoplankton. And usually, hovering near, or already scurrying about the green layers like kids around some huge table of Saint Patrick's Day confections, are the copepods and other zooplankton.

The unfathomed patchwork structure of the plankton world deceives the senses of an observer who looks out over a turbulent ocean from shore, or from a ship, or who gazes at the peaceful, homogeneous expanse below a high-flying aircraft. Perhaps more than anywhere else in the sea, paradox resides in the plankton world. Incredibly complex, integrated drifting communities, some extending over hundreds to thousands of square kilometers, result from life activities on the infinitesimal scale—the interception of invisible shafts of sunlight and many modes of nutrient absorption, consumption, rejection, excretion, attraction, repulsion, synergism, and antagonism in the space of a period on this page.

The web of transactions in this world of "simple" life easily rivals the U.S. economy in complexity. Late in the season, variations in horizontal and vertical distribution reach a maximum in the pelagic communities. In the words of Ramón Margalef, an expert in planktonology, patches of plankton in this last stage of development "change from moment to moment like clouds in the sky."

Fall and winter bring dormancy to the pelagic forests. Most of the "leaves" have died and drifted down to darkness, and the nutrients no longer actively upwell from below. To be sure, all the life is still there, ticking over slowly in gelid repose, waiting for the return of long days and high sun and the slow rush of the upwelling sea, like a renewal of sap flowing up to the canopy.

Down in the multiple worlds within worlds of the plankton, the human mind awkwardly gropes for intellectual crumbs. Events of great significance, perhaps the fate of a nascent red tide, may hinge on a whiff of molecules or a fractional shift in temperature or light intensity. Many planktonic secrets remain to be discovered. These will not readily give themselves up to man's understanding. They may long remain elusive because laboratory culture flasks and the present analytical approaches cannot capture all of the essential qualities of an upwelling sea rolling westward mile after mile and micrometer by micrometer.

Red Tides

Certain kinds of phytoplankton, the dinoflagellates, tend to form very large patches known as red tides. Sometimes these patches or dense blooms are several kilometers wide. Often they are oriented parallel to the coastline. Red tides arise from the rapid multiplication of the algal cells, which may occur as free individuals or else form short chains of cells. Peak population densities reach millions of cells per liter of sea water.

Although red tides have been under study for more than 100 years, scientists are still unsure of many aspects of their biology; in particular, the precise origin of blooms cannot yet be explained. It is known that the motile red tide organisms, propelled by the animated whiplike hairs known as flagella, actively seek concentrations of dissolved nutrients. An active population will move up or down in the sea over many meters. When the cells find preferred nutrient levels they will stop, often forming a sharply defined layer which registers on oceanographic instruments as a chlorophyll maximum zone.

How the patches stay together at sharp horizontal edges is the real mystery. Planktonologists invoke physical concentrating mechanisms such as eddying currents, but no one actually knows. Those who have observed dense red tides close up marvel at the sight of water the color of tomato soup which demarcates suddenly as if someone began painting at a boundary line across the sea surface.

One extremely interesting attribute of some red tide organisms is bioluminescence. The biochemical basis of light production by the tiny single-celled plants has been found to be similar to that of fireflies. Dinoflagellates appear to light up primarily in response to physical disturbances in their immediate surroundings. At night the effect can be spectacular in a breaking wave, and fish swimming through bioluminescent phytoplankton leave trails of cold green light. The latter phenomenon has led biologists to speculate that algal bioluminescence may be a defensive mechanism. This "burglar alarm" hypothesis suggests that throwing millions of tiny spotlights on nocturnal filter feeders in the plankton patch exposes the culprits, for example anchovies, to their predators. Such algal feeders may dislike the brightly lit surroundings and depart for darker waters. Not all dinoflagellate species possess the ability to luminesce, however, and the reason why remains unclear.

The development of red tides at the surface often follows heavy rains and excess river runoff to the sea. Higher than usual nutrient concentrations reach coastal waters at such times, and this enrichment has long been suspected of triggering red tides. Numerous correlations between red tides and the increasing incidence of marine pollution have also come to light in recent years. Toxic dinoflagellate blooms are becoming common in the vicinity of burgeoning sewer outfalls in marine environments such as Tokyo Bay, Japan, and Oslofjord, Norway. The growth of *Gonyaulax catenella*, the predominant red tide organism in Pacific Northwest waters, is stimulated by detergents containing NTA (nitrilotriacetic acid).

Many species of dinoflagellates exhibit alternating life-styles in which a free, drifting planktonic existence is followed by a sedentary, benthic way of life. This general scheme is common to many marine creatures, but unlike most of them, the bottomed-out dinoflagellates live in a strange form of suspended animation called resting stages, or cysts. They neither move nor grow. Passively defensive, they surround their single-celled bodies with a shell-like coating similar to that encasing the pollen grains of higher plants. This material is one of the toughest substances known, immune to most of the chemical forces wielded by man and nature. Boiling acids fail to etch it, and the encysted cells can pass unharmed many times through a variety of grinding, churning stomachs and the powerful digestive juices of sediment-feeding animals.

After a time, which may be years (no one really knows), some subtle signal calls forth a new planktonic generation from the drab little cysts which have been found on the continental shelf by the thousands per gram of sand.

Recently some biologists have proposed that red tides begin with such mass synchronous hatching of cysts which have accumulated over several years from successive small inconspicuous dinoflagellate populations. The releasing signal may involve changes of temperature, salinity, or nutrient concentrations favorable to the growth of the algae, but again, no one yet knows for sure.

If it were not that a few species of dinoflagellates are highly toxic to a variety of higher forms of life, including man, red tides would probably never excite more than a handful of academic specialists and occasional bemused boaters. However, among dozens of harmless species in North American coastal waters, a total of four now account for sporadic losses of millions of dollars in the tourist and seafood industries. Two of these species have caused fatal human poisonings.

In New England, *Gonyaulax excavata* (formerly called *G. tamarensis*) has become widely pestiferous only since 1972. In that year discovery of the toxic organisms along the Maine, New Hampshire, and Massachusetts coasts, together with a few suspicious fish and bird deaths, led to a condemnation of the clam fishery for several weeks. Several cases of red tide-related illness were reported, but this prompt action probably averted a serious public health problem. *G. excavata* has been of concern in Canadian maritime waters for over twenty years because of a number of human fatalities from the eating of contaminated shellfish.

The poisonous alga has appeared off New England as far south as Cape Cod every summer since 1972. Some scientists speculate that increasing amounts of sewage and thermal pollution may have made New England waters newly favorable to the noxious *G. excavata*.

In the Gulf of Mexico, destructive red tides are attributed to two species, *Gymnodinium breve* and *Gonyaulax monilata*. The greatest biological impact of red tides in this region seems to be on fish of all kinds. Doomed fish caught in these red tide waters, mainly off the Florida and Texas Gulf Coasts, exhibit bizarre behavior. Single fish swimming normally suddenly shoot to the surface, thrash violently half in and out of the water. They appear to gasp for air, then fall over dead. Whole schools of mullet have been observed suddenly to "stand" on their tails at the surface, spout small fountains of water, then collapse and die. Secondarily, the tourist industry succumbs for lengthy periods as masses of rotting fish wash in on the beaches.

Gulf of Mexico red tides are rarely associated with serious human illness. However, intense respiratory irritation, with symptoms of coughing, sneezing, and burning sensations, has been experienced by people on the beach and boaters. These symptoms presumably derive from a kind of natural air pollution—algal toxins whipped off choppy red tide-laden water by the wind.

Along the Pacific coast occur the red tides most dangerous to man. The organism to watch, among numerous harmless ones in this region, is *Gonyaulax catenella*. This species, which usually forms chains of cells, becomes abundant only from northern California (San Francisco) northward. Its occurrence is extremely spotty. Large stretches of coast may not see a poisonous red tide for years. Then one will materialize in the ocean like a rosy cloud at sunset.

The season of blooming for *G. catenella* is July through September. During the day, a bloom capable of laying down a lethal and temptingly baited trail of nerve poison may not be noticed at all. This species seldom develops the extreme water-reddening population densities achieved by others. But at night along the shore in scattered areas from Point Reyes to the Aleutians, the algae signal a warning. Pacific coast Indians knew from experience that the beautiful green sprays of light shimmering along the breakers meant that shellfish were not to be eaten.

To man and most other vertebrates tested, paralytic shellfish poison, or PSP, of *G. catenella* is one of the most acutely toxic substances known. It is some fifty times more potent than curare, the famous substance used on blowgun darts by Amazonian Indians. PSP appears to consist of more than one compound; probably a family of related organic chemicals is involved.

One measure of *G. catenella's* devastating potential against human life is seen in its use by the Central Intelligence Agency's modern political headhunters. After being distilled and concentrated, the algal toxin was applied to the tips of the Agency's assassination darts. The most sophisticated weapon in this line was so tiny that a human victim might not realize he had been struck. In theory (since the Agency claims no darts were ever fired at humans) the victim would feel nothing, but the infinitesimal amount of pure PSP injected would work in minutes. There would come a trembling and numbness in his lips, then perhaps fingertips and toes; quickly, because of the concentrated nature of the chemical and direct entry to the bloodstream, paralysis would rise in a wave from the extremities to immobilize the limbs. On the street, in a car, an elevator, or even back in his office, the victim would collapse and die of respiratory failure as paralysis seeped into his chest muscles and diaphragm.

In all known cases of poisoning from PSP, these same symptoms tend to occur, but the onset of poisoning appears only after a prolonged time interval ranging from two to twelve hours. In these cases the victims had eaten shellfish from the vicinity of a toxic bloom. Residence time in the digestive system before the toxin reaches the bloodstream and individual quirks of physiology account for the delay in onset of illness.

The severest symptoms of paralytic shellfish poisoning yield to the simplest treatment, if it is kept up long enough. Although a badly affected person cannot breathe or move, he will remain otherwise healthy if provided with artificial respiration. In the absence of hospital equipment, mouth-to-mouth will do. Recovery usually occurs rapidly around twenty-four hours after the first appearance of symptoms, and there are no known permanent aftereffects.

The severest cases of poisoning, including death, have occurred after the eating of mussels and clams collected in waters of high salinity. Oysters grown far back in brackish bays, for example in the Puget Sound system, almost never come in contact with *G. catenella*. Poisoning is most closely associated with bivalve mollusks because these creatures feed by filtration, and they sieve enormous numbers of *G. catenella* cells from the water. The bivalves themselves have evolved a tolerance to PSP, and in the soft bodies of mussels and clams the toxin becomes greatly concentrated. Exceptionally noted for its ability to store highly concentrated PSP is the butter clam, *Saxidomus gigantea*, common in the Pacific Northwest. The CIA used *S. gigantea* as its primary source of dart poison.

Although bivalves are the most seriously contaminated organisms on the North Pacific coast, others, including crabs and snails, have been found to harbor enough PSP to be dangerous if eaten by humans. Perhaps these latter creatures pick up the toxin by preying on very small bivalves.

The patchy occurrence of PSP contamination can be baffling. Clams and mussels from beds only a kilometer apart are known to vary enormously in toxicity. One may yield perfectly safe provender; the other may harbor death. In addition, PSP is known to linger in clam meat for weeks after the last vestiges of *G. catenella* have moved through a particular area.

Every year on the Pacific coast, people sicken (and occasionally die) from PSP. Almost never is the illness traced to restaurants. Most often it seems to happen to tourists. At high risk seem to be college students on wilderness outings and nature-loving heartlanders from Des Moines or Tulsa who have never heard of red tides and who become distracted at a critical point in their reading of Euell Gibbons. Novice foragers along the coast from California to Alaska should check with local health authorities or perhaps seasoned fishermen concerning the edibility of local shellfish. The wisest course would be to follow the old Indian rule and abstain from clams and mussels from the time of the first auroral displays in the summer surf until the autumn.

The Kelp Forests

There is another kind of algal forest in the sea, and a diver in certain places off La Jolla, Monterey, San Juan Island, Amchitka and many points in between would know why it can be described as a forest. In these places the stature of the dominant plants, extending from the bottom at a depth of ten to twenty-five meters to the surface, compares quite favorably with trees. The terms that refer to this marine community—groves, stands, canopy, understory—also bespeak its similarity to a terrestrial forest.

Kelps are the largest algae, at the opposite end of the scale from phyto-plankton. Yet it is interesting to observe that spatially the "forest" cover of kelp is infinitesimal compared to that of the phytoplankton. The giant algae grow in a very narrow belt, while the diffuse canopy of the phytoplankton, although normally not extending very deep, spreads across the entire surface of the water planet.

Kelps are cold-water plants. A handful of species is usually characteris-tic of a given region, but as a group kelps are found worldwide where summer water temperatures do not rise much above 20° C. Along the coast of eastern North America, lush growth does not extend south of Cape Cod, although scattered stunted plants may be found at times to northern New Jersey. North American kelp achieves its greatest range and diversity on the Pacific Border. The cooling influence of the California Current allows kelp to flourish all along the continental borderland to northern Baja California.

The huge kelp plants, typically *Macrocystis* in southern California, *Nereocystis* in Puget Sound, and *Laminaria* in the perenially icy waters of the far north, as well as the species of lesser stature which form understory bushes and scrub, are not all that meets the trained and properly equipped eye of a marine botanist. Like most creatures in the sea, kelps lead a double life, but their transmutation is stranger than any in the long animal parade of larval and adult couplets, or even the shift between cyst and swimmer in red tide organisms.

Early kelp biologists were baffled by the plants' beginnings until some-one noticed a proliferation of tiny capsules, now called sori (singular, sorus) along the edges of the thick leathery "leaves," or blades. The sori resembled seeds, albeit small ones for so strapping a plant, but further surprises waited.

Mature sori are only containers for much smaller "seeds," sixteen to sixty-four of them per sorus; the number is always an exponential multiple of two, but varies for different species. These microscopic "seeds" are more properly termed zoospores, for they can swim using tiny hairlike flagella. Moreover, within their single-cell bodies the zoospores have altered the basic cellular numerology of the kelp plant, reducing to one-half the number of chromosomes carrying the genes of a particular species.

Consider that cells of the big kelp contain perhaps thirty chromosomes arranged in fifteen pairs. Each member of a pair is very similar to its mate, although many slight differences may be found. Such differences are based in subtle patterns in the components of DNA (deoxyribonucleic acid), which stretches, twists and kinks its way throughout each chromosome and specifies heredity in a million interlocking ways. It is enough to note that slight differences do occur between the so-called identical chromosomes in a given pair.

The importance of the zoospore is that its formation is accompanied by an unpairing of the chromosomes. Unlike normal cell division, as in the vegetative growth of a plant—division in which all the chromosomes reconstitute, divide, and distribute themselves in new cells—the zoospores effect a *reduction* division. Each of the first two produced within the developing capsule has one chromosome from each of the parental plant's pairs. Almost immediately these two cells divide into four. By a subtle process called crossing over, in which paired chromosomes exchange whole segments just before the initial reduction division, each of the first four zoospores may possess slightly different combinations of genes.

The first four zoospores then further divide, each passing on copies of its unpaired chromosomes until the sorus-capsule is filled with spores (16, 32, or 64 of them). Now carrying half of the chromosome complement in the rest of the big plant's cells, each spore contains the essence of kelp at its lowest common denominator. Stripped to this essential genetic cargo and possessing a prepackaged energy supply and propulsive flagella, they are ready for a momentous and hazardous journey through inner space.

At some unknown signal, the sori themselves are launched. They fall from the kelp canopy by the millions and drift downward and away on unknown trajectories. Even as they fall they open, and the tiny spores begin to sputter forth into the void. Some zoospores are scattered to the surface currents and probably make their way among the phytoplankton, traveling many kilometers before reaching bottom. But in dropping whole capsules, the kelp plant hedges its bets, and many zoospores may remain when their vehicle touches down gently on the sea floor within or near the parental forest. These zoospores emerge onto ground already proven capable of supporting a healthy stand of plants.

After their landfall, the tiny cells swarm over the ground and begin to establish a settlement. Another attribute of the kelp colonists is that they are evenly divided into males and females. Each spore settles and germinates into a strange little male or female plant called a gametophyte. It is the alter ego (or egos) of the mighty but sexless sporophyte of the giant kelp. It is also a whole separate generation which, until fairly recently, has been poorly known to biologists because gametophytes are microscopic, short-lived, and difficult of access.

All known kelp gametophytes are tiny, look-alike plants. Barely discernable to the eye, the minikelps appear under the microscope as tasselated bunches of whiplike filaments composed of only a few cells. The male plants seem to have smaller cells and possess more branches than the females. Most of what is known about gametophytes comes from laboratory cultures, although after active shedding of sori in a kelp forest, they must grow for a time like microscopic grass across the dim sea floor.

The female plants produce a number of special encapsulating cells. Each contains an egg which ripens as its surrounding chamber swells, then finally bursts. The egg is extruded from the chamber, but remains hanging from the outer edge. Meanwhile, the male gametophytes have also been sexually active. Buds called antheridia grow at the tips of the male's branches. Each bud releases a tiny spermlike (or pollenlike) cell with twin flagella, and then the male dies.

Now the climax of a strategic and monumental process is at hand. The strategy of all sexual reproduction is the recombination or shuffling of genes, which increases the chances for future fitness in a species. From generation to generation different combinations of genes produce new and different survival properties which organisms and species need in order to cope with a changing world.

Many simple organisms—bacteria, phytoplankton, protozoa, and even sea anemones, flatworms, and some higher plants—retain the ability to reproduce asexually, usually making carbon copies of themselves through simple bodily division. But they also exhibit the sexual mode, showing that the need for regularly edited copies is felt throughout the animal and plant kingdoms. Radical changes in new editions of organisms are rare. Most are very slow to change, and many generations may pass before the completion of some very complex selection processes. Unfortunately for organisms living in the modern era of exceptionally swift environmental change, nature has no way of speeding up the editing and review schedules.

Like a gnat searching at moss-level in a sequoia grove, the kelp "sperm" seeks an egg hanging from the female gametophyte. When the two fuse, their chromosomes join pair to pair, reconstituting the original number and configuration in the big sporophyte plant. The likelihood is great that the essential shuffling has occurred, that the two contributing gametophytes originated from colonizing zoospores which fell from different big plants. Thus inbreeding is minimized; there is a marriage of chromosome complements which came from different parts of "town," so to speak, perhaps even different towns or states.

The kelp now becomes a vegetative phenomenon. The minute fertilized egg begins to divide. It grows on top of the female gametophyte plant, which is soon lost from view. Simultaneously, a matlike proliferation of cells begins to spread across the bottom, and a vertical blade grows upward. The bottom mat will branch into a broad, tough, irregular network, the holdfast. This looks like an exposed tangle of roots, but its only function is to anchor the plant to the rocky bottom.

The upward-trending shoot becomes a stem or frond. In the common giant kelp of southern California, *Macrocystis pyrifera*, the frond sprouts blades, or photosynthetic "leaves," at regular intervals. The growth of *Macrocystis* is one of the foremost wonders of the underwater world, for the huge fronds elongate at rates exceeding thirty centimeters per day, faster than any other plant known. In their prime, the giant algae have been known to add twenty-five meters in a sustained growth spurt over 120 days.

Macrocystis plants eventually sprout numerous fronds, most originating near the bottom from a single base stem. Up to 130 separate upward-growing fronds, including young shoots, have been counted in a single sporophyte. The average number, however, is more like thirty or forty. When these long streamers, sprouting thin, pointed, photosynthetic blades, reach the surface, they continue to grow for a time and coalesce with others into a leafy canopy ten to thirty meters above the sea floor.

The fronds are buoyed by tiny gas-filled floats called pneumatocysts. *Macrocystis* possesses a small pneumatocyst at the base of each leaflike blade, and a single mature plant has thousands of them supporting the long streaming fronds. Pneumatocysts are much larger in some other west coast kelps, notably *Pelagophycus* and *Nereocystis*. The former has a single pneumatocyst which supports the whole plant. Here the growth form is very different from that of *Macrocystis*. *Pelagophycus* features a single, smooth, whiplike stalk rising from the holdfast to the surface where it terminates in a gas-bulb having a capacity up to 2.6 liters. Like a leathery balloon, this large pneumatocyst supports two diverging masses of blades which hang down from the surface like a huge frayed curtain.

While *Macrocystis* appears to hold the absolute record, prodigious algal growth is common in other species. The large brown alga *Cystoseira* (not a true kelp) in Monterey Bay is an example. It maintains a perennial basal stalk extending less than a meter high from the bottom. Seasonally, the plant sends aloft a reproductive frond. This grows ten or fifteen meters, and then dies when its sexual effort is spent. The big kelps of the Pacific Northwest and Alaska are also known for impressive records of growth.

How do these plants achieve such phenomenal growth, up to hundreds of times faster than trees? Part of the answer must be that physical support comes easily for kelp. Budding small fleshy floats demand far less energy and bulk resources than producing the thick, heavy structural stems needed by large land plants. Also, plants in the sea are surrounded by the fertilizing nutrients; they don't have to absorb them through roots laboriously searching through many cubic meters of stony soil in constant, tangled competition with neighboring plants.

The main competition among plants in a kelp forest seems to be for light, and it is not always the largest species which get the upper hand. Off Amchitka Island in the Aleutians, several species of *Laminaria*, straplike kelps which do not reach the surface in water over a few meters deep, commonly dominate over a large surface canopy-forming species, *Alaria fistulosa*. This species is capable of growing from depths of twenty-five meters or more, but it appears that *Alaria* is shaded out by the others, for its densest growth occurs only in the shallowest, most disturbed (hence fairly open) areas near the shore. In experiments in which diving biologists with pruning shears cleared the regular subsurface *Laminaria* canopy from patches at several depths, the giant *Alaria* sprouted quickly and grew to form extensive coverage. Just the opposite occurs in southern California, where *Macrocystis'* great surface canopy apparently shades out local understory species.

Self-shading also limits growth when a canopy becomes too thick. Young giant kelp plants can only grow around the edges wherever their parent sporophytes are thickly settled. Often the new sprouts find less than favorable bottom—for example, shifting sand or areas that are too deep or shallow —and new growth is effectively prevented until clearings appear in the mature stand.

In its prime, with plants several years old, a large mature stand of kelp rivals a tropical rain forest for teeming animal life. As usual, the forest floor has the greatest abundance and diversity of inhabitants. Conspicuous creatures include flowerlike anemones, large starfish and sea urchins, crabs and snails. The most famous snail found here is certainly the abalone, of which there are several species. Within sediment spaces bounded by rocky bottom, sometimes in astonishing numbers, are found tube-dwelling worms. One of these, *Diopatra*, extends its tube above the surface of the sand as a kind of stubby chimney. In an apparent attempt to camouflage this exposed part of its dwelling, *Diopatra* glues sand grains, small shells and the like around the outside. In the kelp beds the attached debris often includes bits of *Macrocystis*, which apparently provide the omnivorous worm with snacks as well as concealment. Specialized rock-boring bivalves also live within the bottom by the millions. These modified clams riddle the soft sandstone and mudstone terraces and shallow shelves off California. Over centuries they may affect bottom features and even the rate of coastal erosion, but they probably have little effect on the life of a kelp grove.

Across the rocks and low ledges, among the silent leathery "trunks" of kelp, prowl the octopus and numerous bottom fish. Above the bottom amid waving shafts of sunlight and algae, fish become the dominant inhabitants in terms of size and status in the food web. At times, the leafy spaces seem empty; in another moment fish may materialize in the bronze glades like mythical forest spirits.

The daily bread of many of these fish are the small encrusting organisms: tiny hydroids, crustaceans, mollusks, worms, and bryozoans abound on the surfaces of the big plants. The wavering aisles among the fronds are like a well-stocked supermarket for the finny browsers. Vegetable bins are as well supplied as meat counters, for several kinds of lesser algae grow attached to the larger plants.

Along the deep outer edge of a California kelp stand there is a chance of an encounter with the top carnivores in the marine jungle. Like great shadowy birds of prey, sea lions and sharks patrol the kelp fringe. The former is generally more common than the latter, or perhaps merely more conspicuous.

Many kinds of sharks are more scavengers than predators. The vultures of the sea, these silent, stubby-winged spectres glide in to forage on the deed, the weak, and the vulnerable. There are exceptions, however. In California waters the great white shark *Carcharodon carcarias,* with un-vulturelike aggressiveness, preys on seals and sea lions. This species has also attacked human swimmers and divers, possibly mistaking them for its normal prey, from La Jolla to the Farallon Islands off Marin County in northern California. Several of these encounters have been fatal.

Other species of sharks also frequent the Pacific Border. Santa Catalina Island is a gathering place for blue sharks, *Prionace glauca*, a slender, graceful species posing little, if any, danger to man. Biologists at California

State University at Long Beach, who attached sonic transmitters to some of the big fish, discovered that the blue sharks of Catalina behave in a consistent diurnal pattern. During the day, sharks dispersed widely in the sea between the island and the mainland; then at night they tended to regroup near the island. The best estimates indicate that hundreds of sharks come in with the darkness and roam very close to Catalina's shoreline, perhaps seeking fish and other prey which emerge from the cover of kelp and boulder beds at night.

Orcas, or killer whales, are sometimes seen off southern California, though they are more common farther north. These are the pre-eminent predators of the planet. They feed primarily on other mammals—seals, sea lions, and porpoises. They seem fiercely intelligent, and strangely, not unfriendly to man. Eskimo epics notwithstanding, the case for orcas attacking humans lacks reliable documentation. There are intriguing accounts of sled dogs, trapped on small ice floes, being attacked, while their equally vulnerable human owners were ignored or spared. The scuba diver population of Puget Sound continues to grow and thrive despite routine sightings of orcas including social gatherings of the "killer" fraternity, or *familia,* numbering in the dozens. No attacks on divers have been recorded.

A diver with large predators on his mind feels a great sense of security near or within a kelp forest, a mental state that may be shared by many creatures there. There may be not only an awareness of safety from the big gliding shadows that snatch the unwary along the edge of the kelp, but also an overall elemental coziness. Dense kelp breaks and tames the most furious storm swells. On a raging night, a sea otter tucked into *Macrocystis* fronds near the middle of a great stand must feel snug indeed. Of course his or her water bed may be set at 10° C. in winter, but a sea otter is quite comfortable sleeping cold.

Other smaller creatures below in the dark, twining fronds and on the sea floor probably experience the storm only in occasional drafts of water and a muffled distant roaring of surf on some unprotected beach. John Muir's experiences in the High Sierra are called to mind. Never using a tent on his excursions, Muir sheltered from storms and the bitter night winds in dense brushy thickets, "where the branches were pressed and crinkled overhead like a roof and bent down around the sides . . . The night wind . . . at first only a gentle breathing, but increasing toward midnight to a rough gale . . . fell upon my leafy roof in ragged surges like a cascade, bearing wild sounds from the crags overhead."

Storms ultimately destroy the kelp forests, but at the same time they provide for renewal. Weakened by erosive activities of urchins, snails, and perhaps crabs, burrowing clams, and other creatures, a holdfast will give way in a storm. Kelp cutters and their boats also unintentionally loosen and detach the holdfasts, further contributing to the mortality of California's stands of *Macrocystis*.

Loose kelp begins to drift through the kelp bed, entangling other plants. Some of these cannot stand the added drag, and they too break away. Even entangled plants which remain attached to the bottom usually die. The multiple fronds of drifting and intact plants become so knotted and interwoven that separation is impossible. Diver-biologists have observed as many as eighteen giant kelp plants hopelessly entwined in one mass, like a huge, ragged ball of yarn. Eventually the dead and dying vegetation will tear loose and disappear. The plants wash in on the beach to the bemusement of tourists, or perhaps the last tattered remains sink to a canyon tributary where a grand burial is provided by a turbidity flow rushing into the Santa Barbara Basin.

After an especially severe storm, old kelp beds in which plants with crumbling holdfasts were fairly common suffer drastic thinning. Dozens of drifting plants initiate a chain reaction of entanglement and mortality that may eliminate most of a stand.

The extent to which sea urchins threaten kelp forests is controversial. Whether enhancement of urchin populations in recent years is caused by humans is still more controversial. While urchins do attack kelp, notably and most seriously the holdfasts, it is clear that the spiny creatures are not universally destroying the kelp beds, even in southern California. Local population explosions of urchins, such as the one off Point Loma, near San Diego, have not been explained, however.

Kelp and sea urchins have coexisted for a long time, and one hopes they will continue to do so. Potentially and directly more dangerous to the kelp in the sea off California is the increasing pollution, ranging from oil to hot water. A man-induced pathogen, parasite, or industrial disease of kelp could be far more serious than the nibblings of urchins. The enemies, tolerances, and requirements of the tiny gametophytes are virtually unknown. More research and great environmental concern are needed in and around the kelp forests.

On the nearly barren bottom from which the great adult sporophytes have been stripped, or severely thinned, there is a rapid, almost magical reawakening. A soft effusion of sunlight reaches the sea floor where deep shade had prevailed for perhaps five or six years. Young sporophytes sprout like weeds in a field. But this is a most vulnerable time. The greatest losses of the tender plants are to grazing fish and shifting bottom sediment. Unlucky sprouts are buried and smothered by ripples of sand that travel as slow waves across the bottom.

The early thinning, however, is beneficial. In a few months only a relative handful of survivors remain, and now they are spaced well apart. The plants shoot upward along refracted rays of light, bronze melding into bronze. Within the year the local environmental cycle will be complete with the re-establishment of a unique community of life. This silent, hanging forest between the somber sea floor and the tossing sunlit surface becomes a leafy, living matrix, embedding and enmeshing many lives all along the Pacific Border.

Oceanic Oil: Coping

Off southern California, in an elongate area of some 2,600 square kilometers (1,000 square miles), roughly from Point Conception to Point Fermin, petroleum seeps quietly from a number of scattered points on the sea floor. The oily emanations have probably gone on for a long time. Exotic Pleistocene animals, saber-toothed cats, dire wolves, and their hooved prey, may have sniffed cautiously at lumps of asphalt which drifted in to prehistoric beaches and rocks. Many of these same creatures later perished in other encounters with the same stuff. Their bones have been found in the gooey petroleum seepage which formed on land near Los Angeles, and is today called the La Brea Tar Pits. Still later, but long before huge production platforms marred the view from the Santa Barbara hills out over the Channel, coastal Indians pondered the provenance of beached tar lumps in a place now known as Coal Oil Point. They even took advantage of the asphalt which washed ashore. Accounts by early Spanish settlers report that the Indians used it to caulk their canoes.

According to petroleum geologists, southern California has one of the highest rates of submarine petroleum seepage in the world. In the region of major known west coast seeps (the 2,600 square kilometers mentioned above), estimates of escaping oil range from 100 to 900 barrels per day (a barrel of oil contains 160 liters, or 42 gallons). At the upper estimated rate, southern California contributes about eight percent of the world's natural marine petroleum pollution (an estimated 11,300 barrels per day).

Major oil-bearing beds off southern California often lie close to the surface. For example, the Dos Cuadros bed, from which emanated the famous 1969 Santa Barbara oil well blowout, intersects the sea floor in some places. Most hydrocarbons at the very surface have long ago leached away, but large extant oil concentrations have been found just 100 meters down in the sedimentary strata. This fact, together with the prevalence of strike-slip crustal movement, which cracks the thin confining rock like an eggshell, accounts for the extremely high regional rate of oil seepage. Although it is largely unexplored, the long stretch of borderland off Baja's Pacific coast is also rated as a zone of high potential for oil seepage. It is probable that loci of important seeps shift repeatedly in such a chaotic tectonic environment, but petroleum has apparently been dribbling naturally, if spottily, into the sea here for millions of years.

In the latest microsecond of geological time, however, the rate of marine oil leakage has rapidly increased. Human activities now release ten times more oil to the world's oceans than do natural seeps. In United States coastal waters the man-made petroleum pollution is more than twelve times the natural.

Coping with oil in the sea has become a new problem for man and one of sharply increased severity for marine organisms. The following discussion is a sequel to the previous chapters on oceanic oil (in the New England section), which dealt primarily with the acute and obvious aftereffects of uncontrolled oil spills, and emphasized fairly gross sensitivities of marine animals to petroleum pollution. It summarizes the fledgling technology of oil control and cleanup in the sea and speculates on the ability of marine life to cope with oil in highly sophisticated ways which are just becoming apparent.

The only presently reliable technique to clean up large oil spills in open water involves the use of large flexible floating barriers called booms. Booms operate either by being moored in the path of a drifting oil slick or else by being towed actively behind a pair of ships. Either way, the boom operators try to trap the floating oil in a U-shaped pocket, as if the boom were a kind of ponderous trawl fishing at the surface. Once caught, a slick tends to pool up in the pocket where it can be pumped into a waiting tanker-barge.

Limitations on the effectiveness of booms are the rate of spillage and the time until the boom and collecting barges are put into service. Also critical are the velocity of the current in the area and the sea state, or size of the waves encountered.

The current and the waves can drastically crimp the pollution fighters' best laid plans no matter how quickly the men and equipment arrive on the scene. Even the best of booms fails in very modest currents. Failure is due mainly to a phenomenon termed "head-wave loss," which begins when the moving water below a contained (hence stationary, or nearly so) oil slick draws bubbles and blobs of oil down at the head or upstream edge of the slick. Some of the oil bubbles rise again to rejoin the undersurface of the slick closer to the boom. Thus oil tends to migrate continuously deeper into the confining pocket. Inevitably some of the oil reaches the boom's lower edge, is pulled along with the undercurrent and escapes. The stronger the current, the more rapid the loss. Once loss begins, the head of the slick comes steadily toward the pocket or U of the boom; eventually leakage is complete.

Engineering analysts find that two knots (3.7 kilometers per hour) is the highest current velocity for the operation of modern booms without severe head-wave loss. Furthermore, choppy seas induce much head-wave loss at currents well below two knots, and the maximum sea state for operating a boom reliably and safely is about 1.5 meters (five feet). Theoretically it is possible to design megabooms, which would perform more reliably in stronger currents and higher seas, but because of logistical and power requirements in transport, deployment, and operation, the experts are skeptical about their development.

In a series of computerized scenarios, scientists from the Massachusetts Institute of Technology's Offshore Oil Task Group have projected outcomes of attempts to contain and clean up large oil spills that might be expected from modern and future sources, especially supertankers. In the scenarios, three kinds of locations were considered: a major oil terminal, a secondary port having only very small barges available for receiving the spilled oil, and finally a remote site. Other variables in the computer programs were boom and barge deployment times and capacities, and the spillage rate of oil. The maximum current velocity was assumed to be one knot, and the spills to have occurred in protected waters with negligible wave action.

As expected, the "remote area" spill was harder to control than those in the other hypothetical sites considered. Even at a relatively low spillage rate of 100,000 gallons (380,000 liters) per hour, 55 to 60 percent of the oil from a large (10 million gallon) spill would ultimately be lost.

The most critical factors governing success of the computerized cleanup simulations were the size and availability of tanker-barges to remove oil collected in the boom. In the remote area scenario, it was assumed that small barges (3,500-ton capacity) would not begin to arrive until twenty-four hours after the onset of the spill. Under this constraint, the largest boom (conceived as having a two million-gallon capacity), even if deployed as little as one hour after the initial mishap, would be ineffective. More than half the oil would be lost.

Even in a spill at a major oil port, the barge arrival time was terribly critical. The analysts considered that at the time of a spill nearby barges might be full and have to be offloaded before becoming available for the cleanup. If the delay ran as long as twelve hours, with a high spillage rate of 500,000 gallons per hour, 90 to 95 percent of the oil would be lost—this despite the optimistic achievement of boom deployment in the first hour after the spill. The conclusion of the MIT study of oil cleanup prospects looks to the future with cautious optimism. In summary, the computer scenarios predict that if a rapid-response, ready-alert system is maintained so that booms and containment crews reach spill sites in one or two hours, and barges arrive in no more than five hours, a 75 percent recovery can be effected in protected waters.

The depressing gap between cleanup responses in a computerized spill and in a real emergency was seen after the October, 1974, spill at the large oil-handling terminal at Bantry Bay, Ireland. This spill of crude oil, estimated at 2.4 million liters (650,000 gallons) went on overnight and was not even noticed until the next day when the local harbor was filled with oil. Winds began to drift the oil out of the bay. Containment on the water was too little, too late. Even before shore cleanup efforts could be mobilized, oil came in along thirty-five kilometers of beach. Extensive ecological damage was noted; in particular, intertidal and subtidal seaweeds were killed by both oil and the detergents used in the beach cleaning.

The unprogrammed reality of a remote area spill became starkly evident after the *Metula* disaster in the Straits of Magellan, also in 1974. The *Metula*, one of the class of very large crude carriers (VLCC), which will service the Alaska pipeline, hit the rocks at full speed, fourteen knots. The huge vessel, which normally takes between three and four kilometers to stop in open water, ground to a halt in 250 feet. There was an immediate gush of 1.6 million gallons (6,000 tons) of oil from the split bow compartments.

Later the hull opened in several more places. After more than two months, the grounded vessel, tortured by a tidal range of up to seven meters and five- to six-knot currents, had lost over 50,000 tons of crude oil into the choppy waters. At one point the released oil covered 2,600 square kilometers of sea. Hundreds of kilometers of beach were smothered with black goo up to several inches deep.

No cleanup effort whatsoever was made after the *Metula* spill. Over a period of several months, the oil companies involved sent several scientific observers, as did the Chilean government. The reports differed widely. After an aerial survey one expert reported very little oil on the beaches. Another walked miles of beach in several areas, and found oil in a layer up to eighteen inches thick, hidden beneath a thin veneer of pebbles and sand. Water in waves receding from the high tide mark shimmered with rainbow hues.

The U. S. Coast Guard also sent observers and trainees in the months following the spill. They brought new equipment, such as a portable, high capacity pump, and they assisted in the offloading of *Metula*'s unspilled oil into smaller tankers. The Coast Guard's main objective was to gain experience for the assembly of mobile oil-spill control teams in the U. S.

It is heartening to note that the Coast Guard is working to develop a rapid response system for dealing with oil spills. But while expert cleanup personnel can now be mobilized quickly and airlifted to trouble spots anywhere in the country, the heavy equipment they need, the ships from which they operate, and especially the collection barges still arrive like the proverbial slow boat to China.

It is disheartening to note that the ability to cope with an oil spill in waters where currents exceed two knots and waves are over five feet high is practically nil. This in effect writes off serious at-sea cleanup efforts along most of the open coast most of the time from the Aleutians to Mexico. In particular, it denies a hope of salvaging a *Metula*-style disaster in the beautiful and dangerous Straits of Juan de Fuca between Vancouver Island and Washington's Olympic Peninsula. In the next few years, increasingly heavy tanker traffic will shuttle between the Alaska Pipeline terminal at Valdez and inner Puget Sound refineries. The giant crude carriers will routinely encounter five-knot currents; sometimes they reach seven knots. The tankers will also encounter fog and other ships. In the inner Puget Sound straits (Rosario and Haro) leading to the refineries, the tankers will encounter hazardous bottom topography and rocky islands. Cleanup crews facing a large spill in these areas will encounter tragic frustration.

Another, somewhat less effective, and markedly less environmentally acceptable technique for combating oil spills is the use of dispersants. Dispersants are basically detergents. They do not remove the oil, but sink it, emulsify it, or disperse it from a coherent mass into tiny droplets in sea water. To a certain degree a choppy sea will physically disperse oil. Simple turbulence breaks up a slick into a frothy brown mixture of oil and water known to cleanup crews as "chocolate mousse." The addition of a dispersant is supposed to finish the job, producing a mixture with such minute droplets that marine bacteria can quickly surround and decompose both oil and dispersant.

Unfortunately, the most effective dispersants tested so far have had severe side effects on marine life. The harsh detergent action of these chemicals not only dissolves oil but attacks sensitive living tissues. It is especially devastating to many kinds of small phytoplankters. Their thin cell membranes are largely made of fatty substances called lipids. The living cells simply burst as the detergent dissolves their membranes. Having added a few ppm of dispersant to a drop of sea water under the microscope, an observer witnesses a macabre scene from inner space as tiny cells scattered across the circular field wink out in silent micro-explosions of protoplasm.

Numerous dispersants have been found to be toxic to fish. Some of these compounds cause acute reactions more quickly and at lesser concentrations than the oil itself. There is evidence of dispersants interfering with the functioning of the nervous system of fish. The physical coordination of swimming and the cycle of activity coordinated with the tide were disrupted in a species of flounder by certain dispersant compounds.

Finally, the much touted use of specially bred and artificially seeded bacteria to decompose spilled oil is still in its infancy. Difficulties abound. Used in conjunction with dispersants, bacteria suffer from dissolution effects as much as phytoplankton. If a slick remains coherent, on the other hand, bacteria cannot get enough oxygen or else experience a nitrogen deficiency, which curtails protein formation, growth, and reproduction. The microbes are unable to penetrate the mass of oil, and decomposition occurs only around the edges.

Another important constraint is the water temperature. Bacteria are active directly in relation to the temperature of their surroundings. A given strain seeded into tropical waters may attack oil with great vigor; in the cold, dark winter sea off the Olympic Peninsula, it may fizzle sluggishly.

In time a drifting slick will be consumed, but so will one which has not been treated, and time is not in the favor of marine life and shores in the path of an oil slick.

The largest and most famous oil pollution incident on the Pacific Border is the blowout in the Santa Barbara Channel which began on January 28, 1969. Between 10,000 and 50,000 barrels of crude oil were estimated to have leaked into the sea over the first ten-day period. Very high leakage continued until mid-March. As late as July, several hundred barrels per day still emerged from a large crack in the sea floor beside the sealed well.

Some of the heavy oil washed ashore, coating beaches, rocks, and birds. Masses of oil caught in the kelp canopies, and much undoubtedly sank to the bottom. There was no attempted cleanup at sea. Most of the job of coping at Santa Barbara was left to the marine creatures, and in most cases their successes and failures were never ascertained.

Some obviously important local marine communities such as the kelp forests received surprisingly little study. A few curious divers poked around the fringes of the kelp at risk to their wet suits (oil dissolves neoprene rubber), and gave accounts to news reporters. But quantitative ecological studies by scientists from the University of Southern California and the University of California at Santa Barbara were limited to open water fish (away from the kelp) and shore organisms living between the tides (chiefly mussels and barnacles). Besides failing to pursue a thorough investigation of the kelp community, researchers treated the rich bottom life growing on subtidal rocks or within the sediments just offshore in a highly cursory manner.

Max Blumer, the oil expert from Woods Hole, Massachusetts, has pointed out that the Santa Barbara study ignored subtidal crustaceans, which seem to be the most oil-sensitive creatures in the sea. Blumer has stated that certain amphipods, small shrimplike organisms, show sublethal effects of petroleum hydrocarbons at levels below which the substances register on the most sophisticated analytical equipment.

The Pacific Border

A number of marine ecologists have criticized the post-spill research at Santa Barbara for its failure to apply up-to-date quantitative measures. In several essential instances, both dealing with the subtidal and intertidal zones, the study used imprecise methods without replicate sampling or control observations of marine communities in areas which were not touched by the oil.

A better-planned research effort in the Santa Barbara Channel after the spill might have shed much light on the comprehensive effects of oil spills in open coastal waters. Intriguing observations in Mexican waters suggest an enhancement of growth in kelp which had been touched by an oil spill. It may be that kelp has a high tolerance to oil; it produces a mucus-like substance which seems to keep oil from touching the actual surface of the plant. Researchers believe, however, that enhancement of growth may have resulted from a selective kill of grazing animals such as sea urchins, which can suppress the kelp's growth below what it could achieve if it weren't being constantly gnawed and nibbled.

In the case of Santa Barbara's fish, the wrong ones were studied, although it is easy to understand why the research was carried out as it was. The fish sampled were ones that could be easily caught using a trawl in the open reaches of the channel. By nature these pelagic species move about over great distances; they easily avoid an area containing a noxious stimulus like spilled oil. It is not surprising that such fish were found to be little affected in the months after the Santa Barbara spill. Harder to see, harder to catch rocky-bottom species and those inhabiting the kelp forests were subject to no quantitative study despite the casually reported finding of small tar lumps in the guts of sea perch. This discovery should have prompted a sampling program to explore sublethal effects and long-term problems such as petroleum-induced cancers in fish and their predators. Nothing of the sort was attempted.

Starry flounder

After the Santa Barbara event, little time and effort were spent to find out what was happening along the sea floor beneath the huge floating blotches of oil, especially in the nearshore area where churning waves, sand, and organic detritus might have brought tons of oil to the bottom. Criticism should be tempered here, however, for at the time everyone believed that the acutely toxic SAD (soluble aromatic derivatives) compounds all quickly evaporated from a slick at the surface. Yet, after only a qualitative study which left out major components of the fauna, the leader of the U.S.C. oil ecologists declared there had been no damage to Santa Barbara's subtidal bottom communities. The researchers then concentrated on the hardy intertidal mussels.

In September, 1969, scientists from the Woods Hole Oceanographic Institution discovered an immense kill of bottom organisms down to at least ten meters (thirty feet) after a small oil spill in Buzzards Bay off Cape Cod. When their data, which demonstrated mortalities in dozens of kinds of marine creatures, had been assembled one of them remarked that if they had limited their study to mussels they would have concluded that spilled oil was of little consequence to marine life. A temporary depression of reproductive effort was the only apparent symptom suffered by the mussels.

Some interesting hints of marine fish adapting to live with chronic exposure to oil have been found recently. These 1975 experiments were carried out by researchers from Woods Hole in local environs, but the findings may have wide applicability. The subjects were killifish, *Fundulus heteroclitus*, a hardy species of coastal harbors and estuaries.

One group of killifish studied, the "experimental" group, came from Wild Harbor, the center of the 1969 Cape Cod spill, where oil still could be squeezed by hand out of bottom mud five years later. The control group of fish came from an unpolluted estuary a few miles away. Immediately after the spill, Wild Harbor killifish were killed or moved away, but within a few months a sizeable population reappeared. Their habit of living near the bottom and feeding on bottom organisms and detritus, however, apparently brought about a continual low-level contact with residual oil in the sediments. This in turn stimulated some previously unsuspected adjustments in metabolism.

After passing into the bloodstream of a fish via the gills or gut, oil (and its chemical breakdown products) is not easy to trace. The scientists chose to examine livers from the two fish populations, because this organ has long been known as an important site for the detoxification of assimilated poisons ranging from heavy metals to alcohol. The liver was the first logical place to look for hidden effects of exposure to petroleum hydrocarbons.

There were no gross signs of liver damage in the experimental fish, so the analysts probed toward the innermost hepatic recesses—the area between and within closely packed cells at the edge of resolution by refined chemical techniques and the electron microscope. The scientists were especially interested in lipids, a family of substances in the larger category of fats. Several kinds of lipids having different metabolic uses are common in fish liver. Some lipids are energy-storing compounds; others attract and dissolve complex organic compounds, including organochlorine pesticides, and probably petroleum hydrocarbons. Exotic substances in such chemical custody may be held in the body, and in some cases they are apparently mobilized in the blood, still attached to their lipid guardian molecules, and excreted.

Still another kind of lipid, stiffer stuff called phospholipid, forms a major component in cell membrances. And when the liver analyses were finished, the quantities of phospholipid in the two different populations of killifish were found to be strikingly different.

Some of the experimental fish had nearly an order of magnitude (10 times) more phospholipid than the controls from the clean estuary. The experimentals were also conspicuously deficient in triglyceride, a lipid which functions chiefly as an energy store. It was furthermore interesting to note that if the researchers had not probed as deeply as they did they might have concluded "no effect" because the total lipid content of the two populations was the same.

Electron microscope pictures of extremely thin slices of the fish livers revealed in a huge proliferation of specialized membranes within cells of the experimental fish. These cells were crammed with the squiggly rumpled fragments called endoplasmic reticulum, a kind of membrane known to form sites of intense protein production.

The researchers' interpretations of this clear but quiet little sublethal backwater of an oil pollution impact are not yet firm. At first glance, abnormally large quantities of phospholipid in the Wild Harbor fish could mean that petroleum hydrocarbons are damaging cell membranes somewhere in the fish, and much phospholipid is needed continually for regenerative efforts.

But the overabundance of phospholipid-rich endoplasmic membranes, seen in the liver cells with the aid of the electron microscope, tends to contradict this first interpretation. These membranes' primary role in protein formation suggests that detoxifying enzymes (which are proteins designed for highly specific chemical jobs) are being produced at a high rate. Such enzymes could work to neutralize the poisonous action of petroleum anywhere in the fish's body.

An idea suggested by another scientist was that the fish might be effecting a cleanup by producing large amounts of phospholipid, which is the most detergentlike among the several lipid types available. Free phospholipid could capture hydrocarbon molecules in the bloodstream, enabling fish to continuously purge their bodies of oil. Keeping the toxic hydrocarbons mobile by continuously flushing them out of the body would prevent a dangerous buildup in vital tissues.

As an example of natural adaptability to an uncommon form of stress, the inner coping of the killifish is inspiring. The natural world is extremely flexible and resilient. Biologists probably will find that some other marine creatures incorporate subtle measures and mechanisms for living with oil. Logically, organisms inhabiting the vicinity of natural seeps off California may have acquired interesting adaptations of this sort long ago.

It is possible too that because of the present ubiquity of man-made oil pollution, especially in epicontinental waters, chronic sublethal manifestations may be appearing in shallow water marine life everywhere. The killifish symptoms represent only the first discovery of its kind, and this over only a fraction of the creature's spectrum of physiological response (or perhaps vulnerability is a better word). Researchers should be especially attentive to potential disruptive effects of oil on behavior and chemical communications, which are vital for every living thing in the water from algae to fish. A severe threat of this sort faces lobsters in New England waters, but other marine organisms remain untested.

Some would be encouraged by the killifish story, and, indeed, it would appear premature to say that the oceans are dying from oil pollution. But uncritical optimism over nature's self-cleansing abilities is equally unfounded. Every organism which must alter its metabolism to deal with the spreading pollution threat pays a hidden price. Perhaps the cost of the killifish's increased phospholipid reserve is somewhat poorer egg production, or less stored energy for times of food shortages, or reduction in pools of those adaptive enzymes necessary to adjust to sudden changes in salinity or temperature.

There are many ways in which a fish, which must expend metabolic energy to combat deleterious effects of pollutants, becomes slightly less fit for normal environmental vicissitudes. Unfitness may be exacerbated when animals or plants are in dynamic phases of their life history—for example, during the brooding of young, times of molting, or the larval period of rapid growth. Because of the heightened metabolic demands of these activities, creatures suffering added stress from pollution may abort young, falter and be caught by predators, or even die outright. This dilemma can be appreciated by contemporary humans: during city smog alerts, school children are warned against strenuous exertion.

So far, as suggested by the killifish example, marine organisms may be more effective and ingenious in their particular ways of coping with oil in the sea than man has been, but because of the extrametabolic demands imposed by oil on marine life, together with the spectre of synergistic effects and depressing trends in abuse of the sea by man, the outlook for a healthy ecology on the continental shelf is dubious. There is a tendency toward overextension of organic abilities—a pushing to the limits of adaptability—which might in time spell doom for most of the creatures condemned to reside indefinitely in a slightly oily sea.

A Pollution Potpourri

T he reputation of the Pacific Border for diversity is legendary. California in particular is blessed with an Olympian physical diversity: golden beaches and lofty mountains; deserts and temperate rain forests and alpine/arctic climate zones; vast wildernesses to great cities. Matching the physical diversity is the state's immense cultural and social diversity. Some bless this, while others curse it. The latter sentiment, however, must be unreservedly applied to what is happening to the regional coastal zone in the wake of intense human activity—the expanding effects of oil production, dredging and filling, municipal waste disposal, pesticides, trace metals, and thermal pollution. An unfortunate diversity of pollution has appeared on the submerged California borderland.

Within a strip extending inland from the coast only fifty kilometers (thirty miles) live most of the more than 20 million citizens of California. The actual figure is 85 percent or 17 million people on the coastal strip—one-thirteenth of the population of the United States. Most Californians are concentrated in two areas: the urban centers around San Francisco Bay and that unique catchment of humanity known as southern California, roughly between Santa Barbara and San Diego. In various ways, the high population of these areas has been responsible for the steady decline in quality of California's natural submarine environment.

Some of the worst degradation of the borderland has come from simple physical abuse. Unlike the Atlantic coast, a relative scarcity of estuaries prevails along the Pacific Border, yet these productive epicontinental environments have suffered the same fate as those on the east coast. Leaving out San Francisco Bay for the moment, at least 50 percent of California's estuaries, lagoons, and salt marshes have been destroyed by dredging and filling. Of the remainder, 62 percent have suffered severe damage from pollution. These startling statistics were reported in the journal *New Scientist* (24 April 1975) in an article which summarized a recent report of the California Coastal Zone Commission.

San Francisco Bay, perhaps the most unique and multifariously valuable part of California's borderland (former Secretary of the Interior Stuart Udall called it "the greatest single resource in this region") has been treated as a dumping ground and landfill site. Since 1860 more than 40 percent of the Bay's surface area has been filled for subdivisions and airports. Such extensive filling has probably grossly altered the marine ecology. The fauna in some areas of San Francisco Bay has been termed "depauperate" by the marine ecologists Joel Hedgpeth and Jefferson Gonor. The scientists suspect this was not formerly the case. For example, Indian shell middens discovered at various points around the Bay give evidence of a diverse and abundant prehistoric mollusk fauna.

Unlike many other human impacts, the filling of San Francisco Bay is not qualitatively a new thing. Over many millenia of stable sea level, substantial filling of the Bay would occur naturally because of the erosion of surrounding hills and inflow of remotely derived sediment from the Sacramento and San Joaquin River systems. Man has hastened the natural filling process by several orders of magnitude.

Ironically, some west coast marine geologists are concerned with a type of physical disruption much the opposite of what is happening in San Francisco Bay. This is perhaps the most basic form of environmental alteration imaginable—the shutting off of the sand supply to the open coastal zone. Unlike the broad, flat, stable Atlantic and Gulf coastal regions, where active sand transport from rivers out over the continental shelf has virtually ceased, the Pacific Border, dipping steeply into the sea, has a delicately balanced sand budget. Sand reaches west coast beaches primarily from streams, especially during infrequent floods. Recently scuba divers and observers at greater depths in submersibles have watched cascades of sand moving down California's submarine canyons. This transport, they believe, may be occurring on a massive scale, a steady sliding, slipping movement of bottom material from the shallow nearshore zone into the deep basins.

The scientists fear that dams on some west coast rivers are dangerously disturbing the sedimentary steady-state. At the mouths of southern California's small but seasonally active streams, the same problem occurs because of the dredging of boat basins, which act as unnatural sediment catchments. In short, much of the coast is starving for sand. If this problem is as severe as some geologists think it is, then many nearshore sand beds and beaches may winnow away in the currents and surf and disappear down the canyons. Only continuous replenishment with sand, which sometimes moves from major sources along the coast for a thousand kilometers, keeps the erosion from happening. If sand flow from the rivers is interdicted indefinitely, coastal erosion may make up the difference as the beaches narrow and the full force of Pacific winter storms reaches soft sandstone bluffs and formerly secluded dunes.

From Santa Barbara to San Diego, loosely contained within the gently curving arc of coast, lies the southern California Bight. Like its east coast counterpart, the New York Bight, this stretch of shallow sea is the most polluted area of the Pacific Border. Also, as in the New York Bight, southern California's marine pollution may be funneling into the deep sea. Here, however, a number of submarine canyons perform this function instead of the single giant conduit provided by New York's Hudson Canyon.

The main difference between southern California's glut of marine pollution and that on the continental shelf off New York is the dispersion of the waste materials. Huge centralized dumps for sludge and other solids do not exist off California. Instead, enormous pipelines carry municipal and industrial wastes directly out to sea. Some outfalls are more than ten kilometers offshore. Several pipelines serve greater Los Angeles. Orange, Ventura, and San Diego Counties, as well as industrial conglomerates, also have spiked large pipelines into the sea.

The huge sewer lines carry a gruel of suspended solids and dissolved organic and inorganic matter, some components inert, some toxic. Emerging on the sea floor, the wastewater is lighter than the cold sea water and the effluent plume rises until it reaches the thermocline. Here, however, in the manner of an atmospheric inversion, the sewer water becomes trapped, for it is denser than the surface layer of the sea. The wastewater plumes, millions of liters per minute, spread out along the underside of the thermocline like great stratus clouds. Noxious fallout in the form of precipitates on water-borne particles rains back to the bottom for many kilometers along the prevailing paths of marine currents.

The reactions of marine life to the waste discharges off California resemble those off New York. Evidence of fin rot disease has been found in at least thirty species of bottom fish from coastal waters off Ventura, Los Angeles, and Orange Counties. A type of flatfish known locally as Dover Sole, *Microstomum pacificus,* is the species most affected. At times the frequency of occurrence of fin rot and tumors in this species has reached 80 percent. Diseased fish are most common off the Palos Verdes Peninsula and have been caught from just off the beach to depths greater than 200 meters.

The awareness of marine pollution off southern California goes well beyond obvious fin rot in coastal fish. Despite the diffusion of marine wastes disposal and the physical and geological complexities of the area, more is known about fates and impacts of major marine pollutants here than in any other area of similar size on the United States coastal shelf. A large proportion of this emerging environmental knowledge has come from studies by scientists at the Southern California Coastal Water Research Project (SCCWRP) in El Segundo and Scripps Institution of Oceanography at La Jolla.

One of the less expected findings, confirmed recently after several years of work, is that much of the waste material entering the sea off greater Los Angeles comes out of the air, carried by dust particles or rain. Two classes of "hard" pollutants that are most common in the aerial fallout are organochlorines and toxic metals.

DDT (with its equally toxic derivative DDE) still contaminates the sea off California despite near cessation of this insecticide's use in 1971. Atmospheric fallout of DDT in the southern California Bight is now estimated at 1.5 metric tons per year. About the same amount flows into the Bight from the combined wastewater effluents, and still more comes in from streams which flow strongly after storms. Nevertheless the organochlorine influx has decreased sharply since 1971, when 19 metric tons of DDT reached this small, crescent-shaped corner of the sea from Los Angeles County's discharge alone. (Most of it was traced to a chemical plant which specialized in pesticide production.)

Progress indeed has been made since 1971, but some scientists worriedly point out that southern California's marine sediments are still loaded with DDT/DDE, an estimated 200 metric tons in the upper twenty centimeters of a sixty-square-kilometer strip off Palos Verdes. No one knows how long the poison will take to decompose, nor the full extent of its threat to regional marine life.

While the flow of new DDT is down, PCB contamination in the Bight remains dangerously high. PCB discharge in wastewater now exceeds that of

DDT by approximately three and one-half times. One other organochlorine, the potent carcinogen dieldrin, maintains an ominous presence in southern California's great flush to the sea. Wastewater concentration of dieldrin usually reaches 100 parts per trillion, an amount that is not at first startling alongside DDT or PCBs. But on closer examination, this amount is ten or twenty times higher than the greatest concentrations so far detected in estuaries receiving drainage from dieldrin-soaked agricultural land anywhere in the United States. Given the tendency toward biomagnification in marine food webs, such strong and narrowly focused injections of dieldrin into the marine environment near pipelines may present a serious cancer hazard to fish, birds, and mammals, including man.

An interesting quirk of pollution in the southern California Bight is related to the weather. Surface (river) runoff of pesticides, PCBs, and other toxic materials occurs almost entirely during the few stormy days of the year. Sudden injections of pollution reach the coastal zone, and these may produce intense local reactions which probably would not occur if the same amount trickled evenly into the sea throughout the year. No research has been done on the impact of such heavy seasonal dosage. The greatest effects might be looked for in small harbors.

Organochlorines affect marine life off California in the same ways as in the Gulf of Mexico. The phytoplankton which soak up DDT and PCB from the water are first hit almost instantaneously, endangering the tiny plant cells themselves.

Off the Pacific Border, phytoplankton commonly contain from one to several parts per million of PCB, DDT, and DDE combined. This is not as high as some organochlorine measurements in phytoplankton from the Atlantic (twenty-two ppm in the Gulf of St. Lawrence and greater than one ppm in oceanic waters far from land). Recent studies indicate that any cells contaminated in the low ppm range are well within the danger zone. The growth of one very sensitive species of diatom was suppressed by a cell concentration of only 2/10 ppm. Four or five other species were all strongly affected by five ppm and probably considerably less.

Experiments on several phytoplankton species growing in the same culture show that the more sensitive ones are weeded out when the culture is "stressed" with low levels of organochlorines. PCBs have been found more potent in this regard than DDT/DDE. Merely 100 parts per trillion (1/10 ppb) of PCB in seawater changes the species composition of phytoplankton communities set up in the laboratory. Although the diversity of the communities diminished as the more sensitive species succumbed, the overall "chlorophyll" level, and hence photosynthesis, remained about the same, indicating the hardier phytoplankters had actually increased in numbers and replaced those which had disappeared. Thus the effect of very low levels of PCB in the marine environment would probably be impossible to detect by crude chlorophyll studies, but might be very apparent to fish or crustacean larvae which depend specifically on one of the sensitive phytoplankters for food.

Biological oceanographers have found cases of declining phytoplankton diversity in areas of chronically high organochlorine contamination. They fear that changes in phytoplankton communities may have profound effects on food webs, even if oceanic photosynthesis remains relatively stable.

Higher up in the food web, organochlorine poisoning has hit California's fish, birds, and marine mammals. Disturbingly, the huge, invisible weight of DDT in the sediments off Palos Verdes has contaminated Dover Sole throughout this entire region to twice the level (five ppm) permitted in seafood by the U.S. Food and Drug Administration.

Gross evidence of fish intoxication by pesticides has been found in recent SCCWRP studies, and as in the case of killifish inhabiting an area of oil-contaminated sediment the tale is told by the liver, in this case, that of the Dover Sole. Chlorinated hydrocarbons are strongly associated with lipids, and DDT and related compounds concentrate to an overwhelming degree in liver tissue. Under extreme contamination, the liver becomes greatly enlarged from a proliferation of fatty material necessary to neutralize the organochlorines.

Livers from Dover Sole caught off the Palos Verdes Peninsula are measurably larger than those in the same species from other localities. In Palos Verdes fish with fin rot, livers were nearly twice the size of livers in healthy specimens from Santa Catalina Island, which served as a control area. This finding has led the SCCWRP scientists to suspect that fin rot is linked in some way to organochlorine contamination.

Another part of the SCCWRP study reveals that a wave of the remnant DDT off Palos Verdes appears to be migrating southward into Orange County waters. During 1975, the researchers found a fivefold increase in the concentration of DDT in Dover Sole off Orange County. Ruling out increased discharge of DDT in this area, they believe that the pesticide must be coming from the north. This, the report concludes hopefully, means that gradual dispersion of the awful concentration of DDT in Palos Verdes sediments is taking place. How long the process will take and how far the stuff will reach (Mexico?) before it essentially disappears remains a question.

Fishery quarantines due to high DDT levels have been occasionally imposed for some time off California. When DDT was heavily used, numerous catches (chiefly mackerel) were condemned by the FDA. One might suppose that a lesson was well learned, but sadly this was not the case. During 1974, decisions were made somewhere high up in the political wilderness to permit "crisis use" of DDT over widespread areas of commercial forest in the Pacific Northwest. This was done despite the fact, well documented in *Audubon* magazine, that safer and just as effective chemicals were available for the job at hand. A far wider and deeper crisis than ever imagined by the timber lobby is spreading with DDT on the submerged Pacific Border.

As in the Gulf of Mexico, predators of fish have been poisoned by pesticides in California waters, although mortality has been suffered primarily by the young.

Breeding on the Channel Islands off southern California, sea lions (*Zalophus californianus*), whose body burdens of DDT/DDE range into the hundreds of ppm, have shown an increasing incidence of premature births. Many of the short-term pups, which are born up to four months early, are unfurred. The pathetic little creatures lack normal muscular coordination; their breathing is irregular and they die soon after birth. Female sea lions which have given birth prematurely have organochlorine residues two to eight times higher than those which carry their young to full term.

California brown pelicans (*Pelecanus occidentalis californicus*), like their congeners in the Gulf of Mexico, have suffered a drastic decline in numbers. The major food of pelicans in southern California waters is the anchovy. In the late 1960s, extremely high levels of pesticides, primarily DDE (up to an average of 4.3 ppm in 1969), were noted in these small pelagic fish of the California Current.

The northernmost major pelican rookeries on the Pacific coast are found on Anacapa Island and nearby Santa Cruz Island, about 110 kilometers west of Los Angeles, and on Isla Coronado Norte off northwestern Baja California. From a total of 1,125 pelican nests surveyed at these sites in 1969, only a total of four fledged young emerged at the end of the season. Pesticide concentrations in intact eggs sampled from the breeding colonies averaged over 900 ppm. Eggs found broken (due to thinning of the shell caused by DDT/DDE) contained on the average more than 1,200 ppm.

Since 1969-70 the breeding success of pelicans has steadily improved. The pesticide level in anchovies has declined twenty-eightfold and that of pelican eggs ninefold. In 1974 the fledgling survival was nearly one per nest, although this was still 30 percent too low for population stability.

But the hope for pelicans on the Pacific Border to achieve that stability may be in vain. If continued application of DDT and other hard pesticides is allowed from time to time and place to place in the forests and croplands whose drainage ultimately reaches the irresistible southward pull of the California Current, there is no hope. The anchovies will continue to carry enough poison to assure the pelican's gradual demise, at least off southern California, and perhaps, speeded by growing foreign reliance on organochlorines, a wave of extinction will creep along the Baja and Central American coasts. The insidious toxic fallout will continue to contaminate everything from phytoplankton to the sea floor and its unsuspecting creatures. In devious ways, which appear imminent in the Gulf of Mexico, sublethal effects will envelop man himself.

The history of marine pollution by toxic metals has become well-known off California. Again, better documentation exists here than anywhere else in the marine purview of the United States. In addition, California scientists have made much progress in understanding biological fates and impacts of the metals, although more research needs to be done.

Within cylindrical cores of neatly laminated sediment from the Santa Barbara Basin is recorded a short, unhappy history of southern California's age of pollution. The record is not comprehensive. It omits, for example, the gaseous constituents of smog and most of the choking organic burden in sewage. In selected aspects, however, the sedimentary record solidly and soberly reflects the changing quality of the regional environment on land, in the epicontinental sea, and even in the air.

Mercury and lead are especially good indicator pollutants since they rapidly settle from overlying waters into the sediments. Mercury levels deposited in the Santa Barbara Basin began to increase about 1900. Lead concentrations began to rise steeply in the 1940s.

Oceanographers from Scripps believe that aerial transport of these metals forms a major pathway for contamination of the marine environment.

For example, an estimated 18.4 metric tons of lead is daily spewed into the air by internal combustion engines in the Los Angeles area. Like pesticides, metals in the air are brought back to earth (or sea) by rain and dust. Also, as in the case of pesticides and PCBs, atmospheric fallout appears to contribute about as much lead to coastal waters as do the combined wastewater effluents of southern California.

In the marine environment, lead seems to be one of the less threatening pollutants, at least according to the present rather imprecise ecological perceptions. However, anthropogenic lead is entering the sea off southern California at twice the rate derived from natural sources, such as erosion of ore deposits. Man's input of mercury into the southern California Bight is now equivalent to nature's. Both lead and mercury should continue to be monitored, and creatures near the top of their food webs should be checked for the deleterious (perhaps synergistic) effects these elements have on them.

The problem of mercury seems to be especially critical for pregnant humans, sea lions, porpoises, and whales. Unlike many kinds of toxic substances which are screened out by a biochemical barrier in the placenta, methyl mercury is known to get through and enter the mammalian fetus from the mother's bloodstream. The delicate fetal systems may be much more sensitive than the mother's.

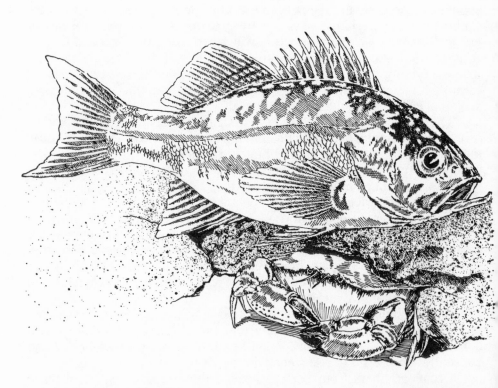

Black rockfish

Methyl mercury's terrible effects on the human nervous system first appeared in Japan and were traced to the eating of contaminated fish. The U.S. FDA has set a "guideline" limit of ½ ppm mercury in fish for human consumption, but the guideline is largely ignored. Large fish, such as tuna and swordfish, often exceed the limit, although some of their mercury burden comes from natural sources and arises from biomagnification high in the food web. In parts of Australia where shark is common fare, much concern has arisen over mercury levels up to three ppm in the most popular edible species.

Once again those at greatest risk are insatiable fish lovers, or more commonly poor people subsisting on protein they have caught or cheap shark picked up at the pier. Fish dinners a few times a month are unlikely to hurt anyone, but at least one article in a prominent medical journal (*New England Journal of Medicine,* Vol. 285, No. 1, pp. 49-50, 1971) has warned pregnant women to avoid regular consumption of fish with mercury contamination reaching even half that posted by the FDA. For comparative reference, the 1965 poisoning at Niigata, Japan, in which six persons died and forty-one others were maimed, was caused by fish with mercury concentrations averaging 1.0 ppm.

Unprecedented levels of another metal, the exceedingly toxic cadmium, have recently caused concern on the Pacific Border. Chronic cadmium poisoning in man results in kidney disease and bone degeneration. As in the tragic case of the mercury-induced Minamata disease, cadmium effects are known primarily from Japan. The strange malady known as *itai-itai* (ouch-ouch) disease begins gradually with pain in the joints. Eventually, however, skeletal damage results in grotesque postural deformities. The upper body becomes sharply bowed or bent double. Meanwhile, portions of the kidneys have been destroyed. In many cases these severe symptoms were linked to long-term consumption of rice containing approximately 1 ppm cadmium.

Recently, researchers from San Jose State College and Moss Landing Marine Laboratories have discovered consistently high levels of cadmium in plankton off Baja California. The excessive cadmium contamination was originally discovered in routine samples taken just south of San Diego. The measured values of the metal in the plankton proved to be up to three times higher than any previously sampled on wide-ranging cruises along the Pacific coast and between Hawaii and California. The new cadmium values off Baja also greatly exceeded those taken in earlier studies by other scientists in Atlantic and Caribbean waters.

The Moss Landing investigators sought to confirm their results. They took extra precautions in sampling, using a rubber dinghy which they rowed several hundred meters away from their ship in order to avoid catching flecks of paint and rust in the plankton net. They used nylon and plastic fittings in their equipment, except for brass net rings substantially coated with fiberglass.

Back in the laboratory the results were confirmed overwhelmingly. Almost all the samples taken south of San Diego contained more than 10 ppm cadmium; the values ranged up to 20.9 ppm. The high concentrations were not confined to nearshore waters either. Sixteen to 17 ppm were recorded 500 kilometers off the central Baja coast.

What baffles the plankton detectives most is the sudden jump in cadmium concentration just south of San Diego. If anywhere, peak values should be found near the major wastewater discharges from San Diego north to Palos Verdes. The huge effluents form the most conspicuous regional marine source of cadmium, totalling fifty metric tons per year. But calculations indicate that after mixing occurs in the California Current, fifty tons of cadmium would be diluted to normal levels in sea water before reaching Baja California. Furthermore, discounting the scientists' expectations, plankton samples off Los Angeles contained only 3.5 to 3.9 ppm cadmium.

The reason for the buildup of cadmium in the sea south of the border is currently unknown. Writing in the journal, *Science* (Vol. 190, 28 November 1975), the researchers who discovered this puzzling pollution phenomenon conclude: ". . . the plankton data do suggest that an extraordinary situation in regard to this toxic element may well exist off Baja California. The reasons for its occurrence should be investigated."

Kelp and other large seaweeds are also known to concentrate cadmium to excess. Values well into the parts per million range have been measured in kelp around the British Isles. In these cases the concentration of cadmium had been multiplied by several thousand times over that in the sea water.

Toxic symptoms from assimilated cadmium may soon appear in top marine predators such as sea lions and sea otters. Already, analyses of kidney tissues of these two creatures have revealed respective concentrations of 570 and 960 ppm of the metal.

There is a ray of hope here, however. A University of British Columbia scientist has discovered three separate cases of detoxifying enzymes which protect against the effects of cadmium. Once again the liver has come up with the life-saving formula. Heavy-metal-binding proteins called metallothioneins were found in livers of the grey seal (*Halichoerus grypus*), the Pacific fur seal (*Callorhinus ursinus*), and the Pacific rock fish (*Sebastodes caurinus*). The enzymes, moreover, are inducible. In experiments with rockfish, injection of cadmium chloride resulted in increased levels of metallothionein.

Such natural mechanisms of pollution prophylaxis in marine organisms are impressive. Perhaps similar properly designed research should focus on human subjects as well, although it is uncertain whether man's physiology affords him as much innate protection from hazards of his own making.

The final major marine pollution topic of interest on the Pacific Border is thermal pollution. A number of large coastal power plants have been proposed for the region. Some of these, such as the giant Diablo Canyon nuclear facility near San Luis Obispo, California, are faulted for more than mere discharge of hot water. California's earthquake-prone coastal belt makes nuclear power plants riskier here than anywhere else in the country. Unique thermal impacts on coastal ecology, however, are an already proven threat.

Kelp is especially sensitive to warming of the water and shows a marked cycle of "condition" with the seasons. Biologists and divers have long been aware that *Macrocystis* looks healthier in winter than during the summer. In winter, the blades are fresh-looking, relatively smooth and free of encrustations. In summer, the blades tend to be heavily encrusted; their edges are often ragged from grazing by animals.

Careful study, however, has shown that off the open coast of southern California, summer temperatures are actually ideal for the growth of the big sporophyte plants. *Macrocystis* reaches peak photosynthesis around 21°C. The poor summer condition is thus not a temperature effect per se, but seems due primarily to the onslaught of many canopy-dwelling animals whose activity is heightened by seasonal warming of the water. Usually the period of destructive grazing lasts from four to six weeks in late summer. Notably, however, between 1957 and 1959, unusually warm conditions lasted through much of the year. The results were devastating. Kelp beds nearly disappeared over wide areas, and they did not recover until the temperature cycle returned to normal. The magnitude of the loss produced a direct economic impact on the kelp harvesting industry.

Very large thermal effluents in the vicinity of kelp beds will alter the ecology, establishing warmer than usual conditions the year round. Near the large nuclear plants now in the construction or planning stages, areas of significantly elevated temperature (one or two degrees above the surroundings) will extend over dozens of square kilometers. With the boost in activity afforded even by such small thermal increments, the animals may well get the upper hand and eventually overwhelm large areas of kelp forest. If tampering with the underwater seasonality becomes widespread, sensitivities of the giant plants and their little known gametophytes may become even more pronounced in more northerly waters.

A few years ago when the electrical energy demand projections were doubling every ten years, some futurists predicted, perhaps overzealously, that by the year 2000 large nuclear plants would be built every ten miles along the California coast. Were such a thing to come to pass, the resulting network of heated plumes and patches on the continental borderland might create an environmental debacle. On a regional scale, the loss of kelp forest habitat for hundreds of dependent species could be classified an ecocatastrophe. Almost nothing is now known about these matters, and extreme caution should be exercised in considering large coastal thermal effluents.

In southern California, humans as well as kelp have begun to suffer directly from noxious creatures stimulated by artificial warming of the water. When a small thermal effluent from a power plant at Los Alamitos went into operation, stingrays and sharks from warmer southern waters migrated to the area in large numbers. Ironically, the Los Alamitos plant had been heralded as an attraction for people to enjoy warm water swimming and surfing. Instead the beaches were closed periodically while the undesirable and potentially dangerous creatures were seined out of the bathing area.

The sea off western North America appears vast, puissant, unassailable. It seems immutably large and deep and clean. Its ceaseless heavy whisper on the shore, the normal conversational tone of the water planet, seems as self-assured as ever. To a migrating Miocene tern, the glittering steepening swells near the end of its immense oscillatory journey looked then as now. To the sonar consciousness of once great pods of grey whales, the main features of the rugged borderland never changed detectably over a lifetime, although a leviathan resurrected from its watery grave every few thousand years might have noticed a slight, steady shifting of certain underwater landmarks.

These manifestations of permanence and continuance, however, are misleading. Rock and water will continue to behave as always, even when there is no living thing to notice. Most of what is beautiful and valuable in the sea, however, is created by the creatures which have evolved in the spaces between the waves and rocks, and which have developed wondrous dwellings and communities in the filtered sunlight.

The beautiful and valuable, vital and vulnerable places lie very close to the ocean's surface and to its edge. These sensitive areas, conspicuously the realms of the algae—from phytoplankton to giant seaweeds—have changed a thousandfold in the last fifty years. For a while the changes remained invisible, but their effects are now breaking out at all levels in the marine communities. The creatures of the Pacific Border must feel the changes in ways that can only be imagined approximately: a creeping paralysis in tiny green cells; a wet leprous itch or tumerous throbbing somewhere on a streamlined body; a premature slippage of fetal membranes, a gush of warm fluid, and maternal bewilderment on wet rocks above cold sea spray. These are the new environmental realities on the Pacific Border.

The Shores of Inner Space

It seems like a parody of a NASA launch, proceeding from an odd mirror-image perspective. Two humans are sealed in a small capsule poised above a blue abyss. There is an instrument check and a communications check, but when liftoff comes it is accomplished without fanfare. No countdown, just a harsh clanking as steel hooks and cables are unleashed. Then NEKTON, awash in the swells, scuttles away from the side of the ship.

The trip through inner space will be a short one, only six or seven hundred feet, but we will land on a small part of planet earth never before seen by human eyes.

I would be going far deeper than I had ever gone wearing scuba gear. From the submersible I would descend to country I had only imagined on previous surface cruises over the outer continental shelf. My eyesight would sift through darkening water and reach the remote sands far below. Travelling these plains and rimlands at the edge of the sunless deep would be comparable to visiting another planet, a world inhabited by exotic and beautiful beings, but one immediately lethal to human life unprotected by technological contrivance.

What follows are excerpts from a diary I kept during the Outer Shelf Benthic Surveys conducted by biologists from the U.S. National Marine Fisheries Service (NMFS) in July, 1974. As a guest member of the scientific team, I made two dives in the submersible NEKTON into the world of a submarine canyon at the very edge of the continental shelf.

11/VII/74 Thursday

We are several hours late departing Woods Hole. Finally everything is aboard and secured, including a couple of new batteries picked up at the last minute in town. The batteries are for the bright yellow submersible, NEKTON, which is tied down on the rear deck.

We finally leave Great Harbor about 5:30 PM. The ship is a ninety-five foot steel catamaran, decks bridged a few feet above the waterline. It is starting to go to rust but seems stable. The twin hulls step steadily through a moderately choppy Vineyard Sound. I can detect no sign of seasickness after eating a dinner of comfortable volume—roast chicken breast with rice and fresh peas.

Near sunset, southeast of Chappaquiddick Island, there is a whale. First we see spouts in the air—maybe ten or twelve feet high—then closer, slow rhythmic flaps of huge fins. Hard to estimate size (a few feet long?). The fins, one seen at a time, rise to the vertical, hold in position, wave gently for a second or two, then lower again without haste into the water. There is apparently only one large whale, but a smaller object seems to be in the water nearby (a mother and calf?).

The shadows of the wave crests are lengthening over the water. Nantucket is lost in twilight haze to the east. Martha's Vineyard is now a long, low, featureless inkblot on a rosy horizon, and I imagine the last whales on earth, resting on the summer sea near the islands which played such a large role in their destruction.

12/VII/74 Friday

A slowly brightening morning. The light begins bluish gray. Seas are still gentle, but now a definite underpinning of long-period swell is apparent. We are close to 100 miles south of Martha's Vineyard, nearing our station over the head of Veatch Canyon.

From my bunk, through the open door of the deck van, I can see a corridor of sea. Continually slipping sideways, it appears empty to the horizon, but then a shearwater flashes past very close to the ship. From the deck, just after sunrise I count a dozen sooty shearwaters and about that many small petrels. The sun is a few degrees above the horizon and casts an ethereal light, rouging the breasts of shearwaters.

We wait to have breakfast in shifts, and everyone becomes better acquainted. First names are easily learned. Dick is chief scientist. Under forty, he is a senior biologist with NMFS and one of the foremost diving scientists in the country. Joe is Dick's theoretician, technical expert, and aide-de-camp. He is also a biologist with NMFS, somewhat older than the rest of us, soft-spoken, and affable. Rounding out Dick's group are Cliff, Ken, and Roger. They are younger than the average on board, and are expert scuba divers and trained biologists as well. Around the lab they are known as Dick's dragoons. Cliff is not as mellow as the other two, but all three are eager for action, discussing at breakfast the chances for making hazard pay.

The submarine people, Rich and Jerry, are westerners with quiet drawls that stand out in this crowd of sharper New England voices. Both are easygoing; Rich is the more outgoing. They have the competent air of pilots, but in addition to their work for the corporation which leases NEKTON, both are professional geologists. Rich has a Ph.D. and a university position in Colorado; Jerry is finishing a Master's in California.

Ted is in the Ocean Engineering Department at the University of New Hampshire. Like me he is a guest scientist on the cruise. He is working on a scheme for ocean disposal of baled solid wastes from cities. The connection with the NMFS project is the possibility that reefs of baled wastes may attract large numbers of fish, but the idea is in its infancy. Ted has brought several small bales, about two feet high, to be placed on the sea floor by NEKTON. These prototypes will be marked with a pinger and Ted plans to recover them for study in a year.

The ship's crew of four, together with the vessel itself, are on hire from a charter company in New Jersey. Except for Arnold, the cook, the crew is barely conspicuous at breakfast. Tony, the captain, appears briefly, munching a bologna sandwich, and takes a cup of coffee up to the bridge. The others are Angus, very large with white curly hair and a strong Scottish accent, and

Ozzie, the mate, a tall, gaunt, and very quiet fellow.

Our first operation is to set a marker buoy to serve as a reference point in the diving area. This is emplaced in 600 feet of water on the east flank of Veatch Canyon, close to the rim. We are several miles seaward of the actual head of the canyon which cuts deeply into the continental shelf. A few hundred yards due west of the buoy it is 1200 feet deep.

A fairly detailed chart of the bottom, made by echo sounder, shows complicated terrain; there are several bluffs and promontories projecting outward from the canyon rim. Between these features, side canyons and tributaries run down the slopes toward the main axis. The chart recalls a topo-sheet depicting any typical small canyon system in the southwestern United States, but down there, with fifty-foot visibility, explorers will experience the equivalent of evening fog on a mountain trail.

Joe and Rich have the first dive. It is a reconnaissance trip to locate what the NMFS group terms "pueblo" habitat: steep-sloping ground, sometimes nearly vertical, composed of thick clay. Numerous animals, chiefly large lobsters, crabs, and tilefish, have dug or scoured burrows in the clay. The multi-pitted canyon walls, containing holes from the size of a quarter up to three feet in diameter, a strange face peering from early every one, resemble a weird cliff-dwelling community. Dick's team was the first to discover the underwater pueblos last year on the western side of Veatch Canyon. Their initial estimates make this the richest habitat on earth for lobsters. The present objective is to survey upper Veatch Canyon more thoroughly, documenting on video tape and film the types of terrain and all large fauna with potential fishery status. Depending on available time, submersible transects will also be run into several other canyons farther east on the outer edge of Georges Bank.

After two hours, Joe and Rich are back. The whole dive from launch to recovery has been fairly uneventful for this experienced duo. They do not find anything like the pueblo area they saw last year. It may be there, however. Just before coming up, they ran over some clay bottom at 650 feet. The next pair of divers should go deeper.

Joe puts his video tapes on the playback console in the deck van, and we watch TV footage shot within the hour directly below us. His most interesting sequence shows a squid, perhaps a foot long, holding and eating a small flounder. Fastidiously, it works steadily around the anterior part of the fish, cuts the head off and drops it, then with its unseen beak begins the meal in earnest.

Video tape footage does not seem to give the sharp definition of film. Joe is ribbed as being a reject from the *Undersea World of Jacques Cousteau*. But the footage obtained does allow good general survey work and immediate appraisal of the results.

Wind comes up strongly in the afternoon. White caps are all over the sea so Dick and Jerry cannot be picked up for an hour after surfacing from their afternoon dive. Their first attempt at docking failed, and NEKTON's rudder was damaged slightly when it bumped the ship hard in a swell. They bob like a waterlogged cork, as the ship maneuvers to stay fifty or sixty yards away. Finally the dragoons reach the sub in a Zodiac rubber boat. They attach lines from the ship, and secure their hazard pay at the same time. Dick has been badly seasick, and Jerry is close to it as they crawl out of NEKTON's stuffy, smelly interior. The sub had gone through some 90° rolls at the surface.

Shearwaters are gone with the shifting weather; the petrels, however, stay with us. They are the only obvious life to be seen out over the windy wastes. I begin to feel seasick after indulging in a late afternoon beer. I do not make it to dinner—pork chops and potatoes. In the evening with a very heavy stomach I feel a bit morose, anticipating a week of unpleasant weather, instability, and fasting. Trying to fall asleep against the rolling of the catamaran, I wonder where the petrels go on stormy nights.

13/VII/74 Saturday

Awake feeling better—even hungry. The sea has calmed noticeably. After a merazine pill for security, breakfast is fine. We are steaming back to the marker buoy. Our nocturnal strategy is to run about ten miles in on the shelf to reach a depth of about 350 feet where the ship can anchor. Unlike other kinds of cruises I have participated in, the submarine work is only practical and safe in daylight. The captain thinks the anchoring option saves more fuel than if we were to drift and/or maneuver all night.

Sometime during the night a shark was hooked on a rope line set out by Dick's trio. Ozzie, the tall mate, says he hauled it in about two in the morning. It is a male blue shark, seven or eight feet long, slender and smooth. It hangs over the side, lashed by the tail to the winch arm. Claspers flap gently with the ship's motion. The snout and one large, lidless eye are awash. The other eye has been torn out by the hook.

On station near the marker buoy. Dick is disturbed by the dead shark, pronounces it an eyesore (to groans of disgust), and orders it cut loose. Ken and Rich have the first dive. They will carry the first of my two test racks to the bottom.

My objective and reason for being here is to study the accumulation over time of a host of stationary animals. These are known collectively as fouling and include sponges, coelenterates, bryozoa, barnacles, tunicates, and many others. Fouling is pestiferous, adds to a ship's weight and drag in the water, and impairs the function of other long-term underwater equipment, but it is also extremely important as browze for fish, small crabs, and lobsters. Dick is interested in fouling from the standpoint of total productivity of the canyon area. In a year's time we hope to recover my test racks which hold an array of six-inch ceramic and wooden panels. Counting and measuring the sessile creatures which have settled on the panels will give qualitative and quantitative estimates on an important section of the marine food web never before tabulated on the outer shelf.

Ted's project has been coupled to mine, quite literally. It seems efficient to tie his small bales of trash to the bases of my racks. Then both experiments can be emplaced at the same time by the submersible. His pingers are tied to the racks, and small incompressible marker floats which will remain about twenty feet above the bottom are also attached.

The first test rack goes down without a hitch. On the bottom Ken and Rich maneuver it a few hundred feet to a small ledge on a steep canyon slope at

720 feet. In the midst of pueblo habitat, this is the first fouling/bale-dump station. But communications are somehow scrambled; after they return with video footage, it is clear that they left the rack upside down.

Communications between the sub and the surface are accomplished with hydrophones. The unit on board the ship operates through a transducer which is hung over the side during a dive. Sound waves carry voices directly through the water, which is a far better conductor than air. A good human shout would carry at least ten kilometers down there.

It is my turn to dive. Jerry is the pilot. The sub is about ten feet long, shaped like a fat torpedo, with an entrance hatch atop a small conning tower amidships. I crawl in first. As the scientific observer I will crouch or lie on the floor, the belly of the fish. It is padded with a foam mattress and is comfortable enough. My views are through a number of Plexiglas ports in the nose. I can see forward, down at an angle, up at an angle, and to the sides. Jerry sits on a small stool directly below the hatch. I can see his hands covering the controls, but his head sticks up just out of my sight into the conning tower. He has a 360° view through a circlet of ports.

Even before we are unleashed from the ship, we begin very badly by dropping the second test rack. It is gripped insecurely and slips out of NEKTON's claw and goes down through blue water surprisingly fast.

In less than five minutes we follow. We are about a hundred feet from the ship when Jerry begins to bleed the buoyancy chambers, and we settle slowly beneath the swells. The exact moment of submergence is hard to gauge.

The surface waters within are a brilliant blue in the cool crystal sunshine. Even looking downward, I see a blue radiance as if from some diffuse but powerful source of light hidden in the depths. The water is full of soft-looking particulate matter of assorted sizes and shapes. One of Dick's assistants refers to this as sea snot, but by certain geometric subtlties and movement, some of it declares itself to be living. I can see swimming salps up to a foot long, comb jellies, and an occasional pulsing medusa. Several of these true jellyfish, bell-like in shape, are motionless with tentacles extended radially. This behavior is known as "sink fishing." The creatures resemble living plankton nets falling through the water. They are small, however, and the invisible turbulence of our descending bulk startles them into swimming with bursts of contractions like a rapid blinking of the eyes. Another species, considerably larger, pulses continuously like some futuristic metronome. It is transparent and trails long graceful tentacles.

We are passing 300 feet and the view toward the surface is a fading blue green; below is deepening dusk. Jerry switches on an outside light which reveals the water to be filled with organic particles; the scene recalls a snowstorm on a perfectly still evening. Only here the flakes are falling gently upward past the viewport as the sub descends.

Steadily, gently falling, we approach 600 feet and pass it. Still no bottom. Now in the soundless world outside all seems dark beyond our artificial spray of light. An occasional slender salp weaves across the path of the lifeless flakes like some wandering comet among a sea of regimented stars, having strictly linear motion.

Then there is a brightening, yellowing reflection of our lights from below, and we can see bottom from perhaps 25 feet above. This is similar to the way the bottom materializes to the eye on a deep scuba dive. Uncertain shapes resolve into mounds, depressions, sandripples, then small organisms as we settle on a sloping, sandy plain 675 feet down.

Jerry taps the depth gauge to make certain of the depth, then reports our landfall to people in a different world far above us. They acknowledge with staccato voice and matter-of-fact attitude. Our gentle impact seems to have raised a thick cloud of silt, but it clears fairly quickly. The organic snow is still in the water. Now that we are stationary, this image seems normal, and the big flakes move with a noticeable horizontal component, carried with a slight current across the sandy plain.

The terrain in view shows no major relief, but it is incredibly pocked and dimpled and mounded. Castings and small animals are everywhere. There may be hundreds of macroscopic fauna per square meter. Small anemones, sea pens, and worm tubes reveal the largest numbers. On the side where our lights shine through the soft precipitation, the visibility is perhaps twenty-five feet. On the unlit side of the sub is a scene reminiscent of a moonlit night. Details are blurred, but without the lights one seems to see a longer distance over a dimly reflecting bottom of vague shapes and shadows.

The outside thermometer indicates 10°C. The walls of the sub are now cool and moist, beginning to condense moisture from the air. It is very quiet as we watch the placid stands outside. The psychological depths are less placid, however, and I feel a tinge of fear. One quarter inch beyond the curving steel wall the silence presses very heavily. If anything should cause a cracking of this metallic egg we would not survive. At 675 feet the pressure is sufficient to crush head sinuses and collapse our rib cages. Even if we had time to reach the scuba tanks and regulators, stowed with the spare batteries behind Jerry's seat, safety is highly unlikely. We would have to wait for the sub to flood in order to open the hatch. Then a rapid pressurized ascent from this depth would probably trigger a fatal case of the bends.

Jerry is quick to answer my first "what if" question. He flatly states that submersibles are safer than airplanes and especially cars. NEKTON has five separate ways to get to the surface in the event of entanglement or systems failure. These even include dropping the whole propeller assembly if necessary.

We are moving slowly now, a couple of feet per second up the gentle slope. We will try to find the dropped test rack. After consultation with the people on the surface, we have estimated its general location. Our lights play over two lobsters, a few meters apart. They are hunkered down in shallow holes. I wonder what sensory impressions they record as our monstrous craft with lights glaring, faces staring, and motor whirring passes by.

I try taking some video footage of the general terrain and animal life as we travel. The whole area seems relatively flat. There are a few of the tall, sand-dwelling anemones, *Cerianthus*, and then some large crabs appear, running about as fast as we are moving. They are wary and stay on the very periphery of bright visibility. These crabs seldom reveal their full form. They assume variable shapes because of white reflecting surfaces on their anterior shells and claws, which glow brightly. A branching soft coral of the *Al-*

cyonium type has an almost fluffy look, its polyps fully extended. A single small starfish represents its kind out here in the open spaces.

We have stopped to search for sonar targets. The sub's gear is not extremely sensitive, but Jerry thinks the rack will provide a fair reflection if it is not in a gully or behind a ridge. Through the lowest viewport I see a spurt of movement, very close to the sub. It is a slow eruption, a mini-volcano of sediment produced by the inner rumblings of a hidden worm.

I try to imagine the incredible biomass that would appear if the sediment were to be winnowed away to a depth of a few centimeters. The communities in the soft bottom are intricate in time and space. Ecologists exploring marine bottoms have found that only a handful of species, one or two kinds of bivalves and worms, can colonize firm virgin sand. Arriving as tiny larvae, these are adapted to penetrate the tightly packed, nearly sterile grains. They loosen the subsoil and begin to contribute organic matter to the surface layers. These pioneering species are filter (or suspension) feeders, drawing their nourishment from the overlying water column.

Gradually other creatures arrive and settle in the softening bottom. Organic matter deepens; associated bacteria and protozoa enhance its nutritive value for a variety of deposit feeders: worms with elaborate gills, sipunculids, burrowing crustaceans, bivalves, echinoderms, and many predators. Eventually local invertebrate cities coalesce into a megalopolis of tubes, tunnels, and inhabited interstices stretching for many kilometers. These delicate communities, a living veneer within the solid shelf, may take years to develop.

Moving again. Several hot prospects on the sonar have turned out to be boulders, no doubt dropped here by melting ice from the vanished glaciers which would once have been visible across a dry continental shelf to the north. The extensive deposits of clay, which now form the areas of pueblo habitat, were also brought here by rivers of glacial meltwater.

One of the boulders is in a shallow depression. The surface of the rock is covered with anemones and hydroids. It looks like a flower arrangement, the former being carnation-like, the latter, a species of *Tubularia*, looking like exotic daisies with pink centers. The *Tubularia* are the biggest I've seen, over ten inches long.

The most striking aspect of the scene is a dense population of tube-dwelling polychaete worms. The tubes are greenish, about an inch high and slightly thinner than soda straws. They project straight up from the sand around the flowery boulder so thickly they resemble a close-cropped lawn. They stop abruptly within a meter from the base of the rock. There must be a commensalism here if not a symbiosis. The presence of the rock and its coelenterate populations provides some essential component, possibly edible fallout, in the ecological niche of the polychaete.

Jerry has a very strong sonar target which means an object is nearby, and we head toward it. I try to pierce the outer darkness ahead and to the side. We have been close to the 600-foot level for some time, up on the flat shelf east of the canyon. The visibility is better than when we landed, here perhaps forty feet.

Jerry says, "It's a ghost trap." We cruise up to it and see two lobster traps tangled together in a snarl of rope. There is no connecting line to the surface. The traps are wood, and both are old and battered, with numerous slats broken or missing. They no longer pose a threat to lobsters and crabs. Ironically they are providing a lair for a large hake, *Urophycis*, which seems to have hollowed out a shallow crater beneath the slats. Jerry maneuvers the sub so I can get good video shots, and the fish turns to face us continually.

We have been underwater for two hours. There is no sign of the missing rack and the search seems fruitless. My legs are horribly cramped somewhere back in the video recording gear around and behind the pilot's seat. There are no more good sonar targets in this area. We decide to surface, and notify our friends 600 feet overhead. Just before signing off, we hear a rapid series of clicks on the sonar phone, then another series, then several more. Each burst only lasts two or three seconds. Jerry thinks they may come from nearby dolphins.

There is a hiss of compressed air into a ballast tank. The upward movement is very slow at first, before the air begins to expand. From a few meters above the bottom I can look back and see the single eight-inch wide track of our base runner extending across the sand into obscurity. Then we are again in a grayish murk, with uncertain depth perception. A greenish tinge shows in the upward-directed port at about the 500-foot level. The view grows gradually in brightness until at 100 feet all is blue around us. The undulating surface is visible from 50 feet below, and we rise rapidly, breaking through to the world of sunshine and turbulence. I think of the still, dim world far below and of its abundant creatures which have never known the vibrant blue swells. Most of them are tethered for life to the edge of the continent in the near-darkness and cold.

It is quite rough and the sub rolls and tosses smartly. They have already launched the Zodiac in case of problems. We can see it with a crew of grinning dragoons following us closely. But there is no trouble, and I do not even get seasick. We come alongside the ship under our own power and are picked up in ten minutes. On deck there are greetings and camaraderie for the novice diver (me), a little patronizing, but enthusiastic.

The clicks we heard just before starting for the surface probably came from pilot whales. A group of five or six of these fifteen- to twenty-foot creatures was sighted from the ship about the same time as we were using the phone. But the communicator at the surface heard nothing, so the whales were probably focusing their biological sonar directly on NEKTON. Hearing unusual noises, including Jerry's voice, coming from the bottom, they were "eyeing" us with sound waves through hundreds of feet of dim water.

At night small petrels, apparently blinded by the bright lights nearby on deck, twice flutter into my open cabin. They are docile and utter no sound when I catch them and release them into the night away from the light.

14/VII/74, Sunday:

After breakfast the shark hunters butcher two small blue sharks for their unimpressive jaws and tails. The carcasses are tossed over the side and sink, oozing oil and blood.

On the morning dive, Roger and Rich go deep into the canyon, partly by mistake. We monitor their descent on the sonar phone, expecting to hear of touchdown at 650 or 700 feet. But a deep current apparently carries them past the projected landing site. Rich reports passing 800 feet, with no bottom, then 850. Finally, NEKTON settles onto coarse sand and gravel at 920 feet.

The submersible's nominal limit is 1,000 feet. According to the leasing company, it has been tested empty, hanging from a cable, to three times that depth. Rich thinks it would be safe to 2,000 feet.

On this dive, an extensive and spectacular pueblo area is located on a canyon wall, centered near 750 feet. Rich thinks it is continuous with the clay zone where the first test rack was placed, but the two divers do not relocate the experimental site in this extremely jumbled and confusing country.

Their video sequences are superb. Huge lobsters and tilefish, *Lopholatilus chamaelonticeps*, flicker across the screen. One of the lobsters is backed into a large, crumbling, fifty-five gallon drum, lying on its side. The creature's tail may well be touching the back of its cylindrical home. Its claws bulk big as hams. The animal's frontal aspect half fills the mouth of the drum, and Dick estimates that this matriarch may be seventy-five years old and weigh fifty pounds.

About noon a loggerhead turtle appears for a few minutes around the ship. It has several accompanying small fish that cannot be seen clearly (pilot fish?). Ozzie, the tall thin mate, has a hunting bow on board with an attached reel and line and some heavy-duty fishing arrows. He materializes fully equipped, ready to let fly at the turtle, but is dissuaded by a chorus of dissenting yells. He shrugs and dematerializes.

Ted and Jerry make the afternoon dive. They spend their bottom time in another search for the dropped test rack, now disgruntledly referred to by everyone as "the trash" or "the garbage." They fail to find it.

Late in the day we meet an offshore lobster boat, a thirty-five or forty footer from Beals Island, Maine, operating out of Rhode Island for the summer. She is "manned" by two young men and two young women. They are intrigued by the submersible on our rear deck. A brief shouted conversation results in Dick and Ken going across in the Zodiac with two six packs of beer and half a bottle of scotch. In return we receive a dozen and a half fine lobsters. Ken, Roger, and Cliff are from Maine, and they know how to treat lobsters. The cardinal rule is to boil them in sea water, not fresh water, not even salted fresh water. With the Maine trio's guidance, Arnold the cook prepares a lobster extravaganza for the evening meal.

After dinner and before sunset we watch with interest a number of ships on the horizon. More and more appear, headed in our direction, and it becomes clear that they are part of the foreign fleet. From the hazy northeast they gather like huge seabirds on the water. They appear to concentrate due north of our station at the edge of the shelf, and we are forced to make our nightly run to an anchoring place well to the east.

At night I stay on deck for a long time watching what appears as a city of lights stretched across several kilometers of horizon. It is a city of low uniform height, and it is a city in motion. The lights crisscross, wax, and wane toward the unseen horizon. The fleet must consist of at least 40 ships, possibly representing several countries. They are working over the innermost head region of Veatch Canyon, perhaps six to eight miles from the shelf edge.

It is somewhat unnerving to go to bed. The ships twinkling and milling around in the night are huge compared to ours. I imagine a small petrel eyeing a horde of albatrosses in a feeding frenzy. I would like to see what the bottom looks like after the fleet has finished its massive assault on the sands below.

To the entire community of bottom organisms in the path of the heavy trawls, the effects must be worse than saturation bombing by a fleet of B-52s. The wonderful, galleried structure of the sea floor is ripped into a slurry of silt and shreds of soft animal tissue. A choking pall of mud rises high over the survivors, then slowly settles to smother fish eggs and broken sediment dwellers which provide a short-lived feast for roving scavengers.

All the delicate patchiness, the symbioses and commensalisms, the complex spatial patterns, which play an essential role in the mass synchronous breeding of sessile animals and which develop only after years, are destroyed.

Is it possible for oceanic Edens, such as Georges Bank and the Gulf of Alaska, to become man-made deserts as have areas of the Middle East, where once continuous forests and a sylvan fauna ran over the now barren hills? We do not know for sure how resilient and persistent the undersea communities will be. Widespread natural catastrophism is rare on the outer shelf. The last time the Georges Bank region suffered an environmental impact across its entire breadth was during the Wisconsin glaciation. If very wide areas of the continental shelf are continually scraped and stripped of the natural sediment texture and structure, key organisms may disappear, great fisheries may decline to the vanishing point, and no one can predict how long it will take for recovery to occur.

15/VII/74, Monday:

When I get up and emerge on deck, there are already several watchers. They are not looking at the fishing fleet which is still out there, but rather at Ozzie, the mate. He has strung up still another shark and is shooting blunt practice arrows into it with his powerful bow from a few feet away. At this range he seldom misses, and he jerks the arrows back out with the attached line. The big fish's sleek side is full of dripping holes. We are offered turns, but no one takes him up on it. Ozzie has on an imitation buckskin vest, complete with fringe, which he often wears. After this incident he is dubbed "Natty Bumpo" or "the sharkslayer" by one of Dick's team.

I am paired with Rich for the morning dive. This will be the last trip devoted to the now infamous garbage. We have given up trying to find the dropped rack, but will concentrate instead on finding our way back to the first one which was placed in a pueblo area at 720 feet. This will be a practice run, anticipating the hoped-for recovery next year.

We plan to begin well north of the area in which we expect the rack is located. Our initial descent is too slow—an underestimate of weight—and Rich suspects we might be carried far afield by currents. We resurface from 300 feet and rendezvous with the Zodiacians, who hand Rich twenty pounds of lead through the open hatch. This maneuver may be slightly against regulations. Rich advises me not to shift my weight while the hatch is open. A wave breaking into the sub could send it down through blue water like a stone.

We resubmerge without incident and go down more quickly now through the layers of deepening twilight. The transition to grayness comes more rapidly than on my previous dive, but overhead the green glow lasts until we are well below 400 feet. We reach bottom with a noticeable bump on a moderate slope at 650 feet.

During our last moments of free fall we see a rope to our left, arching upward out of view. It is apparently part of a lobsterman's long-line gear, but we do not see a trap. Rich immediately heads down slope to find the 720-foot contour along which we will run to the garbage.

We are running down over a uniform sandy bottom with abundant small sized fauna and lots of scallop (*Placopecten*) shells. The slope seems to steepen as we descend. This may be the most prominent and northerly of the tributary canyons which were plotted using the ship's echo sounder. Through the forward port I see what looks like a worn fragment of a large, sculpted Renaissance fountain, or a giant oyster shell about four feet long and three feet wide. This object has a shallow concavity, and it is encrusted with *Tubularia* and anemones. The latter are all light colored and fairly small, except for a giant of a distinctly different species which looks like a fleshy Venus's-flytrap. Its crown consists of two rounded lobes. The longest measurement across its top must be ten inches.

Rich compares the elaborate anemone roost to a huge fossil bone, part of some titanic creature's hip girdle or a whale's shoulder. My other thought is that this object may be a large flake from an old algal reef such as occurs off North Carolina. But we agree that we really cannot positively place it.

We are now on the 720-foot contour, starting south over sandy bottom on perhaps a 20° slope. For what seems a long time we cross sand whose surface is dominated by a small pinkish shrimp and shell-less hermit crabs. Broken scallop shells, with an occasional one whole but empty, are common through an area extending several hundred meters along our course.

Rich says he has seen several squid ahead, jetting out of our path. Suddenly on our brightly lit side and slightly above us I see two of them, swimming side by side, silently matching our pace. Their slender, highly reflecting bodies seem almost artificial from a few meters away. At this distance their organic jet propulsion seems to move them without obvious flexion or effort. Seemingly watchful and curious, they proceed in perfect formation like an imagined escort of UFOs.

This is the closest I have come to squid free in the underwater world. I have seen them in aquaria and a few times while scuba diving, when they seemed far more wary. Once for a split second I glimpsed one flying, or rather gliding, through the air on a stormy night at sea.

Woods Hole scientists have confirmed the belief that *Loligo peleai*, a common shelf species of squid, remain near the bottom during the day and rise into mid-water regions to roam actively in small groups at night. These small wolves of the nighttime sea track prey with short, forward-pointing tentacles, stalk close, then flick out their long pair of tentacles in a lightning movement and pull in the victim, usually a small fish. Like wolves, they seem to sense the fitness of their prey. There is a distance factor in their hunting strategy which conserves energy. They ignore creatures which keep more than a meter away from their cruise path.

Some of the daytime observations of squid are even more interesting. The students of squid behavior report that the animals routinely find buried prey such as crabs or shrimp in a sandy bottom. The jet-propelled hunter, which looks as if it never stands still, has the patience to remain motionless for minutes above the sand. It watches for the tiniest movement. Then using its siphon, the squid blows away flurries of sand and will even dig with its tentacles to secure its dinner.

Most intriguing of all is a systematic search pattern described by Dr. Frank Bowles of the Marine Biological Laboratory at Woods Hole. The squid moves back and forth in lawn-mower fashion, producing a constant agitation of the sand with the siphonal water-stream. This motion appears to have the same function as an owl's hunting call, which is to startle prey into a slight revealing movement.

I am not sure what species of squid we are looking at; neither is Rich. We decide to stop to see what the pair that has been shadowing us with such precision will do. They stop also, but only briefly. Then still together, they turn and move slowly into the darkness.

The density of life here is fantastic; we are still cruising on a sandy, moderate slope. Small fish and crustaceans are everywhere. One of the commonest bottom fish is four to six inches long, cigar shaped, with vertical gray bars and scattered iridescent blue green spots on its back. Small and large flounder have become common; they are up to fifteen inches long. Lobsters and crabs occur in depressions, or stalk ghost-like at the edge of the gloom. Several times we see squid again—hovering and watching, but none follow us.

We begin to find indications of clay habitat. Firm-looking lumps and small hummocks emerge through the mantle of sand here and there, and I see the first tilefish, a small one about two feet long. The first dun-colored clay areas are only perhaps thirty meters or so across, and then we are on sandy substrate again. The exposed clay bottom has a different fauna from the sand. Gangly galatheid crabs seem tied to the clay. Pink-hued shrimp and the shell-less hermit crabs largely remain on the sand. But there are more lobsters in the clay.

We have followed the 720-foot contour generally south, but at times our course has swung from nearly west to nearly east, and we have been able to recognize the terrain plotted from the ship. Having gone around a large westerly trending terrace, we seem to be coming back toward the southeast. The terrain is steepening noticeably. On the downhill side to our right, the view is truly mysterious. Our lights are swallowed up within a few meters. A small crab moves downslope, becomes lost in the shadows. How far is it to the bottom of the canyon, or tributary, or whatever else is represented by this abyss, which has remained in darkness for thousands of years?

The clay terrain has become extensive and more rugged. The first big tilefish appears, and now a huge lobster faces us from a cavern in a clay bank. Ahead are several more tilefish. Bulky phantoms, they are shy and move out of our way. Most swim rather slowly, but we see one four-footer suddenly sprint and dive headlong into a barrel-sized opening in the clay bottom, as if into a foxhole under fire.

This is pueblo country. It is very steep overall, with a chaotic topography of ledges and eroded clay cliffs. It is dominated by giant tilefish and lobsters and is so spectacular that one does not readily focus on the smaller biota. But burrows are everywhere and most of them are occupied. The galatheid crabs are abundant, as are rosefish up to eight inches long. A conspicuous sedentary resident is a polychaete with a medusa's mop of long slender tentacles, snaking and writhing in every direction over the bottom.

We continue to move slowly along the rugged, plunging clay slope and Rich suddenly says, "I can see it." He clicks on the sonar phone and sings, "We found the garbage."

NEKTON coasts to a halt beside the rack, and I see it is upside down and listing slightly to one side, as shown in the earlier video tape. In this position the pinger is shielded over nearly a whole hemisphere by the upturned bales of waste material. The acoustic signal is probably smothered to a great degree. We decide to try to turn it over.

The mechanical arm of NEKTON is manually controlled, simple to operate, but requires a lot of muscle at this depth. Over 300 pounds per square inch presses inward on our hull, and the metal rod with the claw on its end has a cross-sectional diameter of three-eighths of an inch. Using a rope and pulley device, Rich forces the arm to extend, and I manipulate the rack outside with the claw. For a minute the job looks impossible, but then I try pushing the contraption down the slope. Slowly, it turns over into the upright and correct position. The float line is still partially tangled around the top of the rack. However, the marker float rises about twelve feet above the rig, and we decide not to fool with it further.

We report success to "Mission Control" and they want us to come up, but Rich and I argue for a brief survey of the bottom surrounding the garbage site. Permission comes back through a very short chain of command, and we drop slowly downslope.

Below a vertical wall at 740 feet we come upon an incredible sight. NEKTON's bright lights shine on a cliff face alive with nimble, jumping figures. They are large shrimp of a type I've never seen before—hundreds of them, about five inches long, reddish brown with a bright white stripe down each side. The long delicate antennae flick incessantly. The movement of the creatures is electric in its nervous intensity. They are probably startled to their innermost synaptic reflexes by the impossible glaring lights which confront them in the darkness. The water here seems very clear. There is a totally alien air to the visible world revealed by the sub's lights—dim ridges and slopes of soft talus, with candy-colored shrimp dancing on the near cliffs.

It is a place of superlatives. Beyond and below the hallucination of shrimp we enter a zone of large caves. From one of them, a lobster emerges, facing in our direction. It is huge, perhaps bigger than the one filmed by Roger, which was hanging out of the fifty-five-gallon drum. Its antennae semaphore at us, and then without hesitation, the creature lumbers right down the little hill below its burrow to the ledge where we rest. I can see its tail through the lower forward port, and its anterior body through the side port as it rears up against the sub. Rich can see its antennae playing over the conning tower ports in front of his face. Incredible! Is it totally unafraid? An animal with no natural enemies, and no fear of the unknown? Is it just attracted to our lights with the witless arthropodan fervor of a moth? Rich immediately says the latter conjecture is invalid because no other lobsters have done this. He thinks it wants to see if NEKTON is good to eat.

After about a minute of close inspection, the lobster leaves us. Without haste it walks downhill into the dark, the Duchess of Veatch Canyon, off to inspect another part of her demesne. We would love to follow, but are called urgently by the voices from above. They want us to surface now.

As we lift off with infinite slowness, Rich turns off all the lights, inside and out. As our eyes adjust, the visibility starts to expand slowly, and a silver gray world begins to widen below. Twilight at noon. It is hard to tell how fast we are rising. According to the sub's gauge, we must be forty feet above the bottom now, and have a deceptively clear view of unidentifiable landforms in irregular patches of light and dark. We seem to be caught in a current that was not noticeable on the bottom, and we glide gently through fluid dusk over a landscape that appears as if it could be miles below. Rich thinks our drift is up the local tributary canyon since we remain in sight of the bottom for so long a time.

About seventy-five feet from the bottom, all visual contact with the terrain below us is lost. We are again in free-fall upward through gradually greening grayness. In the clear water near 100 feet, Rich releases some air, slowing our ascent, and we accompany a universe of tiny scintillating bubbles toward the surface. This is a stunning sight in the open, intensely blue surface waters, an utter contrast with the pressing gray of the nether layers.

The sudden turbulence truly seems a two-dimensional phenomenon, almost a surprise after two and one-half hours of perfect calm below. We pitch and roll toward our rendezvous with the ship.

This was my last direct contact with the bottom world on the outer continental shelf. Further dives were made by others into Veatch Canyon, as well as two others, Hydrographer and Oceanographer Canyons, which form prominent notches on the shelf edge farther east. The bottom which was explored at these latter two sites featured broad areas of gravel and fields of boulders, indicating a relative proximity to the prehistoric glaciers. A rich fauna inhabited these rockfields as well. There were fleshy crimson anemones, *Tealia*, like flowers sprouting from gray stones; five-armed and multi-armed starfish were far more common than on the softer bottoms I had surveyed.

On one transect to the 1,000-foot level in Oceanographer Canyon, Joe and Rich were accompanied by a school of perhaps seventy-five spiny dogfish, a small type of shark. The dogfish milled around NEKTON in every direction, careening in close to the sub's observation ports, and out again beyond the field of view. Their excited but confused behavior recorded on Joe's tapes contrasted sharply with the cautious watchfulness and military bearing of the squid I saw. But Joe made the point that the behavior of bottom animals observed from a submersible with brilliant lights and making strange noises may not represent normal or natural behavior. Joe's feeling was that the divers should sit in one place for a while, adjust to the gloom, and possibly use infrared snooperscope equipment or something similar which the animals would not sense.

During the remainder of the cruise, I continued to share the discoveries of the others through their video recordings. But nowhere was there encountered a diversity of bottom topography and abundance of life to match that in the pueblo country of Veatch Canyon. If portions of the outer continental shelf are to be preserved as unique and valuable natural areas, this wondrous submerged canyonland should be in the first rank. Nevertheless in many of the views of exotic bottom country and creatures, there was a depressingly familiar intrusion, and I kept a litter log.

During twenty-two short trips to the bottom on the outermost shelf and its canyons, I and others saw and recorded: dozens of beverage bottles and cans, numerous one-gallon paint cans, seven fifty-five-gallon drums, tangled wire and pieces of heavy cable from fishing gear and ships' rigging, assorted sections of nylon netting, the entire cod end of a trawl, endless tangled rope, myriad pieces of cardboard, a sunken radar reflector, and numerous ghost traps, some made of wood, and some of plastic-coated wire.

That certain lightweight refuse from ships reaches bottom quickly was vividly recorded by Ken. From NEKTON one afternoon he filmed shrimp fighting over what looked like lifeless white worms. On closer inspection, these turned out to be strands of leftover spaghetti which the cook had jettisoned only an hour earlier, after lunch.

The shrimp's bounty was probably quick to disappear, but much of the rest of the trash scene on the outer shelf made me think of a very dirty city park. More appropriately, the defilement of this rich marine wilderness 150 miles from the nearest city is akin to creating a rubbish dump in a remote and spectacular area of a national park. When one considers that our view of several tiny tracts is probably typical of a vast portion of the continental shelf, the equivalent prospect is the finding of junk through forests, in clear streams, strewn across meadows, and up to ledges and remotest crags—in the mind's eye, distributed haphazardly over the entire face of a Yellowstone, Yosemite, or McKinley.

Hardly questioned in the wardrooms and boardrooms, dumping from thousands of ships creates a litter problem that goes beyond aesthetics: oil, toxic chemicals, and plastics kill marine life, from mammals, birds, and sea turtles down to fish larvae and the tiny free cells on which everything depends. Even marine research institutions are guilty of routine dumping at sea.

On the last evening of the cruise there were more small petrels than ever around the ship. We may have drawn these birds from hundreds of square miles of ocean. When the cook appeared with the day's trash and dumped it over the side, they came in to the calm lee of the ship like pigeons, and proceeded to dabble and dip daintily for meat scraps amid the styrofoam cups, PVC and polyethylene wrappers, waxy cardboard milk cartons, and aluminum cans.

Sea lion bull

World Without Summer

For at least several million years, with perhaps a brief respite or two, marine world at high latitude has been controlled largely by ice. Frozen seas and glaciers were apparently dominant features in the far north seven million years ago in the Pliocene. Before that, the record skips back more than 30 million years, simply because no samples of arctic sea floor sediment have yet been taken for these eons. But marine geologists, working from a unique research vessel, the drifting ice island T-3, have recently come up with some early and surprising slices of Arctic Ocean history. In long cores from the deep sea floor were the abundant remains of warm water phytoplankton, their tiny immutable skeletons under the microscopic spotlight testifying to an arctic sea once mild and teeming.

This early organic Arctic lasted many millions of years from late Cretaceous time into the Eocene, but at some time during the missing 30 million years between the Eocene and the early Pliocene, winter gained the upper hand. Except for what paleoclimate specialists believe was a very long and warm interglacial period between 2.7 and 2.4 million years ago, most of the arctic sea has remained perenially ice encrusted and ecologically restrained.

This is not to say that ice conditions have been static, however. The ice is in constant motion, shuffling and eddying like the cloud masses in a huge, slow storm pattern. Biologically, there is life and structure and movement, but survival demands nearly inanimate patience in darkness beneath meters of ice, or sheer hardiness beneath centimeters of blubber. From algae to mammals, very few species represent their particular kind here, and the food webs are lean.

Below the sea ice in winter, microscopic golden green cells wait for the return of light. Several species of diatoms actually live within the lower 30 centimeters of the ice. Others grow attached to its lower surface. The diffuse grayness gradually brightens through the early spring and finally triggers an explosion of cell division. For a few weeks productivity leaps to match that of months in milder seas. During the height of the hidden bloom, myriads of amphipods, small shrimplike crustaceans with flattened sides, migrate up from the dark bottom to graze these fertile underfields in inverted concert with the caribou moving through lush June tundra.

On the arctic shelf large seaweeds are rare. They cannot tolerate the ice-scoured shallows; neither do they grow in water deeper than about ten meters. Deep in the world without summer a strange marine vegetation takes over on suitable bottoms of shelving-rock, cobbles, and even small pebbles. All these surfaces are covered with a layer of fleshy, living crusts. There are a number of species, but the biology of this unique forest is almost unknown, for these environs have been glimpsed by biologists only in the past decade.

The dominant crustose algae range far down rocky underwater slopes eighty or ninety meters below the surface in the dim, silent cold. Scientists have not yet reached these depths for direct visualization, but they speculate that this plant life may have striking, special adaptations for life in the poorest light and perennial cold (about -2°C). On the fringe of hostile inner space, these small cushiony creatures seem close to the realm of exobiology.

In the larger rivers of Alaska's North Slope—Canning, Sagavanirktok, Kuparuk, and Colville—which flow from the Brooks Range to the sea, adult arctic char, *Salvelinus alpinus*, and their developing eggs are confined through eight dark months below the ice in deep, spring-fed pools. The eggs themselves are protected from even the most extreme freezing conditions, for they remain within the coarse gravel of the stream bed, sustained by slow subterranean flows. Found only in the Arctic, char are large streamlined fish, closely related to trout and salmon. With the thaw and breakup of the ice, the surviving adults and larger juveniles return to the sea to forage and fatten until the next late summer run to spawn and overwinter. Also in the spring, about the end of May, the fry emerge into the elemental turbulence of a river half in the fluid state, half in the solid. Many of them are swept out of the densely populated spawning gravels and distributed for many kilometers along the streams. They remain fresh-water creatures for an average of four years before the anadromous urge brings them down to enter the circumpolar feeding grounds of the arctic continental shelf.

South of the range of the char in a system of milder streams and seas, the salmon live similar lives. Pacific salmon native to North America comprise several species. They range from the Bering Sea to northern California, although some of their ocean migrations reach Japanese coastal waters. Atlantic salmon from eastern Canadian rivers seek rich oceanic feeding grounds off the west coast of Greenland.

Widely scattered in time and space, taking their cues from the advance and retreat of solar radiation and ice, are the most conspicuous inhabitants of the black and white wilderness. They are the marine birds and mammals. But even these creatures, which are superficially independent of the cold, must accommodate their lives to the rule of ice.

The Arctic pack ice covers an area of about 10 million square kilometers. In the polar sea the average thickness of ice is three to four meters. The permanent or multi-year ice sometimes extends inward over the continental shelf, and in winter it abuts the seasonal coastal ice. Powerful winds and currents force the closing of leads, or open channels, and newly forming ice in such places is heaved above and below the surface into pressure ridges. The submerged portions, or keels, of pressure ridges extend as deep as forty-five meters and scour the shallow sea floor as the pack ice shifts and jostles nearly continuously.

The pack ice is in constant, complex motion. The ice island T-3, with its small military and scientific outpost, began its manned journey in 1952 near the North Pole. It has drifted thousands of kilometers, circling the Beaufort Sea twice in great slow gyres. Since 1970 it has spun out across the Canadian Arctic toward Greenland. The open channels, or leads, including extremely large ones up to 500 square kilometers in area known as *polynas*, also move

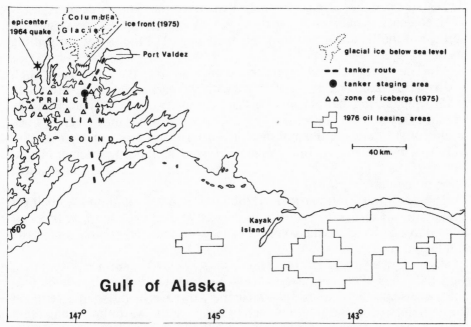

Northeastern Gulf of Alaska: Prince William Sound and environs, including prospective offshore oil field.

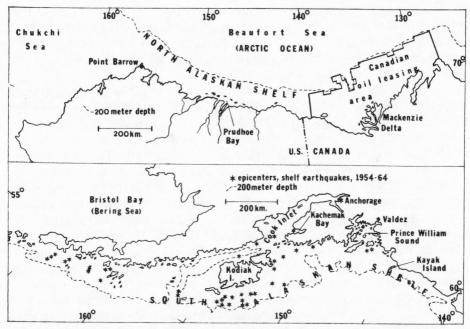

Coast and Continental Shelf of Arctic Alaska and Northwestern Canada; and South Alaskan Coast and Continental Shelf, innermost Aleutian Islands to Yakutat Bay.

through the packlike streaks of open sky in overcast. The ice cover is never total. Recent estimates suggest that even in winter, between two and ten percent of the Beaufort Sea remains open as part of the system of shifting leads.

In late spring, the ice along the shore and over the continental shelf begins to break up and move offshore with the permanent pack. From late June to September, the cold, sere shallows lie open for miles off places such as Prudhoe Bay and the Mackenzie Delta. However, winds may push big floes around on the outer continental shelf all during its open season, from the end of July to early October. But summer below is an illusion, a sleight of sun. Endless days of light, sifting through thinning ice and, for a time, dark water, bring no perceptible warmth.

South of the Arctic proper, in the Gulf of Alaska and on the shelf off northeastern Canada, the ice is less pervasive, but even here, at times, it looms large and impacts the affairs of marine life and (potentially) man on the continental shelf.

Drifting icebergs, which bulk much larger below the surface than above, plow the sands of the continental shelf. Northeast of Belle Isle, Newfoundland, side-scanning sonar has shown iceberg furrows on the shelf, averaging thirty meters wide and over six meters deep. Some were three kilometers long. In Alaska, this phenomenon is probably confined to the shallower portions of fiords, since icebergs are rare on the Alaskan outer shelf, but the tremendous ice plows may have reached far south on the Pacific Border in the past when glaciers swooped in many places to the open coast.

An iceberg, scraping and scuffing across the shelf, calls to mind the action of huge modern fishing trawls. Disruption of sediments and the sedentary community is similar, but the damage icebergs do is not as comprehensive. A crab would probably outrun one, and the floating ice does not actively seek out the most productive places.

Icebergs are spawned where glaciers meet the sea. These sites are often at the heads of deep fiords, especially on the south coast of Alaska, and in the turbid depths along a plunging frozen cliff occurs another manifestation of the ecological rule of ice. Slow but widespread melting of the glacial front far below the surface causes fresh water to rise buoyantly. This initiates an upwelling as sheets of sea water are entrained or pulled from the depths with the fresh. These plumes may arise from hundreds of meters down and bring significant amounts of deep regenerated nutrients to the near-surface algae.

Finally, the ice and climate in boreal and arctic regions bring an intense seasonal pulse of runoff from the land into the sea. For months, virtually constant marine conditions exist along the frozen coasts. Then suddenly come immense inundations of fresh water, silt, and organic matter into the waters of the continental shelf. Organisms in the way must be ready to accommodate themselves, take what advantage they can, or die.

Ecologists have long been intrigued by the relationship of biotic diversity to latitude. As one proceeds from the tropics toward the poles, a fairly steady diminishment occurs in the numbers of species of animals and plants both on land and in the sea. While there are some imperfections in the pattern, due to overlaps in biogeographic zones and migrating species, the extremes which are represented by an equatorial rain forest versus tundra, or a coral reef versus a boreal or arctic estuary, are very apparent.

In the ocean, biological samples collected over broad areas have indicated that the variable abundance of species is based largely on the stability of physical conditions. The simple inference that warm surroundings promote high diversity and cold the opposite is thus not strictly correct. Only in the last decade, vastly improved techniques for remote sampling and direct viewing via submersible have shown that the frigid, dark, but utterly constant deepsea floor rivals the tropics in its diversity of animal life.

It seems then that many species evolve gradually and coexist in places of long-term environmental harmony and equilibrium. Here biological rather than physical factors control the ecology. Scientists use the phrase "biological accommodation" to describe such ecosystems where life builds upon life in a concentrated welter of organic economics. Food webs become wide and hugely intricate. Resources are diversified. Natural communities assume great stability. Should one prey species diminish unexpectedly, perhaps because of disease, predators have five more to rely on.

By contrast, the diversity of life decreases with a progressive incidence of environmental disturbance. To live exposed to sharp and broad fluctuations in temperature, salinity, sunlight, and available organic matter is extremely demanding of organisms' energy reserves, protective mechanisms, and staying powers. Perhaps the key concept here is predictability. Creatures of the northern shallow seas must be able to survive many unexpected contingencies. And the forces exerted by climate and ice are not the only physical disruptions.

In the summer, a surprising and totally unpredictable factor governs marine communities in the nearshore zone from the Gulf of Alaska southward. Enormous drift logs bound in the surf and batter wide swaths through beds of mussels and algae. In the Pacific Northwest this is believed to be a major mechanism providing clearings for the renewal of growth, comparable to reforestation after wind or lightning damage in a forest.

Even earthquakes, which are commonest along the south Alaskan shelf from Prince William Sound to Kodiak Island, disturb the marine ecology. The great Alaskan earthquake of Good Friday, 1964, raised beaches and intertidal clam flats two or three meters, stranding the clams on some parts of the coast, and *tsunamis*—huge ocean waves caused by earthquakes—swept uncountable tons of soil, rocks, trees, and a few smashed boats, buildings, and other artifacts into the sea. What effects earthquakes have well off the coast down in the hidden galleries of the continental shelf is uncertain.

The adaptation of life to the harsh, unpredictable zones of the earth's surface is termed physical accommodation. Communities in the places that are difficult to live in are far less stable than in the tropics. Food webs are sparsely structured. Any given species relies on relatively few sources of food, sometimes just one or two, and a loss of one species can have serious repercussions, bringing down a tier of others like a house of cards.

The world without summer is understood less well than any other marine environment. The first detailed natural history of a marine invertebrate (a small clam) in southern Alaska's Prince William Sound was published as late as 1973. The lives of most subtidal marine creatures along this coast, not to mention the Arctic, are still little known.

Warm Life in a Cold Sea

T hrough the long days of short summer, the ocean rim of northern North America hosts one of the most spectacular assemblages of birds and mammals on earth. This combination of migratory and resident animals is more diverse than in the Antarctic. The creatures are large and exotic. Like the remaining megafauna of the African plains, some species, such as walrus and the eider, form herds and flocks that roam seasonally past wide and seemingly bleak horizons. Others are solitary or form small groups. These include the world's only seagoing bears, the sleek furred hunters which dwell along the edge of an unparalleled algal jungle, and the huge albatrosses from the south which in summer soar nearly to the Arctic Circle. Although not generally abundant and spottily distributed, the warm-blooded communities of the continental shelf from the Gulf of Alaska around the top of the continent to the Gulf of St. Lawrence represent the last of the wild Pleistocene, the "Age of Mammals" which is about to come under the total rule of one species.

The exotic creatures of North American seas have persisted longer than their ponderous counterparts on land, but they have diminished drastically in numbers during historical time. Certain fabulous creatures of the northern shelf have already disappeared. The last flightless great auk, the "penguin" of the north, died on some treeless rocky island near Iceland in the middle of the last century. This last bird may have succumbed unnoticed, but along Canada's east coast, multiple thousands of its kind were once clubbed by sailors for food and sport, eaten in the egg, and near the end cut up for fish bait.

In the Bering Sea and Gulf of Alaska, Steller's sea cow, *Hydrodamalis gigas*, probably disappeared around the same time as the great auk. Believed to have weighed ten tons, this wonderful animal formerly ranged at least as far south as Monterey, California. Some modern researchers speculate that this giant kelp-eating manatee had a special relationship with the sea otter, which once also ranged along a vast stretch of coast around the North Pacific.

The sea otter, *Enhydra lutris*, itself was nearly made extinct. The animals are now found in what biogeographers call a disjunct distribution. As of December, 1974, the northernmost established population off California was in the kelp off Sunset Beach, Santa Cruz County. Occasionally, individual otters have been seen farther north along the California coast, and new breeding colonies may develop. However, at present 1,700 nautical miles separate California's sea otters from their nearest naturally established kin in Prince William Sound, Alaska.

A recent census of sea otters puts the California population at somewhat over 1,600. Over an immense Alaskan range, extending far out along the Aleutian Chain but not touching every island, the known northern population comprises about 120,000 animals. Experts in comparative anatomy believe that the California population may be a separate subspecies, a judgment based mainly on variations in skull characteristics. If the experts are correct, the small southern population is unique and endangered wildlife.

The Alaskan sea otter still lives in pristine wilderness. In the absence of hunting pressure exerted by man, these mammals thrive. Their lives are bound to great stands of seaweed, and several of the significant factors in their ecology are touched upon in the following scenario.

Off an outer island in the Aleutians a large female sea otter nuzzles her tiny pup and a moment later dives into a dense leathery fringe. Two meters below the surface, she angles outward and pushes through the edge of an algal curtain and continues padding silently down. The vegetation hangs straight in the water beside the animal, a visual barrier, a comforting presence. Outwardly the hazy gulf seems about to shout of vast apprehensions, but today there is no ominous chatter of orcas out toward the Aleutian Trench. The silence is as pure as the clear frigid sea, and the graceful animal is all ease as she reaches a scrubby bottom and slides under the weeds hiding coarse gray sand and rocks.

Three hundred meters above the level of the sea, a young bald eagle, still in dirty brown plumage, surveys a world of water rolling from the far horizon through an undulating algal reef to a nearby beach of rounded stones. Beyond the beach the land begins to rise, past low hills toward a mounded mountain dribbling summer streamers of snow like whipped cream on a volcanic pudding. A small flock of eiders bobs on the waves just off the dense algal canopy. Earlier the eagle stooped once at them, but the ducks arched into a swell and were gone. They reappeared fifty meters away along the algal fringe, opposite the two otters, and the eagle climbed again into the sky.

The bird can see the otters clearly. When the mother dives the reasoning circuits in his small brain stutter over the possibilities. He is immature and very unsure, however, and he makes a wide circle.

Fifteen meters below the surface, the big otter weaves over a dim forest floor. Her flank brushes a boulder, and the fur leaves a small swirl of microscopic bubbles hanging in her wake. Suddenly breaking into a small open lead from the outer sea, like a clearing in dense woods, the otter startles a foraging eider. The duck backpeddles in the water, its feathers ruffling with the unexpected movement. It turns and disappears with furiously pumping legs toward the surface.

Half concealed under a dead algal frond is a large green sea urchin, doughnut-sized. Using a stone the size of a coffee cup, the otter bashes the urchin with a sure, light touch. Cracked in several places, but not quite broken open, the prey is scooped up and the predator turns toward the canopy.

As the otter begins its upward climb, precisely retracing its descent, the eagle commits itself. Its cautious path is not a straight drop, but a long shallow glide toward the small mammal which is half exposed in a coarse woven matrix of vegetation. Descending, the bird seems to move faster and faster. He sees the small pup twist fitfully in the fronds. Thirty meters out, sensing success, the swooping eagle begins to brake, tail turning down, wing muscles tensing for a slow strike in this uncertain terrain.

The lithe, one-and-one-half-meter body of the female otter pushes through the choked, softly-lit canopy, and then she emerges into harsh, cloudy-brightness beside her cub. In a gust of explosive flapping, the eagle comes to a standstill two meters away, treading air with flexing talons. With a harsh hiss the otter throws herself on her back over the pup. Despite an open mouth and muscular paws in the air, she too seems vulnerable, her languid physique unsuitable for close, brutal combat. Her size is enough. Within seconds it is over; the big bird rises with heavy wingbeats that briefly and rhythmically airbrush small water sectors in the weed mass directly below.

The otter slides to one side, places her baby on top of her abdomen. Then she arches to the other side and picks up the cracked urchin from the dense fronds where it was dropped at the moment of surprise. Placing it on her chest, she picks it apart slowly, sucking with relish at the innards.

Within historical memory the sea otter ranged from the northern islands of Japan through the Aleutians and down the North American coast to Baja California. Now only remote remnants of this immense range are occupied in the Soviet Kuril and Commander Islands, the Aleutians and southern Alaska, and a small isolated section of the central California coast. Recently small numbers of sea otters from the Aleutians were transplanted to Oregon, Washington, and British Columbia waters.

Based on recent studies at Amchitka Island in the Aleutians, a hypothesis has emerged concerning the sea otter's control over the local ecology of kelp and other large algae, together with its associated animal community. Off Amchitka the large sea otter population (twenty to thirty animals per square kilometer of habitat) is estimated to consume annually at least thirty-five metric tons of prey organisms per square kilometer. Sea otters have catholic tastes in seafood. Their known prey ranges from fish and crustaceans to sedentary abalone, and even to deep-burrowing clams, but sea urchins are one of the staples.

Off Amchitka and its neighbor islands, urchins are scarce in depths shallower than twenty meters. The only places where the spiny creatures may be seen in any numbers are in deep cracks among the rocks, and even in such refugia few reach a large size. Where the urchins are rare, kelp and other algae form an almost continuous vegetative cover near the shore. In depths of fifteen or twenty meters, two canopy levels often occur, one at the surface and one a meter or two above the bottom. The diversity of animal life in the amber jungles is higher than on open bottom.

In another group of islands separated from Amchitka by 400 kilometers of open water, including some deep ocean passes, the situation is very different. Around this group, called the Near Islands, there is an almost continuous carpet of sea urchins in the shallows. They reach a large size, nine centimeters in diameter. With their five-tined central mouths pressed against the bottom, they graze like fat, bristly caterpillars, and they seem to be primarily responsible for the distinct lack of conspicuous algae below the intertidal zone. In the Near Islands sea otters were completely eliminated by Russian fur hunters in the late eighteenth century. Breeding populations of otters have not yet returned, and now scientists think that this may account for the great difference in the marine communities around the Near Islands as compared to Amchitka.

At times, feathered divers take some of the otters' largesse. Eiders and other diving ducks are now known to reach impressive depths. Along the coast of Norway, biologists have documented them on the bottom between twenty-five and fifty meters, feeding on worms, crustaceans, and in particular certain kinds of fish eggs which form benthic mats. In such deep water, the birds may be in a hurry, for they gulp sand and gravel along with the fish eggs. Off Amchitka Island, eiders are known to take urchins as well; generally, however, these are small, and the birds' poaching probably has little effect on the mammals' food supply. Also, birds are probably limited to foraging in relatively open water because of poor maneuverability and perhaps an avian weed claustrophobia.

Where the sea otters consume tons of urchins, the seaweeds are lush and thick. This fact leads in turn to speculation that the otters were important to the survival of the giant kelp-eating sirenians. After the pogrom against the otters, the algal forests may have deteriorated, and the sea cows starved. Large stands of algae enhance the local marine productivity, species diversity, and community stability. In the otter's fiefdom, there are many more fish than over urchin-scoured bottoms. Fish-eating harbor seals move in and coexist with the otters. Even bald eagles are more common on islands where the kelp zone is healthy than where it is barren.

Eagles in the Aleutians subsist to a great extent on fish. Several recent observations at Amchitka prove that the fierce birds catch live sea otter pups when their mothers leave them at the surface to dive briefly for food. Typically the eagles wait on shore, watching from a high perch, then swoop down on their prey when the coast is clear.

Unlike seals and whales, sea otters are insulated by a layer of air trapped beneath fine, dense water-repellent fur. This, plus a high resting metabolic rate, provides comfort in frigid surroundings. They have no blubber. The creature's wonderfully valuable fur nearly caused its extinction, and incidentally provided the stimulus for the early explorations of the Alaskan coast by Russians. At its peak the sea otter hunt extended to southern California. To pursue the agile creatures in their kelp-girt realm, the Russian captains employed (most often forcibly) Aleuts with their *baidarkas* (equivalent of the Eskimo kayak), and transported them as far as the Channel Islands off Santa Barbara.

In winter sea otters can be affected adversely by severe freezing conditions. This happens nearly exclusively to the extreme northern populations in the Bering Sea. If prevented from reaching open water and food, the otters quickly die. Like some seals, they seem to become disoriented away from the edge of the sea. After rapidly advancing ice fronts have cut off all the cracks and channels to safety, living sea otters have been found wandering in an emaciated condition several kilometers inshore on the ice. Others have been found dead.

Sea otters have been called "tool-using animals," although what this implies about their level of intelligence remains unclear. (Are they smarter than dogs?) In the Aleutians, sea otters remain close to the security of the nearshore algal blanket. They seem almost never to dive below twenty meters, even though the abundance of urchins and other tasty food increases markedly just below that depth. In California, however, some observers report that they commonly reach thirty meters and deeper. The algal forests thin out below twenty meters, and fear of the sudden focus of a sharp-pulsed sound pattern and the rush of huge predatory shapes may govern the creatures' behavior, for orcas are more common around the Aleutians than off California.

The sea otter stands as a fragile symbol of warm-blooded life in the northern seas. In Alaska, the sleek creatures with their wiry whiskers are tied precariously to the long, narrow band of kelp that traces the contours of a wild coast at the inception of rapid development. In California, the otters exist solely at the sufferance of man. Unprotected by law, they could be exterminated by abalone fishermen in a few weeks, but the abalone saved would be scarcely noticeable. Large abalone have become rare on the entire coast, not just where there are small enclaves of otters.

Sea otters are as vulnerable today as they were in the decades of the great hunts, although today the greatest danger is likely to come from sticky patches of floating oil. Its fine fur matted and gummy, the insulating air layer diminished or lost, an oiled sea otter dies of numbing cold, the same fate suffered by most oiled birds.

The thin line between life and death in the northern ocean is further symbolized by the continental shelf itself, whose foreshortened growing season and lean food web rule the lives of all large marine creatures here. During the high arctic summer, reliable mammalian navigation and foraging is possible only on the shelf, and during the rest of the year the ice is thinnest there. The largest arctic whale, *Balaena mysticetus*, the bowhead, and even its Eskimo pursuer are primarily shelf creatures.

Named for its tremendous arching skull, the bowhead is the only large whale to remain throughout the year in the Arctic. Each spring the whales, which reach twenty meters or more in length, migrate along the northwest coast of Alaska. They stay very close to the shore ice, and lazily follow the northward melting along the continental shelf.

The bowheads commonly move singly or in small groups of two or three. Sometimes one will be accompanied by a small flock of white belugas, toothed whales resembling large porpoises. At times, the northward migration is halted by unbroken ice, and numerous whales gather and play, awaiting the opportunity to travel on. At such times, Eskimos, who are exempted from the International Whaling Convention, catch as many as they can use for their subsistence needs.

Although the voice of the bowhead remains unrecorded by science, Eskimo hunters have heard it, apparently coming through the ice of open water. They describe it simply and exquisitely as sounding "like a guitar playing inside the water."

By June, the bowheads of the western Arctic round Point Barrow and disappear along the arctic shelf. Nobody knows where they go. They reappear at Point Barrow again in September, traveling the other way, just ahead of the southward-moving pack ice. Some of the big adults lag behind the rest and risk entrapment, but the soft-voiced giants are built like icebreakers, and they have no dorsal fin to get in the way. Where there is no open water, they have been seen crashing up through new ice over a foot thick in order to breathe. In the fall, the bowheads disappear into the Chukchi and Siberian Seas.

According to information gathered by the whale conservationist Scott McVay, the overall population of bowhead whales in the western Arctic is between one thousand and two thousand. A separate population of bowheads also exists in the Canadian Arctic, but there have been very few recent sightings. It appears that despite the cessation of commercial whaling for bowheads more than fifty years ago, they have not recovered significantly.

In the summer, migratory gray whales and orcas sometimes appear along the northwestern Alaskan coast. In addition to the bowhead, the only true whales of the Arctic include the beluga and the near-mythical narwhal, *Monodon monoceros*, the unicorn of the sea. When mature this elusive toothed species is only four to five meters long. Except for anatomical knowledge of beached specimens its biology is practically unknown.

Besides the whales, numerous seals of several species, sea lions, and walruses inhabit the shallow northern seas. Like the whales, most of them vocalize underwater. Some of these acoustic adaptations appear devoted to echolocation, but the marine mammalogist G. Carleton Ray thinks seals also stake out territories with their underwater warbles, siren tones, shrieks, and roars. At times recordings made beneath the ice reveal a pandemonium. How territorial boundaries are drawn with sound or communicated to others, however, remains to be deciphered.

Alaskan coastline

Much of the scientific study of marine mammals has been phenomenological. For example, captive seals apparently can fall asleep underwater, although how this accomplishment serves the animals in their natural environment is unclear. In the same vein, we are intrigued but left wondering at the soulful singing and the alien psyche behind the play of whales: the benign play of the southern right whale, which teases and tickles its baby with a big strand of kelp, and the apparently sadistic play of orcas, the big-brained cats of the sea, whose bloody games of catch with young seals and sea lions have been documented recently on film.

Even the physical mechanism behind the sound production of most whales is unknown. What voice box produces the ocean-spanning, 150-decibel bursts of the great rorquals? The cetologist Roger Payne, in a March, 1976, lecture at the University of Hawaii, described these leviathan shouts as having a "stupefying intensity . . . the listening equivalent of placing your head a yard behind a jet engine at full rev." Some biologists believe rorquals may receive even very faint sounds by amplifying them through resonance in their large chest cavities. Sperm whales may be able to focus their chatter through an acoustic oil-lens in their heads. Such explanations behind the phenomena however, are mere speculations at present. How tragic if something wonderful should become apparent when it is too late to save its living source.

There is still so much to be learned here, so much incredible behavioral content and adaptive context in the world of sea mammals. It seems somehow imperative to understand the sleeping seals and singing whales. If man is to explore the ocean from within, he will have to strip away his terrestrial biases. Our free fellow mammals in the sea perceive the realities of our shared planet far differently than we. We cannot afford to lose their eyes and ears and voices.

The continental shelf of Alaska and the Arctic remains the last stronghold of marine mammals around North America. It is almost as important as a reservoir of seabirds. The marine environment of the far north is as fragile and subject to long-term damage as the tundra and alpine zones. Nearly every life linkage is essential; survival margins are slim; nothing is wasted. The old Eskimos knew this, but they were leaner folk than those who follow them on the frozen shelves and stormy gulfs with oil rigs and factory ships. To preserve the remaining sea otters, the seals, and the whales in their rightful places; to assure the perpetual return of eiders, guillemots, and the great albatross, the entire northern marine ecosystem must be protected with scrupulous care.

The Last Underwater Frontier

T he salmon moved into the waters of the continental shelf sometime during the short night. Although it traveled as part of a small group, the fish did not have the instinct of a tightly schooling species. It was powerful and fast and its behavior sprang from an urge of the species, channeled through individual motivation.

It now sensed several new things. The pattern of turbulence from the surface swells had become slightly less regular, as if the ocean currents were being compressed, flattened by the shoaling sea floor. In the early light, the clarity of the water seemed slightly reduced over that of previous days, back beyond memory in the open North Pacific. There was another memory, though; hauntingly it played in the fish's brain. It had not faded; it seemed stronger now and flowed from the sea with each respiring gulp, and entered the hidden channels of olfactory nerves. The taste of home teased and tugged the lithe spotted swimmer toward the distant coast.

Within sight of snowy peaks, a scattered array of ships churned heavily in leaden swells. Most of the vessels trailed thick, taut cables, which angled into the water. One ship dwarfed the rest; it had a strange shape, and it did not move. It lay on the water like a primitive caricature of the human figure, a body with no arms, but with legs represented by a long split extending into the stern. Cleaving gently into this rectangular Y-slot of protected water, one of the smaller ships was entirely enclosed, and within minutes began discharging its cargo of fish. Nearby, below, the salmon felt the throbbing of many powerful engines, but somehow it did not encounter a trawl.

Nearing the coast, the fish began to find patches of drifting ice. About the same time the waterborne odors proliferated and became stronger. Humic and resinous tastes of bogs and forests reached into the sea in thousands of fluid zephyrs and tide-wafted tendrils. If these had been visible they might have resembled the streams of yellow pollen flowing in the air above thousands of square kilometers of dark evergreen hills. But if the individual odors and combinations of odors in the water could be portrayed as colors, there would be an almost infinite variety with minute degrees of shading. Within the streamlined head, the fish brain was sorting these stimuli with a finer accuracy than the human eye deals with the many shades of color.

Beneath a small drifting ice field, there was a sudden change. The light seemed dimmer, and the fish's olfactory world began to distort. The creature struggled to hold its level of awareness in the presence of new cloying odors in the water. Beneath a thin film of old brown oil trapped under the ice, the bewildered salmon swam erratically; questing back and forth, it attempted to restore its former perception of place and direction.

Before anesthetization was complete, the fish emerged from under the ice and passed as if through a curtain into unadulterated sea. Slowly the chemical fog cleared from its head.

Along the coast, the searching fish found more and more of its kind. At entrances to bays and fjords they swam excitedly in large numbers, adjusting to the forces of strong tides and freshening water.

Recognition came swiftly and surely with the ebbing tide. Late on a still evening, the fish followed many others into a gradually shoaling sound with a surface like a dark mirror. The lack of normal turbulence in the water as well as the ebbing tide saved many fish in the rear echelon of the run. They felt the strangling vibrations of the others and tasted the secretions of fear flowing down toward them in the tidal current.

The remnant of the run turned and swam along the huge curving gill net. In the half-light they were close enough to see drowned diving birds hanging limply and many trapped fish struggling with failing muscles, gulping and gasping faster and faster until numbness seeped through each small brain like the slow winter thickening of the water.

The salmon scenario dramatizes in a summary fashion some of the present and future interactions of man with the remaining least disturbed portions of the North American continental shelf. Overfishing and oil pollution loom as the major offshore problems at high latitude. The salmon, of which there are several species, is a good representative organism with which to begin this chapter because these fish are already among the most threatened creatures in northern marine and freshwater ecosystems.

The freshwater life history of salmon is widely familiar--the rush to spawn in clear, cold upland streams, sometimes hundreds of kilometers from the sea. After spawning, Pacific salmon of the genus *Onchorynchus* always die, while Atlantic salmon, *Salmo salar*, may return to the sea and live to spawn during several succeeding years. Eggs develop slowly, and after emergence the young fish remain for an average of one to two years in fresh water. For most salmon the ocean phase begins when the fish are fifteen to twenty centimeters long, and this part of the salmon's life is less well known; the migrations of some species still have not been fully explored by biologists.

Young salmon, called smolts, have the ability to remember the last whiff of estuarine water which they experience before going to sea. The memory remains fresh, locked in the deceptively shallow recesses of the piscine mind for one, two, even three years, while the fish seek rich oceanic feeding grounds as distant as 5,000 kilometers from their home streams. When they have matured and the reproductive urge waxes strong, the powerful swimmers begin to make their way back along routes known best to themselves. How far out their exquisitely miniaturized olfactory computers can sense the home water, picking up its flavor amid thousands of other combinations, is not known, but the fish arrive unerringly in the right place in the right season.

However, fewer return every year. Probably the species in greatest danger is the Atlantic salmon. Fishery analysts in the NMFS fear that unless a prodigious effort is made to revive some of New England's northern rivers, *Salmo salar* will soon be gone from U.S. waters for good. This species has already vanished over most of its formerly immense range on the other side of the Atlantic, from northern Spain around the British Isles and Scandanavia to Arctic Russia. Industrial pollution, the siltation of spawning areas as the result of negligent forestry, and overfishing have left only a handful of breeding populations in remote northern streams.

The big silvery ocean trout (the Atlantic salmon is more closely related to trout than to the several species of true Pacific salmon) is now making its last stand in Canada. But even here, record low returns and recruitment (production of young) have been noted since 1973. Canadian biologists are virtually certain that the intensive fishing for Atlantic salmon on the high seas off West Greenland is responsible for the present decline of spawning stocks. This largest feeding area for salmon in the Atlantic was discovered in 1960. In succeeding years, the West Greenland catch increased by nearly fifty times to a record 5.8 million pounds in 1971. This level of fishing pressure, the Canadians believe, cannot be sustained and already severely endangers future production of Atlantic salmon in Canada.

In the North Pacific, the greatest catchers of salmon have been the Japanese. They also work on the high seas, hanging their huge gillnets in the water from large ships. Near the coast and in the bays and fjords gillnetting is also the preferred method of American and Canadian fishermen, albeit on a much smaller scale. Longlining with baited hooks is also practiced.

Pacific salmon treaties, chiefly concerning Japan, Canada, and the United States, have been negotiated and renegotiated in recent years. Many Alaskan fishermen, chiefly those who depend on the great runs funneling into Bristol Bay north of the Aleutians, still think the Japanese offshore fleet is taking an inordinate quota of "American" salmon. Unfortunately the Japanese catch is, in a sense, wasteful because the fish taken are typically less than half the size they would have attained upon completing the marine phase of their life cycle.

While salmon swirl at the center of North Pacific fishery controversies, the less-well-known bottom fish in the rich Gulf of Alaska may present an even greater conservation problem. The once populous, huge, and delicious Pacific halibut are greatly reduced and other species may be declining fast. Great difficulties appear at both the biological and regulatory ends of the modern fishing poll in the North Pacific. According to William L. Sullivan Jr. of the U.S. State Department's Bureau of Oceans and International Environmental and Scientific Affairs, biological knowledge of North Pacific stocks is in a primitive state, as compared to that in the North Atlantic. At the same time, the Northeast Pacific Fisheries Commission (NPFC) is not well established. As of 1975, its membership did not include all the nations fishing in the area.

Sullivan emphasizes that the functioning of NPFC does not compare favorably to its North Atlantic counterpart, ICNAF. Regulation of the catch and the tabulation of the species and numbers of fish caught are very poorly coordinated in the North Pacific. The Russians, for one, Sullivan believes, have probably greatly underestimated their catch records.

Compared to the North Atlantic, wide parts of which have been fished with increasingly sophisticated hardware since before Columbus, the northeast Pacific is a new frontier. Primitive subsistence methods of coastal Indians, Eskimos, and Aleuts, which reached barely a day's paddle onto the shelf, first gave way to American and Canadian trawlers in the 1930s. Now almost overnight have come the technological fleets which roam vast areas.

The probable next stage in the exploitation of living marine resources moves toward an oceanic future shock. Among the most portentious developments is the concept of the "island mother ship": already on the drawing boards, such vessels would replace the present generation of factory ships. They could remain on the fishing grounds for up to four years.

A Polish proposal envisions a mother ship 220 meters long. It would accompany a fleet of 40 trawlers, each 45 meters long and capable of landing 1,000 tons of fish per day. The mother's stern would be split in a squared-off Y-shape to allow protective docking of trawlers and special transports. A mother ship would take on raw fish, process it, and then transfer it to the transport vessels, which would ferry the catch home and return with supplies for the fleet.

Although the island mother ship would seldom move about, it would support the equivalent of a factory town devoted exclusively to processing fish. This would require an estimated 100,000 tons of diesel fuel per year, a prohibitive prospect, so the Polish design calls for the mother to be nuclear powered. Its swarm of trawlers could use electric accumulators, charged by the mother vessel, for at least part of their energy needs.

If such awesome creations as island mother ships ever get off the drawing boards and on the ocean, they may be hard to stop. Once shelf fisheries became unprofitable, or protected, the new matriarchal fleets could probably literally clean up on the continental slopes in deep international waters.

Two University of British Columbia analysts, one of them a mathematician, recently showed that the extinction of fishery resources can be profitable. Diminishing returns will not necessarily halt overexploitation short of extinction because rarity may make certain species extremely valuable as has happened with the abalone. Other examples of fisheries proceeding steadily toward the vanishing point include certain species of whale, and perhaps the Pacific halibut and Atlantic yellowtail flounder.

Even in the far north, endangered creatures such as the bowhead whale and various seabirds remain in some jeopardy. Eskimos have traditionally hunted these creatures, and they have been given dispensations from protective federal laws and international treaties. Today they continue to pursue their old ways for subsistence purposes, even in areas designated as wildlife refuges.

However, there is now a blurring of the boundaries between technological and primitive methods of hunting and fishing. Snowmobiles and outboard motors are in widespread and efficient use on the northwest Alaskan coast. Here at the edge of the Bering Sea, the eggs of seabirds are popular fare. The motorized equipment permits people to reach the outlying nesting islands far more easily and frequently than before. This is laudable from the point of view of safety and efficiency, but it is reasonable only if there does not come a large increase in the population of egg gatherers.

The bowhead whale problem is more acute. Once their huge quarry is sighted from the edge of the spring ice, a modern crew of Eskimo whalers still paddles out in a big *umiak,* because the underwater noise produced by a motor would frighten off the whale. But having closed in, the Eskimos attack the whale with a modern harpoon bomb. Sometimes several of these internally exploding grenades are needed to finish off a big bowhead. To their credit, the Eskimos waste very little of a landed leviathan. To their discredit, according to Scott McVay, they fatally wound and lose five bowheads for every one actually captured.

Eventually some lines may have to be drawn even for subsistence consumption of our rarest natural resources. If Arctic coasts truly begin to develop, at the ends of radiating networks of roads embracing great tracts of oil-rich tundra, local populations may grow at a startling pace. Might the hunt for the bowhead someday feature spotter planes or hovercraft, crossing ice and open water alike?

With further development and exploitation along subarctic and arctic coasts will come greater pressure on all the marine wildlife. Even populations of creatures which are not pursued directly can be devastated. Birds are especially hard hit.

Pieces of plastic and rubber bands are now being consumed by northern seabirds such as puffins and auklets, with fatal constipating effects. Most of this trash in the sea must come from ships. Gill nets routinely entrap and kill murres, puffins, shearwaters, and fulmars in the North Pacific. Off West Greenland the Danish gill net fishery alone has been responsible for the deaths of an estimated one-half million thick-billed murres in a single year, a number believed to represent one-third of the annual production of this species in the western North Atlantic.

While the exploitation of living marine resources in the north has at least some historical perspective, and is subject, at least in theory, to fairly effective control, the other major resource found here beneath the shore and shallow sea bed presents regional problems totally without precedent.

Offshore oil development and the coming operation of a major oil terminal at Valdez are the most troublesome aspects of the new northern industrial revolution. Sporadic oil development has already begun beneath Alaskan

Short-tailed albatrosses

223

waters. In 1963 commercial quantities of oil and gas were confirmed in Cook Inlet. More than fifteen producing wells now yield the expected low-level petroleum contamination in this deep, cold environment. An environmental expert from the Exxon Corporation has estimated the Cook Inlet spillage at 0.03 percent of the oil produced.

A large field of platforms rising from the prime salmon waters of Kachemak Bay, just off Cook Inlet, has been the recurring nightmare of fishermen for several years since the early 1970s. Now it is about to happen.

Kachemak Bay, near the town of Homer on the Kenai Peninsula, is one of Alaska's most productive marine embayments. Besides serving as a migratory route for all five species of Alaskan salmon, the bay provides prime fisheries for two species of commercial shrimp and three species of crab, including *Paralithodes camtschatica*, the Alaskan king crab. Biologists at Alaska's Auke Bay Laboratory of the National Marine Fisheries Service believe that shrimp production in Kachemak Bay may be equivalent to, or even exceed, that of some of the most productive areas of the Gulf of Mexico.

In mid-1976, the kill of fish and valuable crustaceans in Kachemak Bay was set to begin suddenly. An exploratory drilling rig became stuck in sub-bottom strata and oil engineers estimated that the only sure way to salvage the expensive platform was to blast through its legs above the bottom with explosive charges. Underwater explosions kill and injure marine life up to several kilometers from the blast site. This kind of unforeseen impact is likely to become more frequent in Alaskan waters.

Early in 1976, U.S. Secretary of the Interior Thomas C. Kleppe surprised many environmentalists as well as energy analysts by deciding to lease large undersea tracts for oil development in the Gulf of Alaska. This, together with the development of inshore areas such as Kachemak Bay, raises the possibility of disruption of salmon runs because of chemical interference with the fishes' olfactory homing mechanism. Very limited behavioral research has been done on the salmon's sensitivity to oil in sea water. In experiments at

Spectacled eider

the NMFS laboratory at Auke Bay, salmon fry reacted to and even tried to avoid as little as 1.6 ppm of Prudhoe Bay crude oil in water. Big fish returning to spawn could be just as sensitive. At least two petroleum fractions, the low-molecular-weight paraffins and the aromatics, are known to produce anesthesia or narcosis in a wide variety of organisms. A large oil spill or simple, widespread, low-level contamination, hanging in the water across the continental shelf, conceivably could block thousands of fish from reaching their home rivers. Even if the navigational disruption is only temporary, effects on the delicate timing of egg production and spawning could reduce the reproductive effectiveness of runs in streams throughout southern Alaska.

That oil and seabirds do not mix is known to everyone, but this modern law of nature has so far received little attention in the North Pacific. Among the most susceptible birds are the densely flocking migrants, especially eiders and other sea ducks. Hundreds of thousands of birds from the Gulf of Alaska to Puget Sound will at various times of year be in the potential drift path of oil from tanker accidents or blowouts. Even the Alaskan offshore birds, the solitary soarers which include the magnificent spring and summer visitors, the black footed and Laysan albatrosses, may not be out of danger. The petrels, shearwaters, and albatrosses, all close relatives, have unusually low body temperatures and presumably low metabolic rates, which means they could be affected severely by even a very light oiling. Losing only a small proportion of insulating protection, they might succumb to hypothermia or irreversible chilling, while a bird with a higher metabolic rate would survive.

The Gulf of Alaska, with its fearsome storms and frequent earthquakes, is quite possibly the worse place on earth so far slated for large-scale petroleum production. The CEQ report of 1974 described the Gulf as extremely difficult and dangerous with regard to the safety of men, equipment, and the marine environment. If petroleum is actually found beneath this wild and turbulent mantle of water, sand, and stone, the CEQ opined it should not be developed until theoretical and technological uncertainties were cleared from a path in which small blunders could lead to a swath of wreckage, bodies, and oil across the cold continental shelf.

Geologists have plotted the belt of recent major earthquake activity in an offshore band parallel to the coast from Kodiak Island to Prince William Sound. Other known fault zones lie farther east, principally in the coastal mountains of the Chugach-St. Elias region. Much of the continental shelf and deeper bottom here has not been explored by anyone but occasional fishermen. New faults beneath the shelf may await discovery by seismological fingers feeling through the concealing sands.

The resistance of oil platforms, submerged well heads, or pipelines to the crumpling forces of a strong earthquake, or a minor one for that matter, have been little tested.

The oil industry in Alaska faces a frontier of nemeses. If the Gulf of Alaska is the worst place to drill on the ice-free continental rim, then Valdez is the worst site for an oil shipping terminal in the United States. When oil from the present North Slope fields begins to flow through the Alaska pipeline, between two and three large crude carriers will load at Valdez every day. Watched by numerous sea otters, the ships will enter Prince William Sound, whose marine biology remains little known. The tankers will proceed northward toward spectacular mountains which conceal irresistible geological forces capable of moving miles of rock, ice, and water. Finally the ships will turn into the Valdez Arm, a long fiord leading to Port Valdez, which itself forms an elongate embayment, roughly fifteen kilometers long by six wide.

In 1973, a 500-page report called *Environmental Studies of Port Valdez* was issued by the University of Alaska. This study of the natural environment was the only one to be done in the area before a total commitment was made to develop Valdez. The research project, which was sponsored by the Alyeska Pipeline Service Company, with additional support from the U.S. Sea Grant Program and the University of Alaska's Institute of Marine Science, covered chemical, biological, and geological parameters. But there were some omissions.

While concentrating strongly on phytoplankton and primary production, the report virtually ignored the next link in the food web, the oil-sensitive zooplankton. Only relatively few data relevant to zooplankton were taken in the program, which showed an overall seasonal bias. It is easy to sympathize with scientists trying to do fieldwork in a difficult maritime climate, but the parade of superships and dangers of oil contamination will not cease during the winter.

Although the bottom environment was considered, and its creatures fairly thoroughly tabulated, the report did not discuss the effects of oil in the water, especially oil coating the abundant, fine, suspended matter, much of it glacial rock flour carried down by streams. Conspicuously missing too was a consideration of the buildup of oil in the bottom sediments. No matter how clean the industry intends to keep the oil terminal, small slicks will inevitably reach the little Valdez basin and the fjord leading to the sea. This oil will enter from the proposed ballast-water treatment facility in the port and from impossible-to-control sources such as rain running off the giant tankers which will always be in port. Once it reaches the soft cold sediments, the oil will remain for decades.

Most surprising of all was the total omission of nekton in the Valdez biological study. The cold, turbid waters of Port Valdez nurture many young fish which contribute to valuable commercial populations in nearby waters.

The most serious single flaw of the Valdez environmental investigation is a geological one. It can be argued that the extremely important oversight lay outside the geographical jurisdiction of the study, but here, as on any frontier, a myopic view can be dangerous. The problem that was overlooked is the huge, 1,100-square-kilometer Columbia Glacier, which now flows in chunks and enormous ice splinters into Prince William Sound just west of the Valdez Arm. In 1973, just after the University of Alaska study group released the *Environmental Studies of Port Valdez,* glaciologists from the U.S. Geological Survey (USGS) began to have suspicions that the Columbia Glacier might be about to break up in a massive retreat.

Presently meeting the sea at the head of a deep, foreshortened bay and eventual fjord-to-be, the Columbia Glacier terminates in an impressive cliff between six and seven kilometers wide and rising 100 meters or more above the surface of the water. In summer, the icefalls from the face of the cliff sometimes produce enough of a ripple to rock the small sight-seeing ferries which ply inner Prince William Sound. During 1973 the professional glacier watchers first noticed that huge cavities had formed along the western part of the glacial front.

During the summer of 1974, the USGS scientists went to work. Using a small, unmanned, radio-controlled platform, they managed to obtain depth measurements along the frontal cliff of the glacier. Their data showed that the moraine, the giant bar of rocks, gravel, and sand deposited at the front of an active glacier, was very narrow and apparently did not extend far beneath the ice.

With special sonar equipment set up at various points atop the huge river of ice, the scientists found that for some 30 kilometers in back of the terminal cliff the glacier extended far below sea level. In places the great mass of ice above the sea continues on down to bottom out in an awesome hidden fjord 600 meters (2,000 feet) deep. Another summer or two of probing deep into the glacier's anatomy is necessary to see how well the ice is supported by transverse ridges of rock. If there are no substantial exoskeletal underpinnings beneath the long extension of the glacier leading to Prince William Sound, instability could develop rapidly.

Under physical conditions where a high mass of ice is not supported and confined, it will not stand up. And if it is not being "nourished" by sufficient snowfall to offset summer wastage, a glacier will begin to retreat. Glaciologists believe that these conditions may be about to combine to make the retreat of the Columbia Glacier one to remember.

Late in the summer of 1975, unusually massive icefalls occurred near the center of the ice-cliff facing Prince William Sound. The USGS observers think this could be the warm-up exercise for a stupendous ice show in which 220 cubic kilometers (fifty cubic miles) of the glacial mass could be discharged into the sound during the next thirty to fifty years. If what the scientists term "this drastic retreat" does indeed begin, the terminus of the glacier could fall back a kilometer or two each year. Eventually a stable position would be reached far inland at the head of the fjord.

Ice by the cubic mile caving into Prince William Sound clearly presents certain obstacles to supertankers, and in fact the obstacles are already there. In the late summer and fall of 1975, they reached the proposed shipping lanes in modest numbers of hundreds—icebergs. Most of them are small, a few meters across, and of shallow draft. But each berg's several-thousand-ton mass, when hit at fifteen knots, is capable of crumpling a tanker's hull like tinfoil. The largest Columbia-spawned bergs, which can presently escape across the thirty-meter-deep moraine-shoal in front of the glacial snout, could, no doubt, "total" a supership.

The Coast Guard is highly concerned over the increasing iceberg threat. It already plans to build a radar station overlooking Valdez Arm and requires radar for all oil transports entering Prince William Sound. Regular ice patrols by Coast Guard boats and planes will probably be essential, however, because radar easily misses small bergs, especially when the water is choppy. At such times even the human lookout may not notice until it is too late. Some icebergs contain large quantities of enclosed rock which lessens buoyancy, and they drift quietly just below the surface.

In front of the vast crystalline cliff, the prevailing currents set toward the entrance of the Valdez Arm and on into the central sound. If the ice does begin to break up with unglacial swiftness, hundreds of thousands of bergs at a time may drift into the sound. Indeed, a single cubic kilometer of ice will yield the equivalent of a million icebergs, each with a thousand-cubic-meter bulk. By USGS estimates, four or five times this much ice may fall each year. Small bergs could clog Prince William Sound like a bathtub full of ice cubes. Or, seen from the air, they will float southwest and south in free, curving paths; luminous on the dark water, they will drift toward the oncoming tankers like the stars of one universe meeting another.

Twenty-five kilometers west of the Columbia Glacier is an unobtrusive spot near the northwestern corner of Prince William Sound. It marks the epicenter of the Good Friday, 1964, Alaskan earthquake. In places around the sound, the ground moved ten meters or more. At a number of localities along the rugged south Alaskan coast *tsunamis* over thirty meters high swept ashore carrying everything in their path to oblivion. The small town of Valdez was devastated by the quake.

The Port of Valdez, Prince William Sound, and the south Alaskan shelf are precarious enough in the declining years of petroleum, but the final bane of the oil industry may prove to be the arctic shelf. On Canada's Mackenzie Delta, facing the Beaufort Sea, nearly two dozen highly successful oil strikes have been made since the late 1960s. Abundant quantities of natural gas also appear to be present. Together with scattered arctic islands, the deep frozen sands of the Mackenzie Delta cover what now appears to be the richest source of conventional energy in Canada. As in the case of the United States' mammoth Prudhoe Bay field to the west, the oil-bearing formations extend out beneath the Beaufort Sea. Some petroleum prospectors have tentatively ventured that the whole area could be another Gulf of Mexico—under ice.

The possible consequences of a large oil spill in the Arctic Ocean are now taxing the predicting capabilities of the experts. Given the awful weather and the highly mobile sea ice, moving in great gyral patterns, flexing and shearing, forming and closing leads of open water, neither oil industry scientists nor their critics, notably from the U.S. Geological Service and academia, seem reasonably confident of the future. There seem to be only worst-case possibilities.

The first possibility is a well blowout on the arctic shelf. If this occurred in late summer or fall, shortly before the freezeup, Canadian experts point out that the well could run wild for nine or ten months. Stopping a blowout on the open shelf of the Beaufort Sea after freezeup is now considered impossible. The usual technique is to drill another hole close by the first and force great gouts of heavy drilling mud down to plug the area around the underground openings, thus holding back the reservoir pressure. But the drilling equipment on the open shelf cannot be left in place during the winter, since it would be swept away by the shifting ice. An average well, running out of control for nearly a year, would spew nearly 90,000 cubic meters of crude into dark, frigid water beneath the ice.

Along the underside of the ice, the oil would tend to spread in a thin layer over hundreds to thousands of square kilometers. Underwater pressure ridges would intercept the flow, and channel it in unpredictable directions. A spotty pattern could result, encompassing a much wider area than a coherent slick. One USGS scientists has calculated that the movement of the ice would exceed the spreading rate of the slick in water. The gyral circulation of ice moving over the site of the spill could pull the oil into a widening spiral smear which might eventually span a large portion of the Beaufort Sea.

If part of a slick should reach the surface of open water and be exposed to turbulent conditions, the oil would emulsify into tiny persistent droplets. If again carried beneath the ice, in particular the multi-year ice which lies beyond the edge of the shelf, this ultra thinned oil-in-water suspension ("chocolate mousse") could cover immense areas.

The motion of the so-called permanent arctic ice not only involves the large-scale gyral sweeps, the shearing motions, and the translation through the pack of the leads, at speeds of up to forty kilometers per day. There is also a slow, vertical upwelling of annual layers through the entire floating skin of the polar sea. The average thickness of arctic ice is three to four meters. This oceanwide veneer is in a continuous, dynamic equilibrium. Each winter about a meter of new ice forms at the bottom, and each summer about a meter melts and evaporates from the surface. Another important factor is that almost no precipitation falls in this polar desert. The result is that a given layer of the sea ice is continuously upwardly mobile. In three or four years, it migrates from the underside to topside. Oil will do the same.

A thin film of crude trapped beneath the pack ice will be frozen in and incorporated during the first winter. With each summer's melt, it comes closer to the surface and finally appears, dark and absorbant of heat.

The albedo, or reflectivity, of pure sea ice is very high. The ice reflects most of the solar energy it receives in the near-continuous radiance of the high-Arctic summer. But a film of oil will lower the albedo greatly.

Sophisticated estimates of an ice field's response to diminished albedo were published in 1971 in the *Journal of Geophysical Research* (Vol. 76, pp 1,150-1,575). The study indicates that a 10 percent reduction of albedo in summer would cause a 60 percent thinning of the ice's equilibrium thickness. Lowering the albedo by just 20 percent results in the disappearance of the ice after two years. A 10 percent loss of albedo over one square kilometer with a crude oil film of expected thickness, would require only ten cubic meters of oil.

One should keep in mind the likelihood that in the jumble of pressure ridges and open-water leads, the oil might well break up into numerous patches. According to ice scientists with the U.S. Geological Survey and the University of Washington, each patch of oil is capable of initiating the melting of an area of ice ten times the size of each oil patch.

These same scientists have also made calculations on the second possibility concerning oil in the Arctic Ocean, that of expected chronic contamination. Based on typical operational data from oil industry sources, the analysts believe that oil spillage in the Beaufort Sea would be on the order of 0.1 percent of production. They assume there will be many more drilling platforms, and more hazardous conditions than now exist in Cook Inlet, where Exxon's estimate is 0.03 percent spillage. Tentative estimates by USGS have placed recoverable offshore petroleum reserves in the Beaufort Sea between 4 billion cubic meters and 10 billion cubic meters and therefore the haphazard chronic spillage should fall between 4 million to 10 million cubic meters. For patches of oil with the expected thickness of one millimeter, the cumulative area covered by oil will reach between 400,000 to 1 million square kilometers, or from 20 to 50 percent of the surface of the Beaufort Sea.

Beyond this the experts' mental maps of the future state of the Arctic Ocean become fuzzy. Truly massive melting could ensue beyond the bounds of the oiled ice. Dark open water absorbs heat nearly as well as a dark oil film. A large amount of summer radiation which is now reflected would be absorbed as heat in the ocean. If a large amount of ice melted, it might not reform readily. Winter freezing might not redress the former balance between seasonal gains and losses of heat. A new equilibrium state in the thickness and extent of the pack ice could become established, and this might have unpredictable consequences for world climate and seaside habitation. These speculations have all been made by arctic experts recently. So far they are just speculations.

Oil companies have been relatively quiet about the prospects for cleaning up ocean spills in the Arctic. Even in the fairly open shelf waters of summer, cleaning up would be difficult because of the presence of random ice floes. Like small moving islands, these can appear at any time to hamper boom crews. Oil spilled in the leads opening into the pack ice would get away from all but an immediate cleanup effort. As in an artificial boom, it would tend to escape under the ice by the mechanism of head-wave loss. Even above the ice, winter cleanup, according to scientists who have tried it with a few barrels of oil in Coast Guard tests, would be extremely difficult and hazardous to men and equipment.

The physical sensitivity of the arctic ice-pack environment to oil is exceeded only by the biological sensitivity of this realm's deceptively hardy creatures. Pollution of the open leads in the ice would be deadly for mammals and birds concentrated from thousands of square kilometers of surrounding territory. Off the Mackenzie Delta in spring before the breakup of the ice, up to 175,000 eiders and old squaw ducks congregate in the narrow water spaces.

According to an assessment in the journal *Science* (5 March 1976), contamination from a large blowout off the Mackenzie could affect hundreds of kilometers of the Alaskan coast as well as the Canadian. It could lead to massive losses of fish, such as Arctic char, as well as birds and marine mammals. Ice algae and the planktonic food for the last bowhead whales could disappear over the entire regional shelf. As shown by Swedish and American scientists, the extremely slow rate of biological degradation of oil in cold sea water means that spills in the Arctic Ocean will remain relatively unchanged for fifty years.

There is one further dangerous possibility. The Arctic acts as a giant condensing trap for airborne chemicals, such as pesticides and radioactive isotopes. These substances continually reach the Arctic in thinly polluted winds from the south. The steep temperature gradient of the far north, known to meteorologists as "the cold wall," wrings the last precipitation from the air, and the toxic materials gradually build up in ice and life at the top of the world. Thus with the progression of time and seasonal thaws, the far northern seas form an ultimate receptacle for the gaseous trash of faraway ecological abominations.

The coming of oil with its carcinogens may bring about synergisms with cold-wall pollutants that will reach through the food chain to arctic mammals, poisoning the once pristine diet of the coastal Eskimo. How soon this will happen, or how serious it might be, cannot be told. Such science is very new here.

The arctic shelf is a special place, fragile and tautly woven in its ecological fabric. In the arctic marine world, the rule of ice and physical accommodation has permitted the existence of only relatively few species for millions of years. Now dark decades of oil are descending on the arctic, and all must make new accommodations or die.

Marine Wilderness: Ideals and Imperatives

Ecological interactions between man and the sea have increased to an extent that challenges comprehension, especially in the more developed places on the earth's surface, such as the coast of North America. Try to encompass in your mind the magnitude of coastal change that has been wrought in the mere three and one-half centuries since the essentially organic culture of the North American Indian dominated this area. Then remember that 90 percent of this change has occurred in the last fifty years and 90 percent of that in the last fifteen. Then realize that, because natural change is extremely slow, and wilderness conditions are optimal for communities of most creatures, practically every added increment of change has been detrimental to the marine system. As a calculus for the future this is a grim prognosis.

Perhaps the worst of it is that we don't yet understand most of the detailed happenings on the continental shelf. We know relatively little of what lives on the shelf, how marine creatures live, where they are abundant, and where they are scarce. We know less concerning the ultimate effects of man's activities on marine life. And we know least about the vital linkages among organisms in the food webs. The sickening or death of one or more obscure supportive species may bring down many of the sea's living things which are recognized as valuable to human beings.

It is possible to imagine marine scientists as weavers in some primitive society which, as a kind of religious exercise, is engaged in making a tapestry of intricate design and gigantic proportion. All of the weavers have started in different areas; sometimes small knots of people work in the same place and fill in the pattern at a faster than average rate. The quality of the weave, the artistry and elegance of the result is highly variable; sometimes whole sections have to be redone. Other portions remain in a shoddy state for some time, while still others have been brilliantly executed.

The scientists are trying to model the extant (or perhaps ideal) natural fabric whose structured patterns are ultrarefined and near perfect. The conceptual copy now being fashioned will never match the original in detail and integrated function (even when simulated by computer), although it does improve with time. The outstanding aspect of the model tapestry in its present state is the amount of blank space between known physical and biological sections, which are islands in an ocean of ecological ignorance.

Environmental change is proceeding through the normally somnolent ecosphere like a chain reaction. The rate of extinction has become many times that seen in the past. Even the spectacular die-offs in the North American Pleistocene and the Age of Reptiles occurred over thousands and millions of years respectively. In the present era, thousands of species have become threatened with extinction in mere decades. Many of these are already gone.

As of January, 1976, the U.S. Interior Department's list of "endangered" or "threatened" species totaled 435 worldwide. Scientists from the Smithsonian Institution, in a report prepared for Congress in 1975, recommended that nearly 3,000 more species of plants be added to the list. Other researchers, notably in marine fields, believe that many more species are in trouble. These scientists consider the preponderance of terrestrial creatures on the endangered list, as well as the list's modest length, to be misleading. The hidden life of the continental margin may be disappearing as rapidly as the more conspicuous creatures on land.

Some researchers look beyond the endangered species concept and see the advent of endangered ecosystems. That large and vital ecological units are already threatened is apparent when one considers the tragic decline of American salt marshes. Numerous marine ecologists now point to Georges Bank, already painfully plucked and scraped for its thin layers of living wealth and about to be drilled for oil, as an example of a remote marine ecosystem being pushed toward collapse. They point out that the shallow northern Gulf of Mexico and portions of the sea off Southern California could also be stressed beyond natural tolerance levels. A massive oil spill in Pacific Northwest or Alaskan waters could create systematic havoc, and recovery would be terribly slow and perhaps incomplete.

Belatedly, there are some new ideas that offer hope of preserving at least a few small wilderness enclaves on the continental shelf. Hidden along the green water rim are areas as unique and valuable as Acadia, Everglades, Big Thicket, the North coast Redwoods. The lobster canyons of Georges Bank achieve such status; so do Hudson Gorge, the ancient reef at the Carolina shelf edge, and the monadnock country of the northwestern Gulf of Mexico. Selected kelp forests and fjords from California to the Aleutians likewise qualify as irreplaceable national assets. Although numerous breeding sites of marine mammals and birds have been set aside, their migration routes and wintering sites should receive equivalent protection and become marine sanctuaries. Even places that humans do not find physically spectacular should be preserved because, for example, the teeming interstices of the sandy shelf and the crevice communities of marine boulder fields are like no other life zones on earth. Marine sanctuaries should be designated wilderness areas. Commercial fishing should be prohibited. Even the kinds of recreation allowed should be carefully limited. In relatively shallow places such as the northwestern Gulf, shipping should be routed around sanctuary perimeters. Potential polluting developments such as offshore ports, pipeline terminals, and thermal outfalls should be many kilometers distant.

Detailed ecological studies should be done on proposed areas to make sure their boundaries are large enough to include a self-sustaining natural system. Special problems may be encountered with migratory species which move beyond sanctuary boundaries into unsafe areas, as do wandering herds in the large African parks. In some cases, marine sanctuary studies should set pollutant buffer boundaries. Potentially dangerous shipping and industrial projects might have to keep a minimal distance which would vary with the nature of the impact. Thermal fields should be fairly easy to calculate. The dispersal of and danger from specific chemical substances or solid microparticles would be more difficult to estimate.

On the continental shelf we are at the same relative position as we were when a land frontier of great natural wealth and beauty lay before us. Because of ecological ignorance, much of the wealth and most of the beautiful vistas, which the great midland ecologist Aldo Leopold compared to a prairie sea, have been lost to dust storms, sheet and gully erosion, and more recently nitrate-fertilizer poisoning in the fresh water. Our continental shelf is narrower and more precariously situated than was the prairie wilderness. Lying next to the most populous segments of the country, the shelf—unlike the west—will be "won" not over generations of hardscrabble pioneering but in a few years of mighty technological turmoil.

The establishment of marine sanctuaries should not be viewed as merely satisfying the whims of a few scuba aesthetes, marine scientists and submersible buffs. From general ecological principles and more specific biomedical needs have come powerful reasons for preserving the widest possible variety of marine habitats.

The new conservation rationale springs from the conviction of scientists that the accelerating rate of extinction will severely narrow future options for man. The biotic diversity of a wilderness environment is a storehouse of genetic variability. In a sense, such areas are vast libraries which have randomly accumulated works of stupendous importance as well as trivia. Especially well represented are "how to do it" manuals for better living. They are intricately programmed and provide directions for running the most sophisticated machinery known, but their secret formulas, which deal with every contingency of life on earth, can be translated and used by man.

Terrestrial genetic diversity has been of inestimable value in plant breeding. Genes that resist disease or drought have been introduced from wild grasses into corn, wheat, and other food crops. But already plant geneticists lament the loss of hundreds of species of wild vegetation from which desirable food crop qualities might have been borrowed.

On the continental shelf natural genetic diversity may be extremely important to the future of mariculture, the farming of the sea. Mariculture lags behind agriculture by a century or more, but recent attempts at the selective breeding of oysters and shrimp show promise that it is catching up. Wild populations of these creatures on the shelf probably harbor genes that will increase growth rates of farmed varieties and improve resistance to waterborne diseases and parasites.

In the last decade or so an even more concrete value has been placed on wilderness, for it has proved to represent a surprising stockpile of medical drugs which as yet has only begun to be inventoried, especially the sea, where pharmacological explorers have discovered substances with brand new disease-fighting properties for use in the human body. New antibiotics are being developed from sponges; an anti-tumor substance has been found in tunicates; other marine organisms now supply anticoagulants and agents for cardiovascular therapy. Especially notable is the imminent development of powerful new cancer treatments from such unlikely sources as starfish and seaweeds.

In Australia, the infamous crown-of-thorns starfish, *Acanthaster planci*, has been found to contain a substance with remarkable tumor-inhibiting capabilities. The seaweed story is even more intriguing. Early in 1976, University of Hawaii researchers discovered that a chemical substance called aplysiatoxin, isolated from the marine blue green algae, *Lyngbya*, shows a high degree of activity against leukemia. The potential new drug gets its name from its co-occurrence in the sea hare, *Aplysia*, which feeds on the blue green alga. The sea hare stores aplysiatoxin, and may itself become a valuable source of the compound.

Drug companies have displayed a steadily mounting interest in testing marine creatures for new antibiotics. The work has barely begun. The living continental shelf may be a unique pharmacopia containing cryptically packaged compounds, some unfortunately in short supply, which may hold the promise for curing or alleviating most of man's remaining physical illnesses. Some thinkers even suggest that certain marine immortals such as sea anemones may hold the secret of a vastly extended human life span.

Hearing such things, people nowadays tend to say: "But why take the time to catch sea hares, collect algae or whatever? We can simply raise them on a large scale in captivity and satisfy our drug needs that way." Of course this is how it will be done, but what will be the next creature from the wild continental shelf to prove priceless to our health?

It seems worth noting that more and more cancer-causing chemicals are trickling into the shallow seas from human sources just as we are discovering vital antidotes in the resources of nature. What a pity and what irony to scrape, dredge, choke, poison, and scald out of existence myriads of living resources that may save us from epidemics of our own making. By preserving large areas of pristine habitat on land and in the sea we are investing in the most precious currency for ourselves, our children, our grandchildren. The true conservative today is not someone who favors the laissez-faire activities of big business but rather one who opposes such activities if they threaten one of the most basic of human needs, which is a world of clean air and water, uncontaminated soil and biota.

Eventually, perhaps, an extensive marine sanctuary program may be recognized as serving rational human interests better than the extraction of offshore oil and the building of offshore power plants. But for now the official priorities all lie with oil fields, supertankers, and offshore ports; with mining marine sand and gravel for more roads; and with industrial fishing which lays waste whole ecosystems.

Still another threat to fragile places and wildlife on the shelf emanates from recreational pressure, a problem which has already become devastating on land. So far, the continental shelf has suffered little of the trampling, stripping, and erosive influences which are destroying New England's alpine zone and areas of the southwest desert, but the onslaught is beginning. Through the 1960s and early 1970s the coral reefs of the Florida Keys were being routinely dynamited by entrepreneurs operating nationwide curio shops. Practically everything they left behind was being plucked by hordes of scuba-diving tourists. In 1975 the federal government declared the reefs endangered and prohibited all taking of live coral. Even this long overdue action may not be enough, for biologists now have discovered widespread evidence that Florida's coral suffers from a unique disease. In areas of heavy underwater sightseeing, a bacterial infection has taken hold, and dead white patches of reef are increasing. The disease, which is rare in remote stretches of reef, seems to begin at sites where coral branches have been scraped or broken. Most of the breakage occurs in the wake of heavily flippered humans.

There is more on the horizon. The problems of Florida's reeflands will spread if underwater access continues to improve. The worst of it could come in the form of a new recreational vehicle. Everyman's minisub, battery powered like the little electrocars now appearing on city streets, will soon appear in the garages of affluence beside the snowmobiles, trail bikes, and hang gliders. Besides taxing the rescue arm of an already harried Coast Guard, the advent of such vehicles spells doom for the beautiful underwater places. Imagine a weekend gymkhana of submerged sea buggies on runners, raising clouds of silt among the beds of flowerlike invertebrates or densely clustered benthic fish eggs.

Such developments pose dangers to underwater sites of historical importance as well. Already divers have located and destroyed ancient wrecks in relatively shallow water. With improved access to the depths, this problem will grow in severity. Even scientists are sometimes guilty of unbecoming behavior. Right after its discovery off Cape Hatteras in 1973, the Civil War ironclad *Monitor*, whose resting place became the first U.S. undersea sanctuary, was violated by a marine geologist's dredge.

In the future, portions of the rapidly developing continental shelf with natural or historical value may come to be viewed as museum pieces. In fact, imaginative proposals have come forth to consider unique habitats as one might a collection of art treasures. Preservation could then proceed from either the governmental or the private sector. The latter case would be unique in the United States. Offering priceless ecological habitat for sale to businessmen would help preserve biotic diversity with the same force that had been destroying it. Since rare pieces of nature will probably grow rarer, their purchase would also be a good investment. Roger Payne, the cetologist, has suggested that natural habitat museums might have boards of directors and trustees, curators, and guards. Whether privately or governmentally owned, not all the collection would be on display. Some "pieces" would be closed to public viewing at certain times, for example, during spawning seasons. Guards might come from an adventuresome volunteer service similar to the Peace Corps.

The museum idea for protecting rare and endangered habitat was first raised with terrestrial areas in mind, but the concept could as easily be applied to the continental shelf. Underwater habitats could be guarded by remote listening equipment combined with scuba and submersibles. Owners, directors, or trustees might gain a strong sense of pride and rare adventure from the occasional viewing of a treasure such as an outer shelf canyon from a small submersible.

All around the North American rim, degradation of the marine environment is proceeding rapidly. The reduction in diversity of life, here caused by overfishing, here by pollution, and everywhere by the loss of wilderness, forms the root of the problem. The gradual collapse of natural communities and food webs is beginning with a wave ringing the continental shallows. From the dying marshes, estuaries, and harbors, this wave is already forming ripples, spreading outward on the continental shelf.

As Barry Commoner has emphasized in his book, *The Closing Circle*, the environmental crisis is not due to man's biological capabilities, which are modest and change only very slowly with time, but rather to his social actions, which change and grow in magnitude with neoplastic rapidity. However, an optimist would also note that unlike most biological properties, social actions are subject to conscious restraint and sustained control. Or are they?

We should stop to ask the sobering question: are humans really any smarter than fish in a breeding tank, or fruit flies with perhaps a generation's worth of life-sustaining resources left? So far there has been no convincing sign of a superior, sustainable eco-intelligence that would set man off from less spectacular creatures. We seem to be entering the first years of global famine, energy shortfalls, and shortages of materials. Pushing population growth, economic growth, and the discredited natural resource policies of the past to their logical limit, man may simply come to a more spectacular end than any other species.

The unifying living ocean is essential to the earth as an ecological unit. The thin bands of ocean around continents and islands are among the richest places on earth. The vast, remote regions of the ocean are like deserts compared to the continental shelves. Man still has time to protect these vital narrow seas and use them wisely for the reasonable needs of a reasonable population. Man looks seaward over the last relatively unspoiled, untrammeled places. He and the continental shelf will survive the environmental crisis together or not at all.

Cultivating the Sea

The world's food supply relative to population growth has reached a phase of diminishing return. The new technological mystique of food production which was to stave off a modern Malthusian reckoning has not lived up to expectations. Vaunted cereal grains which would miraculously multiply the world's supply of bread have produced abundantly only where they have received massive doses of increasingly expensive refined fertilizers and pesticides. The expected miracle of the fishes—a doubling, then a tripling of the oceanic supply—first predicted in the 1950s has also failed to materialize.

Since 1970, despite rapid advancement in technology, the world catch of fish has failed to show a significant increase. It has hovered between 65 and 70 billion tons caught annually; about 55 billion tons of this is from the sea. Slight drops were registered in 1971 and 1972. Now analysts predict that exorbitant fuel costs may cause further drops. The large fleets of nations like Japan are among the hardest hit by fuel prices.

The leveling-off of the catch around 70 billion tons is far short of expectations which held until the late 1960s. Experts had predicted a world catch exceeding 110 billion tons annually before the end of the century. Now it is believed universally by fishery scientists that practically exploitable stocks, with one questionable exception, are being taken everywhere at a level close to the maximum sustainable yield. Some areas are being overfished and their very ecosystems damaged by the sheer intensity of trawling and perhaps the continued removal of important predators. Man himself, as an ingenious predator, has been able to remain external to many of the systems he exploits, but the signs are clear that his most important resource systems are now being stripped and poisoned, pushed to the edge of exhaustion. This is true of some of the best agricultural soils, and it is becoming true generally of the continental shelves. In the end, man, the clever omnivore, may have to adapt his tastes to a narrower menu. Previously unfished, pollution-hardy creatures in the sea, various worms, sea urchins and the like, along with their counterparts on land, could become a necessary diet for much of mankind.

One possible important exception to the dwindling wild harvest in the sea is a small shrimplike creature, technically called a euphausid, but generally and collectively known as krill. In waters surrounding Antarctica, krill are exceptionally abundant. They form patches which sometimes reach many kilometers in diameter, and they have just recently come to the attention of the technological fleets. Exploratory fishing for Antarctic krill has been initiated by the Soviet Union, West Germany, Chile, and Japan. The Russians have the biggest operation so far, and the greatest apparent enthusiasm. They predict a potential sustainable harvest of up to 100 million tons per year. They have test-marketed krill in a homogenized form, unappetizingly translated as "ocean paste." By all accounts, the reception of this processed krill by Russian consumers since 1973 has been poor.

The future of krill in the world protein market depends on many factors: who will eat it, and what incentives will exist to get it to those who may have no choice? There is also the ecologically unsound possibility of using krill for a protein supplement in livestock feed. This suggestion is unsound because ten or more kilograms of krill, which may be worth its weight in diesel fuel for a conventional Antarctic trawler (nuclear ships would change this), will emerge eventually as only one kilogram of, say, pork. Even worse than this, if the price were right, krill could go to the pet food industry in affluent countries, as does much of the present anchovy yield.

The uncertain future of a krill fishery is also worrying those trying to save the great whales from extinction. Migratory humpbacks, the few remaining blue whales, finbacks, and perhaps several other species are probably dependent on Antarctic krill. No one knows exactly how these big baleen whales locate their food. They do not randomly filter sea water as once believed, but probably depend on finding fairly thick patches of their planktonic prey. If humans thin the huge shoals of krill, which together with the most of the last whales are found only around the bottom of the world, we may doom the leviathans just as surely as if the last one were to be harpooned. The Russian calculation of 100 million tons per year as a sustainable yield of krill made no mention of a ration left for the whales.

Few fisheries futurists are now touting krill. Instead, the optimists wax enthusiastic over the possibilities of mariculture. Since the late 1960s, mariculture in the United States has sprung from a handful of backyard garden-sized operations, primarily with oysters and shrimp, to a widespread, highly technological enterprise with enormous subsidy from federal and state governments and large corporations.

Although mariculture is far behind agriculture, in the mid 1970s a few of the more ecologically sound and ingeniously run sea farms are on the verge of making a profit. But even the most rapid development of mariculture is unlikely to solve the looming problem of famine. Most sea farmers are interested in a maximum return on a risky investment. Presently the smart money is in crops for the restaurant market: lobster, shrimp, salmon, and oysters on the half-shell (even the shells must be the proper size and shape, or the oyster is discarded).

The involvement of big business in mariculture raises the ironic possibility of internal conflicts developing over coastal water quality. For example, Weyerhauser and Union Carbide have both invested substantially in the raising of penned salmon in Puget Sound. Releases of pesticides and other chemicals traceable to such companies could have deleterious consequences for salmon. However, if the new aquabusiness should become truly profitable, habitual polluters of the nearshore farmlands could meet stiff criticism, opposition lobbying, and even lawsuits, all backed by hefty corporate muscle.

Beyond the confines of the corporate pens, salmon hold a promise of contributing simultaneously to the world's food supply and to the evolution of an oceanic philosophy. Salmon in the wild are transcendent creatures. They roam far beyond the continental shelf in both landward and seaward directions; they transcend international boundaries, but in the end they always come home again.

It is the oceanic phase of the salmon's life history that is currently exploited by the commercial salmon industry. The high seas fishery for salmon, however, is extremely costly and clearly wasteful in terms of fuel, equipment, manpower, and the salmon resource itself. Recently some fishery scientists have questioned the wisdom of pursuing salmon all over the ocean when the fish can be caught from shore with a method known to the American Indians for hundreds of years.

The Indians made large fish traps shaped like crude funnels, or weirs, near the mouths of rivers. They caught fish which had fattened at sea and were returning in prime condition before the grueling upstream run to spawn. The Indians could control the size of their catch easily. If they wished they could have trapped a whole run in some of the smaller streams, but they took only what they could use, and many fish were allowed to proceed on their urgent mission.

Without fully realizing it, the Indians were practicing ocean ranching, a term referring to the passive use of the sea as open range and cropland. Applied to searoving species such as salmon, ocean ranching is especially useful for conservation because it utilizes the creature's innate ability and urge to return to its point of origin. Another prospect that makes salmon a fishery futurist's dream is the ease with which some species of salmon can now be reared from the egg. Hatcheries can accommodate hundreds of thousands to millions of fish up to roughly twenty centimeters long. At this length they are at the so-called smolt stage at which they normally go to sea, and ocean ranchers can take advantage of the incredible olfactory memory within the small fish's nervous system.

The beauty of the hatchery-based system is that salmon babies can be reared anywhere where high-quality cold water (about 10°C. is best) is available, then transported to a previously chosen release site. After being held for a few days in floating cages immersed in the local estuary, the young fish are imprinted for life on that particular mix of water. The beauty of the salmon's life history is that the fish forage and grow on the open ocean range, then return to a pinpoint geographical location at a predestined season as if on demand.

By combining the human ability to aid salmon reproduction and the survival of young with the fish's ability to grow unaided and essentially cost-free to large size in the sea, the ocean ranching advocates hope to achieve what they term "salmon encroachment." The most optimistic among them talk of a future planetary aquaculture.

Private companies and university researchers in the United States have made test releases of hatchery-reared smolts and have achieved good returns on both the Atlantic and Pacific coasts. Some west coast salmon experts are proposing large-scale releases of Pacific salmon, especially coho (*Onchorynchus kisatch*), in northern New England.

Sadly, chances for hatchery-enhanced establishment of the beleaguered Atlantic salmon, *Salmo salar*, in New England are not good. This species, which once ranged as far south as the Hudson, has now been excluded by pollution and obstruction from all of its former spawning streams in the United States, except for those in northernmost Maine. Atlantic salmon are much more difficult to rear in hatcheries than their Pacific cousins. They grow more slowly, require several times more space, and are more susceptible to disease than the hardy coho.

Japan has embarked on a massive salmon-rearing and release program. A hatchery complex in Hokkaido will soon produce up to 1.3 billion young fish per year. These will be seeded into the relatively unpolluted streams of Japan's northern islands and managed carefully, using the trap-on-return technique.

It appears that salmon restoration and enhancement can only work through close international cooperation, closer than has yet been achieved in fishery agreements and Law of the Sea negotiations. An end to the high seas salmon fishery would save everyone money and provide an incentive to clean up selected estuaries and upland river systems all around the northern hemisphere. This might even help to bring back the wild populations of *Salmo salar*. A truly international salmon enhancement program with its antipollution aspects, together with hatchery and trap-fishery developments should more than make up the jobs lost on salmon-catching ships.

Without doubt the boldest and most farsighted idea for international salmon development has been advanced by Dr. Timothy Joyner and colleagues of the NMFS in Seattle, Washington. Joyner's proposal is to seed smolts of North Pacific species into the far southern hemisphere. No native salmon exist here, so the fish should have no close competition. Releases would be made from points as far south as possible, so that the fish might reach the enormous krill concentrations in Antarctic waters. Krill is excellent food for salmon, and Joyner has visions of fat fish returning in astronomical numbers to release points along the coasts of Tierra del Fuego, the Aukland Islands, and perhaps Kerguelen in the south Indian Ocean.

If such massive salmon production, which Joyner terms a first step toward a planetary aquaculture, does indeed go as planned, there will be an increasingly complex and constructive web of international fishery relationships—in this case, chiefly between Chile, Argentina, New Zealand, and northern hemisphere countries. But there remains a question regarding the stability of the food web in the Antarctic sea. The projected consumption of krill by salmon may starve off the whales.

Although salmon enhancement is perhaps the most dynamic example of large-scale future mariculture, two humbler organisms, mussels and kelp, have the potential for producing ocean crops of enormous bounty.

Mussels are bivalve mollusks, relatives of clams and oysters. Mussels are especially good for mariculture since the best varieties grow in cold water where there are relatively few shellfish diseases and predators. At a given water temperature, mussels grow considerably faster than most commercial clams and oysters.

There are other strategic advantages to farming mussels. In many locations they are the most abundant wild bivalve, and when the veliger larvae reach the point of settling down from the plankton, they have a gregarious tendency. On a properly managed mussel farm, the new crop literally seeds itself next to the coming harvest. Unlike clams, mussels can grow attached to nearly any solid surface. Unlike oysters, mussels do not warp badly when they are allowed to grow in dense clusters, the most economical culture configuration. With their beardlike byssus, a mat of tough strands tipped by sticky adhesive, mussels commonly grow attached to ropes in the water. This provides the crowning suitability for mussels as a commercial crop, for they can literally be farmed in three-dimensional plots.

Modern mussel culture utilizes knotted ropes hanging vertically from surface floats or rafts. Mussels grow in clusters down the lengths of the ropes. The productivity of these hanging sea gardens is nearly beyond belief. In the upper twenty to thirty meters of Puget Sound, Washington State's Lummi Indians, who also rear salmon, have been harvesting 150,000 pounds of mussel protein per acre.

At present few people in the United States eat mussels, although they are very popular in Europe. The worldwide species, *Mytilus edulis,* is generally the most esteemed. Steamed on the half-shell, *Mytilus* has a delicious nutty flavor, and it goes well in many seafood recipes. Mariculture experts such as Dr. Bruce Miller of the University of New Hampshire believe that introducing the American public to mussels is largely a public relations problem. Successful marketing requires psychology and the kind of advertising skill that once transformed the shunned "horse mackerel" into the profoundly popular tuna fish.

Sad to say, most of the present mussel harvest in the United States goes into animal feeds. However, as consumers of phytoplankton, mussels and other bivalves are the most economical and ecologically efficient products of mariculture. Their filter-feeding habit, however, makes water quality an important issue. Although bivalves are fairly hardy in the presence of pollution, they greatly magnify noxious and dangerous substances in their tissues. Contaminated mussels, if placed in clean water, will purge themselves of harmful microbes, but it is known that many chemicals, especially the carcinogenic polycyclic aromatic hydrocarbons (PAH) remain indefinitely in the meat of oysters. Presumably this holds true for other bivalves. Certainly a mussel or oyster farm could be ruined by a nearby oil spill. Trace pollution with pesticides or PCBs would probably be equally disastrous. Large bivalve-growing operations of the future, if they are intended to provide protein for human consumption, will be incompatible with all but the cleanest coastal waters.

The large-scale, open-sea culture of kelp has developed almost overnight. The main financial backing and direct initial participation in personnel, equipment, and logistical support have come from the U.S. Navy. Roots of the idea are diffuse, but the modern kelp-farm concept seems to have emerged not long after the Arab oil embargo.

The Navy has spent considerable time working on modular attachment surfaces for the kelp. The most likely physical system is a nylon mesh or webbing on a lightweight collapsible frame, forming an artificial substrate up to several hundred meters across. The probable configuration will be circular with radiating spokes; a central supporting column may be present, making the whole rig resemble an upside-down parasol. Arranged horizontally about twenty meters below the surface, the circular substrate will form a false bottom from which the kelp will grow upward as if it were in its normal habitat.

But the kelp farms of the future will be planted far offshore in the California Current.

If the pilot experiments prove workable, there are some far-reaching plans for the future. Many small modular kelp farms could be linked together in plantations, extending perhaps for ten kilometers in various configurations. The drag of water on such a huge field of kelp makes mooring it in one place difficult, if not impossible, and it might be necessary to let the neutrally buoyed arrays drift. Substrates could be deployed and planted with kelp "seedlings" somewhere in the Northeastern Pacific. The new groves could be moored until the drag caused by the growing plants became prohibitive, then released to move slowly southward with the California Current.

By sometime in the 1980s this imaginative style of ocean aquaculture might come to resemble a blend of modern high-yield forestry and an old-time cattle drive. The huge drifting sea forests would probably be attended by men on small but seaworthy craft. Constant navigational fixes on such a large, low-lying, maritime obstacle would be needed. Occasionally, tugs might have to steer the algae out of major shipping lanes and away from islands on the approaches to southern California. Finally, perhaps off San Diego, mature kelp would reach the end of the trail. Harvesting and processing might occur at sea in factory vessels, and then the collapsible substrate arrays would be recovered and returned to the starting point of the cycle.

The primary product of this potentially enormous-scale enterprise is not food, nor the traditional gelatin products derived from kelp. The Navy's interest is not to provide cover for submarines. Kelp is seen to offer a living and rapidly renewable energy source.

Using cheap fermentation processes, the seaweed can be converted and refined into clean, powerful fuels. Alcohols and hydrocarbons of low molecular weight produced from kelp would all work well in internal combustion engines. Tons of algae, however, are required to produce a barrel of fuel, and the practicality of kelp power on a significant scale is far from assured. Still, the ocean range is fertile and incomparably vast, and there are other promising possibilities for pioneers. For example, kelp could replace petroleum in providing feedstocks for the plastics industry, and a combined harvest of chemical resources and food might be feasible, the latter in the form of fish and other edibles attracted to and living within the huge floating masses of seaweed.

But before we clear and plow and sow the ocean wilderness, we must look ahead and ask if biological engineering on the scale of planetary aquaculture is beyond criticism. How long can we continue to manipulate the earth's rare inheritance of biotic diversity? What might truly massive injections of some future race of genetically manipulated super-salmon do to certain marine ecosystems? Will crazy quilts of cultured kelp someday make the California Current look like a distorted version of Iowa's corn country? And will high intensity marine farming bring a new wave of aquapesticides, nominally to suppress the shelled and spiny nibblers of the crop, but unintentionally to contaminate the oceanic gyres? Multiple billions of humans can conceivably live on mussels, but living *like* mussels is a less appetizing prospect.

The Industrial Shelf

Along the North American rim, a mass spawning of industrial projects is expected in the next ten years. Power plants, whether built on the coast or offshore, will endanger life on the continental shelf until better methods to prevent entrainment and entrapment are devised. Constructive uses should be sought for the rivers of warmed water which return from the huge generating stations to damage the sea, or dry-cooling should be employed. Some form of intensive aquaculture may be possible in the thermal plumes. However, one scientist writing in the journal *Aquaculture* (1975, Vol. 6, page 8) warns that a buildup of dangerous radioactive ions in seafood near nuclear plants could result in marketing problems under U.S. law. The extent of an actual impact on public health (chiefly concerning cancer) from such seafood remains to be evaluated. New ways to recover usable energy from thermal effluents are needed. The concept of "waste" heat should be abhorrent to a technological society facing an extended energy crisis.

It is hoped that waste disposal on the continental shelf will taper off, but whether it does or not will depend on a conservation ethic, a willingness to steer away from the short-term temptations of a throwaway economy. Recycling and reclamation of wastes from metals to organic fertilizing substances may reverse the deterioration of water quality and cure the already widespread environmental health problems on the shelf. Of course, releases of highly toxic and carcinogenic chemicals to the environment must stop entirely. New breakthroughs, such as the bacterial process for treating PCBs in wastewater, are encouraging, but the corrective research is still decades behind the burgeoning chemical disposal problem. Solid waste disposal from ships is a problem of oceanwide severity to small fish, birds, and perhaps other creatures. This situation could be controlled by the simplest measures: eliminating the use of non-degrading plastics, and installing trash compactors. Vessels operated for oceanographic research should set an example in this respect for the marine community.

But the greatest industrial presence of them all on the continental rim is Big Oil. The extraction of oil on Georges Bank, the Middle Atlantic shelf, off southern California, in the Gulf of Alaska, and perhaps on the Arctic shelf will be the most conspicuous activity. A frenetic shuttling of tankers, laying of pipelines, building of offshore terminals and onshore refineries will follow.

From the halls of the FEA to local chambers of commerce, the planning course being followed for new offshore oil development has been very hastily contrived. Nearly everyone with a political or economic stake in the industrial shelf has urged drilling at full speed, albeit after public hearings on the shelf environment. The environmental hearings, held in 1975 in the regions concerned, were based on scant scientific information, and even missed gravely pertinent facts, such as the New England lobster's strange behavioral sensitivity to certain petroleum fractions. Yet these hearings, before the facts were in, probably consumed more man-hours than were allotted for subsequent actual impact studies of the offshore environments which will be developed. Typically, the impact studies were to be one year in duration. The official, federally-sanctioned study of the bottom fauna on Georges Bank, for example, employed five people, two of them on a part-time basis.

There is a growing feeling among marine scientific observers that the impact studies on the shelf are based on minimal compliance with the law—a mere going through the motions. They believe the quality of regional marine environments is bound to suffer. And some who look beyond the years of declining hydrocarbon production believe that present plans for onshore development will bring some gross human impacts as well.

In the New England region, the possibility of a major oil strike on Georges Bank has brought calls for building new refineries on the pristine northern coast. Much industrial attention is focused on Eastport, Maine. Oil industry spokesmen and some local businessmen emphasize the economic boon to the Eastport area in terms of jobs and economic growth, but many local residents are unsure. Economic analysts from MIT and elsewhere have pointed out that most of the jobs in the construction and operation of a modern oil terminal and refinery do not go to needy but untrained local people. Instead, outside workers are imported by the principal companies and contracting firms.

On the subject of massive industrial development in remote and relatively pristine coastal sites, some hard questions seem overdue. If the terminals and refineries bring growth and change to outlying areas, what will be lost in these areas? Rather than turn a place of increasing rarity, such as Eastport, into an industrial center, why not place new refineries in existing industrial areas?

Some regional developers, oil companies, and politicians envision building new refineries at several scattered points on the New England coast. Searsport, Portland, Boston, and Providence have received prominent attention in addition to Eastport. At present, Providence has New England's only refinery, a small one of 7,000-barrels-per-day capacity. The nearest large refineries are in northern New Jersey.

Scattering oilports and refineries at numerous localities along the coast makes poor sense from the standpoint of dealing efficiently with oil spills. Concentrating the refineries and the pollution-fighting capabilities is ecologically safer and maybe economically sound as well. With regional refineries clustered in a single area, transport routes and transfer points for the supertankers of the 1980s will be fairly precise and limited. The best antipollution equipment can be held ready for deployment at a few strategic coastal points which are accessible to these routes. This would maximize the ability to control spills and minimize potential impacts to spawning grounds, wild and scenic shores, and seaside recreation areas.

One or two centralized petroleum-handling facilities rather than half a dozen would save lots of antipollution money by avoiding costly replication of effort and equipment. If we are serious about stopping the dismal tide of spilled oil, it will be expensive. The MIT Offshore Oil Task Group recommended that a separate basic cleanup system (boom, barges, and personnel) be available to protect each new oil port. Without this local protection, the analysts' computers predicted that nearshore spills could not be reached in time for adequate containment and collection. The MIT group projected that the annual cost of a minimal local cleanup system would probably exceed a million dollars.

New England seems especially vulnerable to scattershot oil development. The outlying coastal areas thrive on summer tourism, largely because of their well-preserved colonial flavor. But a tanker terminal can't be hidden behind a maritime museum. As yet there is no such thing as a quaint oil refinery.

What of the future? We are told that even the largest potential Georges Bank find will be pumped out in fifteen or twenty years. Even Arab oil will be nearly gone in forty. What will happen to the quickly built refinery towns and their economies then? Will the proposed new oil centers simply become ghost towns when the oil is gone, like those small western towns which were founded on short rushes for precious minerals? In a major industrial center it is possible that the idle refineries of the future can be refurbished and used for some other useful capacity, but in outlying places such as Eastport, Maine, this is doubtful.

The question of building New England refineries will be settled on the basis of many factors: economic, scientific, aesthetic, and whimsical. But one thing should be kept in mind. Once growth begins to block in the natural coastal landscape, and once pollution begins to build up in the sediments, there is no going back. The precedents are almost everywhere.

In the Middle Atlantic region, a copious flow of offshore oil is expected from the Baltimore Canyon Trough, and the questions raised about petroleum development on New England's continental shelf could be repeated here. If refineries, tanker traffic, and tar lumps spread along the remaining undisturbed shores, where will we go for a change of scene?

There is another good argument for concentrating refineries, transfer facilities, and perhaps other projects such as power plants into energy enclaves: concentration would help to protect these facilities from coastal and open-water sabotage. Three factors combine to make security on the continental shelf an exceedingly serious issue for the next decade and beyond. First, the technology of diving has achieved great sophistication in the amateur ranks; second, the depressing trend of destructive guerrilla activity in the national and international arena may well escalate with time; finally, the kinds of developments proposed along the continental shelf will have high commercial and strategic value. If these facilities proliferate and become widely dispersed, they will be highly vulnerable as targets.

Offshore oil fields will be especially hard to protect and may be the first installations to invite sabotage or blackmail. In the North Sea, British oil and gas platforms have been threatened several times. One scare was taken seriously enough for the Royal Navy to rush an antidemolition diving team to the scene. Unless buried deeply, pipelines will be very vulnerable. Even relatively deep-water equipment may not be safe because of small submersibles and the ease with which they can be handled. The next ten years may see the advent of the malicious oil spill.

In the Gulf of Mexico, the United States' first offshore "superports" (LOOP and Seadock) are about to be built. Technical experts offer a number of reasons for believing that superports are safer with respect to oil spills than conventional harbors. The reduction of oil tanker traffic in congested harbors is foremost among these. However, the northwestern Gulf of Mexico is already congested with oil rigs. Better sites for superports might have been found farther east, not as far as the pristine Florida shelf, but at least where the huge crude carriers would not have to enter the great watery pinball table of the northwestern Gulf.

Far more oil has already been spilled off Texas and Louisiana than anywhere else on the United States continental shelf. Why then has so little research on Gulf Coast oil pollution reached the readily available scientific literature? Why have no national symposia focused on several massive oil spills in the Gulf in recent years? Why have studies in less oily parts of the country, notably New England and California, contributed more to the public's understanding of the effects of oil in the sea than any done in the Gulf Coast region?

The answer to these questions appears related to the fact that most oil pollution research in the Gulf is funded by oil interests. The purse strings of the petroleum industry are reaching enormous distances. One of the largest organizations of marine scientists in the area is the Gulf Universities Research Consortium (GURC). Founded in 1965, GURC is an affiliation of scientists from twenty-two colleges and universities across the deep south from Florida to Texas, including one in Mexico. The list of eighty corporations providing GURC's research funds includes eighteen oil and gas companies, among them several well-known giants. Nearly all the rest are direct oil-industry affiliates such as drilling companies, pipeline companies, oil tool companies, etc. Organizations such as GURC and the similarly funded Texas A. and M. Research Foundation have tended to monopolize regional scientific investigations of oil pollution. This is especially true in the modern era of tight government funding. An outsider has little chance of obtaining a grant to conduct an independent study. This unfortunate situation must change. If they are to be reliable, future impact studies in the Gulf, for example ecological investigations of large offshore port facilities, should have significant participation by scientists whose work is supported by other than oil industry money.

Like the coastal oil ports proposed for New England, LOOP and Seadock, the projected offshore terminals in the Gulf of Mexico should have full contingents of resident, pollution-fighting men and equipment. As the industrial presence spreads on the shelf and grows in magnitude, the chance of polluting wide and vital areas looms with such enormity that it demands full-time attention. The U.S. Coast Guard has taken on part-time pollution cleanup and environmental law enforcement roles. With its many other duties, however, the Coast Guard is hard pressed to oversee all the widening ripples of marine impact.

The steps taken by the Coast Guard—for example, in developing methods and assembling teams to control toxic materials spills—should be continued and expanded. Because pollution on the shelf could be so pervasive in the future, perhaps a full time national marine environmental service is warranted. Such a group might be thought of as a marine action arm of the Environmental Protection Agency.

Along the Pacific Border, the major looming threat is from tankers which will begin to carry Alaskan North Slope oil in late 1977 or 1978. From an environmental standpoint, transport of this oil would be safer if it didn't go through the dangerous straits into Puget Sound at all, but rather were taken farther south.

Plans already call for huge LNG (liquified natural gas) tankers to carry Alaska's natural gas from Valdez to southern California. Perhaps most of the oil should follow suit. For safety reasons the superships could stay more than 100 kilometers offshore all the way and take advantage of the slight boost afforded by the California Current as well as the usually fine weather on the approach to port.

The same potential antipollution advantages that would accrue to the condensation of refineries on the east coast should also hold on the Pacific Border. The economics, ecology, and aesthetics of large energy facilities should receive thorough public debate. Such facilities might be expected to make areas which are already polluted somewhat more so. However, new methods to control emissions to air and water could, if applied with the current fervor of an industrial TV commercial on the environment, result in a net reduction in pollution in heavily developed areas. These same methods, of course, would be required no matter where new refineries were sited.

So the prime remaining oil-risk factor would seem to be the chance of a superspill. Physically speaking, risks would seem greater in northern fogs and storms (Washington's Rosario Straits and the Gulf of Maine) than off sunnier southern shores. Psychologically speaking, oil spill risks might be felt more acutely near developed areas, such as popular public swimming beaches and seaside estates of corporation heads. This was the lesson of the Santa Barbara blowout. This very principle could make tanker captains a little more cautious on the approaches to southern California than to Puget Sound.

The surprising 1976 decision by U.S. Interior Department Secretary Kleppe to permit petroleum development in the Gulf of Alaska, despite warnings from the federal Council on Environmental Quality and most other government and independent groups familiar with the area, seems likely to spawn some earthshaking environmental reaction. Already disturbed by visions of icebergs and tidal waves in Prince William Sound, Alaskans are now becoming concerned about the unsettling possibilities surrounding the establishment of production platforms on the southern shelf. One wonders about the whole seemingly irrational rush to "drain America first" as the continental shelf leasing program has been dubbed. If our domestic oil reserve is as small as most believe, should we burn most of it in the next ten to fifteen years? The cost of extracting crude from offshore fields in the difficult and dangerous Gulf of Alaska may exceed the price of Arab oil.

The situation in the Bering, Chukchi and Beaufort Seas is even riskier than off southern Alaska. But since petroleum experts believe that continental shelves of the high Arctic may well harbor huge petroleum reservoirs, their attempted development is probably inevitable.

If big oilfields are somehow developed in the environs of the arctic shelf, the thin ecological strands in that part of the world could be strained for decades, or snap and be permanently lost. Chronic pollution or a big spill at sea could literally kill large portions of the northernmost continental shelf.

The spillover from any large new sources of arctic oil probably would have consequences for the lower Pacific Border. New refineries beyond those needed for the Prudhoe Bay field would have to be sited, presumably on the west coast. How much wild underwater borderland will then remain away from the routes of huge crude carriers?

For the present, oil is indeed king of the continental shelf, and will be, probably, for some time to come. The acute threat to unique and irreplaceable localities, the official and unofficial underwater parklands, will come from huge ships and sea floor pipelines. The chronic danger to the entire epicontinental sea will come from a barely perceptible thickening and spreading of oil in water over the years. Within and below the waters of the continental shelf, the wonderfully intricate and vital natural communities will survive only with conscientious human stewardship.

Technology: From Missiles to Mussels

T echnology is the most problematic of human creations. It threatens us, nurtures us, pampers us. It causes future shock as it heals us. Technology has made modern man the world-dominating organism he is. Across the planet it has begun to alter physical and biological systems to a measurable extent. Some decry its darker developments as leading us rapidly to global ecocide. Others see it as our only hope for the future.

So far technology has achieved very little toward reversing the flow of degradation in the marine environment. Even modest examples of a "technological fix"—the premise that scientists and engineers can always come up with the necessary device or formula to save the future from the excesses of the present—have not materialized. We have not yet significantly reduced oil contamination through technology; we have not found effective ways to utilize waste heat, nor can we cure fin rot, although we could end the pollution which seems to cause it.

The growth of exploitative marine technology, on the other hand, has been phenomenal. Much of this has been coupled to the ever more intensive and extensive search for mineral wealth beneath the sea. The development of offshore oil reserves, in particular, has provided a mounting, although indirect, threat to the health of the ocean environment. Direct technological assault on the living sea has come with the invention of fishing methods so powerful they may destroy wide areas of bottom on the continental shelf. A new, more sophisticated line of fishing equipment is just becoming available to those who can afford it. From the comfort of his bridge, the late twentieth-century fisherman can identify and pinpoint his quarry, bag his limit, disgorge the catch into an island mother ship, and go back for more. This gross mechanical ability has matured before the full development of understanding of the fragile fisheries or of the coordination which must exist between man and his total environment.

Technology unrelated to the exploitation of marine resources may still have a disruptive effect. Examples are common. Two to watch in the future are flights of SSTs playing their devastating sonic booms in wide paths crisscrossing the water planet, and bionic sonar, a new invention for orientation and communication by military submarines. Bionic sonar mimics natural sounds in the sea and thus remains undetectable to a listening enemy. Both the SST and bionic sonar pose uncertain, unsettling threats to the behavior of the beleaguered marine mammals.

Nevertheless, there has also been a vast bloom of technology with beneficial uses which may contribute enormously to oceanic conservation. Although immensely powerful, the friendly technology is chiefly passive. By itself, it does not carry the power to clean up or maintain the ocean environment; instead it enhances vision. Primarily through the development of satellites, human beings can now gauge their interactions with nature over the entire surface of the earth. The powerful new perception permits monitoring of the marine environment and the formulation and enforcement of conservation laws with unequaled precision and objectivity.

The prototype for remote surveillance of the ocean is the Earth Resources Technology Satellite (ERTS), first launched in 1972. ERTS' original mission was to define practical, peaceful earthly problems for which space technology might offer solutions; specifically this reconnaissance satellite was to develop new techniques for the survey of planetary resources. Very quickly the 891-kilogram orbiting observatory exceeded original expectations of its worth. In circling the earth fourteen times a day, while photographing a continuous 185-kilometer strip of ground, ERTS proved of special value in economic geology and agriculture.

Numerous geological features, commonly associated with metallic ore bodies and petroleum, have appeared on ERTS photos of previously little-known regions. A variety of crops and forests, diseases of crops, even variations in plant growth and crop yield can be mapped and measured from space.

Many views which were totally unexpected came from the sea. After being photographed from space, huge natural plumes of turbid water on the Texas continental shelf were found to contain concentrations of brown shrimp. Discolored patches and streaks on the sea from various dumping operations in the New York Bight have been recorded numerous times. ERTS can also detect upwellings and algal blooms. The imaging equipment aboard the satellite operates in several bands of visual light and the infrared as well. By means of automatic picture transmission of an upwelling area, for example, thermal differences as small as 2°C. can be distinguished. This same capability also permits delineation of ocean currents such as the Gulf Stream in surroundings of different temperature.

Pictures telemetered to the ground from ERTS readily reveal oil slicks and large effluent plumes. Enhancement of such features can be achieved through an artificial coloring of the original image, which is received in varying tones of gray. Each of the several spectral bands superimposed in a picture is assigned a different color. The result is a highly detailed false-color photograph.

The resolution of ERTS' video-recorded images is quite good. Features as small as ninety meters in diameter can be discerned, and linear tracks only fifteen meters wide can be seen. Movements of large ships such as oil tankers probably could be monitored, although most fishing vessels might be just below the limit of resolution. The wakes of relatively small craft, however, might be visible after computer enhancement of the tiny images.

The routine use of satellites to verify ship movements, spot illegal ocean dumping, monitor marine sanctuaries, and protect offshore fishing grounds is thus on the verge of practicality, although several satellites will be required, simultaneously covering different orbits.

There is even the possibility of much closer inspection from the vantage point of space. Recent declassified data on U.S. military photo-reconnaissance satellites refer to the ten-ton "Big Bird," first flown in the early 1970s. Big Bird can zoom from wide-area coverage to telescopic inspection which shows objects a third of a meter in diameter. One disadvantage is that these extreme close-up views cannot yet be attained by video techniques. These photos must be taken with classical, high-resolution photographic equipment, and film must be recovered in special, parachute-equipped capsules, which are picked up in midair.

The prospects of satellite monitoring for fisheries' purposes are good in light of comparable usages envisioned by the U.S. Customs Service in tracking small fishing and pleasure craft suspected of smuggling drugs ashore along numerous stretches of the U.S. coastline. If the powerful electronic and photo-optical capabilities of Big Bird and its offspring become more generally available and convenient to use, spot checks for illegal catches could be done from space. It should be possible to distinguish lobster from squid, flounder from cod and other species. In time, perhaps, even mesh sizes of nets might be verified by remote sensing. If controlled by the United Nations or another body with international power, such inspections could be used to guard territorial and international fisheries all over the world.

Developments comparable to satellite reconnaissance have appeared in inner space as well. The latest facts and figures are classified, but by the early 1960s the U.S. Navy had already deployed acoustic receivers on both the Atlantic and Pacific margins of North America. This equipment could detect a submarine or surface ship nearly anywhere in the ocean and localize it, at worst, within an eighty-kilometer radius. The underwater listening system has undergone many refinements in the last decade. It now locates with pinpoint precision the test missiles which land in the vast Pacific Missile Range. The recovery of a Soviet submarine off Hawaii in 1974 was possible only because U.S. ears in the sea recorded the explosion which marked the sub's demise. The sound was plotted so accurately that towed cameras later quickly found the sub on the bottom, 5,000 meters down.

Remote tracking of nearly any propeller-driven ship is possible because of an acoustic property termed the "propeller signature." Individual peculiarities of ships' engines and even hull shapes, transmitted as vibrations through the turning propeller, produce sound patterns as identifiable as human fingerprints. Modern passive listening arrays, placed on the outer continental shelf and slope, can detect these particular vibrations coming from thousands of miles away. Such technology should aid the monitoring of marine sanctuaries and specific sensitive fishing areas, for example, spawning grounds. Future fishermen using jet boats and hydrofoils, which might be harder to identify, could be required to carry a sonic signaling device with an assigned frequency or pattern of pulses. Acoustic monitoring could even cover a future krill fishery in the vast oceanic reaches surrounding the bottom of the world.

Beside the satellite and the earphone, there is another, long-established marine monitoring device with great potential for global service. Fashioned differently, but no less intricately than its sophisticated counterparts which record information in the visible and audible spectra, the mussel collects chemical data. Distributed worldwide, these small shellfish absorb and concentrate petroleum hydrocarbons, organochlorines, heavy metals, pathogenic microbes, and even trace atomic fallout such as strontium-90 and plutonium.

The idea of a global "mussel-watch" has received much recent promotion, notably by Dr. Edward Goldberg and colleagues at Scripps Institution of Oceanography in California. The United States EPA and UNESCO have shown interest in the scheme, which promises a continuous, low-cost assessment of marine pollution around the world.

The idea is to let the bivalves do the initial concentrating of the substances. The relative amounts of various pollutants accumulated by mussels in several geographic areas have already been calibrated. A special advantage of mussels is that one species, *Mytilus edulis,* exists worldwide in cool temperate and boreal epicontinental waters. This is also where most industrial nations are, and hence where the greatest amounts of most pollutants enter the sea. In the tropics, other species would have to be used, and their particular rates of uptake of pollutants compared to the standards for *M. edulis.*

U.S. mussel watchers propose that volunteers travel around the country, and perhaps the world, sampling mussels from urbanized to remote areas. Some technical training would be necessary; sampling would have to be precise and uniform. Simple pollutant analyses could be done on the spot, even in remote areas, with portable kits used in a van or boat. Other samples could be preserved in specified ways and sent to sophisticated labs. Different tissues of the mussel—byssus, liver, shell, etc.—accumulate different substances to different degrees. These could provide cross checks on the accuracy of laboratory results.

The mussel-watch idea is beautiful in its simplicity, but some caution may be in order. The mollusks may mislead researchers by metabolizing certain chemicals in still unknown ways. And parallel efforts must be made to understand what a given level of a pollutant in the mussel means to other creatures in the marine food web: algae, fish, and men, to name a sensitive few.

The sudden appearance of a dramatic technological solution to any given large-scale problem is improbable. Gradual improvements in relations between man and the marine environment may come about, however, through many separate developments which will combine approaches from the arcane electronic gadgetry of satellites to the quiet workings of mussels in muddy water.

Law of the Sea

More than any other natural phenomenon, the ocean has been recognized as the earth's greatest single unifying system. The aggregative world ocean constitutes a dynamic, integrating force of enormous complexity. It transforms powerful outside influences, such as radiant solar energy and the movements of celestial bodies, into vital earthly attributes. At the same time, massive exchanges of materials and energy occur worldwide between oceans, the atmosphere, and the land. Even in time, the ocean presents a unifying image. In a sense its waters are older than the ocean floors and most of the continental rocks. Physically, chemically, biologically, the oceans have directed the course of global evolution. Most recently the influence of the sea has controlled many of the activities and aspirations of the world's dominant species. Now man's influence on the sea may be the more powerful.

In the year 1608, a Dutch lawyer named Hugo Grotius wrote a document which came to be known as "Freedom of the Seas." In his preamble he said, " . . . the subject of our discussion is the ocean . . . that ocean which encompasses the terrestrial home of mankind with the ebb and flow of its tides, and which cannot be held nor enclosed, being itself the possessor rather than the possessed." Grotius proposed a three-mile limit to the seaward territorial claims of coastal nations.

For more than three centuries, the world ocean and its resources beyond the three-mile limit were considered extranational. Throughout this time, the sea provided highways, fishing grounds, and battlefields which experienced ever greater use, but the idea of ownership of large areas of the sea received negligible attention. Perhaps it was psychologically impossible for most men, who took days or weeks to cross the open reaches in wet, cold, creaky little ships, to conceive of actually owning such territory. Longing for the security and comfort of landfall, even the most ardent of expansionists from the Elizabethan era to World War II must have thought of the sea as a kind of outer space. Moreover, in practical terms, except at critical straits the sea roads were too broad to defend indefinitely and the fishery resources were inexhaustible, so why bother claiming them?

Freedom of the seas—and by extension, the sea floor—remained a vague form of international law until close to the middle of the twentieth century. In 1945, the first significant move toward national seaward expansion was made by President Harry S. Truman. This relatively little-known Truman Doctrine proclaimed U.S. ownership over the sea bed and its resources out to the edge of the continental shelf. The decree ignored the overlying water with its swimming resources.

The motive behind this extension of jurisdiction over submerged ground was not immediately clear, but in 1946 work began on spindly little platforms which were eventually towed a short distance out to sea, fitted with drilling equipment, and by 1949 oil had begun to flow from shallow offshore wells in the Gulf of Mexico.

After the dramatic American challenge to the notion of oceanic freedom, three South American countries bordering the Pacific waded in a step deeper. In 1952, Chile, Peru, and Ecuador claimed national jurisdiction and full territorial authority over the sea to a distance of 200 nautical miles off their coasts. They laid claim to resources which were both on the bottom and suspended in the water. In particular they were interested in controlling the enormously rich fishery for tuna, among other species, which had been discovered in the upwelling zone offshore.

Soon a number of other countries began claiming territorial waters beyond the traditional three-mile limit. In 1958 and 1960 two conferences were called by the United Nations to consider updating and refining international law as it applied to the sea. The result was a non-binding proclamation which sanctioned the Truman dictum on the continental shelf and reserved the traditional freedom of the high seas for fishing and navigation. At this time, there was little knowledge of what lay on the sea bed, and perhaps under it, beyond the edge of the shelf, and little prescience of the coming burst of marine technology, particularly in the fields of remote sensing and extraction of resources.

Oceanic issues again came to the fore in the United Nations in 1970. A world conference was proposed and planned for 1973 to establish a new legal regime for the world ocean and its resources which lay beyond the bounds of national jurisdiction.

Although three years were allotted for the massive amount of study necessary prior to the 1973 conference, the conference turned into a mere procedural session, and the difficult discussions were put off until the next year. The Law of the Sea Conference finally convened in the summer of 1974 in Caracas. One hundred fifty countries were represented, and no agreements were reached. The Caracas conference became only the first session in a series of ponderous international gatherings—Geneva in 1975, New York in 1976.

At issue is an ocean of resources: valuable fisheries, in particular those for wide-ranging species such as salmon and tuna; potentially huge petroleum deposits beneath several kilometers of water and sediment in the zone of the continental rise; and manganese nodules, potato-sized lumps of metallic ore which cover huge patches of the deep sea floor.

The future of international economics and efficient use of rare metals and a vital protein reserve depends on whether the high seas and deep ocean are regarded as belonging to the world community (*res communes*) or to no one (*res nullius*). A policy which is based on *res nullius* may turn out to be very expensive for almost everyone. There is the possibility of a destructively competitive race among great powers for the last unclaimed wealth on the planet.

Res communes seems the logical and humane choice for our water-filled spaceship earth, which is already running short of critical industrial metals and food. Profit to the world community as a whole would be greatest if ocean resources are extracted in the most efficient and conserving way possible. However, this would require a strong international authority to manage the deep ocean territory. The replication of extraordinarily expensive efforts could be avoided only if cutthroat international competition gave way to a shareholders' market in which auctions for long-term leases or saleable rights to ocean resources might provide some incentive for conservation—a measured pace of exploitation instead of a wasteful rush for immediate profit, one step ahead of the competition.

Without a strong international authority, community ownership of ocean space and resources could easily degenerate into a form of *res nullius*. Such a situation would resemble what University of California ecologist Garrett Hardin has called "the tragedy of the commons," in which public grazing land in seventeenth-century England was destroyed. Each farmer bordering the commons sought to maximize his own return by steadily enlarging his herd which used the free community land. The conservation ethic did not develop in such a society of individuals. No one farmer would limit the pace of exploitation, since his portion of the commons would simply be taken by others. Thus from a number of expressions of rational self-interest, a collective insanity resulted in the ruin of the commons.

The final possibility is to divide the whole ocean into plots owned by the individual nations, but this plan is not without pitfalls. Proprietary control of ocean resources may or may not be ecologically or economically sound depending on the owner's conservation ethic, which is related in complex ways to national wealth and the level of population.

Pollution will tend to spread from its focus into adjoining national sectors. Cynically, a polluting nation might calculate a favorable cost incentive for ocean dumping because neighboring ocean areas would absorb part of the waste.

For practical purposes, the ocean, with its natural flows of water and life, remains essentially a commons, even if it is divided up into private parcels or multiple-use sectors. There seems to be no easy way to avoid a clash of rational self-interests which everybody concerned recognizes as irrational in the end.

Clearly some radically new approaches are needed to avoid a tragedy of the oceans. Responsibility for protecting oceanic resources against destructive plundering must go beyond the stage of non-binding agreements. International amicability is useful, but the availability of sanctions and enforcement may be more important to an oceanic authority of the future. Fisheries for species such as salmon, tuna, and whales, which typically move through several proposed national economic zones, might be controlled by the threat of economic pressure on an offending country. This has already been tried in a small way by a few private groups, but success demands boycotts of larger scope. The use of satellites will enhance the enforcement of laws of the sea, but policing the wide waters will remain expensive.

Finally, whether man uses the precious metals and protein lying beneath the high seas to his best advantage or whether he squanders this marine inheritance in the next few decades may depend on the strength of the United Nations. Leadership by the technological nations such as the United States and the Soviet Union is also essential, for only a few countries among many possess the capabilities for the extraction of resources and environmental protection in the deep seas.

Around the continents, the law of the sea will be left to individual nations, and problems are more acute than in the deep ocean itself. The value of living marine resources and the intricate ecosystems must be clearly identified and protected, and underwater sites of great rarity, beauty and productivity should be accorded equal status with their counterparts on land.

Because of the growth of seaside populations and industry, environmental law in the United States and probably elsewhere has reached an impasse. Who does bear responsibility for the damage done to natural systems? At present, liability for environmental harm that occurs after the approval of an impact study belongs to the federal agency which gave the OK. For example, the tainting of clams in Rhode Island by an EPA-approved dumping operation resulted in a lawsuit against EPA by a seafood company. With the proliferation of industrial development and impact statements, and with the shrinking capacity of the environment to cleanse itself amid ever dirtier surroundings, such litigation is likely to appear at an accelerating pace.

The difficulty of performing an adequate impact study, especially in the marine environment, is enormous. A year is usually allotted for a study which might still be preliminary after ten. Most marine studies merely tabulate the distribution and abundance of visually obvious life in the projected impact area. Sometimes even this is done poorly. For example, when nighttime sampling is omitted, many kinds of creatures are missed entirely, and the numerical data for others are badly distorted. Studies often show a seasonal bias. Very rarely are the extremely delicate larval stages of organisms taken into account. Worst of all, the projected impact conditions are almost never created in model form and tested in a meaningful way on local animals and plants.

The crowning inadequacy is that most impact studies involve a direct client-consultant relationship. A private environmental research lab receives funding for a study from those who have a vested interest in getting approval for a potentially damaging project. The result is a form of directed research, for the consulting lab is often desperate for a contract, and the funding corporation can let its consultant go and hire another if it feels its interests are not being given due consideration. One way to avoid this vicious circle would be for companies to contribute to a regional fund for impact studies to be disbursed by an independent environmental commission. Contracts for impact studies could be awarded on a bidding system, which would also take into account the qualifications of a given research organization for dealing with a specific environmental problem.

Some improvement in the present system is essential. Agencies such as EPA cannot possibly monitor all the original research which goes into an impact study. Much of it has to be taken on faith. In the world of corporate competition, which spawns million-dollar bribes around the world, of what considered value is a clam bed, a shrimp nursery, or stand of kelp? If fishermens' lawsuits go against EPA, the federal agency will face ever-mounting litigation, while the polluting parties remain in business. If EPA wins its cases, then responsibility for environmental harm belongs to no one, encouraging poor-quality impact studies, followed by slipshod environmental management and control policies. In terms of preserving environmental quality, either outcome presages a no-win dilemma.

Until fairly recently, the right to sue was limited to cases in which a concrete adversity existed. Concrete adversity was traditionally interpreted as direct physical or economic injury wrought by one party on another. In 1972, an important environmental case (*Sierra Club* v. *Morton*) came before the U.S. Supreme Court. The Sierra Club sought to halt development of a huge recreational complex, planned by Walt Disney Enterprises, in Mineral King Valley, a wild, remote portion of California's Sequoia National Forest. In this case, however, injury of a non-economic nature was claimed. But there was a further twist. The Club attempted to act as a legal guardian of the valley, and did not make the standard claims that members used the valley, depended on it for specific recreational values, etc.

The court ruled four to three that the Sierra Club did not have the right, or "standing," to sue since it was not claiming a stake in the potential adversity. But the decision did allow clearly for the first time that an individual could go to court in a case of adversity involving an aesthetic issue, and the Sierra Club was encouraged to refashion its suit in the name of a person or persons whose wilderness values were at stake in Mineral King Valley. This was not enough for Justice William O. Douglas, however. In an imaginative dissenting opinion he stated that a perfectly good case of concrete adversity was at hand if the action were revised as *Mineral King Valley* v. *Morton*. The Sierra Club would then simply have to show that it was fit to be a *guardian ad litem* or "next friend," bringing suit on behalf of the valley. Douglas argued that nonpersons such as ships and corporations qualify for this form of legal standing, so why not trees, rivers, and other natural objects?

Douglas' dissent in the *Mineral King Valley* case was based on a 1972 essay by C. D. Stone, a law professor at the University of Southern California. The case received serious discussion in Harvard and Northwestern University law journals. Eventually this "hypothesis of rights" of endangered natural systems and objects may have wide repercussions. If lobsters, menhaden, and shrimp, kelp forests and sea otters were to have legal standing, if lawsuits could be brought in their behalf against specific polluters, the responsibility for damages to the marine environment would fall squarely on the despoiler. Impact studies would then function as powerful guidelines on whether to proceed with a project. If the potential polluter could be sued by the damaged natural entity, through its "friends," there would be a high incentive to perform studies well, to assess the risks as accurately as possible.

Some degree of convergence between human and natural law is now essential. In its crasser manifestations, civilization is an attempt to become independent of the environment, and the humane aspects of this independence are still important—for example, the maintenance of reliable food supplies and freedom from natural disasters and disease—but there is a great overkill. If species continue to become extinct at an accelerating pace, and the degradation of ecosystems spreads, then the long-running "evolutionary play" in the "ecological theater" imagined by G.E. Hutchinson will eventually become bereft of players, props, and possibly the theater itself.

The coexistence of human beings with nature is, in a sense, a trust of universal magnitude. Albert Claude, in his 1975 Nobel lecture, hinted at the depths he has discovered in a living cell: "Life, this anti-entropy, ceaselessly reloaded with energy, is a climbing force, toward order amidst chaos, toward light among the darkness of the indefinite, toward the mystic dream of love between the fire which devours itself and the silence of the cold."

Life is physical nature trying to save itself from itself. Evolving consciousness is a wondrous process, now visibly capped by human beings. But they are endangering this universal experiment. The ultimate sin of pride against natural law would be to reduce wastefully and needlessly the options in the evolutionary process.

Like the calculations of chance for an industrial catastrophe—a head-on collision of supertankers, or a worst-case nuclear accident—our planet itself is an improbability, a million-to-one shot in the dark. With its flowing waters and winds, its slow, stony dynamism which raises spectacular monuments, its gentle sunshine, and its fitness for life, the earth may be as nearly perfect a place as ever will support a reasonable-sized human population whose civilized activities do not overwhelm the restorative natural forces. It is our only home, the only permanently habitable island of a tiny archipelago in an impossibly large sea.

Bibliography

New England I

Atema, J. and D. G. Engstrom. 1971. Sex pheromone in the lobster, *Homarus americanus. Nature* 232:261–63.

Cooper, R. A. and J. R. Uzmann. 1971. Migrations and growth of deep-sea lobsters, *Homarus americanus. Science* 171:288–90.

Emery, K. O. and E. Uchupi. 1972. *The Western North Atlantic Ocean: Topography, Rocks, Structure, Water, Life, and Sediments*. American Association of Petroleum Geologists. Tulsa, Okla.

Herrick, F. H. 1909. Natural history of the American lobster. *Bulletin U. S. Bureau of Fisheries* (Fishery Bulletin) 29:147–408.

Hughes, J. T. and G. C. Matthiessen. 1962. Observations on the biology of the American lobster, *Homarus americanus. Limnology and Oceanography* 7:414–21.

Mann, K. H. 1973. Seaweeds: their productivity and strategy for growth. *Science* 182:975–81.

New England II

Bigelow, H. B. and W. C. Schroeder. 1953. Fishes of the Gulf of Maine. *Fishery Bulletin* 53:1–577.

Boyar, H. C. et al. 1973. Seasonal distribution and growth of larval herring (*Clupea harengus* L.) in the Georges Bank-Gulf of Maine area from 1962 to 1970. *Journal du Conseil* 35:36–51.

De Wolf, A. G. 1974. The lobster fishery of the Maritime Provinces: economic effect of regulations. *Bulletin Fisheries Research Board of Canada* 187:1-59.

Dow, R. L. et al. 1975. Bioeconomic relationships for the Maine lobster fishery with consideration of alternative management schemes. *NOAA Technical Report*, NMFS, SSRF 683:1-43.

Graham, F. Jr. 1973. The lobster is a fisheries disaster. *Audubon* 75(4):105–8.

Graham, M. 1943. *The fish gate*. London: Faber and Faber, Ltd.

Jeffries, H. P. and W. C. Johnson. 1974. Seasonal distributions of bottom fishes in the Narragansett Bay area: seven-year variations in the abundance of winter flounder (*Pseudopleuronectes americanus*). *Journal Fisheries Research Board of Canada* 31:1057–66.

Newton, R. S. and A. Stefanon. 1975. Application of side-scan sonar in marine biology. *Marine Biology* 31:287–91.

Olson, S. B. 1975. Big changes ahead in commercial fishing. *Maritimes* 19. 1:1–3.

Posgay, J. A. and R. R. Marsh. 1970. The numbers of haddock spawning on Georges Bank as estimated from egg surveys. *ICNAC Research Document* 70/83:96–102.

Rusby, J. S. and J. Revie. 1975. Long-range sonar mapping of the continental shelf. *Marine Geology* 19:M41–M52.

Shuck, H. A. 1952. Offshore grounds important to the United States haddock fishery. *Research Report* 32. U.S. Fish and Wildlife Service:1–20.

New England III

Atema, J. and L. Stein. 1972. Sublethal effects of crude oil on lobsters (*Homarus americanus*) behavior. *Technical Report WHOI 72-74*. Woods Hole, Mass.

Atema, J. et al. 1973. The importance of chemical signals in stimulating behavior of marine organisms: effects of altered environmental chemistry on animal communication. In *Bioassay Techniques and Environmental Chemistry*, pp. 177–97. Ann Arbor, Mich.: Ann Arbor Science Publishers, Inc.

Beardsley, R. C. and B. Butman. 1974. Circulation on the New England continental shelf: response to strong winter storms. *Geophysical Research Letters* 1:181–84.

Blumer, M. et al. 1971. A small oil spill. *Environment* 13(2):1–12.

Blumer, M. et al. 1972. Petroleum. In *A Guide to Marine Pollution*, ed. E. G. Goldberg; pp. 19–40. New York: Gordon and Breach.

Blumer, M. and W. W. Youngblood. 1975. Polycyclic aromatic hydrocarbons in soils and recent sediments. *Science* 188:53–5.

Council on Environmental Quality. 1974. *OCS Oil and Gas - An Environmental Assessment*. Wash., D. C. 5 Vols.

Dow, R. L. et al. 1975. The ecological, chemical, and histopathological evaluation of an oil spill site. *Marine Pollution Bulletin* 6(11):164–73.

Forrester, W. D. 1971. Distribution of suspended oil particles following the grounding of the tanker, *Arrow*. *Journal of Marine Research* 29: 151–70.

Gillette, R. 1974. Oil and gas resources: did USGS gush too high? *Science* 185:127–30.

Grigalunas, T. A. 1975. Offshore oil development and the New England economy. *Maritimes* 19(2):5–7.

Kuhnhold, W. W. 1974. Investigations on the toxicity of seawater extracts of three crude oils on eggs of cod (*Gadus morhua* L.). *Berichte Deutsch wiss. Kommission Meeresforschung* 23:165–80.

Mackin, J. G. 1973. *A Review of Significant Papers on Effects of Oil Spills and Oil Field Brine Discharges on Marine Biotic Communities*. Project 737, Texas A&M Research Foundation. Texas A&M University, College Station, Tex., pp. 1–86.

Michael, A. D. et al. 1975. Long-term effects of an oil spill at West Falmouth, Massachusetts. *Proceedings of the Conference on Prevention and Control of Oil Pollution* (March 25–27, 1975) San Francisco, Calif., pp. 573–82.

Offshore Oil Task Group (MIT). 1973. *The Georges Bank Petroleum Study*. Sea Grant Project Office, Mass. Inst. of Technology. Cambridge, Mass. 3 Vols.

Sanders, H. L. et al. 1972. The West Falmouth oil spill. *Technical Report WHOI 72–20*, Woods Hole, Mass.

Sanders, H. L. 1974. The West Falmouth saga, how an oil expert twisted the facts about a landmark oil spill study. *New Engineer* (May, 1974).

Shelton, T. B. and J. V. Hunter. 1975. Anaerobic decomposition of oil in bottom sediments. *Journal Water Pollution Control Federation* 47:2256–70.

Walford, L. A. 1938. Effect of currents on distribution and survival of eggs and larvae of the haddock (*Melanogrammus aeglefinus*) on Georges Bank. *Fishery Bulletin* 49(29):1–73.

Walker, J. D. et al. 1975. Effect of South Louisiana crude oil and No. 2 fuel oil on growth of heterotrophic microorganisms including proteolytic, lipolytic, chitinolytic, and cellulolytic bacteria. *Environmental Pollution* 9:13–33.

Map Sources

Fritz, R. L. 1965. Autumn distribution of groundfish species in the Gulf of Maine and adjacent waters, 1955–1961. *Serial Atlas of the Marine Environment*, Folio 10, American Geographic Society.

Walford, L. A. 1938. Effect of currents on distribution and survival of the eggs and larvae of the haddock (*Melanogrammus aeglefinus*) on Georges Bank. *Fishery Bulletin* 49(29), pages 8 and 33.

Cooper, R. A. and J. R. Uzmann. 1971. Migrations and growth of deep–sea lobsters, *Homarus americanus*. *Science* 171:288–90.

U. S. Department of Interior (Bureau of Land Management). 1975. Map: Frontier Outer Continental Shelf Areas—Georges Bank Trough (shows areas of potential oil reserves).

The Temperate Atlantic Margin I

Cheney, R. E. 1974. Nomads of the Sargasso Sea (more about Gulf Stream Eddies). *Maritimes* 18(3):11–13.

Dolan, R. A. et al. 1973. Man's impact on the barrier islands of North Carolina. *American Scientist* 61:152–62.

Emery, K. O. and E. Uchupi. 1972. *The Western North Atlantic Ocean: Topography, Rocks, Structure, Water, Life, and Sediments.* American Association of Petroleum Geologists. Tulsa, Okla.

Hoyt, J. H. and J. R. Hails. 1969. Pleistocene shorelines in a relatively stable area, southeastern Georgia, USA. *Proceedings Committee Mediterranean Neogene Stratigraphy 1967. Giornale di Geologia* (2) XXXV, fasc. IV; pp. 105–17.

Newton, J. G. and O. H. Pilkey. 1969. Topography of the continental margin off the Carolinas. *Southeastern Geology* 10:87–92.

Newton, J. G. et al. 1971. *An Oceanographic Atlas of the Carolina Continental Margin.* N.C. Dept. of Conservation and Development. Raleigh, N.C.

Perry, W. J. et al. 1975. Stratigraphy of Atlantic coastal margin of United States north of Cape Hatteras—brief survey. *American Association of Petroleum Geologists Bulletin* 59/9, pp. 1529–48.

Swift, D. J. P. 1975. Barrier-island genesis: evidence from the central Atlantic shelf, eastern USA. *Sedimentary Geology* 14:1–43.

Swift, D. J. P. 1975. Tidal sand ridges and shoal-retreat massifs. *Marine Geology* 18:105–34.

The Temperate Atlantic Margin II

Blaxter, J. H. S., ed. 1974. *The Early Life History of Fish.* New York: Springer-Verlag.

Breder, C. M. 1967. On the survival value of fish schools. *Zoologica* 52:25–30.

Caldwell, R. L. and H. Dingle. 1976. Stomatopods. *Scientific American* 234(1):80–9.

Coleman, D. C. and A. C. Mathieson. 1974. Investigations of New England marine algae VI: distribution of marine algae near Cape Cod, Mass. *Rhodora* 76:537–63.

Coleman, D. C. and A. C. Mathieson. 1975. Investigations of New England marine algae VII: seasonal occurrence and reproduction of marine algae near Cape Cod, Mass. *Rhodora* 77:76–104.

Frame, D. W. 1974. Feeding habits of young winter flounder, *Pseudopleuronectes americanus:* prey availability and diversity. *Transactions American Fisheries Society* 103:292–96.

Gehringer, J. W. 1970. Young of the Atlantic sailfish *Istiophorus platypterus. Fishery Bulletin* 68:177–89.

Howe, A. B. and P. G. Coates. 1975. Winter flounder movements, growth, and mortality off Massachusetts. *Transactions American Fisheries Society* 104:13–29.

Humm, H. J. 1969. Distribution of marine algae along the Atlantic coast of North America. *Phycologia* 7:43–53.

Jolley, J. W. Jr. 1975. *Sailfish in Florida waters.* International Game Fish Association, Ft. Lauderdale, Fla.

Kendall, A. W. and J. W. Reintjes. 1975. Geographic and hydrographic distributions of Atlantic menhaden eggs and larvae along the middle Atlantic coast from R/V *Dolphin*, 1965–66. *Fishery Bulletin* 73:317–35.

Norcross, J. J. et al. 1974. Development of young bluefish *(Pomatomus saltatrix)* and distribution of eggs and young in Virginian coastal waters. *Transactions American Fisheries Society* 103:477–96.

Reintjes, J. W. and P. M. Keney. 1975. Annotated bibliography on the biology of the menhadens, genus *Brevoortia*, 1963–73. *NOAA Technical Report*, NMFS-SSRF 687, Seattle, Wash.

Sears, J. R. and R. T. Wilce. 1975. Sublittoral benthic marine algae of southern Cape Cod and adjacent islands: seasonal periodicity, associations, diversity, and floristic composition. *Ecological Monographs* 45:337–65.

Shaw, E. 1975. Fish in schools. *Natural History* 84(8):40–46.

Tyler, A. V. 1971. Surges of winter flounder, *Pseudopleuronectes americanus* into the intertidal zone. *Journal Fisheries Research Board of Canada* 28:1727–32.

Bibliography

The Temperate Atlantic Margin III

Bowen, V. T. 1974. Transuranic elements and nuclear wastes. *Oceanus* 18(1):43–54.

Carpenter, E. J. 1974. Power plant entrainment of aquatic organisms. *Oceanus* 18(1):35–41.

Carpenter, E. J. et al. 1974. Survival of copepods passing through a nuclear power station on northeastern Long Island Sound, USA. *Marine Biology* 24:49–55.

Carter, L. J. 1974. Floating nuclear plants: power from the assembly line. *Science* 183:1063–65.

Clark, J. R. 1969. Thermal pollution and aquatic life. *Scientific American* 220(3):19–27.

Clark, J. R. 1974. *Coastal Ecosystems: Ecological Considerations for Management of the Coastal Zone.* The Conservation Foundation, Wash., D.C.

Hedgpeth, J. W. and J. J. Gonor. 1969. Aspects of the potential effect of thermal alteration on marine and estuarine benthos. In *Biological Aspects of Thermal Pollution*, pp 80–118. Eds. P. A. Krenkel and F. L. Parker. Nashville: Vanderbilt Univ. Press.

International Commission for Northwest Atlantic Fisheries. 1965. Environmental Symposium. *ICNAF Special Publication No. 6.*

Jensen, A. C. 1974. Sport fisheries and offshore oil. *N. Y. Fish and Game Journal* 21(2):105–16.

Kraft, J. C. et al. 1971. Time–stratigraphic units and petroleum entrapment models in Baltimore Canyon Basin of the Atlantic continental margin geosyncline. *Amer. Association Petroleum Geologists Bulletin* 55:658–79.

Olla, B. L. et al. 1970. Prey capture and feeding motivation in the bluefish, *Pomatomus saltatrix. Copeia* 1970:360–62.

Pearce, J. B. 1974. Regional coastal environmental considerations for offshore power plants, Sandy Hook to Atlantic City, New Jersey. In *Modifications*

Thermiques et Équilibres Biologiques, pp. 97–165. Amsterdam: Institut de la Vie, North Holland Publ. Co.

Shelford, V. E. and E. B. Powers. 1915. Reactions of fish in thermal gradients. *Biological Bulletin* 28:315–34.

Speth, J. G. 1975. The hazards of plutonium. *Natural History* (Jan., 1975), pp. 74–82.

U.S. Atomic Energy Commission. 1974. *Final environmental statement related to the proposed Seabrook Station, Units 1 and 2.* (Public Service Company of New Hampshire), Directorate of Licensing, U.S.A.E.C., Wash., D.C.

U.S. Atomic Energy Commission. 1974. *Final environmental statement related to the operation of Oyster Creek Nuclear Generating Station* (Jersey Central Power and Light Company), Directorate of Licensing, U.S.A.E.C., Wash., D.C.

U.S. Geological Survey. 1973. Water resources data for Virginia. Wash., D.C.

The Temperate Atlantic Margin IV

Babinchak, J. A. and J. T. Graikoski. 1974. Fecal coliforms in marine sediments. *Abstract, Amer. Society of Limnology and Oceanography Annual Meeting.* June, 1974.

Carpenter, E. J. and K. L. Smith Jr. 1972. Plastics on the Sargasso Sea surface. *Science* 175:1240–41.

Carpenter, E. J. et al. 1972. Polystyrene spherules in coastal waters. *Science* 178:749–50.

Colton, J. B. 1974. Plastics in the ocean. *Oceanus* 18(1):61–64.

Council on Environmental Quality. 1970. *Ocean Dumping: A National Policy.* CEQ, Report to the President.

Duedall, I. W. et al. 1975. Fate of wastewater sludge in the New York Bight apex. *Journal of the Water Pollution Control Federation* 47:2702–06.

Evseenko, S. A. and M. M. Nevinsky. 1973. Breeding and development of witch flounder (*Glyptocephalus cynoglossus* L.) in the Northwest Atlantic Ocean. *ICNAF Research Document 73/49.*

Geldreich, E. E. 1975. Microbiological criteria concepts for coastal bathing waters. *Ocean Management* 2:225–48.

Gopalan, U. K. and J. S. Young. 1975. Incidence of shell disease in shrimp in the New York Bight. *Marine Pollution Bulletin* 6(10):149–52.

Guarino, C. F. et al. 1975. Land and sea solids management alternatives in Philadelphia. *Journal Water Pollution Control Federation* 47:2551–64.

Keller, G. H. et al. 1973. Bottom currents in the Hudson Canyon. *Science* 180:181–83.

Loder, T. C. 1975. Effects of baled solid waste disposal in the marine environment—a descriptive model. In *Marine Chemistry in the Coastal Environment*, Amer. Chemical Society Special Symposium, 1974.

Mahoney, J. B. et al. 1973. A fin–rot disease of marine and euryhaline fishes of the New York Bight. *Transactions of the Amer. Fisheries Society* 102:596–605.

Pratt, S. D. et al. 1973. Biological effects of ocean disposal of solid waste. *Marine Technical Report*, Series 9. Sea Grant Office, Univ. Rhode Island.

Rowe, G. T. 1972. The exploration of submarine canyons and their benthic faunal assemblages. *Proceedings of the Royal Society of Edinburgh (B)* 73:159–69.

Rowe, G. T. et al. 1974. Time-lapse photography of the biological reworking of sediments in Hudson Submarine Canyon. *Journal of Sedimentary Petrology* 44:549–52.

Royce, W. F. 1959. Decline of the yellowtail flounder *(Limanda ferruginea)* off New England. *Fishery Bulletin* 59:169–267.

Shepard, F. P. 1975. Progress of internal waves along submarine canyons. *Marine Geology* 19:131–38.

Smith, W. G. et al. 1975. Seasonal distribution of larval flatfishes (Pleuronectiformes) on the continental shelf between Cape Cod, Mass., and Cape Lookout, N.C., 1965–66. *NOAA Technical Report*, NMFS-SSRF 691. Seattle, Wash.

Soucie, G. 1974. Here come de sludge. *Audubon* 76(4):109–13.

Tihansky, D. P. 1974. Recreational welfare losses from water pollution along U.S. coasts. *Journal of Environmental Quality* 3:335–42.

Vaughn, J. M. 1974. Human viruses as marine pollutants. *Oceanus* 18(1):24–28.

Ziskowski, J. and R. Murchilano. 1975. Fin erosion in the winter flounder. *Marine Pollution Bulletin* 6(2):26–29.

Map Sources

Stearns, F. 1969. Bathymetric maps and geomorphology of the middle Atlantic continental shelf. *Fishery Bulletin* 68:37–66.

Harrison, W. et al. 1967. Circulation of shelf waters off the Chesapeake Bight. *ESSA Professional Paper* No. 3. U.S. Dept. of Commerce, Wash., D.C.

Guarino, C. F. et al. 1975. Land and sea solids management alternatives in Philadelphia. *Journal Water Pollution Control Federation* 47:2551–64.

U.S. Department of Interior (Bureau of Land Management). 1975. Map: Frontier Outer Continental Shelf Areas - Baltimore Canyon Area.

Smith, W. G. et al. 1975. Seasonal distribution of larval flatfishes (Pleuronectiformes) on the continental shelf between Cape Cod, Mass., and Cape Lookout, N.C., 1965–66. *NOAA Technical Report* NMFS-SSRF 691. Seattle, Wash.

Kendall, A. W. and J. W. Reintjes. 1975. Geographic and hydrographic distributions of Atlantic menhaden eggs and larvae along the middle Atlantic coast from R/V *Dolphin*, 1965–66. *Fishery Bulletin* 73:323.

Pearce, J. B. 1974. Regional coastal environmental considerations for offshore power plants, Sandy Hook to Atlantic City, New Jersey. In *Modifications Thermiques et Équilibres Biologiques*. Amsterdam: Institut de la Vie, North Holland Publishing Co. pp 97–165.

Bibliography

Gulf of Mexico I

Borchert, H. and R. Muir. 1964. *Salt Deposits*. New York: Van Nostrand.

Bright, T. J. and L. H. Pequegnat. 1974. *Biota of the West Flower Garden Bank*. Houston: Gulf Publishing Co.

Burke, K. 1975. Atlantic evaporites formed by evaporation of water spilled from Pacific, Tethyan, and southern oceans. *Geology* 3:613–16.

Emery, K. O. and E. Uchupi. 1972. *The Western North Atlantic Ocean: Topography, Rocks, Structure, Water, Life, and Sediments*. American Association of Petroleum Geologists. Tulsa, Okla.

Emiliani, C. et al. 1975. Paleoclimatological analysis of late Quaternary cores from the northeastern Gulf of Mexico. *Science* 189:1083–88.

Garrison, L. E. and R. G. Martin Jr. 1975. Geological structures in the Gulf of Mexico Basin. *Geological Survey Professional Paper 773*, USGS, U.S. Dept. of Interior.

Kennett, J. P. and N. J. Shackleton. 1975. Laurentide Ice Sheet meltwater recorded in Gulf of Mexico deep-sea cores. *Science* 188:147–50.

Gulf of Mexico II

Adkins, G. 1972. A study of the blue crab fishery in Louisiana. *La. Wildlife and Fisheries Commission Technical Bulletin 3*.

Barrett, B. B. and M. C. Gillespie. 1973. Primary factors which influence commercial shrimp production in coastal Louisiana. *La. Wildlife and Fisheries Commission Technical Bulletin 9*.

Barrett, B. B. and M. C. Gillespie. 1975. 1975 environmental conditions relative to shrimp production in coastal Louisiana. *La. Wildlife and Fisheries Commission Technical Bulletin 15*.

Cook, H. L. and M. A. Murphy. 1970. Early developmental stages of the brown shrimp, *Penaeus aztecus*, reared in the laboratory. *Fishery Bulletin* 69:223–39.

Copeland, B. J. and T. J. Bechtel. 1974. Some environmental limits of six Gulf Coast estuarine organisms. *Contributions in Marine Science of the Univ. Texas* 18:169–204.

Crance, J. H. 1971. Description of Alabama estuarine areas—cooperative Gulf of Mexico estuarine inventory. *Alabama Marine Resources Bulletin*, No. 6.

El Sayed, S. Z. et al. 1972. Chemistry, primary productivity, and benthic algae of the Gulf of Mexico. *Serial Atlas of the Marine Environment*, Folio 22. Amer. Geographic Society, N.Y.

Farfante, I. P. 1969. Western Atlantic shrimps of the genus *Penaeus*. *Fishery Bulletin* 67:461–591.

Franks, J. S. et al. 1972. A study of nektonic and benthic faunas of the shallow Gulf of Mexico off the State of Mississippi. *Gulf Research Reports* 4(1):1–148.

Gaidry, W. J. III. 1974. Correlations between inshore spring white shrimp population densities and offshore overwintering populations. *La. Wildlife and Fisheries Commission Technical Bulletin 12*.

Gunter, G. and K. McGraw. 1973. Some analyses of twentieth century landing statistics of marine shrimp of the south Atlantic and Gulf states of the United States. *Gulf Research Reports* 4(2):191–204.

Hedgpeth, J. W. 1953. An introduction to the zoogeography of the northwest Gulf of Mexico with references to the invertebrate fauna. *Publications of the Institute of Marine Science of Texas* 3:109–224.

Kernek, S. P. and D. J. Kimeldorf. 1975. X-ray induced behavioral reactions and detection mechanisms in the shrimp. *Physiology and Behavior* 15:1–5.

McFarland, W. 1963. Seasonal change in the number and the biomass of fishes from the surf at Mustang Island, Texas. *Publications of the Institute of Marine Science of Texas* 9:91–105.

Moore, R. H. 1975. Occurrence of tropical marine fishes at Port Aransas, Texas, 1967–1973, related to sea temperatures. *Copeia 1975*(1):170–72.

Subrahmanyam, C. B. 1971. The relative abundance and distribution of penaeid shrimp off the Mississippi coast. *Gulf Research Reports* 3(2):291–345.

Subrahmanyam, C. B. 1971. Descriptions of shrimp larvae (family Penaeidae) off the Mississippi coast. *Gulf Research Reports* 3(2):241–58.

Temple, R. F. and C. C. Fisher. 1965. Vertical distribution of the planktonic stages of penaeid shrimp. *Publications of the Institute Marine Science of Texas* 10:59–67.

U.S. Department of Interior, Fish and Wildlife Service. 1954. Gulf of Mexico, its origin, waters, and marine life. *Fishery Bulletin* 55(89).

White, C. J. 1975. Effects of 1973 river flood waters on brown shrimp in Louisiana estuaries. *La. Wildlife and Fisheries Commission Technical Bulletin* 16.

Wickham, D. A. and F. C. Minkler III. 1975. Laboratory observations on daily patterns of burrowing and locomotor activity of pink shrimp, *Penaeus duorarum*, brown shrimp, *P. aztecus*, and white shrimp, *P. setiferus. Contributions in Marine Science of the Univ. of Texas* 19:21–35.

Gulf of Mexico III

Dobkin, S. 1961. Early developmental stages of pink shrimp, *Penaeus duorarum* from Florida waters. *U.S. Fish and Wildlife Service Bulletin* 61(190):321–49.

Harriss, R. C. and J. Mathis. 1974. Mangrove detritus and heavy metal cycling in the Florida Everglades. *Abstract, Amer. Society of Limnology and Oceanography. Annual Meeting.* June, 1974.

Hoffmeister, J. E. 1974. *Land from the Sea: the Geologic Story of South Florida.* Coral Gables, Fla.: Univ. of Miami Press.

Idyll, C. P. 1965. Shrimp nursery: science explores new ways to farm the sea. *National Geographic* 127(5):636–59.

Kuenzler, E. J. 1974. Mangrove swamp systems. In *Coastal Ecological Systems of the United States*, eds. H. T. Odum, B. J. Copeland, and E. A. McMahan. The Conservation Foundation, Wash., D.C, Vol. 1, pp. 346–71.

Odum, W. E. and E. J. Heald. 1972. Trophic analysis of an estuarine mangrove community. *Bulletin of Marine Science* 22:671–738.

Rehm, A. and H. J. Humm. 1973. *Sphaeroma terebrans:* a threat to the mangroves of southwestern Florida. *Science* 182:173–74.

Walsh, G. E. 1974. Mangroves: a review. In *Ecology of Halophytes*, eds. R. J. Reimold and W. H. Queen, pp. 51–172. New York: Academic Press.

Gulf of Mexico IV

Anderson, J. W. et al. 1974. Sublethal effects of oil, heavy metals and PCBs on marine animals. In *Survival in Toxic Environments*, eds. M. A. Q. Kahn and J. P. Bederka Jr., pp. 83–121. New York: Academic Press.

Anonymous news article. 1975. Texas passes legislation paving way for Seadock offshore terminal. *Ocean Industry* 10(7):85.

Blumer, M. and J. Sass. 1972. Oil pollution: persistence and degradation of spilled fuel oil. *Science* 176:1120–22.

Blumer, M. et al. 1973. The environmental fate of stranded crude oil. *Deep Sea Research* 20:239–59.

Carter, L. J. 1973. Deepwater ports: issue mixes supertankers, land policy. *Science* 181:825–28.

James, W. R. et al. 1975. Effects of an offshore crude oil unloading terminal on the marine environment. *Marine Technological Society Journal* 9:(1):27.

Mostert, N. 1974. *Supership.* New York: Knopf.

St. Amant, L. 1970. Biological effects of petroleum exploration and production in coastal Louisiana. In *Santa Barbara Oil Symposium: Offshore Petroleum Production—an Environmental Inquiry*, spons. by U.S. National Science Foundation and Marine Science Institute, Univ. California, Santa Barbara, pp. 335–54.

Sterling, G. H. and G. E. Strohbeck. 1975. The failure of the South Pass 70 Platform B in Hurricane Camille. *Journal*

Bibliography

of Petroleum Technology (March, 1975):263–68.

Stone, J. H. et al. 1972. *Louisiana Superport Studies*. Center for Wetland Resources, La. State Univ., Baton Rouge.

Gulf of Mexico V

Bendix, S. 1974. Environmental mutagens. *Science* 184:188–89.

Bent, A. C. 1922. Life histories of North American petrels and pelicans and their allies. *U.S. National Museum Bulletin* 121:1–335.

Bidleman, T. F. and C. E. Olney. 1974. Chlorinated hydrocarbons in the Sargasso Sea atmosphere and surface water. *Science* 183:516–18.

Bidleman, T. F. and C. E. Olney. 1975. Long–range transport of toxaphene insecticide in the atmosphere of the western North Atlantic. *Nature* 257(5526):475–77.

Bourne, W. R. P. and J. A. Bogan. 1972. Polychlorinated biphenyls in North Atlantic seabirds. *Marine Pollution Bulletin* 3(11):171–75.

Broecker, W. S. 1975. Climatic change: are we on the brink of a pronounced global warming? *Science* 189:460–63.

Cairns, J. 1975. The cancer problem. *Scientific American* 233(5):64–78.

Carter, L. J. 1974. Cancer and the environment I: a creaky system grinds on. *Science* 186:239–42.

Casida, J. E. et al. 1974. Toxaphene insecticide: a complex biodegradable mixture. *Science* 183:520–21.

Charzarach, S. et al. 1975. Acute toxicity of the insecticides toxaphene and carbaryl, and the herbicides propanil and molinate to four species of aquatic organisms. *Bulletin Environmental Contamination and Toxicology* 14:281–84.

Childress, U. R. 1969. Levels of concentration and incidence of various pesticide toxicants in some species from selected bay areas. *Coastal Fisheries Project Reports for 1968,* Texas Parks and Wildlife Dept., Austin, pp. 1–21.

Cunningham, P. A. and M. R. Tripp. 1975. Factors affecting the accumulation and removal of mercury from tissues of the American oyster, *Crassostrea virginica. Marine Biology* 31:311–19.

Dowty, B. et al. 1975. Halogenated hydrocarbons in New Orleans drinking water and blood plasma. *Science* 187:75–7.

Drake, J. W. et al. (Environmental Mutagen Society). 1975. Environmental mutagenic hazards. *Science* 187:503–14.

Duke, T. W. et al. 1970. A polychlorinated biphenyl (Arochlor 1254) in the water, sediment, and biota of Escambia Bay, Florida. *Bulletin Environmental Contamination and Toxicology* 5:171–80.

Epifanio, C. E. 1973. Dieldrin uptake by larvae of the crab *Leptodius floridanus. Marine Biology* 19:320–22.

Epstein, S. S. 1974. Environmental determinants of human cancer. *Cancer Research* 34:2425–35.

Fisher, N. S. 1975. Chlorinated hydrocarbon pollutants and photosynthesis of marine phytoplankton: a reassessment. *Science* 189:463–64.

Fisher, N. S. 1976. Pollution toxicity tests and the problem of interacting variables. *Ecology,* forthcoming.

Gillette, R. 1974. Cancer and the environment II: groping for new remedies. *Science* 186:242–45.

Gochfield, M. 1975. Developmental defects in common terns of western Long Island, N.Y. *Auk* 92:58–65.

Grimes, D. J. and S. M. Morrison. 1975. Bacterial bioconcentration of chlorinated hydrocarbon insecticides from aqueous systems. *Microbial Ecology* 2:43–59.

Hansen, D. J. 1974. Arochlor 1254: effect on composition of developing estuarine animal communities in the laboratory. *Contributions in Marine Science of the Univ. of Texas* 18:19–33.

Harvey, G. R. 1974. DDT and PCB in the Atlantic. *Oceanus* 18(1):19–23.

Jaworski, E. 1972. *The Blue Crab Fishery, Barataria Estuary.* Publ. No. LSU-SG-72-01, Center for Wetland Resources, La. State Univ., Baton Rouge.

Korn, S. and R. Earnest. 1974. Acute toxicity of twenty insecticides to striped bass, *Morone saxatilis. Calif. Fish and*

Game 60(3):128–31.

Leffler, C. W. 1975. Effects of ingested mirex and DDT on juvenile *Callinectes sapidus* Rathbun. *Environmental Pollution* 8:283–300.

Liang, T. T. and E. P. Lichtenstein. 1974. Synergism of insecticides by herbicides: effect of environmental factors. *Science* 186:1128–30.

Longhurst, A. R. and P. J. Radford. 1975. PCB concentrations in North Atlantic surface water. *Nature* 256(5514):239–40.

Lowery, G. H. 1974. *Louisiana Birds*. La. State Univ. Press, Baton Rouge.

MacIntyre, F. 1974. The top millimeter of the ocean. *Scientific American* 230(5):62–77.

Marx, J. L. 1974. Drinking water: another source of carcinogens? *Science* 186:809-11.

Maugh, T. H. II. 1975. Chemical pollutants, polychlorinated biphenyls still a threat. *Science* 190:1189.

Nimmo, D. R. and L. H. Bahner. 1974. Some physiological consequences of polychlorinated biphenyl and salinity-stress in penaeid shrimp. In *Pollution and Physiology of Marine Organisms*, eds. F. J. Vernberg and W. B. Vernberg, pp. 427–43. New York: Academic Press.

Petrocelli, S. R. et al. 1975. Biomagnification of dieldrin residues by food–chain transfer from clams to blue crabs under controlled conditions. *Bulletin of Environmental Contamination and Toxicology* 13:108–16.

Petrocelli, S. R. et al. 1975. Controlled food–chain transfer of dieldrin residues from phytoplankters to clams. *Marine Biology* 31:215–18.

Petrocelli, S. R. et al. 1975. Seasonal fluctuation of dieldrin residues in the tissues of the marsh clam, *Rangia cuneata*, from a Texas estuary. *Texas Journal of Science* 26:443–48.

Portnoy, B. L. et al. 1975. Oyster-associated hepatitis. *Journal Amer. Medical Association* 233(10):1065–68.

Proctor, N. H. and J. E. Casida, 1975. Organophosphorus and methyl carbamate insecticide teratogenesis: diminished NAD in chicken embryos. *Science* 190:580–82.

Roberts, D. 1975. The effect of pesticides on byssus formation in the common mussel, *Mytilus edulis*. *Environmental Pollution* 8:241–54.

Sheridan, P. F. 1975. Uptake, metabolism, and distribution of DDT in organs of the blue crab, *Callinectes sapidus*. *Chesapeake Science* 16:20–26.

Smith, J. N. 1972. *The Decline of Galveston Bay*. The Conservation Foundation, Wash., D.C.

Weis, P. and J. S. Weis. 1974. Schooling behavior of *Menidia menidia* in the presence of the insecticide sevin (carbaryl). *Marine Biology* 28:261–63.

Weis, J. S. and P. Weis. 1975. Retardation of fin regeneration in *Fundulus* by several insecticides. *Transactions of the Amer. Fisheries Society* 104:135–37.

Map Sources

Osborne, K. W. et al. 1969. *Gulf of Mexico Shrimp Atlas*. U.S. Dept. of Interior, Bureau of Commercial Fisheries, Circular 312.

Garrison, L. E. and R. G. Martin Jr. 1975. Geological structures in the Gulf of Mexico Basin. *Geological Survey Professional Paper 773*, USGS.

The Pacific Border I

Barr, S. M. 1974. Structure and tectonics of the continental slope west of southern Vancouver Island. *Canadian Journal of Earth Sciences* 11:1187–99.

Calder, N. 1972. *The Restless Earth*. New York: Viking.

Elders, W. A. et. al. 1972. Crustal spreading in southern California. *Science* 178:15–24.

Emery, K. O., 1960. *The Sea Off Southern California, A Modern Habitat of Petroleum*. New York: Wiley.

Hammond, A. L. 1975. Minerals and plate tectonics: a conceptual revolution. *Science* 189:779–81.

Heirtzler, J. R. 1974. The slow and steady surprise. *Oceanus* 1–7 (Winter, 1973–74).

Bibliography

Isaacs, J. D. and R. Schwartzlose. 1975. Active animals of the deep sea floor. *Scientific American* 233(4):85–91.

Nafi-Toksöz, N. 1975. Subduction of the lithosphere. *Scientific American* 233(5):89–98.

Shepard, F. P. 1975. Submarine canyons of the Pacific. *Sea Frontiers* 21(1):2–13.

Sholkovitz, E. and A. Soutar. 1975. Changes in the composition of the bottom water of the Santa Barbara Basin: effect of turbidity currents. *Deep Sea Research* 22:13–21.

Soutar, A. and J. D. Isaacs. 1974. Abundance of pelagic fish during the 19th and 20th centuries as recorded in anaerobic sediment off the Californias. *Fishery Bulletin* 72:257–73.

Turner, D. L. et al. 1973. Radiometric ages of Kodiak Seamount and Giacomini Guyot, Gulf of Alaska: implications for circum–Pacific tectonics. *Science* 182:579–81.

The Pacific Border II, III, IV

Arehart-Treichel, J. 1975. Combating the red tide. *Science News* 108(5):74–79.

Fogg, G. E. 1966. *Algal Culture and Phytoplankton Ecology*. Madison: Univ. of Wisconsin Press.

Huntsman, S. A. and R. T. Barber. 1975. Evidence for modification of phytoplankton growth by excreted compounds in low density populations. *Journal of Phycology* 11:10–13.

Kulin, L. D. et al. 1975. Oregon continental shelf sedimentation: interrelationships of facies distribution and sedimentary processes. *Journal of Geology* 83:145–75.

Lasker, R. 1975. Field criteria for survival of anchovy larvae: the relation between inshore chlorophyll maximum layers and successful first feeding. *Fishery Bulletin* 73:453–62.

Lillelund, K. and R. Lasker. 1971. Laboratory studies of predation by marine copepods on fish larvae. *Fishery Bulletin* 69:655–67.

LoCicero, V. R., ed. 1975. *Proceedings of the First International Conference on Toxic Dinoflagellate Blooms*. Massachusetts Science and Technology Foundation, Wakefield, Mass.

McDonald, J. E. 1952. The Coriolis Effect. *Scientific American* 186(5):72–78.

Peterson, W. T. and C. B. Miller. 1975. Year to year variations in the planktology of the Oregon upwelling zone. *Fishery Bulletin* 73:642–53.

Strickland, J. D. H. 1969. Remarks on the effects of heated discharges on marine zooplankton. In *Biological Aspects of Thermal Pollution*, eds. P. A. Krenkel and F. L. Parker, pp. 73–77. Nashville: Vanderbilt Univ. Press.

Sverdrup, H. U. et al. 1942. *The Oceans*. Englewood Cliffs, N.J.: Prentice-Hall.

Symposium on Upwelling. 1974. *Tethys* 6(1 and 2).

Winter, D. F. et al. 1975. The dynamics of phytoplankton blooms in Puget Sound, a fjord in the northwestern United States. *Marine Biology* 29:139–76.

The Pacific Border V

Dawson, E. Y. 1966. *Marine Botany*. New York: Holt, Rhinehart, Winston.

Jupp, B. P. and E. A. Drew. 1974. Studies on the growth of *Laminaria hyperborea*: biomass and productivity. *Journal of Experimental Marine Biology and Ecology* 15:185–96.

Kain, J. M. 1964. Aspects of the biology of *Laminaria hyperborea* III: survival and growth of gametophytes. *Journal Marine Biological Association U.K.* 44:415–33.

Lowry, L. F. et al. 1974. The distribution of six species of gastropod molluscs in a California kelp forest. *Biological Bulletin* 147:386–96.

Nelson, D. R. 1974. Ultrasonic telemetry of shark behavior. *Naval Research Reviews* 27(12):1–21.

Phillips, R. C. 1974. Kelp beds. In *Coastal Ecological Systems of the United States*, eds. H. T. Odum et al., pp. 442–87. The Conservation Foundation, Wash., D.C., Vol. II.

Rosenthal, R. J. et al. 1974. Ecology and natural history of a stand of giant kelp, *Macrocystis pyrifera*, off Del Mar, California. *Fishery Bulletin* 72:670–84.

The Pacific Border VI

Anonymous. 1974. Interview with Coast Guard Commandant Siler. *Ocean Industry* 9(11):38–39.

Baldini, I. and F. Cugurra. 1974. Ichthyotoxic effects of some antipollution products. *Water Research* 8:323.

Baldwin, M. F. and P. L. Baldwin. 1973. Oil and Puget Sound. *Living Wilderness* 37(123):14–23.

Blumer, M. 1972. Submarine seeps: are they a major source of open ocean oil pollution? *Science* 176:1257–58.

Cullinane, J. P. et al. 1975. The effect of oil pollution in Bantry Bay. *Marine Pollution Bulletin* 6(11):173–76.

Easton, R. 1972. *Black Tide*. New York: Delacorte.

Farrington, J. W. 1975. *Oil Pollution and the Coastal Environment, Report for Impact of Pollution on Estuaries*. Prepared for U.S. Environmental Protection Agency.

Gibbs, C. F. et al. 1975. Quantitative studies on marine biodegradation of oil II: effect of temperature. *Proceedings Royal Society of London B* 188:83–94.

Ladner, L. and A. Hagstrom. 1975. Oil spill protection in the Baltic Sea. *Journal Water Pollution Control Federation* 47:796–809.

Mostert, N. 1975. Age of the oilberg. *Audubon* 77(3):18–43.

Offshore Oil Task Group (MIT). 1973. *The Georges Bank Petroleum Study*. Sea Grant Project Office, Mass. Inst. of Technology, Cambridge, Mass., Vol. 2.

Pulich, W. M. et al. 1974. The effects of a No. 2 fuel oil and two crude oils on the growth and photosynthesis of microalgae. *Marine Biology* 28:87–94.

Rehwoldt, R. et al. 1974. Toxicity study of two oil spill reagents toward Hudson River fish species. *Bulletin of Environmental Contamination and Toxicology* 11:159–62.

Sabo, D. J. and J. J. Stegeman. Provisional title: Study of sublethal effects of petroleum hydrocarbons at the biochemical level in *Fundulus heteroclitus*. In *Pollution and Physiology of Marine Organisms*, Vol. 2, eds. Calabrese and Vernberg. New York: Academic Press, forthcoming.

Santa Barbara Oil Symposium: Offshore Petroleum Production, an Environmental Inquiry. 1970. Sponsored by U.S. National Science Foundation and Institute of Marine Science, Univ. of California, Santa Barbara.

Steinhart, C. E. and J. S. Steinhart. 1974. *Blowout, a case study of the Santa Barbara oil spill*. Belmont, Calif.: Duxbury Press.

Straughan, D. et al. 1971. *Biological and Oceanographical Survey of the Santa Barbara Channel Oil Spill, 1969-1970*. Univ. Southern California, Allen Hancock Foundation. 2 vols.

Valentine, J. W. and J. H. Lipps. 1970. Marine fossils at Rancho La Brea. *Science* 169:277–78.

Wildash, D. J. 1974. Arrestant effect of polyoxyethylene esters on swimming in the winter flounder. *Water Research* 8:579–84.

Wilson, R. D. et al. 1974. Natural marine oil seepage. *Science* 184:857–65.

The Pacific Border VII

Anderson, D. W. et al. 1975. Brown pelicans: improved reproduction off the southern California coast. *Science* 190:806–08.

Bascom, W. 1974. The disposal of waste in the ocean. *Scientific American* 231(2):16–25.

Bascom, W. et al. 1975. *Annual Report for the year ended June 30, 1975*. Southern California Coastal Water Research Project, El Segundo, Calif.

Bruland, K. W. et al. 1974. History of metal pollution in the southern California coastal zone. *Environmental Science and Technology* 8:425–32.

Chow, T. J. et al. 1973. Lead pollution: records in southern California coastal sediments. *Science* 181:551–52.

DeLong, R. L. et al. 1973. Premature births in California sea lions: association with high organochlorine pollutant residue levels. *Science* 181:1168–70.

Bibliography

Duce, R. A. et al., eds. 1974. *Pollutant Transfer to the Marine Environment.* National Science Foundation Pollutant Transfer Workshop, Deliberations and Recommendations.

Fisher, N. S. et al. 1974. Effects of PCB on interspecific competition in natural and gnotobiotic phytoplankton communities in continuous and batch cultures. *Microbial Ecology* 1:39–50.

Hancock, D. A. 1976. Mercury in fish. *Australian Fisheries* 35(1):4–7.

Hedgpeth, J. W. and J. J. Gonor. 1969. Aspects of the potential effect of thermal alteration on marine and estuarine benthos. In *Biological Aspects of Thermal Pollution*, eds. P. A. Krenkel and F. L. Parker, pp. 80–132. Nashville: Vanderbilt Univ. Press.

Hom, W. et al. 1974. Deposition of DDE and polychlorinated biphenyls in dated sediments of the Santa Barbara Basin. *Science* 184:1197–99.

Inman, D. L. and B. M. Brush. 1973. The coastal challenge. *Science* 181:20–32.

Jernelov, A. et al. 1975. Swedish perspectives on mercury pollution. *Journal of the Water Pollution Control Federation* 47:810–22.

Kullenberg, G. E. B. 1975. Ocean dumping sites. *Ocean Management* 2:189–209.

Martin, J. H. and W. W. Broenkow. 1975. Cadmium in plankton: elevated concentrations off Baja California. *Science* 190:884–85.

Middaugh, D. P. et al. 1975. The response of larval fish, *Leiostomus xanthurus*, to environmental stress following sublethal cadmium exposure. *Contributions in Marine Science of the Univ. of Texas* 19:13–19.

Morris, A. W. and A. J. Bale. 1975. The accumulation of cadmium, copper, manganese and zinc by *Fucus vesiculosus* in the Bristol Channel. *Estuarine and Coastal Marine Science* 3:153–63.

Nordberg, G. F. 1974. Health hazards of environmental cadmium pollution. *Ambio* 3(2):55–66.

North, W. J. 1974. Effects of heated effluents on marine biota, particularly in California. In *Modifications Thermiques et Équilibres Biologiques*, pp. 41–60. Amsterdam: Institut de la Vie, North Holland Publ. Co.

Olafson, R. W. 1974. Isolation of heavy metal detoxication proteins from marine vertebrates. *Abstract, Amer. Society of Limnology and Oceanography*. Annual Meeting, June, 1974.

Map Sources

Emery, K. O. 1960. *The Sea Off Southern California, A Modern Habitat of Petroleum.* New York: Wiley. pp 112, 205, 321.

Bascom, W. et al. 1975. *Annual report for the year ended June 30, 1975.* Southern California Coastal Water Research Project. El Segundo, Calif. pp 140, 145, 154.

Alaska and the Arctic I

Appollonio, S. 1973. Glaciers and nutrients in arctic seas. *Science* 180:491–93.

Broecker, W. S. 1975. Floating glacial ice caps in the Arctic Ocean. *Science* 188:1116–18.

Clark, D. L. 1974. Late Mesozoic and early Cenozoic sediment cores from the Arctic Ocean. *Geology* 2:41–44.

Dayton, P. K. 1971. Competition, disturbance, and community organization: the provision and subsequent utilization of space in a rocky intertidal community. *Ecological Monographs* 41:351–89.

Dunbar, M. J. 1973. Glaciers and nutrients in arctic fiords. *Science* 182:398.

Gavin, A. 1974. *Wildlife of the North Slope/a Five Year Study, 1969-1973.* Atlantic Richfield Company.

Goering, J. J. and C. P. McRoy. 1974. Sea ice and under ice plankton. In *Coastal Ecological Systems of the United States,* eds. H. T. Odum et al., pp. 55–70. The Conservation Foundation, Wash., D.C., Vol. III.

Grassle, J. F. and H. L. Sanders. 1973. Life histories and the role of disturbance. *Deep Sea Research* 20:643–59.

Harris, I. M. and P. G. Jellymore. 1974. Iceberg furrow marks on the continental shelf northeast of Belle Isle, New-foundland. *Canadian Journal of Earth Sciences* 11:43–52.

Herman, Y., ed. 1974. *Marine Geology and Oceanography of the Arctic Seas*. New York: Springer–Verlag.

Hood, D. W. and E. J. Kelley, eds. 1974. *Oceanography of the Bering Sea*. Institute of Marine Science, Univ. of Alaska, Fairbanks.

McRoy, C. P. and M. B. Allen. 1974. Ice stressed coasts. In *Coastal Ecological Systems of the United States*, eds. H. T. Odum et al., pp. 17–36. The Conservation Foundation, Wash., D.C., Vol. III.

Matheke, G. E. M. and R. Horner. 1974. Primary productivity of the benthic microalgae in the Chukchi Sea near Barrow, Alaska. *Journal of the Fisheries Research Board of Canada* 31:1779–86.

Paul, A. J. and H. M. Feder. 1973. Growth, recruitment, and distribution of the littleneck clam, *Protothaca staminea*, in Galena Bay, Prince William Sound, Alaska. *Fishery Bulletin* 71:665–77.

Percy, J. A. 1975. Ecological physiology of arctic marine invertebrates: temperature and salinity requirements of the amphipod *Onisimus affinis* H. J. Hansen. *Journal of Experimental Marine Biology and Ecology* 20:99–117.

Reed, J. C. et al., eds. 1974. *The Coast and Shelf of the Beaufort Sea*. Arctic Institute of North America, Arlington, Va.

Wilce, R. 1971. Some remarks on the benthic chrysophytes and the fleshy red and brown crusts. In *Cold Water Inshore Marine Biology*, eds. N. W. Riser and A. G. Carlson, pp. 17–25. Boston: Northeastern Univ.

Alaska and the Arctic II

Bruemmer, F. 1975. A year in the life of a harp seal. *Natural History* 84(4):42–49.

Curry-Lindahl, K. 1975. Conservation of arctic fauna and its habitats. *Polar Record* 17(108):237–47.

Davis, J. and W. Z. Lidicker Jr. 1975. The taxonomic status of the southern sea

otter. *Proceedings of the California Academy of Science, 4th Series,* Vol. XL (14), pp. 429–37.

Dayton, P. K. 1974. Experimental studies of algal canopy interactions in a sea otter dominated kelp community at Amchitka Island, Alaska. *Fishery Bulletin* 73:230–37.

Estes, J. A. and J. F. Palmisano. 1974. Sea otters: their role in structuring near-shore communities. *Science* 185:1058–60.

Gjoesaeter, J. and R. Saetre. 1974. Predation of eggs of capelin *(Mallotus villosus)* by diving ducks. *Astarte* 7(2):83–89.

Hill, D. O. 1974, Vanishing giants. *Audubon* 77(1):56–90.

Kenyon, K. W. 1969. The sea otter in the eastern Pacific Ocean. *Bureau Sport Fisheries and Wildlife, North Amer. Fauna* (U.S. Dept. of Interior) No. 68.

King, W. B., ed. 1974. Pelagic studies of seabirds in the central and eastern Pacific Ocean. *Smithsonian Contributions to Zoology*, No. 158, Smithsonian Inst. Press, Wash., D.C.

Laughlin, W. S. 1975. Aleuts: ecosystems, Holocene history, and Siberian origin. *Science* 189:507–15.

McVay, S. 1973. Stalking the arctic whale. *American Scientist* 61:24–37.

Morris, R. J. 1975. Further studies into lipid structure of spermaceti organ of the sperm whale *(Physeter catodon)*. *Deep Sea Research* 22:483–89.

Morrison, P. et al. 1974. Metabolism and thermoregulation in the sea otter. *Physiological Zoology* 47:218–29.

Myers, N. 1975. The whaling controversy. *American Scientist* 63:448–55.

Payne, R. 1974. A playground for whales. *Animal Kingdom* 77(2):7–12.

Ridgway, S. H. et al. 1975. Sleep and cardiac rhythm in the gray seal. *Science* 187:553–55.

Schevill, W. E., ed. 1974. *The Whale Problem*. Cambridge, Mass.: Harvard University Press.

Schneider, K. B. and J. B. Faro. 1975. Effects of sea ice on sea otters, *Enhydra lutris. Journal of Mammalogy* 56:91–99.

Bibliography

Stirling, I. and E. H. McEwan. 1975. The caloric value of whole ringed seals, *(Phoca hispida)* in relation to polar bear *(Ursus maritimus)* ecology and hunting behavior. *Canadian Journal of Zoology* 53:1021–27.

Warham, J. 1971. Body temperatures of petrels. *The Condor* 73:214–19.

Wilson, J. 1975. Killers in the surf. *Audubon* 77(5):2–5.

Alaska and the Arctic III

Anonymous. 1974. Canada and the Arctic. *The Oil and Gas Journal* 72(5):61–96.

Anonymous. 1975. Conservation report (kill of murres off West Greenland). *Auk* 92:126–36.

Ayers, R. C. et al. 1974. Oil spills in the Arctic Ocean: extent of spreading and possibility of large-scale thermal effects. *Science* 186:843–46. (Includes reply by S. Martin and W. J. Campbell).

Blumer, M. 1971. Scientific aspects of the oil spill problem. *Environmental Affairs* 1:54–73.

Campbell, W. J. and S. Martin. 1973. Oil and ice in the Arctic Ocean: possible large-scale interactions. *Science* 181:56–58.

Carter, L. J. 1975. Icebergs and oil tankers: USGS glaciologists are concerned. *Science* 190:641–43.

Carter, L. J. 1976. Oil drilling in the Beaufort Sea: leaving it to luck and technology. *Science* 191:929–31.

Chasan, D. J. 1975. Salmon, bitter fruit of the Pacific. *Audubon* 77(6):8–23.

Council on Environmental Quality. 1974. *OCS Oil and Gas–An Environmental Assessment.* Wash., D.C., 5 Vols.

Cox, D. C. and G. Pararas-Carayannis. 1969. Catalog of *tsunamis* in Alaska. U.S. Dept. of Commerce, ESSA.

Dunbar, M. J. 1973. Stability and fragility in arctic ecosystems. *Arctic* 26:179–85.

French, R. R. et al. 1975. Ocean distribution of stocks of Pacific salmon, *Onchorynchus* species, and steelhead trout, *Salmo gairdnerii,* as shown by tagging experiments. *NOAA Technical Report*, NMFS-SSRF 689, Seattle, Wash.

Hasler, A. D., ed. 1966. *Underwater Guideposts, Homing of Salmon.* Madison: Univ. of Wisconsin Press.

Hood, D. W. et al., eds. 1973. Environmental Studies of Port Valdez. *Occasional Publication No. 3.* Fairbanks: Institute of Marine Science, Univ. of Alaska.

Karinen, J. F. 1975. Oil spill effects. *Science* 190:215–19.

Lovins, A. B. 1974. The case for long-term planning. *Bulletin of the Atomic Scientists* 30(6):38–50.

Maykut, G. A. and N. Untersteiner. 1971. Some results from a time-dependent thermodynamic model of sea ice. *Journal of Geophysical Research* 76:1550–75.

Netboy, A. 1968. *The Atlantic Salmon.* Boston: Houghton–Mifflin.

Paloheimo, J. E. and P. F. Elson. 1974. Reduction of Atlantic salmon *(Salmo salar)* catches in Canada attributed to the Greenland fishery. *Journal of the Fisheries Research Board of Canada* 31:1467–80.

Panitch, M. 1975. Offshore drilling: fishermen and oilmen clash in Alaska. *Science* 189:204–06.

Rashid, M. A. 1974. Degradation of Bunker C oil under different coastal environments of Chedabucto Bay, Nova Scotia. *Estuarine and Coastal Marine Science* 2:137–44.

Rice, S. D. 1973. Toxicity and avoidance tests with Prudhoe Bay oil and pink salmon fry. In *Proceedings of the Joint Conference on Prevention and Control of Oil Spills,* Wash., D.C., pp. 667–70.

Rogers, G. 1975. Offshore oil and gas development in Alaska: impacts and conflicts. *Polar Record* 17:255–75.

Stratz, R. R. 1975. Migration routes of adult sockeye salmon, *Onchorynchus nerka* in the eastern Bering Sea and Bristol Bay. NOAA Technical Report, NMFS-SSRF 690. Seattle, Wash.

Map Sources

Carter, L. J. 1975. *Science* 190, p. 642.

Carter, L. J. 1976. *Science* 191, p. 930.

Tobin, D. G. and L. R. Sykes. 1966. Relation of hypocenters of Alaskan earthquakes to the geology of Alaska. *Journal of Geophysical Research* 71:1659–67.

U.S. Department of Interior (Bureau of Land Management). 1975. Map: Frontier Outer Continental Shelf Areas— Northern Gulf of Alaska.

Toward an Oceanic Philosophy I

Auburn, F. M. 1974. Convention for preservation of man's cultural heritage in the oceans. *Science* 185:763–64.

Broecker, W. S. 1973. Environmental priorities. *Science* 182(4111): editorial.

Frey, H. R., ed. 1972. *Resources of the World's Oceans*. New York Institute of Ocean Resources, Inc.

Ghiselin, J. 1974. Wilderness and the survival of species. *Living Wilderness* 37(124):22–27.

Holden, C. H. 1974. Scientists talk of the need for conservation and an ethic of biotic diversity to slow species extinction. *Science* 184:646–47.

Humm, H. J. and C. E. Lane. 1974. *Bioactive Compounds from the Sea*. Marine Science Series, Vol. 1. Dekker, N.Y.

Seltzer, R. J. 1974. Research on drugs from the sea starts to move forward. *Chemical and Engineering News* 52 (Dec. 16, 1974). pp 20–23.

Toward an Oceanic Philosophy II

Allen, K. R. 1975. The conservation of marine animals. *Search (ANZAAS)* 6:317–22.

Anonymous. 1975. Article on Antarctic krill fishery. *Australian Fisheries* 34(8):18–19.

Anonymous. 1975. Several articles on salmon aquaculture. *The Commercial Fish Farmer* 2(1):Sept.-Oct., 1975.

Blumer, M. et al. 1970. Hydrocarbon pollution of edible shellfish by an oil spill. *Marine Biology* 5:195–202.

Brown, L. R. 1975. The world food prospect. *Science* 190:1053–59.

Chedd, G. 1975. Cellulose from sunlight. *New Scientist* (16 March, 1975), pp. 572–75.

Ehrhardt, M. 1972. Petroleum hydrocarbons in oysters from Galveston Bay. *Environmental Pollution* 3:257–71.

Gallese, L. R. 1976. U.S. firms are hoping to net big profits in rapidly expanding fish-farm industry. *The Wall Street Journal* (6 Jan. 1976), p. 46.

Joseph, J. and Klawe, W. L. 1974. The living pelagic resources of the Americas. *Ocean Development and International Law* 2(1):37–64.

Kennedy, W. A. et al. 1975. Preliminary experiments in rearing Pacific salmon (1973 parr) in pens in the sea. *Fisheries and Marine Service (Canada)*, Technical Report 541.

Toward an Oceanic Philosophy III

Carter, L. J. 1975. Energy and the coastal zone: pulling and hauling among the feds. *Science* 188:1285–88.

Cichetti, C. J. 1973. The wrong route. *Environment* 15 (June 1973):4–13.

Loftas, T. 1974. The threat to Europe's oil fields. *New Scientist* 63(912): 516–17.

Morgan, J. P. et al. 1974. *Offshore Ecology Investigation, Final Consensus Report*. Gulf Universities Research Consortium, GURC Report No. 138, Galveston, Tex.

National Academy of Sciences, National Academy of Engineering. 1973. *Civil Manned Undersea Activity: an Assessment*. Wash., D.C.

Sylvester, J. R. 1975. Biological considerations on the use of thermal effluents for finfish aquaculture. *Aquaculture* 6:1–10.

Toward an Oceanic Philosophy IV

Anonymous. 1975. Article on the proposed "mussel watch". *New Scientist* 68(970):113.

DiSalvo, L. H. et al. 1975. Tissue hydrocarbon burden of mussels as potential monitor of environmental hydrocarbon insult. *Environmental Science and Technology* 9:246–51.

LaViolette, P. E. et al. 1975. Use of APT satellite infrared data in oceanographic survey operations. *Transactions of the American Geophysical Union* 56:276–82.

Bibliography

Linder, M. J. and J. S. Bailey. 1969. Distribution of brown shrimp *(Penaeus aztecus* Ives) as related to turbid water photographed from space. *Fishery Bulletin* 67:289–94.

Maugh, T. H. II. 1973. ERTS: surveying Earth's resources from space. *Science* 180:49–51.

Maugh, T. H. II. 1973. ERTS (II): a new way of viewing the earth. *Science* 180:171–73.

Maul, G. A. et al. 1974. Computer enhancement of ERTS-1 images for ocean radiances. *Remote Sensing of Environment* 3:237–53.

Spalding, T. R. 1975. The earth resources technology satellites. *Weather* 30(3):70–1.

Stumpf, H. G. 1975. Satellite detection of upwelling in the Gulf of Tehuantepec, Mexico. *Mariners Weather Log* 19:71–74.

Stumpf, H. G. and A. E. Strong. 1974. ERTS-1 views an oil slick. *Remote Sensing of Environment* 3:87–90.

Tsipis, K. 1975. Antisubmarine warfare— fact and fiction. *New Scientist* 65(932):145–47.

Wade, N. 1975. Strategic weapons: verification keeps ahead of arms control. *Science* 187:936–37.

Knauss, J. A. 1974. Marine science and the 1974 Law of the Sea Conference. *Science* 184:1335–41.

Lomhoff, P. G. 1974. Dementia Piscatoria—Sanitas Malta: the International Sea Service. *Ecology Law Quarterly* 4:319–41.

Macbeth, A. (Natural Resources Defense Council, New York, N.Y.). 1975. *Structuring the Legal Regulation of Estuaries.* Unpub. Manuscript.

Mineral Resources of the Deep Sea Bed. 1973 hearings before the Subcommittee on Minerals, Materials, and Fuels of the Committee on Interior and Insular Affairs, U.S. Senate, 93rd Cong., Ist Session, U.S. Govt. Printing Office, Wash., D.C.

Ross, D. A. 1973. What common heritage? *Oceanus* 17 (Summer, 1973), pp. 1–5.

Schindler, W. 1976. The impact statement boondoggle. *Science* 192(4239), editorial.

Stone, C. D. 1974. *Should Trees have Standing? Toward Legal Rights for Natural Objects.* Los Altos, Calif.: W. Kaufmann.

Zerbe, R. O. 1974. Optimal environmental jurisdictions. *Ecology Law Quarterly* 4(2):230–31.

Toward an Oceanic Philosophy V

Archer, A. A. and P. B. Beazley. 1975. The geographical implications of the Law of the Sea Conference. *The Geographical Journal* 141:1–13.

Carter, L. J. 1974. Law of the Sea: fisheries plight poses dilemma for United States. *Science* 185:336–39.

Claude, A. 1975. The coming of age of the cell. *Science* 189:433–35.

D'Amato, A. and J. L. Hargrove. 1974. *Environment and the Law of the Sea, a Report of the Working Group on Ocean Environment.* American Society of International Law, Wash., D.C.

Hardin, G. 1968. The tragedy of the commons. *Science* 162:1243–48.

Hollick, A. L. 1975. What to expect from a sea treaty. *Foreign Policy,* No. 18, (Spring, 1975), pp. 68–78.

Index

Index

Tilefish (*Lopholatilus chamaelonticeps*), 199
Titanium, 54
Tourist industry, 39, 162, 245
Toxaphene, 129, 135, 136
Toxicity, selective, 131
Trace metals, 180
Trade winds, 148
Trapping lanes, 29
Traps, lobster, 28-30
Trawl fishing, 27-28, 29, 30, 31, 34, 239
Tree crabs, 121
Tropical marine life, 56, 73-4, 105
Truman, Harry S., 255
Tube-dwelling worms, 57, 168, 197
Tubularia (hydroid), 197
Tumor-inhibiting drugs, 236
Tumors, in clams, 45
Tunafish, 243
Tunicates, 5
Turbidity currents, 51, 142
Turbulence, 22, 71
Turner, Ruth, 74

Udall, Stuart, 180
Unemployment, 38
UNESCO, 254
Union Carbide, 240
Union of Concerned Scientists, 75
United Nations, 257
United States Bureau of Commercial Fisheries, 119
United States Coast Guard, 34, 174, 227, 248
United States Customs Service, 253
United States Environmental Protection Agency (EPA), 71, 79, 82, 131, 138, 249, 254, 258
United States Food and Drug Administration (FDA), 184, 187
United States Geological Survey (USGS), 37, 96, 226
United States Interior Department, 234, 249
United States National Marine Fisheries Service (NMFS), 17-18, 46, 191-204, 242
United States Sea Grant Program, 226
University of Alaska's Institute of Marine Science, 226
University of Hawaii, 236
University of Miami, 74, 119
Upwelling, 152-53, 154, 156, 252
Uzmann, Joseph, 46

Vancouver Island, 146
Veath Canyon, 193
Veligers, 57-58, 71, 158
Velocity caps, 67
Velum, 57, 58
Virginia coast, 55
Virginia Coastal Current, 55
Virginia Institute of Marine Science, 64
Virus contamination, 81
Viscosity, water, 154
Vocalization, 217, 218
Volcanoes, 145

Walrus, 10, 212, 217
Walt Disney Enterprises, 259
Washington, 30
"Waste" heat, 245
Wastes: chemical, 84, 245; disposal of, 78-86, 180, 181-82, 245; industrial, 83-84; nuclear, 75-76; solid, 85
Water circulation, 106
Water temperature, 4-5, 18, 55, 59, 71, 150, 152, 175; and growth, 18, 24; and lobster industry, 30; and nuclear power plants, 67-68, 70, 72; and zonation, 2, 4-5
Weather: and pollution, 183; underwater, 37
Well blowouts, 228
Well heads, 225
West Germany, 239
Wet suits, 4
Weyerhauser, 240
Whales, 10, 53, 58, 169, 216-18, 222-23, 230, 240, 242
Whelks, 58
White mangroves (*Laguncularia racemosa*), 120
White shrimp (*Penaeus setiferus*), 110, 116
Wilderness areas, 234
Wind, 38, 148, 152, 230
Windowspot, 82
Winter flounder (*Pseudopleuronectus americanus*), 78, 82
Witch flounder (*Glyptocephalus cynoglossus*), 86
Woods Hole Oceanographic Institution, 43-44, 83, 84, 177
Woodwell, George, 138
Worms, tube-dwelling, 57, 168, 197

X-rays, detection of, 116

Index